Foreign Commerce Handbook (17th Edition)

by Ann Dwyer Maffry

**International Division
Chamber of Commerce
of the United States**

—

Foreign Commerce Handbook (17th Edition) (6244)

Price: $10.00 each. Discounts available on orders of 10 or more

Order from and make checks payable to:
  Chamber of Commerce of the United States
  1615 H Street, N.W., Washington, D.C. 20062

Add 6 percent sales tax for deliveries made in the District of Columbia.
Add appropriate sales tax for deliveries in California.

Copyright © 1981 Chamber of Commerce of the United States
Library of Congress Catalogue Card No. 22-23199
ISBN No. 0-89834-027-6

Contents

3. Congressional Committees

Senate

House of Representatives

Foreword

The freer international flow of goods, services, capital, people and ideas has been a goal pursued by the Chamber of Commerce of the United States since its founding in 1912. In the ensuing 69 years, the world has witnessed a tremendous growth in international trade and investment, resulting in unprecedented levels of economic and social development in industrial and industrializing societies.

An important spur in this development was and remains the availability of relevant, accurate information about programs and services that exporters and investors can utilize. In helping to fill this need, the U.S. Chamber has continually issued the *Foreign Commerce Handbook* since 1922. The *Handbook* has been used by people in business, the professions and government, both in the United States and abroad, as a reliable guide to information sources for developing international business.

This, the second printing within eight months of the 17th edition of the *Foreign Commerce Handbook,* is a direct response to the demand by exporters and investors for a work which addresses their expanding information needs. Designed to assist the novice as well as the veteran international trader, the *Handbook* shows where to turn for organization services and up-to-date published information on all important phases of international trade and investment. The International Division of the U.S. Chamber of Commerce stands ready to assist users of this book with any inquiries they may have regarding specific aspects of international business.

The U.S. Chamber's International Division staff expresses its thanks to the following individuals: Ann D. Maffry, for her diligent research and writing efforts; John L. Caldwell, who served as Vice President of the Division and who had the foresight to call for the *Handbook's* revision and expansion to meet the business community's needs for the 1980's; and finally John Volpe, who managed the production and design of this 17th edition of the *Foreign Commerce Handbook.*

Michael A. Samuels
Vice President, International

Part I. International Business and Foreign Trade Services (Organizations and Institutions)

This section is a functional guide to the principal national and international agencies and organizations, public and private, that offer international business and foreign trade services, provide information and issue analysis, or play an international economic policy-making or regulatory role. Purely domestic functions are omitted.

A. United States Government

1. Executive Office of the President

The Executive Office of the President (EOP) permits the President to accomplish the many tasks under his responsibility and to assert centralized control over disparate administrative agencies in both financial matters and substantive policy. The sheer size of the executive branch's business has led to reorganization efforts over a period of decades aimed at achieving greater efficiency and more harmonious execution of administration policy. Even when Congress has balked at sweeping reorganization proposals, it has tolerated tightening of executive control in the EOP.

The President's constitutional prerogatives in treaty-making and other negotiating activities give the EOP significant influence in foreign relations, especially in international trade matters. Although the President and Congress work closely together, the former possesses wide-ranging powers in this field, powers which have been enhanced under the 1979 trade reorganization plan.

The President's staff is lodged in the EOP, which was established in 1939. Among its major component staff units are the Council of Economic Advisers, the Office of Management and Budget (until 1970 the Bureau of the Budget) and the National Security Council, which does not offer information services to the public.

Council of Economic Advisers
Old Executive Office Building
Washington, D.C. 20506
Tel. (202) 395-5084

The *Council of Economic Advisers* (CEA) Chairman and two other members are appointed by the President and confirmed by the Senate. The Chairman, who holds Cabinet rank, is the President's principal economic adviser. The CEA provides advice on the macroeconomic and microeconomic effects of various policies and proposals. The CEA is the lead office in developing forecasts on the U.S. economy. In the international area, the current CEA Chairman also is Chairman of the Economic Policy Committee of the Organization for Economic Cooperation and Development (OECD), and the CEA participates in the Ad Hoc Working Group on Energy of the OECD. In addition, the CEA provides analyses, economic advice and recommendations on issues of trade policy and on other areas of foreign economic policy.

Office of Management and Budget
Executive Office Building
17th and Pennsylvania Avenue, N.W.
Washington, D.C. 20503
Tel. (202) 395-3000

The *Office of Management and Budget* (OMB), though not particularly visible to the public, is a highly influential agency on international commercial issues. OMB's International Affairs Division helps determine budgetary priorities in such areas as: foreign assistance, Law of the Sea, trade policy, East-West trade and the policies and programs of the Export-Import Bank and the Overseas Private Investment Corporation.

1

Three branches under the International Affairs Division exclusively review major international programs. The Economic Affairs Branch is responsible for reviewing foreign aid programs (Agency for International Development, PL 480, food aid, U.S. contributions to international financial institutions), trade financing programs (Eximbank) and the budgets of agencies primarily responsible for international economic activities (Office of the United States Trade Representative). In its capacity as adviser to the OMB Director, this branch is concerned with trade, monetary and investment policy and deals with specific issues such as international energy policy and international commodity agreements.

The State-International Communication Agency Branch reviews budgets of the agencies responsible for the conduct of foreign affairs and U.S. contributions to the United Nations. This branch is also concerned with Law of the Sea issues.

The International Security Affairs Branch is responsible for foreign military credit sales and cash sales programs, as well as the United States Arms Control and Disarmament Agency budget.

Office of Federal Procurement Policy
126 Jackson Place, N.W
Room 9013
Washington, D.C. 20503
Tel. (202) 359-5803

The Office of Federal Procurement Policy Act established the *Office of Federal Procurement Policy* (OFPP) within the Office of Management and Budget to improve the economy, efficiency and effectiveness of the procurement processes by providing overall direction of procurement policies, regulations, procedures and forms. The establishment of the OFPP implemented the first recommendation made by the Commission on Government Procurement (COGP) in its report to Congress in December 1972. The OFPP authority applies to procurement by executive agencies and recipients of federal grants or assistance of: property, other than real property in being; services, including research and development; and construction, alteration, repair or maintenance of real property.

Among the principal purposes served by OFPP are:
- To serve as a focal point for all procurement matters (policies, procedures, regulations and forms) involving more than one executive agency.
- To furnish advice to the Congress on the impact of proposed legislation, helping to preclude the passage of piecemeal legislation which would conflict with elements of other legislation or with national objectives accomplished through the procurement process.
- To provide a source for government-wide procurement data.
- To dispense advice to Congress on the effectiveness of existing procurement policies and to recommend new legislation to update and improve current statutes.
- To function as the focus for interpretation and implementation of procurement legislation or related legislation such as the Buy American Act, which is implemented through the procurement process.
- To act as the primary executive branch source of advice on the U.S. procurement system and on other procurement matters involved in implementing the International Government Procurement Code, which is part of the Trade Agreements Act of 1979.

Office of Science and Technology Policy
Executive Office Building
Washington, D.C. 20500
Tel. (202) 456-7116

Creation of the *Office of Science and Technology Policy* (OSTP) was proposed by President Ford in 1975 and established by an act of Congress the following year. The OSTP is pledged to "serve as a source of scientific and technological analysis and judgment for the President with respect to major policies, plans and programs of the federal government."

The OSTP Director, appointed by the President, has the primary function of providing "advice on the scientific, engineering and technological aspects of issues that require attention at the highest level of government."

The OSTP staff of about two dozen people is headed by three Associate Directors, one for each of the following groups of activities: National Security, International and Space Affairs; Natural Resources and Commercial Services; and Human Resources and Social Economic Services. Under these Associate Directors, a small group of policy analysts covers such concerns as oceans and atmosphere, resources, energy, toxic substances, agriculture and intergovernmental science and technology affairs.

President's Export Council
Washington, D.C. 20230
Tel. (202) 377-5719

The *President's Export Council* (PEC) was established in 1973 to serve as a national advisory body to the President. In May 1979, the PEC was reconstituted and the membership broadened. It consists of the heads or representatives of the Departments of State, Treasury, Agriculture, Commerce and Labor, the Office of the United States Trade Representative and the Export-Import Bank, and three members from both the House of Representatives and the Senate. In addition, 28 private citizens selected from industry, agriculture and labor are appointed by the President to serve on a voluntary basis without compensation. The PEC, operating through the Secretary of Commerce, advises the President on matters relating to export trade. Its subcommittees have been set up for more detailed analysis and recommendations in the following areas: export administration, export expansion (incentives/disincentives), export promotion, agriculture, the multilateral trade negotiations (MTN), the General Agreement on Tariffs and Trade (GATT) and East-West trade.

Although the Commerce Department's international trade- and investment-related activities are for the most part concentrated in its International Trade Administration (ITA), other elements of the department also become significantly involved in international commercial questions.

Office of the United States Trade Representative
1800 G Street, N.W.
Washington, D.C. 20506
Tel. (202) 395-4647

During 1979 the President developed a plan for a major reorganization and strengthening of the international trade functions of the executive branch. Reorganization Plan No. 3 of 1979, effective January 2, 1980, was designed to expand exports, promote greater coordination between trade and other policy objectives, improve enforcement of U.S. trade laws and otherwise upgrade government trade activities in response to the multilateral trade negotiation (MTN) agreements. (see organization chart, p. 5)

This reorganization consolidates both U.S. trade policy leadership and all trade negotiation responsibilities in the Office of the United States Trade Representative (USTR), the successor to the

3

Special Representative for Trade Negotiations (STR) which was established pursuant to the Trade Expansion Act of 1962 as an agency in the Executive Office of the President. The USTR continues to hold Cabinet and ambassadorial rank.

By transferring some responsibilities from the Departments of State and Treasury, the reorganization consolidates the day-to-day operation of the government's nonagricultural trade functions in the Department of Commerce. (see Department of Commerce, p. 7)

The reorganization also broadens the mandate and membership of the interagency advisory organization established in accordance with the Trade Expansion Act of 1962.

Responsibilities of the U.S. Trade Representative

With the advice of the interagency Trade Policy Committee (TPC), the Trade Representative has primary responsibility for developing and coordinating the implementation of international trade policy. This policy determination function now applies to a broad range of trade issues, including:

- Expansion of U.S. exports.
- Matters concerning the General Agreement on Tariffs and Trade (GATT).
- Trade, including East-West trade, and commodity matters dealt with either in other multilateral organizations or bilaterally.
- Import remedies, including countervailing duty and anti-dumping issues.
- Direct investment matters to the extent that they are trade related.
- International trade issues involving energy.
- Policy research on trade, commodity and direct investment matters.

The Trade Representative also has primary responsibility for the conduct of all international trade negotiations. In addition to the multilateral and bilateral trade negotiations already assigned to the USTR, his office is now responsible for negotiations relating to commodities and to East-West trade. The new negotiating responsibility includes:

- All GATT activities, including implementation of the recently concluded trade agreements.
- To the extent they primarily involve trade and commodity issues, activities of the Organization for Economic Cooperation and Development (OECD), the United Nations Conference on Trade and Development (UNCTAD) and other multilateral institutions.

Under the reorganization, the USTR became Vice Chairman of the Overseas Private Investment Corporation (OPIC) and a nonvoting member of the Export-Import Bank and a member of the National Advisory Committee on International Monetary and Financial Policies.

Two Deputy Trade Representatives serve in the Washington and Geneva offices, respectively, with each holding the rank of Ambassador. Under the reorganization of trade functions, the Geneva Deputy is U.S. representative to the GATT and is also responsible for all negotiations regarding trade and commodities under the UNCTAD. The Washington Deputy is responsible for trade policy coordination and for negotiations outside the GATT and UNCTAD. (see organization chart on page 5)

4

UNITED STATES TRADE REPRESENTATIVE: Offices and Functions

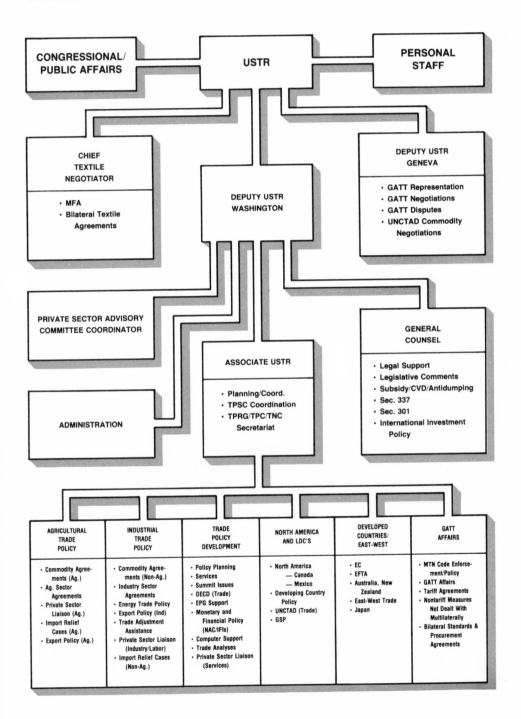

CONGRESSIONAL/PUBLIC AFFAIRS

USTR

PERSONAL STAFF

CHIEF TEXTILE NEGOTIATOR
- MFA
- Bilateral Textile Agreements

DEPUTY USTR WASHINGTON

DEPUTY USTR GENEVA
- GATT Representation
- GATT Negotiations
- GATT Disputes
- UNCTAD Commodity Negotiations

PRIVATE SECTOR ADVISORY COMMITTEE COORDINATOR

ASSOCIATE USTR
- Planning/Coord.
- TPSC Coordination
- TPRG/TPC/TNC Secretariat

GENERAL COUNSEL
- Legal Support
- Legislative Comments
- Subsidy/CVD/Antidumping
- Sec. 337
- Sec. 301
- International Investment Policy

ADMINISTRATION

AGRICULTURAL TRADE POLICY	INDUSTRIAL TRADE POLICY	TRADE POLICY DEVELOPMENT	NORTH AMERICA AND LDC'S	DEVELOPED COUNTRIES/ EAST-WEST	GATT AFFAIRS
• Commodity Agreements (Ag.)	• Commodity Agreements (Non-Ag.)	• Policy Planning	• North America	• EC	• MTN Code Enforcement/Policy
• Ag. Sector Agreements	• Industry Sector Agreements	• Services	— Canada	• EFTA	• GATT Affairs
• Private Sector Liaison (Ag.)	• Energy Trade Policy	• Summit Issues	— Mexico	• Australia, New Zealand	• Tariff Agreements
• Import Relief Cases (Ag.)	• Export Policy (Ind)	• OECD (Trade)	• Developing Country Policy	• East-West Trade	• Nontariff Measures Not Dealt With Multilaterally
• Export Policy (Ag.)	• Trade Adjustment Assistance	• EPG Support	• UNCTAD (Trade)	• Japan	• Bilateral Standards & Procurement Agreements
	• Private Sector Liaison (Industry/Labor)	• Monetary and Financial Policy (NAC/IFIs)	• GSP		
	• Import Relief Cases (Non-Ag.)	• Computer Support			
		• Trade Analyses			
		• Private Sector Liaison (Services)			

2. Executive Branch

Many branches or divisions of U.S. government departments and independent agencies are concerned with foreign commerce. Some actively promote U.S. foreign trade and offer direct services to firms, such as information and counseling. Others serve certain segments of foreign commerce or determine relevant policies or practices. Still others enforce regulations or implement policies that generally affect trade and the economy.

Only those particular functions that have a distinct bearing on international economic and commercial affairs are described here. For more complete information on other U.S. government activities, consult the *United States Government Manual* or contact the individual departments or agencies. (see Bibliography)

a. Executive Departments

Department of Agriculture
14th Street and
  Independence Avenue,
  S.W.
Washington, D.C. 20250
Tel. (202) 655-4000

The *Department of Agriculture* (USDA) plays a major role in the development of U.S. foreign agricultural policy and in market analysis and promotion for U.S. agricultural exports. It also administers agricultural import regulations.

Within the department, most trade policy issues, market support programs and import-related questions fall under the jurisdiction of the *Foreign Agricultural Service* (FAS) (Rm. 5074, Tel. 477-3448) and the *Office of the General Sales Manager* (OGSM). The primary responsibility of the FAS is to develop new and expand existing markets for U.S. agriculture. Using information gathered worldwide, FAS assesses and reports on foreign competition and trade barriers, identifies marketing opportunities, provides input for U.S. trade policy formulation and helps staff trade negotiations.

Four offices, each headed by an Assistant Administrator reporting to the FAS Administrator, together carry out these various functions.

1. The *International Trade Policy* office assists the Trade Policy Staff Committee in the Office of the United States Trade Representative (USTR), consults with the private agricultural sector and analyzes U.S. and foreign agricultural trade impediments.

2. The *Foreign Market Development* office primarily has a promotional function, cooperating with private farm groups in the organization of trade fairs, sales missions and the employment of other marketing techniques. Seven Marketing Directors specialize in individual commodities: cotton, dairy and poultry, fruit and vegetables, grain and feed, livestock and products, oilseeds and products, tobacco and seeds.

3. The *Foreign Commodity Analysis* Office assesses world agricultural production and supply and demand conditions. Like the Foreign Market Development Office, it is organized into seven commodity groups.

4. A fourth office provides Washington liaison with 130 agricultural attaches in 70 U.S. embassies, who report on local and regional farm conditions, national and regional policies and marketing opportunities and who assist with U.S. promotional efforts in their areas.

The *Office of the General Sales Manager* (OGSM) was established in 1976 to improve the department's export policy development, marketing of commodity exports and management of aid programs. It also administers export programs for commodities in ample supply in the United States and helps foreign traders conduct barter transactions through which farm products are exchanged for material produced abroad and needed in the United States. Programs administered by this office to accomplish these objectives are the Public Law 480 Programs and the Commercial Export Programs.

Under the *Public Law 480* programs, the OGSM facilitates the sale of agricultural commodities for long-term credit. In this program, the OGSM is responsible for developing government-to-government agreements, including commodity composition and payment terms. It is also responsible for the donation of farm products to foreign governments, to intergovernmental and voluntary agencies and to the World Food Program. Information from private exporters of agricultural commodities on their export sales and related transactions is also collected and published weekly.

Among the *Commercial Export Programs* is the *Agriculture Department's Commodity Credit Corporation* (CCC) *Export Sales Program* (GSM-5), which provides financing of export sales of U.S. agricultural commodities on a deferred-payment basis for periods from six months to three years. The department each month announces the commodities eligible for financing under this program and the rate of interest to be charged.

The OGSM *Noncommercial Risk Assurance Program* (GSM-101) offers protection to U.S. exporters, in the event of noncommercial risk defaults on foreign bank-issued letters of credit covering U.S. agricultural export credit transactions financed by private entities, for credit periods not to exceed three years.

Also within the Department of Agriculture are other sections with international representatives. The Economic Research Service's *Foreign Demand and Competition Division* works on long-range research and has geographical divisions and its *Foreign Development Division* works on technical foreign aid.

The department's *Agricultural Marketing Service* administers grain export inspections and import grades and its *Animal and Plant Health Inspection Service* checks imports for disease, in addition to monitoring plants, meat and poultry at ports of entry.

Department of Commerce
14th Street and
  Constitution Avenue,
  N.W.
Washington, D.C. 20230
Tel. (202) 377-3808

The responsibility of the *Department of Commerce* (DOC) is to foster, promote and develop the domestic and foreign commerce of the United States. Reorganization Plan No. 3 of 1979 brought to the department an even greater emphasis on trade in both its international and domestic aspects and reinforced its mission of increasing the international competitiveness of U.S. industry. The reorganization, which took effect January 2, 1980, created a new *International Trade Administration* (ITA), where the department's functions as they relate to foreign trade and investment are centered. The new ITA replaces and expands the unit formerly known as the Industry and Trade Administration (also ITA) and earlier as the Domestic and International Business Administration (DIBA). The President, announcing the new arrangement, said that "under this executive order, the Secretary of Commerce will be responsible uniquely and in an unprecedented way for the promotion of exports and for ensuring that agreements on imports and the laws concerning imports will be enforced."

The reorganization focuses policy-making responsibility for nonagricultural trade in the Office of the United States Trade Representative (USTR) and vests major responsibility for the day-to-day operations of trade policy in the Commerce Department. Significant functions handled until now by other agencies were shifted to Commerce as part of the reorganization. One of these is the network of commercial attaches that promotes the sale of U.S. goods and services overseas. This 162-person unit, newly named the Foreign Commercial Service, had been part of the State Department. At the same time, Commerce received more than 100 staff members of the Treasury Department who had responsibility for enforcing the antidumping and countervailing duty laws. These statutes are aimed at policing the entry of foreign goods priced below fair market value or subsidized by foreign governments.

ITA's activities are overseen by the Under Secretary for International Trade, who is responsible for overall development and management of the Department's trade functions. Reporting to the Under Secretary are the Deputy Under Secretary for International Trade, who handles the day-to-day management of ITA, and three Assistant Secretaries, responsible for International Economic Policy, Trade Development and Trade Administration, respectively. Each Assistant Secretary is supported by two or more Deputy Assistant Secretaries (see organization chart, page 9), each of whom directs one ITA subunit. The Deputy Assistant Secretary for East-West Trade, for example, directs ITA's East-West Trade unit and is in charge of the offices, comprising that unit. (see organization chart on page 9)

As part of the Administration's trade reorganization, a new *Bureau of Industrial Economics* (BIE) was established to provide information and analyses on the nation's industrial structure and its relationship to the economy.

The reorganization is intended to add a new dimension to industrial and sectoral analyses. BIE will operate under the general supervision of the Department's Chief Economist, who is responsible for monitoring and analyzing the overall economy. Macroeconomic and microeconomic analyses are coordinated to provide better analytical support to other Commerce agencies and to the entire executive branch of government.

BIE absorbed many of the functions of the former Bureau of Domestic Business Development. In addition, the Office of Industrial Economics, a small unit set up two years ago in the Office of the Chief Economist, has become part of BIE.

In general, BIE will:
- Provide information on industrial structure, production processes, national and international markets and industry-government relations and maintain an automated data base of industrial statistics.
- Produce analyses on the general economic outlook for industries and on trends in industrial productivity, growth, prices and capital formation.
- Analyze the impact of government regulations, tax changes and other policies on individual industries or groups of industries.
- Examine export and import trends by industry and assess the impact of tariff and nontariff changes on U.S. industry.
- Determine industrial productive capability in national emergencies.

The Commerce publications that will become the responsibility of BIE include: *U.S. Industrial Outlook, Construction Review, Printing and Publishing Quarterly, Copper Quarterly, Forest Products Review* and *Containers and Packaging*. The annual *U.S. Industrial Outlook* provides forecasts and data for most of the industrial sector. The *Industrial Economics Review,* which was recently inaugurated by the Office of the Chief Economist to carry analytical articles on the industrial sector, will also become a BIE responsibility.

DEPARTMENT OF COMMERCE   International Trade Administration

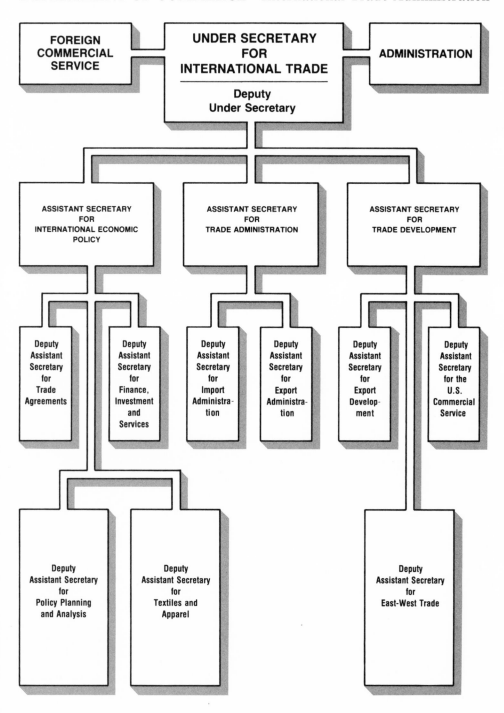

FOREIGN COMMERCIAL SERVICE

UNDER SECRETARY FOR INTERNATIONAL TRADE

Deputy Under Secretary

ADMINISTRATION

ASSISTANT SECRETARY FOR INTERNATIONAL ECONOMIC POLICY

ASSISTANT SECRETARY FOR TRADE ADMINISTRATION

ASSISTANT SECRETARY FOR TRADE DEVELOPMENT

Deputy Assistant Secretary for Trade Agreements

Deputy Assistant Secretary for Finance, Investment and Services

Deputy Assistant Secretary for Import Administration

Deputy Assistant Secretary for Export Administration

Deputy Assistant Secretary for Export Development

Deputy Assistant Secretary for the U.S. Commercial Service

Deputy Assistant Secretary for Policy Planning and Analysis

Deputy Assistant Secretary for Textiles and Apparel

Deputy Assistant Secretary for East-West Trade

Foreign Commercial Service

The *Foreign Commercial Service* (FCS) assists American business abroad through counseling, marketing data, project development assistance and liaison with foreign government agencies. It provides direct support to Commerce's overseas promotional activities such as trade missions, trade fairs and procurement conferences. It is responsible for the development of marketing and commercial intelligence, through the Worldwide Information and Trade System (WITS), for dissemination to the American business community.

Members of the FCS serve as part of U.S. embassy staffs and report directly to the ambassador or chief of mission in each country. FCS develops trade leads, identifies potential agents and develops other commercial intelligence for transmittal to the East-West Trade and Export Development units and to the U.S. Commercial Service in Washington. It also develops information and reports on foreign commercial and industrial trends. The commercial intelligence data obtained by the FCS is disseminated in part through the WITS. The FCS supports Commerce units in import and export administration and monitoring of multilateral trade agreements. It also assists U.S. business in resolving trade complaints against foreign firms and governments.

The Foreign Commercial Service is headed by a Director General who represents the Department on the board of the Foreign Service and in other matters relating to the commercial responsibilities of the Departments of State and Commerce.

Assistant Secretary for International Economic Policy

The *Assistant Secretary for International Economic Policy* is responsible for developing and operating an effective trade policy implementation mechanism within the department and for operating a variety of trade and investment programs to improve the U.S. trade position.

The Assistant Secretary provides the overall direction and coordination of international economic policy formulation, research and analysis within the department, advising the Secretary and Under Secretary on such policies and programs.

The Assistant Secretary is principally responsible for the follow-up, implementation and monitoring of the multilateral trade negotiations (MTN) and closely coordinates with other involved offices and agencies in educating U.S. business on the rights and opportunities resulting from the MTN.

The Assistant Secretary supports the department's activities in international trade, economic and investment matters and is an active participant in U.S. representation before the General Agreement on Tariffs and Trade (GATT), the United Nations Conference on Trade and Development (UNCTAD) and other multilateral deliberations and negotiations. The Assistant Secretary establishes and supervises the implementation of the department's interagency policy role in the National Security Council (NSC), United States Trade Representative (USTR) and other organizations.

Specific entities operating under this Assistant Secretary's direction are as follows:

Trade Agreements

The Trade Agreements unit is the department's primary source of trade policy development and support. It identifies key trade policy issues, develops departmental positions and is responsible for implementation of the MTN and other trade agreements for all non-agricultural matters.

Its activities include implementation and monitoring of MTN tariff and nontariff agreements, as well as investigation and resolution of problems in foreign country application of those agreements. Another of its functions is the development of information and cases arising under the MTN, including the operation of the Trade Complaint Center, the central contact point to which business brings complaints and problems regarding MTN and other trade agreements, and where the private sector receives advice on recourse and remedies available to it. Operation of the private sector advisory process (Industry Sector Advisory Committees—ISACs) under the expanded scope of Trade Policy Committee (TPC) coverage—including investment, East-West trade, etc.—also is administered by this office.

In the import relief area, the Trade Agreements unit provides staff analyses for the TPC in reviewing and considering sections 201, 301 and 406 import relief cases, monitors relief actions and develops departmental policy on orderly marketing agreements.

The Trade Agreements unit develops a continuing program for examination of post-MTN issues for negotiation or consultation, identification and cataloguing of foreign trade practices, such as those affecting trade in "services." It recommends policy objectives for departmental officials to present in interagency and international forums. In addition, it develops plans for educating the U.S. business community on general and specific trade opportunities resulting from the MTN.

Another major function is participating in and, as appropriate, leading negotiations and/or renegotiations of, bilateral and multilateral trade agreements, such as the expansion of MTN code agreements, commodity agreements, orderly marketing agreements, international sector agreements, etc. Other activities include the examination of U.S. access to raw materials and other resources located abroad and the recommendation of appropriate U.S. action in this area. The Trade Agreements unit is organized into three offices: Trade Policy, Commodity Policy and International Economic Relations.

Finance, Investment and Services

The Finance, Investment and Services unit (FIS) develops and implements policies and examines laws, regulations and practices in the financial and investment areas to determine their effect on U.S. business operations abroad. It recommends changes to improve U.S. competitiveness, monitors and analyzes foreign investment in the United States and leads a new department program in support of U.S. service industries' operations abroad.

FIS represents the department in international finance and development assistance affairs, especially those affecting export expansion. This role includes providing analyses and staff support for departmental representation on the National Advisory Council (NAC) and other bodies dealing with export finance, export and investment guarantees and export credit insurance. It analyzes transactions of domestic and international trade financing institutions from the perspective of effects on U.S. trade. It compares U.S. export finance practices with foreign practices and recommends needed changes. It also provides staff support for secretarial membership on the Export-Import Bank board.

FIS develops recommendations to improve the access of some 20 U.S. service industries to foreign markets, representing the department at interagency and international groups dealing with service industry problems. It coordinates closely with each of these service sectors and associations.

It examines the effect of U.S. tax laws and practices on U.S. competitiveness (DISC, foreign tax credits, taxation of U.S. overseas personnel, R&D). It conducts comparative analyses of foreign competitive practices and makes recommendations for changes in

U.S. treatment of export associations (Webb-Pomerene) and trading companies.

Representing the department in matters relating to U.S. direct investment, FIS analyzes investment trends and consults with business on U.S. regulations and international practices affecting investment. It recommends actions in bilateral and multilateral negotiations on investment and develops positions on multinational corporation (MNC) issues, providing staffing for departmental participation in MNC code issues and investment disputes. It advises on programs, policies and legislation affecting investment abroad and analyzes the economic effects on such investment. Also, it operates statutory programs to monitor and analyze foreign investment in the United States and identifies problems and recommends remedial action as necessary.

The FIS unit is divided into two offices: Foreign Investment in the United States, and International Finance, Investment and Services.

Policy Planning and Analysis

This unit conducts research and analysis on U.S. trade and on all factors affecting future trade prospects, developing policy recommendations to enhance the international trade competitiveness of the United States. It is the principal source within the department for developing positions on international positive adjustment policies and on international sectoral issues. On the basis of its own research and analysis as well as that of the new Bureau of Industrial Economics (BIE) and other parts of the government, this unit forecasts future trade trends and is responsible for developing longer-term policy options for U.S. trade and investment.

In conducting policy analyses of positive adjustment issues and international sectoral issues, the Policy Planning and Analysis unit draws on microeconomic and industry analyses of BIE, using these studies and data along with other information to formulate and evaluate policy options and to recommend policy positions. It develops positions to take on international positive adjustment policies in the Organization for Economic Cooperation and Development (OECD) and other forums and focuses on sectoral issues related to multilateral trade negotiation (MTN) implementation and to other trade and investment agreements and policies. In addition, it participates in or will head U.S. delegations to international meetings concerned with sectoral or positive adjustment issues.

In supporting the development of faster U.S. export growth and a stronger competitive position, this unit examines the effects of trade incentives and disincentives of the United States and other governments. It serves as the central contact point for collecting and evaluating information on the likely effects of changes proposed to improve the U.S. export position, developing policy options and recommendations.

The Policy Planning and Analysis unit also forecasts longer-term trade developments, with particular emphasis on identifying future trade problems that will face the United States. It identifies longer-run trade and investment policy objectives, basing these on both its forecasts and its program of research into U.S. trade and the factors affecting U.S. competitiveness. It evaluates the effectiveness of U.S. trade and investment policies and compares these with major competitor nations, and uses mathematical models to simulate the effects of future policy alternatives and provides the planning framework for trade policies and programs.

The Policy Planning and Analysis unit develops and maintains computerized data bases and provides trade and international economic statistics to other parts of the government and to U.S. business.

This unit is organized into two offices: Planning and Research, and International Sectoral Policy.

Textiles and Apparel

The Textile and Apparel unit is responsible for the economic well-being of the U.S. textile and apparel industries, domestically and internationally. Its major efforts include: negotiating bilateral textile and apparel import restraint agreements and in cooperation with other relevant agencies, monitoring imports from controlled (agreement) countries and uncontrolled countries; providing staff and technical support to the Committee for the Implementation of Textile Agreements (CITA); and promoting the expansion of exports of textiles and apparel.

This unit prepares monthly performance reports which show imports compared to restraint levels for each bilateral agreement country. Problems of implementing the agreements are analyzed and brought before CITA for resolution. This unit makes special tables and analyses used by U.S. negotiators of textile and apparel agreements. To accomplish this, it gathers and reports basic statistical data on imports. It prepares monthly reports on the overall import picture, comparing current monthly data with prior years and it is concerned with monitoring imports from uncontrolled countries. It classifies problems arising under agreements and trains foreign officials in U.S. classification procedures.

In addition, this unit provides current economic data and analyses of conditions in the domestic textile and apparel markets, including the impact of imports on these markets. It is responsible for the textile and apparel export expansion program and, in conjunction with the Office of the United States Trade Representative (USTR) and other organizations, reduction of nontariff barriers. Finally, it provides structural assistance to the industry in the form of new technology, research and development and management training.

Assistant Secretary for Trade Development

The *Assistant Secretary for Trade Development* carries out the department's policies and programs to promote world trade and to strengthen the international trade and investment position of the United States.

To this end, the Assistant Secretary oversees: the department's participation in international trade fairs, trade missions and other trade promotions abroad; programs conducted within the United States to expand the export-consciousness of American firms and to facilitate entry into international trade; and efforts to provide assistance to American exporters through the U.S. and Foreign Commercial Services. With respect to East-West trade, the Assistant Secretary is responsible for conducting the department's trade and investment expansion programs in communist countries and for the formulation and analysis of policies with respect to U.S. commercial policy in those countries.

The *International Trade Administration* (ITA) offers an enormous variety of services to help U.S. business sell its goods and services in international markets, too many to list in full here. For complete details, contact the responsible offices in Trade Development.

Following are descriptions of some of the specific programs and activities falling under the Assistant Secretary's jurisdiction:

Export Development

ITA's Export Development unit has primary responsibility for planning the export development programs in noncommunist countries. Its mission is to expand U.S. exports. It develops promotional programs conducted by the U.S. and Foreign Commercial Services and provides them with analytical and technical support.

This unit performs program planning and evaluation activities for the Assistant Secretary and has responsibility for determining program priorities for the U.S. and Foreign Commercial Services. It supports overseas promotional activities through management of Export Development Offices, development of overseas trade missions, sponsorship of special missions and other trade and investment activities. This unit, particularly its staff of country commercial experts, is responsible for counseling services to U.S. business on foreign markets, for market research and for technical support to other Commerce units.

Export Development staffs Commerce information programs, including the Worldwide Information and Trade System (WITS). Such information will be disseminated through the U.S. and Foreign Commercial Services for use by the U.S. business community. This unit also conducts a nationwide campaign on export awareness through specialized counseling, seminars, publications, joint industry/government activities and assistance in competing for major overseas projects. The Foreign Commercial Service stages promotional events and the U.S. Commercial Service assists in identifying participants for them.

Additionally, this unit coordinates program activities of the President's Export Council, which provides private sector advice to the Secretary and the President on export expansion issues. (see page 3)

The Export Development unit is broken down into four offices: Country Marketing, Export Marketing Assistance, Export Planning and Evaluation and Export Promotion. (see also Government Assistance)

East-West Trade

The East-West Trade unit helps American firms conduct business in communist countries, develops and explains East-West trade policy, strengthens governmental mechanisms for expanding trade with the nonmarket economies and expands understanding of issues and opportunities in East-West trade.

This unit conducts the day-to-day bilateral commercial contacts with embassies and other communist government entities in the United States. It supports Cabinet-level joint economic commissions, seeks resolution of commercial problems and assists in the development of commercial policy toward individual communist countries. It collects, analyzes and disseminates information about economic conditions, trade-related laws and regulations and market opportunities and advises U.S. firms on country-oriented trading problems. It also maintains day-to-day liaison with private U.S. bilateral councils established with these countries.

This unit offers practical services to help U.S. firms promote and market products in communist countries. It conducts briefings on "how to do business," arranges contacts between U.S. business and foreign trade organization officials, disseminates information on business opportunities in communist countries and assists U.S. firms in transaction problems involving federal agencies. In addition, this unit plans, recruits for and manages trade promotion events such as fairs, technical sales seminars and catalog shows in communist countries.

Lastly, this unit formulates, analyzes and makes recommendations about legislative and broad policy issues arising in East-West trade. It studies trade potential, balance-of-payments projections, econometric modeling of communist economies and the economic impact of East-West trade on the United States, its communist trading partners and other nations. It also maintains a major statistical data base on East-West trade and provides analyses of trade trends.

East-West Trade's three offices are: Country Affairs, Trade Development and Policy and Planning.

U.S. Commercial Service

The U.S. Commercial Service represents the Commerce Department in dealings with the U.S. business community. It provides U.S. business with information, technical assistance and counseling on export and investment matters and assists in identifying potential U.S. exporters and participants in overseas promotional events.

The U.S. Commercial Service administers a system of 44 District Offices, located in commercial centers throughout the United States. It offers U.S. firms counseling on overseas marketing, technical export information, guidance on marketing opportunities and advice on marketing strategies. It conducts seminars, workshops and conferences and utilizes Export Development and East-West Trade information services, including the Worldwide Information and Trade System (WITS). The service assists in obtaining commercial information from U.S. firms for use in Export Development planning and evaluation and advises the business community of significant trade developments, trade policy issues and technological developments.

The U.S. Commercial Service also publishes *Commerce Business Daily*.

There are 42 *District Export Councils* (DECs), which serve as the local contact with the business community in stimulating export expansion in their respective areas and work in cooperation with the department's District Offices.

Assistant Secretary for Trade Administration

The *Assistant Secretary for Trade Administration* has overall responsibility for the management and operation of the principal programs involving the regulation of imports and exports. The Assistant Secretary advises the Under Secretary and the Secretary on policies and programs relating to trade administration.

The Assistant Secretary is responsible for import administration: antidumping investigation and enforcement and countervailing duty investigation and enforcement. The Assistant Secretary is directly assisted by an Office of Antidumping and Countervailing Duty Policy.

The Assistant Secretary also is responsible for export administration: export licensing and enforcement, including national security, foreign policy and short supply export controls.

Finally, the Assistant Secretary oversees a number of special regulatory programs: antiboycott compliance, industrial mobilization, foreign trade zones and several other statutory import programs.

Following are more detailed descriptions of specific programs and activities for which this Assistant Secretary is responsible.

Import Administration

The Import Administration unit handles the investigation of antidumping and countervailing duty cases. Following investigation, this unit makes formal recommendations on individual cases.

15

In countervailing duty cases, the unit investigates and determines whether a subsidy is being provided with respect to the manufacture, production or exportation of merchandise imported into the United States. As part of the same process, the *International Trade Commission* (ITC) investigates and determines whether an industry is materially injured or threatened with material injury. If both of these determinations are positive, a countervailing duty is imposed in the amount of the net subsidy found to exist.

In antidumping cases, this unit investigates and determines whether merchandise is sold or is likely to be sold in the United States at less than fair value. As in countervailing duty cases, the ITC investigates material injury. If both determinations are positive, an antidumping duty is imposed equal to the amount by which fair foreign market value exceeds the U.S. price of the merchandise.

In addition to these two functions, the Import Administration unit also includes the following import related activities:

—The foreign trade zone program evaluates and processes applictions by port communities seeking to establish limited duty free zones as part of local economic development programs.

—Special statutory import programs related to the import of quota allocation watches and watch movements from U.S. territories and the import of education, scientific and cultural materials by nonprofit institutions pursuant to the Florence Agreement.

Within Import Administration are located the Offices of Compliance, Policy and Investigations.

Export Administration

The Export Administration unit is responsible for export controls for reasons of national security, foreign policy and short supply. The major functions of the program are policy planning, licensing, compliance and short-supply monitoring and licensing.

The policy planning function includes developing and coordinating recommendations on export control policies and programs, reviewing export license applications that present particular foreign policy on security issues and coordinating with other executive branch agencies on licenses and policies requiring interagency review.

The licensing function comprises the development of export control procedures and regulations, technical analysis and review of products, participation in interagency review of license applications, statistical and analytical reports of export licensing activities and formal issuance of licenses.

The compliance function includes the investigation and prosecution of export control violations.

The objective of the short-supply function is to restrict the excessive export of items in domestic short supply and to reduce the inflationary impact of foreign demand.

In addition to export controls, this unit manages the antiboycott and industrial mobilization programs.

The antiboycott program involves the administration and enforcement of the foreign boycott provisions of the Export Administration Act and monitoring of the impact of foreign boycotts on the United States. This includes the investigation and enforcement of compliance with the law as well as the processing of boycott reports.

The industrial mobilization program monitors and assures timely availability of material and products essential to industrial performance on contracts for national defense. This includes stockpile management of strategic and critical materials and an emergency preparedness function designed to identify industrial products and facilities which are essential to mobilization readiness, national defense or post-attack survival and recovery.

The Export Administration unit comprises three offices: Export Administration, Antiboycott Compliance and Industrial Mobilization.

Bureau of Economic Analysis

A comprehensive and detailed view of economic transactions between the United States and foreign countries through the balance-of-payments accounts is made possible by the *Bureau of Economic Analysis* (BEA). Major types of transactions covered are: merchandise trade, travel, transportation, income on international investment, U.S. government military and other services, U.S. private services, private remittances, foreign aid programs, short- and long-term private capital flows and changes in foreign official assets in the United States and U.S. official reserve assets.

Balance-of-payments estimates are published quarterly in the *Survey of Current Business,* the BEA's monthly journal of research and information. Regional and country breakdowns are published, showing bilateral balance-of-payments estimates for major trading countries.

BEA also prepares international investment estimates, both for U.S. direct investment abroad and for foreign direct investment in the United States.

Maritime Administration

The *Maritime Administration* (MarAd) is responsible for promoting and maintaining a U.S. merchant marine capable of meeting U.S. commercial shipping needs and national security requirements. MarAd assists the maritime community in the areas of ship design, construction, development of advanced transportation systems and equipment and promotion of the use of U.S.-flag vessels. It also provides financial support to help U.S. shipbuilders and ship operators narrow the cost advanges enjoyed by foreign counterparts.

MarAd conducts a large-scale research and development program to ensure that U.S.-flag ships incorporate the advanced technology that will enable them to provide shippers with efficient and competitive service. Government-industry cost sharing is a key element of the cooperative program, which is aimed largely at increasing the productivity of the U.S. maritime industry.

In addition, MarAd carries on a dynamic market development program designed to increase the U.S.-flag carriage of U.S. ocean-borne foreign trade. It provides marketing information and cargo data to U.S.-flag vessel operators and maintains contact with U.S. export and import communities to familiarize them with the benefits of "shipping American."

Bureau of the Census
Department of Commerce
Washington, D.C. 20233
Tel. (202) 568-1200

The *Bureau of the Census,* in addition to its better-known work in the population area, compiles and publishes official figures on U.S. foreign trade. Statistical data on U.S. exports and imports are collected from Shipper's Export Declarations and import entries. These forms are filed by exporters and importers with Customs officials and transmitted to the Bureau of the Census. These statistics are designed to serve the needs of both government and nongovernment users.

Government uses the foreign trade statistics: to develop the merchandise trade figures in balance-of-payments accounts; to analyze major movements and trends in international trade; to evaluate and plan export expansion, agricultural assistance and other programs; and to measure the impact of tariff and trade concessions under the General Agreement on Tariffs and Trade (GATT). The foreign trade data also are used extensively as the statistical base to implement and analyze operations under various international trade agreements.

Nongovernment users in industry, finance, research institutions, transportation and other fields use the foreign trade data: in appraising the general trade situation and outlook; in share-of-the-market analyses and market penetration studies; in product and market development for measuring the impact of competition; and, in general, as one of the statistical bases for determining marketing policies.

The statistics compiled by the Bureau of the Census include information on the dollar value and net quantity (pounds, gallons, square yards, etc.) of U.S. imports and exports of commodities by all methods of transportation combined and shipping weight and value of shipments made by vessel and by air. Data are shown by country of origin and destination and Customs districts through which merchandise enters and leaves the United States. Separate statistics are presented on trade with Puerto Rico and U.S. possessions and on trade of the Virgin Islands with foreign countries. Beginning with the January 1948 statistics, data are available on exports (excluding military shipments) and general imports adjusted for working-day and seasonal variations. (see also Statistics, Foreign Trade)

Department of Defense
The Pentagon
Washington, D.C. 20330
Tel. (202) 695-3240

The responsibility of the *Department of Defense* (DOD) is to provide for the military security of the United States. Its foreign trade and investment-related functions are centered mainly in the offices of the *Under Secretary of Defense for Research and Engineering* and the *Assistant Secretary of Defense for International Security Affairs*.

The Under Secretary of Defense for Research and Engineering is the primary adviser to the Secretary of Defense on research, engineering and acquisition of weapon systems and communications, command, control and intelligence resources. The focal point in his office for international activities is the office of the *Director for International Programs*.

The Director for International Programs is responsible for all international activities in DOD related to research and engineering, including defense-related international cooperative efforts and NATO rationalization activities. The director also is responsible for reviewing all proposed sales of defense-related articles and services abroad from a "technomilitary" point of view.

The function of the office of the Assistant Secretary of Defense for International Security Affairs is to assess the impact of international political, economic and military developments on the military security of the United States. Its foreign commerce and investment functions are centered mainly in the office of the *Deputy Assistant Secretary of Defense for International Economic Affairs* and the *Defense Security Assistance Agency*.

The Deputy Assistant Secretary for International Economic Affairs has prime responsibility for identifying national security objectives and developing, preparing and coordinating related Defense positions, policies, plans and procedures in the field of international economic affairs. This officer is the principal adviser to the Assistant Secretary for International Security Affairs (ASD/ISA) on all international economic policy matters of Defense interest. International economic issues covered include: East-West trade, export and munitions controls, technology transfer, foreign investment in the United States (security implications for firms with classified contracts), import protection (where imports may affect capabilities of U.S. industries to meet military needs), energy requirements of the United States and its allies, human rights, arms cooperation in NATO and the domestic and foreign economic impact of global arms transfers. This office represents Defense on interagency international economic committees and supports the ASD/ISA and the Secretary of Defense in senior economic policy forums.

The Defense Security Assistance Agency directs, administers and supervises the execution of programs, authorized by the Foreign Assistance Act of 1961, as amended, and the Arms Export Control Act, through which the United States transfers defense articles, defense services and training to foreign governments by grant or sale.

Department of Energy
Forrestal Building
1000 Independence Ave.,
S.W.
Washington, D.C. 20585
Tel. (202) 252-5800

The *Department of Energy* (DOE), established in 1978, brought together the many fragmented energy programs and offices created over the years in the federal government. DOE is designed to carry out in a coherent and effective manner the elements of the nation's energy policy.

The activities of DOE most directly related to foreign commerce are administered by the Office of International Affairs, the Economic Regulatory Administration and the Federal Energy Regulatory Commission.

The *Office of International Affairs* has primary responsibility for the administration of cooperative energy programs, including negotiating bilateral agreements with other countries for the joint development and exchange of new energy technologies; advising the Export-Import Bank of the United States on all proposed transactions involving the export of energy-related equipment, services and resources; cooperating with the Department of Commerce on matters relating to controls on energy exports; and the monitoring of international trade in energy resources, the world energy equipment market and, in accordance with the Federal Energy Administration Act of 1974, foreign investment in U.S. energy sources and supplies.

The *Economic Regulatory Administration* has been given the authority to control all exports and imports of natural gas from and into the United States, administer the department's oil pricing, allocation and import programs and regulate the transmission of electric power between the United States and foreign countries.

As the successor to the Federal Power Commission, the *Federal Energy Regulatory Commission* has inherited among its other duties the responsibility for establishing and enforcing rates and charges for the transmission and sale of natural gas and electric power imports and for issuing and enforcing the certificates of public convenience and necessity for construction and abandonment of import-associated facilities.

Department of Health and Human Services
200 Independence Avenue,
S.W.

The Food and Drug Administration, under the *Department of Health and Human Services*, formerly the Department of Health, Education and Welfare (HEW), has among its responsibilities the enforcement of the Federal Food, Drug and Cosmetic Act, the

Washington, D.C. 20201
Tel. (202) 245-6296

Fair Packaging and Labeling Act, the Radiation Control for Health and Safety Act and the Public Health Service Act. Its activities are directed mainly to insure safety, effectiveness and wholesomeness and to promote truthful and informative labeling of consumer products covered by these laws.

The *Bureau of Biologics*, under the Food and Drug Administration, administers regulation of biological products shipped in interstate and foreign commerce.

The department's *Center for Disease Control* has the responsibility of directing and enforcing the nation's foreign quarantine activities and regulations.

Department of Housing and Urban Development

Office of International Affairs
451 7th Street, S.W.
Washington, D.C. 20410
Tel. (202) 755-5770

The *Department of Housing and Urban Development's* (HUD) international interests are administered by the *Office of International Affairs* (OIA). Established in 1944, OIA is primarily concerned with information exchange. The objectives of such exchanges are twofold: first, in conformity with U.S. national policy to provide a decent home and a suitable living environment for every American family, OIA facilitates the acquisition of ideas and methods derived from foreign experience which may benefit Americans and American cities; second, OIA supports U.S. foreign policy through formal and informal agreements for exchange of data with other nations and through participation in multilateral activities which reflect U.S. concerns and responsibilities in the international community.

As the nature of data has become more complex and the volume of material available from abroad has increased, the OIA information system has evolved into a computer-based process called the Foreign Information Retrieval System (FIRS). The system is designed to identify, acquire, process and make available current technical, program and statistical data for dissemination to and use by a wide variety of persons and institutions.

Over the years, OIA has built an extensive collection of documentation on a variety of subjects reflecting a broad range of foreign activities and domestic priorities. This collection is added to daily by receipt of material from international organizations, bilateral partners, national and private institutions and individuals. Bilateral arrangements include exchanges with Canada, the Federal Republic of Germany, France, Great Britain, Japan, Mexico, Spain, Sweden and the U.S.S.R. However, informal arrangements result in data from almost every country in the world. International organizations generating valuable data include various elements of the United Nations System—UN Economic Commission for Europe; Committee on Housing, Building and Planning (ECE/HBP); UN Habitat Centre; and the UN Environmental Program; as well as the Organization for Economic Cooperation and Development (OECD) and the Committee on Challenges to Modern Society (CCMS).

Department of the Interior

C Street between 18th and 19th Streets, N.W.
Washington, D.C. 20240
Tel. (202) 343-1100

Various offices and bureaus within the *Department of the Interior* administer international activities and programs having an impact on foreign commerce. These focus on economic and commercial information and its exchange, international conventions and agreements, international meetings and conferences, technical assistance, training programs and research and development. Brief descriptions of these subject areas follow.

Economic studies and resource assessments are prepared by department specialists in cooperation with other U.S. government departments and agencies to develop national plans for the development and conservation of domestic natural resources.

Information exchange takes place on both a formal and informal basis, with numerous department personnel participating in exchanges through scientific and professional organizations. In addition, the department administers bilateral and multilateral activities to encourage formal data exchanges on an international basis.

The department often provides official delegates and advisers to assist the Department of State in negotiating international conventions and agreements. The representatives may be either technical or administrative experts with knowledge of department technological capacities.

The department supplies advisers and representatives to U.S. delegations attending international meetings and conferences. Technical information is provided in the formulation of policies and positions in such meetings, with the department often furnishing leadership and advice in conference planning.

Department specialists in such fields as resource planning, land management, wildlife preservation or control, mines and minerals, parks, geology, hydrology, irrigation, power development and desalination are often detailed to foreign countries to assist in the optimum use and development of natural resources. Technical assistance programs are administered by the department under contract arrangements with the Department of State, the United Nations or foreign governments.

Natural resource and environmental training programs are provided by the department for foreign nationals, ranging from the ministerial level to students. Such training, conducted either in the United States or abroad, may involve in-service training in federal government facilities, on-the-job training or special arrangements with universities. Although training is administered by the department, it is under contract to the Department of State, the United Nations or affiliate organization, a foreign government, a foundation or an independent international organization.

Three types of research and development are carried out by the department in foreign countries: bilateral or multilateral cooperative research programs, foreign assignment of U.S. technical experts under development programs and current research and development contracts awarded by the department to agencies in foreign countries.

Department of Justice
10th and Pennsylvania
Avenue, N.W.
Washington, D.C. 20530
Tel. (202) 737-8200

The responsibility of the *Department of Justice* is to enforce federal laws, to conduct criminal and civil investigations and to defend the United States in court. Its principal foreign trade functions are located in the *Antitrust Division*, the *Criminal Division* and the *Civil Division*.

The *foreign commerce section* of the Antitrust Division is responsible for conducting investigations and filing civil suits or seeking grand jury indictments for violations of the antitrust laws in the foreign trade area. The antitrust laws are designed to protect competition and prohibit anticompetitive and monopolistic practices or agreements among competitors.

Within the Criminal Division, the *Fraud Section* enforces criminal laws against bribery abroad including the Foreign Corrupt Practices Act. The *Customs Unit* handles import penalty cases and the *Internal Security Section* enforces the law that requires those representing foreign powers or agencies to register as foreign agents. The division's *Office of International Affairs* handles extradition of fugitives to and from the United States and is responsible for mutual assistance with foreign countries in connection with criminal investigations here or abroad.

The *Office of Foreign Litigation* in the Civil Division renders international judicial assistance to foreign and international tribunals, represents the United States in foreign tribunals in cases brought by or against the United States or against government personnel stationed abroad for acts performed in the course of their government service and asserts sovereign immunity in suits against foreign states in American courts where the Department of State has recognized such immunity.

Department of Labor
200 Constitution Avenue, N.W.
Washington, D.C. 20210
Tel. (202) 523-8165

The *Department of Labor* has responsibility for a wide range of significant international activities, coordinated largely through its *Bureau of International Labor Affairs* (ILAB). The bureau's primary concerns are to promote the concept of fair trade and international fair labor standards in global economic policy, assist in formulating trade investment and economic policies affecting U.S. workers (with particular attention to the relation between competitive foreign imports and domestic employment) and advise the President on the labor implications of trade legislation, trade agreements and international labor developments.

In addition, it helps represent the United States in bilateral and multilateral trade negotiations and on international bodies such as the Organization for Economic Cooperation and Development (OECD) and the General Agreement on Tariffs and Trade (GATT). It also coordinates the U.S. position in the International Labor Organization (ILO) and administers the trade adjustment assistance program.

There are seven offices under this bureau:

1. *Office of Foreign Economic Policy.* This office is divided into three groups:
   a. *The Trade Policy Group*—develops and coordinates departmental positions on foreign economic policy issues and departmental participation in interagency trade consultations.
   b. *The International Commodities Group*—works on labor aspects of international commodity arrangements.
   c. *The Advisory Committees Group*—coordinates labor union advice on multilateral trade negotiations and on other trade matters.

2. *Office of Trade Adjustment Assistance.* The bureau administers the expanded trade adjustment assistance program authorized under the Trade Act of 1974. The program provides cash allowances and other benefits to workers adversely affected by increased imports. This office has two units:
   a. *Investigations and Reports*—investigates adjustment assistance cases involving workers adversely affected by import competition.
   b. *Trade and Industry Analysis Division*—performs research to determine the number of workers who might be eligible for adjustment assistance in the industries petitioning the International Trade Commission for import relief.

3. *Office of International Organizations and Technical Assistance.* This office oversees the department's dealings with the ILO and is responsible for technical assistance programs.

Participation in the work of various international organizations is another major ILAB concern. Most international organizations have a direct or indirect effect on labor and business abroad through policies adopted and influence exerted in the various nations. This, in turn, has many implications for the U.S. domestic scene. The Labor Department plays a key role in the Organization for Economic Cooperation and Development (OECD).

The Department of Labor is responsible for all U.S. participation in the manpower and social policy matters of the OECD and provides the U.S. delegate to the Organization's Manpower and Social Affairs Committee. It also assists other U.S. agencies responsible for OECD committees dealing with questions of economic growth, investment, trade and other economic and social issues.

The Labor Department also carries out an active program of technical cooperation with various developing countries. Through the Department of Labor International Technical Assistance Corps (DOLITAC), it makes available to these countries advisers and technical specialists with competence in such fields as manpower planning, labor statistics, employment service operations and skills training to assist ministries of labor and related agencies in strengthening their programs in these areas. Such activities are funded by the Agency for International Development, various international aid-donor agencies and by the recipient countries.

4. *Office of Foreign Labor Affairs.* Two groups comprise this office:

    a. *Area Affairs Group*—monitors international labor topics.

    b. *Foreign Publications Group*—publishes monographs and foreign labor profiles on subjects relating to international labor affairs.

5. *Office of Foreign-Financed Programs.* Within this office, self-financed training and development cooperation programs for foreign countries are coordinated.

6. *Foreign Economic Research Staff.* The bureau has established a comprehensive economic research and analysis program to better understand and deal with impact of foreign economic policies on U.S. workers. Subjects researched by this group cover a variety of issues: effects of trade and foreign investment on U.S. employment levels, impact of transfer of technology on the domestic labor market and nontariff barriers used by U.S. trading partners.

7. *The Office of International Visitor Programs.* This office covers trade union and government exchange activities.

The *Bureau of Labor Statistics* conducts comparative studies of the labor force, compensation, productivity and other labor conditions in the United States and abroad and monitors U.S. trade with the rest of the world.

Department of State
2201 C Street, N.W.
Washington, D.C. 20520
Tel. (202) 655-4000

Because of its foreign policy responsibility and authority, and the increased emphasis on the commercial element of U.S. diplomacy by recent administrations, the *State Department,* along with Treasury, occupies a leading position in the development and exercise of U.S. foreign economic policy and its importance to the American trading community.

The State Department's primary objective in the execution of U.S. foreign policy is to promote the long-range security and well-being of the United States. The department collects and analyzes information relating to U.S. overseas interests, makes recommendations on policy and future action and takes necessary steps to carry out established policy. It engages in continuous consultations with other states, negotiates treaties and agreements with foreign nations, speaks for the United States in the United Nations and in major international organizations in which the United States participates and represents the United States in international conferences.

Major programs in the field of foreign commerce are implemented only after consideration by interdepartmental committees composed of representatives of the Departments of State, Commerce and Agriculture and other interested agencies. Nevertheless, most activities of the State Department have some impact on foreign commerce and on specific economic and commercial policies.

The *Bureau of Economic and Business Affairs* has primary responsibility within the Department of State for formulating and implementing policies regarding foreign economic matters, trade promotion and business services of an international nature, and coordinating regional economic policy with other relevant bureaus. Responsibilities of this Bureau are divided among the following areas: *International Finance and Development* (including the *Offices of Business Practices, Development Finance, Monetary Affairs* and *Investment Affairs*); *International Trade Policy* (including the *Offices of International Trade and East-West Trade*); *International Resources and Food Policy* (including the *Offices of Fuels and Energy, International Commodities* and *Food Policy and Programs*); *Commercial and Telecommunications Affairs* (including the *Offices of International Communications Policy* and *Commercial Affairs*); and *Transportation Affairs* (including the *Offices of Aviation* and *Maritime Affairs*).

Regional Bureaus. Under the direction of an Assistant Secretary of State, regional bureaus are each assigned responsibility for U.S. foreign affairs activities in a specific major region of the world. They are: *Bureau of African Affairs, Bureau of Inter-American Affairs, Bureau of European Affairs, Bureau of Near Eastern and South Asian Affairs* and *Bureau of East Asian and Pacific Affairs.* Country "desk" officers maintain day-to-day contact with overseas diplomatic posts and provide country-specific economic and political analyses and commercial counseling to U.S. business. The Assistant Secretaries are responsible for advising the Secretary in the formulation of U.S. policies toward the countries within their regional jurisdiction and for guiding the operation of diplomatic establishments in the countries in their geographic area.

Among the other Department of State functions of particular interest are the following:

- The *Bureau of International Organization Affairs* coordinates and develops guidance and support for U.S. participation in international organizations and conferences.
- The *Bureau of Public Affairs* works for a larger and more effective exchange of information and views on U.S. foreign relations between the department and the American people. It provides information services for news agencies,

makes studies of public opinion, publishes periodicals and pamphlets on current policy and the official historical records of foreign relations, answers inquiries from the public and maintains communications with private groups and organizations interested in international affairs. It also conducts foreign policy information conferences in Washington and throughout the country, fills requests for speakers from the Department of State and answers correspondence on international affairs addressed to the Department of State or the White House.

- Within the *Bureau of Consular Affairs* are: the Passport Office, responsible for controlling American citizens and nationals leaving and entering territory under U.S. jurisdiction; the Visa Office, responsible for the issuance of visas and exit permits to aliens; and the Office of Special Consular Services, concerned with the welfare and protection of American citizens and interests abroad.
- *Foreign Service of the United States.* The prime instrumentality through which the government carries on its work in foreign countries is the United States Foreign Service, which includes ambassadors, ministers, Foreign Service officers, Foreign Service Reserve and staff officers and employees, local employees and consular agents.

  Foreign Service officers and employees in some 300 posts throughout the world have the duty of protecting the interests of the United States in accordance with treaties and international law and of advising, protecting and assisting American residents traveling or having interests abroad. They participate in the negotiation of treaties, conventions and protocols regarding international affairs. They observe, analyze and report on political, social and economic trends of significance in the countries to which they are assigned.
- The *Foreign Service Institute,* operated by the Department of State, trains personnel and officers of the department and the Foreign Service and other federal employees concerned with U.S. international relations. It sometimes utilizes universities throughout the United States for specialized advanced training.
- *United States Mission to the United Nations.* The Mission represents the United States at the permanent headquarters of the United Nations in New York City. It carries out the instructions of the President as transmitted by the Department of State in conducting U.S. participation in the various U.N. organs. Address: 799 United Nations Plaza, New York, New York 10017.
- *Other Special Missions.* The United States also maintains other Special Missions: the U.S. Mission to the Organization of American States, Washington, D.C.; the U.S. Mission to the International Civil Aviation Organization, Montreal, Canada; the Berlin Mission in Germany; the U.S. Mission to the European Communities in Belgium and Luxembourg; the U.S. Mission to the European Office of the United Nations and other international organizations in Switzerland; the U.S. Mission to the International Atomic Energy Agency in Austria; and the U.S. Mission to the North Atlantic Treaty Organization and European Regional Organizations in France.

Department of Transportation

400 Seventh Street, N.W.
Washington, D.C. 20590
Tel. (202) 426-4000

The *Department of Transportation* (DOT) works in partnership with state and local governments and private operators to help develop, maintain and improve domestic transportation services. Many safety standards set by its operating administrations, however, do affect foreign manufacturers and operators of vehicles, vessels or aircraft destined to be sold or operated in the United States.

The Federal Aviation Administration (FAA)

FAA operates the U.S. air traffic control system and establishes practices and procedures to which all pilots operating in American airspace must adhere. The agency issues safety standards which govern the manufacture of all aircraft to be sold or operated in the United States and agency officials serve as government representatives at meetings of various international aviation organizations.

The U.S. Coast Guard

The United States Coast Guard enforces U.S. maritime laws, establishes navigational and operating procedures for vessels sailing in American waters and enforces the conservation law governing fishing in the 200-mile coastal fishing zone.

The St. Lawrence Seaway Development Corporation

The Corporation—in conjunction with its Canadian counterpart—administers the operation and maintenance of the St. Lawrence Seaway.

The National Highway Traffic Safety Administration

This administration sets safety standards governing the manufacture of all motor vehicles destined for sale in the United States.

Department of the Treasury

15th Street and
   Pennsylvania Avenue,
   N.W.
Washington, D.C. 20220
Tel. (202) 566-2000

The *Department of the Treasury*, with its responsibility for formulating and regulating U.S. international financial and tax policy, holds preeminent influence in international monetary, economic and investment matters. Treasury's operations touch on virtually every aspect of U.S. foreign economic relations, including trade and investment, energy, commodity and monetary policy and development finance. The Secretary is U.S. Governor of the International Monetary Fund (IMF) and the international development banks and, with the Deputy Secretaries, chairs or serves on a wide range of government policy advisory bodies and joint economic commissions with foreign countries.

The Treasury offices involved are:

1. The *Office of the Under Secretary for Monetary Affairs* holds principal responsibility for international financial and economic policy-making in the Treasury, except in matters related to taxes and tariff affairs, and has supervisory responsibility over all the department's international activities in the areas of monetary, trade and investment, development finance, commodity, energy and natural resource policy.

2. The *Office of the Assistant Secretary for International Affairs* performs Treasury's staff work in the areas cited above. Specialized support is provided by four Deputies:

The *Deputy Assistant Secretary for International Monetary Affairs* oversees international monetary negotiations and the maintenance and operation of the international monetary system; foreign exchange operations and management of U.S. reserve assets; international banking and capital markets; analysis and forecasting of the global economic outlook and coordination of economic policy among industrial nations. In addition, the Deputy's staff supports U.S. participation in the IMF in those areas of the Organization for Economic Cooperation and Development (OECD) falling within the Deputy's purview and administers the Exchange Stabilization Fund (ESF).

The *Deputy Assistant Secretary for Developing Nations* supervises three offices: *Developing Nations Finance,* with responsibility for formulation of positions and policies on U.S. economic and financial programs toward developing nations; the *Office of International Development Banks* which, among other functions, provides analysis and recommendations on the operations, activities, and policies of the World Bank and other international lending institutions.

3. The *National Advisory Council on International Monetary and Financial Policy* is responsible for coordinating U.S. participation in the international financial institutions and the policies and practices of all agencies of the U.S. government that make or participate in making foreign loans or that engage in foreign financial exchange or monetary transactions.

The *Deputy Assistant Secretary for Trade and Investment* is responsible for international trade and commercial policy, including multilateral and bilateral trade negotiations, trade finance, East-West trade, direct investment and other multinational corporation-related issues.

The *Deputy Assistant Secretary for Commodities and Natural Resources* reviews and develops recommendations on energy and other commodity policy, law of the sea, etc., through the *Office of Raw Materials and Oceans Policy* and the *Office of International Energy Policy.*

4. The *Office of the Assistant Secretary for Enforcement and Operations* formulates policy and supervises the operations of the *U.S. Secret Service,* the *U.S. Customs Service,* the *Bureau of Alcohol, Tobacco and Firearms,* the *Office of Foreign Assets Control* and the *Federal Law Enforcement Training Center,* including enforcement and regulatory matters bearing on foreign trade in alcohol and firearms.

Responsibility for the collection of duties and taxes on imported merchandise, the prevention of smuggling and customs frauds and the administration of certain navigation laws and treaties are all functions of the U.S. Customs, which helps other federal agencies to enforce many of their laws and regulations, such as the export control program of the Department of Commerce.

5. The *Office of the Assistant Secretary for Tax Policy* advises and assists the Secretary and the Deputy Secretary in the formulation and execution of domestic and international tax policies and programs. These functions include international tax regulations and rulings, participation in international tax treaty negotiations and maintenance of relations with international organizations in tax matters.

---

b. Executive Agencies

Civil Aeronautics Board
1825 Connecticut Avenue, N.W.

The *Civil Aeronautics Board* (CAB) is an independent federal agency charged with broad responsibilities for encouraging and developing U.S. civil aviation and for granting authorizations to

Washington, D.C. 20428
Tel. (202) 673-5260

carriers to engage in interstate and foreign transportation. CAB policies are geared to encouraging low fares, increasing competition and strengthening of government regulation to permit individual air carrier managements and the air transportation industry to be more responsive to the demands of the marketplace.

The CAB consults with and assists the Department of State in negotiating agreements with foreign governments for the establishment or development of air routes and services.

Under the Airline Deregulation Act of 1978, the CAB's regulatory powers will be phased out over a period ending January 1, 1985. Meanwhile, to permit maximum competition in air transportation, entry into and exit from air transportation markets will be increasingly eased. The act also protects small community air service and provides for small carrier strengthening, satellite airport service and prevention of "unreasonable" air industry concentration.

Commodity Futures Trading Commission
2033 K Street, N.W.
Washington, D.C. 20581
Tel. (202) 254-6387

The *Commodity Futures Trading Commission* (CFTC) was created in 1975 as an independent agency under the authorization of the Commodity Futures Trading Commission Act of 1974. The Commission has jurisdiction over futures trading on all U.S. commodity exchanges and over trading in commodity options and leverage contracts, including those in gold and silver bullion and bulk gold and silver coins. The CFTC requires exchanges to protect the public with adequate rules and effective enforcement. It reviews and approves rules and may require a market to change its rules or practices and may, in emergencies, direct a market to take necessary actions to maintain or restore orderly markets. It requires a procedure for settlement of customer claims against members and employees of the exchanges.

The Commission also approves all futures contracts and requires that contracts reflect normal market flow and commercial trading practices in the actual commodity and provide for a broad deliverable supply. It may impose a limit on the number of contracts a speculator may trade or hold, including any foreign interests participating in markets under CFTC regulation. It assures that information required of exchanges, such as volume and open interest, is timely and accurate and it monitors market letters, reports and statistics provided by traders, brokers, trading advisers and commodity pool operators. It is responsible for regulating the offer and sale of commodity options (including foreign options offered by U.S. companies required to be registered with the CFTC), dealer options and gold and silver leverage contracts.

The Commission protects customers of commodity professionals by establishing minimum financial requirements and trade practices for registrants and by requiring segregation of customer funds from company funds. The CFTC operates a reparations unit to adjudicate and settle claims.

Environmental Protection Agency
401 M Street, S.W.
Washington, D.C. 20460
Tel. (202) 755-0700

Environmental legislation and the standards and regulations of the *Environmental Protection Agency* (EPA) sometimes have implications for foreign trade. EPA analyzes such measures, together with other U.S. government agencies, to assess their impact on international trade and to assure that any adverse effect on U.S. international commerce is minimized. EPA cooperates with the Departments of State and Commerce to promote the sale abroad of pollution control devices and environmental technology.

The focal point for EPA activities related to foreign commerce is the *Office of International Activities*. The office analyzes agency legislation, regulations and programs for international economic impact and formulates appropriate information exchange programs and consultations; coordinates agency participation in international organizations, such as the OECD, where trade and economic effects of environmental policies are debated; develops reimbursable technical assistance programs with other countries, including initial identification of research and control technology needs; and makes information on foreign environmental policies available to agency experts.

Export-Import Bank of the United States
811 Vermont Avenue, N.W.
Washington, D.C. 20571
Tel. (202) 566-2117

For more than four decades, the *Export-Import Bank of the United States* (Eximbank), an independent U.S. government agency, has been an important source of financing for the sale of U.S. goods and services to purchasers overseas. Created in 1934 by Presidential Executive Order, Eximbank was established on a statutory basis in 1945 with passage of the Export-Import Bank Act. Since then, its operating charter has been renewed periodically, most recently in 1978 when it received a new five-year mandate. It is a financially self-sustaining institution and does not receive appropriations from the Congress. Since beginning operations, Eximbank has paid more than one billion dollars to the U.S. Treasury and has supported more than $90 billion in U.S. export sales.

Today, a growing variety of Eximbank programs assist thousands of American exporters, ranging from some of the world's largest and most experienced international corporations to small firms just beginning foreign trade endeavors. Eximbank financial services support a broad crosssection of products and projects—from industrial raw materials and farm products, computers and farm machinery, to cement plants, power generating plants and commercial jet aircraft.

Its operations generally are divided into two financing "windows." The first is the buyer credit or project financing window, which provides direct loans at fixed interest rates and long terms, as well as financial guarantees of private source loans for heavy capital equipment and capital-intensive projects. The second is the supplier credit window, which offers assistance through medium-term commercial bank guarantees, short- and medium-term export credit insurance, the Cooperative Financing Facility (a network of foreign banks that work with Eximbank) and discount loans.

Project financing supports the exports of "turnkey" projects such as manufacturing, electric power and petrochemical plants and large mining and construction operations. This window also covers "big ticket" product exports including commercial jet aircraft, locomotives and other heavy capital equipment. As of early 1979, project and capital equipment financing accounted for roughly 75 percent of the Bank's $26.5 billion in outstanding financing. The largest part of Eximbank's direct project financing (perhaps as much as 70 percent) assists in financing U.S. exports for creditworthy sales in developing countries.

The supplier credit window, through its various programs, is designed to support less costly transactions where repayment periods are either short-term (up to six months) or medium-term (from six months to five years). In an average year, as many as 3,000 exporters may participate in the supplier credit programs.

The Bank has a financing network with hundreds of U.S. and

foreign financial institutions. These close working relationships have made it possible to extend further its resources in support of American sales abroad.

Credit Insurance. In 1961, the Bank joined with a group of some 50 leading U.S. marine and casualty underwriters to create the *Foreign Credit Insurance Association* (FCIA), which insures the short- and medium-term credits extended by American exporters to their overseas customers against commercial and political risks.

Bank Guarantees. In 1955, Eximbank inaugurated its commercial bank guarantee program, which insures repayment to U.S. banks that extend credit to foreign buyers on behalf of their U.S. customers.

Cooperative Financing Facility (CFF). In 1970, the Bank began building a global network of foreign banks that share in financing sales of American products to overseas buyers.

Discount Loans. In 1969, the Bank introduced a simplified program to assist export-oriented U.S. banks in providing a source of funds during periods of tight money and, more recently, in offering fixed-rate credits to foreign buyers.

PEFCO. In 1970, Eximbank, working with the Bankers' Association for Foreign Trade, established the Private Export Funding Corporation (PEFCO) (see page 76)

Through its *Small Business Advisory Service,* Eximbank provides on-the-spot advice about the availability and use of export credit insurance, guarantees and export financing. The Bank also has a general *Export Counseling Service* that is available to any U.S. business or bank.

Eximbank's network of banking and insurance organizations at home and abroad has made it possible to stimulate private capital participation in export financing and to enhance considerable private sector expertise in the service of U.S. export trade. It provides training and consultation for executives of many private institutions, thereby creating a growing network of export conscious information sources.

For more information on the Export-Import Bank see the booklet, *Eximbank,* describing its financing programs. The Bank also publishes a free newsletter, *Eximbank Record,* ten times each year and issues a comprehensive annual report plus fact sheets about its programs.

Federal Communications Commission
1919 M Street, N.W.
Washington, D.C. 20554
Tel. (202) 632-7000

The *Federal Communications Commission* (FCC) is an independent agency responsible for regulating interstate and foreign commerce in communication by wire and radio under the provisions of the Communications Act of 1934, as amended.

The FCC engages in several activities on an international level, some of which may affect international trade and investment. It seeks to assure that a rapid and efficient worldwide telephone and telegraph service is available at reasonable rates. In fulfillment of this responsibility, the Commission regulates telegraph, telephone, data, telex, television and other communications services provided by submarine cable, satellite communications and, to a limited extent, high frequency radio between the United States and foreign points and between the United States and ships at sea.

The FCC participates in international consultative meetings involving wire and radio communications. It was extensively involved in the 1979 General World Administrative Radio Conference (WARC) of the International Telecommunication Union, a specialized agency of the United Nations located in Geneva, Switzerland, which provided revisions to the international radio regulations and frequency allocations applicable during the period 1980-2000. It also participates in meetings with representatives of other governments to establish efficient methods and procedures for planning international telecommunications facilities.

The FCC is also required to administer the provisions of the Communications Satellite Act of 1962, to foster the establishment and continued operation of a global communications satellite system. The act specifically provides that the economies which satellite technology makes possible should be made available to less developed as well as more highly developed countries.

The FCC also maintains an International Telecommunications Section. It serves as a clearinghouse in the United States for billing, collection and accounting related to settlement of international telecommunications charges by foreign governments to vessels operated by U.S. government agencies, private companies or individuals for marine radiotelephone and radiotelegraph communications through foreign coastal stations.

Federal Maritime Commission
1100 L Street, N.W.
Washington, D.C. 20573
Tel. (202) 523-5911

The *Federal Maritime Commission*, an independent agency, regulates the liner shipping industry operating in U.S. ocean commerce. The Commission was established in 1961 by President Kennedy's Reorganization Plan VII as the successor to commissions and boards having similar functions, dating back to the enactment of the 1916 Shipping Act.

The Commission maintains surveillance over services, rates, practices and agreements of common carriers by water and of other persons engaged in the foreign commerce of the United States. Among other responsibilities, it receives and reviews tariffs specifying freight rates filed by ocean common carriers. It investigates discriminatory rates and practices to ensure that shippers pay the precise legal rates on file with the Commission.

The Federal Maritime Commission requires the owner, charterer or operator of every vessel over 300 gross tons, using any port or navigable waters of the United States, to pay costs arising from spills of oil or hazardous substances. In addition, owners or charterers of vessels offering cruises, or having accommodations for 50 or more passengers, must provide funds to cover passenger liability.

In meeting its responsibilities, the Commission acts as a quasi-judicial body, rendering decisions and issuing orders, rules and regulations governing and affecting all persons subject to shipping statutes.

Federal Trade Commission
Pennsylvania Avenue at Sixth Street, N.W.
Washington, D.C. 20580
Tel. (202) 523-3625

The *Federal Trade Commission* (FTC) is an independent agency established pursuant to the Federal Trade Commission Act of 1914.

The FTC's principal function is to protect consumers and the existence of a free enterprise system through prevention and elimination of unfair methods of competition and unfair or deceptive business acts or practices. Some of the principal offenses against which FTC enforcement actions may be directed are price-fixing agreements, boycotts, illegal acquisitions or mergers, false or misleading advertising, deceptive marketing practices and consumer credit violations. The FTC carries out its enforcement activities through administrative proceedings leading to cease-and-desist orders, trade regulation rules and, to a lesser extent, actions filed in federal courts. Court-ordered civil penalties may be obtained for each violation of an FTC order or rule. The FTC also publishes factual data on economic and business conditions for the use of Congress, the President and the public.

Associations formed solely for the purpose of export trade may obtain limited antitrust immunity by registration with the FTC (Webb-Pomerene associations). The FTC may conduct investigations and proceedings concerning the organization and activities of these associations to ensure that they are not in restraint of trade. In appropriate cases, it may refer its findings and recommendations to the Attorney General for further action.

The FTC has recently expanded its international activities. It has issued several antitrust complaints against foreign corporations, usually in merger matters, and has initiated several investigations of overseas practices of U.S. firms.

Foreign Claims Settlement Commission of the United States
1111 20th Street, N.W.
Washington, D.C. 20579
Tel. (202) 653-6166

The *Foreign Claims Settlement Commission of the United States* is a separate agency within the Department of Justice. Originally established by Reorganization Plan I of 1954, the Commission was recently transferred to the Department of Justice by Public Law (96-209), approved March 14, 1980. The Commission was set up to determine compensation claims of U.S. nationals for imprisonment during specific armed conflicts, and U.S. nationals' claims against foreign governments for compensation for property losses sustained under circumstances determined by Congress. It is currently authorized to receive and determine claims of ex-prisoners of war and American civilians captured and interned during the Vietnam war.

The Commission also is determining property loss claims by U.S. nationals in the German Democratic Republic and the People's Republic of China. Payments on these claims and losses derive from the liquidation of foreign assets blocked in the United States, claims settlement agreements with relevant foreign governments, and appropriations by Congress.

General Services Administration
18th and F Streets, N.W.
Washington, D.C. 20405
Tel. (202) 566-1231

The *General Services Administration* (GSA) was established in 1949 to manage the U.S. government's international business, a responsibility previously spread among dozens of agencies.

GSA is the government's business manager, landlord, real estate agent, maintenance expert, purchasing agent for items ranging from trucks to typewriter ribbons, supplier of telecommunications and computer equipment and services, recordskeeper, office management specialist and recycler or disposer of any leftover or unwanted federal property, from military bases to mops and brooms. It purchases five billion dollars worth of goods and services annually and has 38,000 employees. It has six major departments.

1. *Public Buildings Service.* PBS is the world's largest civilian real estate agency and is responsible for housing more than three-quarters of a million federal workers in buildings it owns, leases or operates. PBS has 18,500 employees and an annual budget of over one billion dollars. It supervises the design, construction, operation, maintenance, repair and protection of about 10,000 buildings.

2. *Federal Property Resources Services.* GSA streamlined its programs for reuse and disposal of excess and surplus federal property in 1978 by uniting them under this single management unit. FPRS controls GSA programs for maintenance and repair of all federal property except real estate, reuse within government of excess real estate and personal property, donation and sale of surplus, real and personal property and acquisition, storage and disposal of strategic and critical materials in the national stockpile.

3. *Federal Supply Service.* FSS procures the many items and services needed by federal agencies for daily operations. During 1978, FSS purchased more than $3 billion worth of office supplies and services, office furniture, cars and trucks for federal transportation, freight services and a myriad of other items ranging from helicopters to fire hoses. FSS also oversees federal travel regulations and audits transportation charges by federal agencies, and manages an 80,000-vehicle motor pool system.

4. *National Archives and Records Service.* NARS collects, preserves and shares America's heritage with its people. Best known of the national records kept by NARS are the Constitution, the Declaration of Independence and the Bill of Rights. But it also has many other historical and genealogical records in its Washington, D.C., headquarters and in 13 records centers around the country. NARS also advises the federal government on records management, and runs six presidential libraries (with two more planned).

NARS also publishes the daily *Federal Register,* which contains federal regulations, determinations and procedures, and the annual *U.S. Government Manual,* which outlines all federal agencies, subagencies, key personnel and programs.

5. *Automated Data and Telecommunications Service.* ADTS manages the government's computer and telecommunications equipment and services and is responsible for acquisition (by purchase or lease), use, retirement and sale of such equipment. It provides and coordinates computer and telecommunications services. ADTS manages the Federal Telecommunications System (FTS), a nationwide network which provides business and emergency communications for federal agencies. ADTS includes the Advanced Record System (ARS), which provides the government with computer-controlled message and data transmission services.

6. *Transportation and Public Utilities Service.* TPUS, the newest GSA service, was formed in January 1979 and is responsible for development and oversight of all GSA programs concerned with transportation and traffic management, auditing government transportation bills, processing of transportation claims by and against the federal government, and operating and maintaining motor equipment and public utilities to meet government needs.

Some special GSA functions are the *Consumer Information Center* (CIC), *Business Service Centers* and *Federal Information Centers.* The CIC puts the expertise of 24 federal agencies at consumers' fingertips through the free, quarterly *Consumer Information Catalog,* which lists more than 200 selected federal publications of consumer interest. The center also produces news stories and broadcast scripts.

The 13 Business Service Centers (BSC) across the country help businesses sell goods and services to the U.S. government—the biggest single customer in the free enterprise system. BSC representatives hold individual counseling sessions, meetings and seminars. There are special BSC programs for women and minorities. The free BSC booklet, *Doing Business with the Federal Government,* explains the general principles and procedures of government purchasing, what each federal agency buys and whom to contact about company products, how and where to obtain necessary forms and papers, how to be notified of upcoming business possibilities and how to make an accurate and profitable bid.

To help people locate the office they need among the 125 federal departments and agencies, GSA operates Federal Information Centers in 38 metropolitan centers; 47 other cities have free telephone access to the nearest FIC. Telephone numbers to call for federal, state and sales tax forms, sales tax information, etc., are also compiled by FIC.

Inter-American Foundation
1515 Wilson Boulevard
Rosslyn, Virginia 22209
Tel. (703) 841-3800

The *Inter-American Foundation* is an independent U.S. government corporation which supports and stimulates social change in Latin America and the Caribbean. Since its creation in 1969, the Foundation has provided more than $83 million for 715 projects in 27 Latin American and Caribbean countries. Projects funded include such activities as worker's self-managed enterprises, credit and production cooperatives, cultural awareness programs and self-help housing. The Inter-American Development Bank (IDB) and the Foundation have entered into an agreement to channel up to $79 million of the IDB's Social Progress Trust Fund resources to Foundation-identified projects.

The Foundation differs from traditional foreign assistance institutions in several important ways: it is free from direct participation in regular government-to-government operations involving short-term foreign policy considerations; it can act quickly and flexibly to assist many organizations often beyond the normal reach of governments; it is responsive to local initiatives and does not seek to direct or control those who receive its grants; and it is capable of making small grants of importance far exceeding their size.

International Communication Agency
(Formerly United States Information Agency)
1750 Pennsylvania Avenue, N.W.
Washington, D.C. 20547
Tel. (202) 724-9103

The *International Communication Agency* (ICA) was officially established on April 1, 1978, when it assumed the responsibilities of the United States Information Agency and the Department of State's Bureau of Educational and Cultural Affairs. Its mission is to conduct international communication, educational, cultural and exchange programs designed to build two-way bridges of understanding between the people of the United States and other peoples of the world. ICA engages in a wide variety of communication activities—from academic and cultural exchanges to international broadcasting, press, film, seminar, library and cultural center programs abroad—to accomplish its goals of presenting a true picture of the United States and its foreign policy to other countries and telling Americans about the world. One of its best known operations is the Voice of America, which broadcasts news, discussions and music to all parts of the world.

ICA also has the responsibility to report to the President and the Secretary of State, as well as to advise the National Security Council on worldwide public opinion as it is relevant to the formulation and conduct of foreign policy.

Securities and Exchange Commission

500 North Capitol Street, N.W.
Washington, D.C. 20549
Tel. (202) 755-4846

The *Securities and Exchange Commission* (SEC) administers the federal securities laws. Its primary goal as mandated by such laws is the protection of investors through disclosure of material information by securities issuers and the maintenance of orderly and competitive securities markets. Each of these securities laws authorizes the SEC to seek remedial relief in cases where violative conduct occurs or is about to occur. In addition, persons alleging that they have been harmed by violators in many circumstances may bring private suits seeking damages and other remedies.

In dealing with foreign issuers in markets, the SEC has recognized that some adjustments of the regulatory scheme are appropriate. For example, it has exempted foreign private issuers from the periodic reporting requirements of the Securities Exchange Act on the condition that such issuers provide certain other information.

In addition, the SEC regulates investment companies under the Investment Company Act. In this regard, foreign mutual funds and other investment companies are prohibited from selling their securities in the United States in a public offering, unless the SEC permits the company to register and make a public offering. Such an offering would be subject to terms or conditions making it legally and practically feasible to enforce the provisions of the Investment Company Act against the company. Foreign investment advisers also are subject to regulation under the Investment Advisers Act and are required to register under that act if they use the mails or any means or instrumentality of interstate commerce in connection with their business as an investment adviser.

The *Foreign Corrupt Practices Act of 1977* requires all issuers subject to the registration and reporting provisions of the Securities Exchange Act to make and keep accurate books and records and to devise and maintain a system of internal accounting control that provides reasonable assurances that certain statutory objectives are met. It also makes it unlawful for such issuers and any domestic concern, directly or indirectly, to pay money or make gifts to a foreign official, foreign political party or candidate for foreign political office for the purpose of improperly influencing a foreign official in order to assist the issuer in obtaining, retaining or directing business to any person.

Because of the scope and potentially broad reach of the securities laws as they relate to financial transactions, these laws must be carefully considered and expert advice should be obtained as to their possible application.

Small Business Administration

1441 L Street, N.W.
Washington, D.C. 20416
Tel. (202) 653-6600

The primary responsibility of the *Small Business Administration* (SBA) is to aid, counsel, assist and protect the small business community of the United States. Its functions as they relate to foreign trade are centered in the *Office of International Trade* and are provided through the SBA's 108 field offices in 98 cities throughout the country. (see list in Appendix)

An individual program of management assistance can be designed to meet the specific needs of current or prospective small business exporters. The program can include: 1) one-to-one counseling by students or volunteers with international trade experience; 2) export management training through co-sponsored workshops and seminars; 3) assistance from professional consulting firms; and 4) management and export marketing publications.

The SBA can provide financial assistance to exporters mainly through its bank guaranty program. Working capital loans can be used for market research, participation in overseas trade promotion events and acquisition of personnel or materials necessary to perform an export contract and for other export-related purposes.

United States Arms Control and Disarmament Agency
320 21st Street, N.W.
Washington, D.C. 20451
Tel. (202) 632-3708

The *United States Arms Control and Disarmament Agency* (ACDA) was created in 1961 by an act of Congress charging the agency with developing acceptable political and technical alternatives to the arms race. Under this charter, ACDA has a central responsibility for the initiation and conduct of arms control negotiations, such as SALT, and other arms control activities. Its functions relating to foreign trade and investment are handled by the units listed below.

The Nuclear Export Division, Non-Proliferation Bureau, is responsible for developing and implementing nuclear export policies and procedures that support the non-proliferation goals of the U.S. government. Under the Nuclear Non-Proliferation Act of 1978, ACDA is required to assess the proliferation impact of any new or amended agreements for peaceful nuclear cooperation negotiated by the United States which enables it to export nuclear-related materials and items to other countries. The Nuclear Export Division of ACDA reviews all export licenses issued by the Nuclear Regulatory Commission, requests for subsequent arrangements by the Department of Energy, requests for authorization to transfer nuclear technology to other countries and any license requests to the Commerce Department which present a potential nuclear proliferation problem.

The Arms Transfer Division, Weapons Evaluation and Control Bureau is primarily responsible for preparing ACDA's advice to the Secretary of State and the President on proposed arms transfers to other countries. The Division prepares arms control impact statements required by the Congress in conjunction with the Administration's annual security assistance request, and impact statements on particular arms sales when requested by the Congress.

The Technology Transfer Group, Weapons Evaluation and Control Bureau has a leading role in preparing advice to the Secretary of Commerce and the President on proposed technology transfers abroad. The Group represents ACDA in interagency technology transfer policy studies and supports the ACDA representative on the Advisory Committee on Export Policy (ACEP) and in subsidiary ACEP committees. The group also prepares arms control impact analyses on cases involving the transfer of technology.

United States International Development Cooperation Agency
21st and Virginia Avenue, N.W.
Washington, D.C. 20523
Tel. (202) 632-8249

On October 1, 1979, the *United States International Development Cooperation Agency* (IDCA) was created as a result of a major reorganization of U.S. development assistance activities proposed by President Carter and approved by the Congress earlier that year.

The Agency includes, as constituent parts, the *Agency for International Development* (AID), the *Overseas Private Investment Corporation* (OPIC) and a proposed *Institute for Scientific and Technological Cooperation* (ISTC). OPIC retains its own board of directors. In addition, IDCA is responsible for the development aspects of U.S. participation in international organizations, including United Nations development programs. It shares with the Treasury Department responsibility for U.S. participation

UNITED STATES INTERNATIONAL DEVELOPMENT COOPERATION AGENCY

MULTILATERAL DEVELOPMENT BANKS

(Department of Treasury)

INTERNATIONAL DEVELOPMENT COOPERATION AGENCY

(Office of the Director)

P. L. 480

(Department of Agriculture)

Chairman

Chairman

DEVELOPMENT COORDINATION COMMITTEE

MEMBERS: AID, ISTC, OPIC, State, Treasury, Commerce, Agriculture, Labor, Energy, OMB, ExImbank, Dep. Spec. Rep. for Trade Negotiations, Asst. to Pres. for Nat'l Sec. Afrs.

BOARD OF DIRECTORS OVERSEAS PRIVATE INVESTMENT CORPORATION

DEVELOPMENT LOAN COMMITTEE

MEMBERS: AID, ExImbank, Treasury, Commerce, State

INTERNATIONAL ORGANIZATIONS With Primarily Developmental Purposes

(Department of State, IO)

AGENCY FOR INTERNATIONAL DEVELOPMENT

INSTITUTE FOR SCIENTIFIC & TECHNOLOGICAL COOPERATION

OVERSEAS PRIVATE INVESTMENT CORPORATION

in the multilateral development banks, such as the World Bank, and shares with the Agriculture Department responsibility for the U.S. Food for Peace Program, under the auspices of AID.

IDCA has two important mandates: first, to assure that international development concerns are considered in the formulation of a wide range of U.S. international policies affecting developing nations; and second, to guide and coordinate development assistance activities, bilateral and multilateral, that the United States supports. (see organization chart, p. 37)

Agency for International Development
1735 North Lynn Street
Rosslyn, Virginia
Tel. (703) 235-9155

The *Agency for International Development* (AID) carries out assistance programs designed to help the people of certain less developed countries develop their human and economic resources, increase productive capacities and improve the quality of human life as well as to promote economic or political stability in friendly countries.

AID's Food For Peace Program administers the donation of agricultural commodities to meet famine or other urgent relief requirements and to promote economic and community development outside the United States.

Overseas Private Investment Corporation
1129 20th Street, N.W.
Washington, D.C. 20527
Tel. (202) 632-1804

The *Overseas Private Investment Corporation* (OPIC) is a self-sustaining agency whose objective is to foster development through the encouragement of U.S. private investment in some 90 friendly developing countries in Latin America, Asia, the Middle East, Africa and Europe.

As incentives, OPIC offers qualified U.S. investors, including financial institutions, political risk insurance, finance services and investment counseling. The programs are extended to new projects or for the expansion of existing facilities which are financially sound and promise to generate host country benefits in the form of jobs, tax revenues, technology transfer, training and foreign exchange revenues. Projects are carefully screened to ensure that they will have no negative effect on the domestic job market or on the U.S. economy in general.

Insurance Services. OPIC's insurance program provides coverage against inconvertibility of local currency earnings and return of capital; expropriation and, in some cases, abrogation of contractual rights; and war, revolution and insurrection.

To private investors, political risk insurance is often an essential element in the decision to make a commitment in a developing nation. Although the investor has the capability to assess the practical business considerations involved, he may find it difficult to judge the country's long-range political climate. OPIC's insurance coverage typically is assured for the duration of project loans or contracts and for 12 to 20 years on equity. Its rates are based on the coverage selected and on its assessment of the risks of the project.

OPIC presently offers insurance protection to U.S. construction and service contractors for letters of credit often required by foreign governments in lieu of performance bonds, particularly in the Middle East.

Finance Services. The major objectives of the finance program are to promote and finance economically and financially viable projects in the developing world, sponsored by smaller and medium-sized U.S. businesses. The three principal means for accomplishing these objectives are OPIC's pre-investment assistance program, the all-risk long guaranty and the direct loan program.

OPIC promotes projects using its pre-investment assistance program which includes a survey program, on a risk-sharing basis, to identify and confirm the viability of projects. Its financing may be in the form of either loans to a project utilizing its own capital or of loan guarantees issued to private U.S. financial institutions. The loan guaranty is an all-risk guaranty for the prompt payment of principal and interest payments. OPIC financing is based on the project's economic and financial viability and usually does not involve a U.S. sponsor's guaranty of the project.

OPIC also offers a number of special incentives designed to help smaller businesses enter international markets and to encourage exploration and development of new sources of minerals and energy.

The Institute for Scientific and Technological Cooperation

The Institute for Scientific and Technological Cooperation (ISTC) was proposed in 1979 as a parallel agency to AID within the restructured development assistance organization (IDCA).

Among ISTC's goals and characteristics are: to strengthen developing country capacity to conduct science and technology research on critical development problems; to focus U.S. and developing country research on ways to meet basic human needs, overcome the worst aspects of world poverty and approach global problems on a cooperative basis; to open up opportunities for cooperative cost-shared work on common problems with important "middle-income" countries; to respond to the expressed desire of developing countries to expand research and find technologies appropriate to their setting; to mobilize existing knowledge and U.S. institutional expertise to address poverty; and to provide a direct link and cooperative relationships with developing country scientists, technologists and institutions.

United States International Trade Commission
701 E Street, N.W.
Washington, D.C. 20436
Tel. (202) 523-0161

The *United States International Trade Commission* (ITC) was created by an act of Congress, approved September 8, 1916, as the United States Tariff Commission. The name was changed to the United States International Trade Commission by Section 171 of the Trade Act of 1974.

The primary duty of the ITC is to investigate tariff and international trade complaints as required by law. It furnishes studies, reports and recommendations to the President, the Congress and other government agencies and also conducts studies, surveys and public hearings and initiates research projects pertaining to the international trade of the United States.

ITC's present powers and functions are provided for largely by the Tariff Act of 1930, the Trade Act of 1974 and the Trade Agreements Act of 1979.

Tariff Act of 1930. Section 337 of the Tariff Act of 1930, as amended by the Trade Act of 1974, prohibits unfair methods of competition in import trade which "destroy, injure or prevent the establishment of a domestic industry, or restrain or monopolize trade within the United States." The ITC determination of unfair practices may be disapproved by the President.

Section 303 of the Tariff Act of 1930, as amended, provides that the ITC determine after investigation whether an industry is being or is likely to be injured, or is prevented from being established by reason of duty-free imports of articles subsidized by foreign governments.

Trade Act of 1974. Under Section 131 of the Trade Act of 1974, the ITC is required to advise the President on the probable economic effect on industries and consumers of duty modification or other import restrictions on articles being considered for possible concessions in trade agreement negotiations. Under Section 503 of the same statute, it is required to advise the President on articles considered for duty-free treatment under the Generalized System of Preferences.

Section 201 of the Trade Act of 1974 authorizes the ITC to investigate whether an article is being imported in such increased quantities as to be a substantial cause or threat of serious injury to a domestic industry and to recommend necessary import relief to the President. Similarly, under Section 406, the ITC determines whether imports from communist countries have caused domestic market disruption and recommends appropriate import relief to the President.

Antidumping Act of 1921. Under Section 201 of the Antidumping Act of 1921, as amended, the ITC reports to the Secretary of the Treasury when it finds injury or potential injury to a domestic industry from importation of merchandise sold at less-than-fair value. The Secretary of the Treasury then imposes a dumping duty on imports of the articles in question.

General. Among publications available from the ITC are results of commodity investigations, an annual report to the Congress on the operation of the trade agreements program, an annual report to the Congress on the ITC activities, *Summaries of Trade and Tariff Information* and statistical reports and surveys of certain industries. Information on publications may be obtained by contacting the office of the Secretary.

United States Postal Service
475 L'Enfant Plaza West, S.W.
Washington, D.C. 20260
Tel. (202) 245-4000

The *Office of International Postal Affairs* is primarily responsible for coordinating mail policy and operational procedures in the *United States Postal Service* (USPS). In addition to this function, the Office makes bilateral international postal arrangements, maintains effective relationships with foreign postal services and serves as the U.S. representative in international postal organizations

---

3. Congressional Committees

Much of the real work of the U.S. Congress is performed in the committees. When a bill is introduced, it is referred to the appropriate standing committee. The committees function with the support of subcommittees. Increases in the rights and power of the subcommittees have grown in recent years with expansion of the legislative workload.

Subcommittees have the power to call hearings and make recommendations to a full committee. The committee, however, considers the bill in its final draft by accepting, rejecting or modifying what the subcommittee has submitted.

There are 17 standing committees in the Senate and 22 standing committees in the House of Representatives:

Senate

Agriculture, Nutrition and Forestry
Appropriations
Armed Services
Banking, Housing and Urban Affairs
Budget
Commerce, Science and Transportation
Energy and Natural Resources
Environment and Public Works
Finance

Foreign Relations
Governmental Affairs
Human Resources
Judiciary
Labor and Human Resources
Rules and Administration
Small Business
Veterans' Affairs

House of Representatives

Agriculture
Appropriations
Armed Services
Banking, Finance and Urban Affairs
Budget
District of Columbia
Education and Labor
Foreign Affairs
Government Operations
House Administration
Interior and Insular Affairs
Interstate and Foreign Commerce
Judiciary
Merchant Marine and Fisheries
Post Office and Civil Service
Public Works and Transportation
Rules
Science and Technology
Small Business
Standards of Official Conduct
Veterans' Affairs
Ways and Means

The Joint Committee on Taxation and the Joint Economic Committee are the only joint Senate-House Committees.

The responsibilities of the standing committees are set forth in the Legislative Reorganization Act of 1946 (Public Law 601, 79th Congress, Second Session) and in S.Res. 4 (95th Congress, Second Session) passed by the Senate in February 1977.

Whenever a congressional committee makes a positive recommendation on the passage of new legislation it has considered, it reports this conclusion to the full membership of the House or Senate. Committee reports are generally available on request from the House and Senate Document Rooms. Published transcripts of hearings conducted by committees are usually available, at varying prices, from the Superintendent of Documents, Government Printing Office, Washington, D.C. 20401. Requests for information may be addressed to the clerk of the particular committee.

The principal committees having jurisdiction over matters relating to foreign commerce and international relations, and a brief summary of their particular responsibilities (apart from purely domestic matters), follows:

Senate Committee on Agriculture, Nutrition and Forestry
Tel. (202) 224-2035
House Committee on Agriculture
Tel. (202) 225-2171

Measures relating to farm exports, agricultural import policy, quotas and standards, agricultural trade development and commodity exchanges.

Senate Committee on Appropriations
Tel. (202) 224-3471
House Committee on Appropriations
Tel. (202) 225-2771

Measures which approve and amend agency spending requests. Subcommittees handle measures relating to State and Commerce Department programs, regular U.N. contributions, all foreign aid programs and U.S. contributions to international trade organizations.

Senate Committee on Armed Services Tel. (202) 224-3871 *House Committee on Armed Services* Tel. (202) 225-4151	Measures relating to research, development and procurement of weapons systems that have international defense ramifications; U.S. overseas military base acquisitions; overseas military construction for U.S. and joint U.S.-foreign nation purposes; conservation and development of naval petroleum and oil shale reserves; stockpiles of strategic and critical materials; military applications of nuclear energy; and oversight of international arms control, disarmament and operation of military commissaries and exchanges.
Senate Committee on Banking, Housing and Urban Affairs Tel. (202) 224-7391 *House Committee on Banking, Finance and Urban Affairs* Tel. (202) 225-4247	Measures relating to banking and currency; export and foreign trade promotion; export controls; international economic policy as it affects U.S. monetary affairs, credit and financial institutions; economic growth, urban affairs and financial assistance to commerce and industry.
Senate Committee on Commerce, Science and Transportation Tel. (202) 224-5115	Measures relating to the merchant marine and ocean navigation; communications; regulation of consumer products and services; coastal zone management; and technology research, development and policy.
Senate Committee on Energy and Natural Resources Tel. (202) 224-4971	Measures relating to all energy matters, except taxes; natural gas and oil imports; relations with OPEC nations; and the Law of the Sea.
Senate Committee on Finance Tel. (202) 224-4515 *House Committee on Ways and Means* Tel. (202) 225-3625	Measures relating to reciprocal trade agreements, customs, collection districts and ports of entry and delivery; transportation and dutiable goods; revenue measures relating to insular possessions; tariffs and import quotas; oversight of the International Trade Commission, the Customs Service and the Office of the United States Trade Representative; and the adjustment assistance program administered by the Commerce and Labor Departments.
Senate Committee on Foreign Relations Tel. (202) 224-4651 *House Committee on Foreign Affairs* Tel. (202) 225-5021	Measures to foster commercial intercourse with foreign nations and to safeguard U.S. business interests abroad (e.g., export controls, export promotion, foreign investment in the United States and international commodity agreements); measures relating to treaties and executive agreements, except reciprocal trade agreements; foreign economic, military and humanitarian assistance; the U.N. and its affiliated organizations; oceans and international environmental scientific affairs as they relate to foreign policy; and international aspects of nuclear energy.
Senate Committee on Governmental Affairs Tel. (202) 224-4751 *House Committee on Government Operations* Tel. (202) 225-5051	Measures relating to the efficiency, economy and effectiveness of all agencies and departments of the U.S. government; and the relationship between the United States and international organizations of which the United States is a member.
House Committee on Interstate and Foreign Commerce Tel. (202) 225-2927	Measures relating to foreign commerce, foreign transportation and the regulation of foreign communications; matters concerning international products standards; foreign investment in the United States; improper payments; oversight of the Department of Commerce; and the regulation of international travel and tourism.

House Committee on Merchant Marine and Fisheries Tel. (202) 225-4047	Measures relating to the regulation of common carriers by water, except matters subject to the jurisdiction of the Interstate Commerce Commission; inspection of merchant marine vessels, merchant marine officers and seamen; navigation and the laws relating thereto, including pilotage; rules and international arrangements to prevent collisions at sea; and registering and licensing of vessels.
House Committee on Science and Technology Tel. (202) 225-6371	Measures relating to science and technology policy, including technology transfer, cargo preference and standards legislation.
Joint Committees: *Joint Economic Committee* Tel. (202) 224-5171	Having no legislative authority, the Joint Economic Committee undertakes studies and holds hearings to focus attention on major economic issues. Its principal function is to make recommendations that other congressional committees can use in drafting their bills. The committee has held several hearings on international economic issues, including transnational corporations, trade and international monetary relations.
Joint Committee on Taxation Tel. (202) 225-3621	Undertakes studies, holds hearings and has jurisdiction over the operation and effects of the federal system of taxation.

Other congressional committees, while not regularly involved in international business matters, also have an impact on international economic policy. Also, several committee jurisdictions may overlap or even compete for attention on the same issue.

---

4. Congressional Services

Congressional Research Service
Library of Congress
1st Street and
Independence Avenue,
N.W.
Washington, D.C. 20540
Tel. (202) 287-5000

Congressional Research Service (CRS) is the Library of Congress' nonpartisan research and reference arm for members, committees and staff of Congress. Founded in 1914, it has since grown steadily in staff and in the demands Congress has made upon it. In the fiscal year ending September 30, 1978, the service responded to more than 300,000 congressional inquiries. The answers were provided by its 542 research specialists, supported by an additional 314 clerical and administrative personnel.

While many of its major studies are published as congressional committee documents, most of its materials are strictly for internal congressional use.

CRS furnishes senators and representatives with analyses of public policy issues, general background reports, development of alternative proposals for solutions to problems and arguments for and against any proposal. However, it will not engage in advocacy of a public issue. It prepares "issue briefs" on major legislation, performs general reference work and provides specialized assistance to committees in preparing for hearings, finding outside witnesses, formulating questions and analyzing testimony.

The CRS is organized into nine divisions, seven of which deal with substantive research, at least four of direct interest to international companies. In addition, the *Office of Senior Specialists* handles longer-range matters, including international economics.

The *Economics Division* studies international trade and investment, multinational corporations, international taxes and U.S. commercial relations with communist countries. In fiscal year 1978, for example, the staff produced reports on such subjects as: reform of the international monetary system, the U.S. trade imbalance, the economic effects of imports on domestic industries in general and U.S., foreign and international trade in energy resources.

The *Foreign Affairs and National Defense Division* studies links between U.S. foreign relations and international economic developments, including such policy issues as: bilateral and multilateral foreign assistance; international finance and trade; the role of foreign investment in sustaining the South African government; impediments to economic and social development in Haiti; and economic conditions in Italy, France and the United Kingdom.

The *Science Policy Research Division's* areas of study encompass international technology assessment, development of hard mineral resources in the deep seabed and energy from the ocean and other alternative sources.

Studies prepared by the *Environment and Natural Resources Policy Division* include the world food trade, foreign investment in U.S. farmland, evaluation of the administration of the ''200-mile law,'' the Agricultural Export Promotion Act, meat import quotas, Soviet maritime activities, oil pollution liability and energy policy options in the face of a threat to national security.

Further information about CRS can be found in the service's annual report, available from the U.S. Government Printing Office or the congressional Joint Committee on the Library. A list of CRS studies in the public domain may be obtained through a member of Congress.

General Accounting Office
441 G Street, N.W.
Washington, D.C. 20548
Tel. (202) 275-6202

The *General Accounting Office* (GAO), as an independent and nonpolitical arm of the Congress, is concerned with finding ways of improving the economy, efficiency and effectiveness of government operations. The Comptroller General of the United States is GAO's chief executive, providing the Congress, its committees and members with information and recommendations based on audits and analyses of proposed and ongoing federal programs.

Continuing study of international business issues is an important focus of GAO's audit activity. Examination of issues involving U.S. trade policy, export controls, foreign assistance, military exports, international banking and investment, international organizations, energy and mineral resources and the general conduct of foreign affairs are some of the major areas of concentration.

Within GAO, the *International Division* is responsible for most of the studies, analyses and audits involving international business issues. Its staff numbers over 230 professionals, including 100 overseas at four branch offices (Frankfurt, Honolulu, Bangkok and Panama City), and it operates under the direction of three associate directors. The Associate Director, Development Assistance, has primary responsibility for evaluating bilateral and multilateral aid programs. The Associate Director, Trade and Finance, directs studies and reviews of U.S. foreign trade policies and practices, Eximbank and Overseas Private Investment Corporation operations, foreign investment and technology transfer issues. Military exports, nuclear safeguards and management of natural resources are major areas addressed by the Associate Director, Security and International Relations.

Other GAO divisions may from time to time become involved in international business issues, for example the *Community and Economic Development Division*, the *Energy and Minerals Division* and the *Program Analysis Division*.

B. Selected Organizations

1. United Nations, Specialized Agencies and Other Organizations/Bodies/Conferences

a. United Nations

United Nations (UN)
Headquarters:
United Nations Plaza
New York, New York
11017
Tel. (212) 754-1234

UN Information Centre:
Suite 209
2101 L Street, N.W.
Washington, D.C. 20037
Tel. (202) 296-5370

The *United Nations* (UN) is an association of nations pledged through signing the UN Charter to maintain international peace and security and to cooperate in establishing political, economic and social conditions under which this task can be securely achieved. Nothing contained in the Charter authorizes the UN to intervene in matters which are solely within the domestic jurisdiction of any nation. The UN formally came into existence on October 24, 1945, with 51 original member nations. Presently, there are 151 members and six other nonmember states that maintain observer missions at the UN and participate only in certain UN activities. The UN operates through six main organs: the *General Assembly*, the *Security Council*, the *International Court of Justice*, the *Trusteeship Council*, the *Secretariat* and the *Economic and Social Council*.

The Economic and Social Council (ECOSOC)

Falling under the authority of the General Assembly, ECOSOC consists of representatives of 54 UN member nations, of which 18 members are elected each year for a three-year term of office. The geographical distribution of ECOSOC is: Africa—14 members; Asia—11 members; Latin America—10 members; Western Europe and other states—13 members; and Eastern Europe—6 members.

The UN Charter assigned ECOSOC wide responsibilities for the implementation and coordination of economic, social, cultural, educational, health and related matters. These responsibilities are carried out by six functional commissions and five regional commissions. The functional commissions are: the *Statistical Commission;* the *Commission for Social Development;* the *Commission on the Status of Women;* the *Commission on Human Rights;* the *Commission on Narcotic Drugs;* and the *Population Commission.* The regional commissions are: the *Economic Commission for Europe* (ECE); the *Economic and Social Commission for Asia and the Pacific* (ESCAP); the *Economic Commission for Africa* (ECA); the *Economic Commission for Latin America* (ECLA); and the *Economic Commission for Western Asia* (ECWA).

ECOSOC may also make arrangements for consultation with national and international nongovernmental organizations which deal with matters within its scope. The benefit of close cooperation with large bodies of unofficial opinion and the benefit of information concerning world needs for action in many areas of ECOSOC's responsibilities are thus obtained.

Certain specialized intergovernmental organizations, working in similar fields as ECOSOC, are brought into relationship with the United Nations. There are 15 such organizations, commonly referred to as specialized agencies of the United Nations. (Brief descriptions of each specialized agency are provided below.) Each agency has its own constitution and receives its basic legal power from the governments which accept its constitution, rather than from the United Nations. Membership in the UN is not a requisite for membership in any one or more of the specialized agencies or vice versa. Although each is an autonomous agency, they work with the UN and each other through the coordinating machinery of ECOSOC.

Sales publications issued by the United Nations are generally available through the Sales Office at the United Nations Headquarters in New York.

---

b. Specialized Agencies of the United Nations

Food and Agriculture Organization
Headquarters:
Via delle Terme di
   Caracalla
00100 Rome, Italy

North American Regional
   Office:
1776 F Street, N.W.
Washington, D.C. 20437
Tel. (202) 634-6215

The *Food and Agriculture Organization* (FAO) was established on October 16, 1945, with the following purposes: to raise the levels of nutrition and standards of living; to secure improvements in the production and distribution of all food and agricultural products; and to better the condition of rural populations, thereby contributing toward an expanding world economy.

In connection with the above-mentioned objectives, FAO supplies member nations with facts and figures relating to nutrition and to the production, trade and consumption of agricultural, forestry and fishery products. Technical assistance is provided also to member governments upon request.

The United States participates in FAO pursuant to a joint resolution approved by the House of Representatives and the Senate on July 31, 1945. An interagency committee advises the Secretary of State on U.S. policy in FAO and implementation of its recommendations.

Inter-Governmental Maritime Consultative Organization
Headquarters:
101-104 Piccadilly
London, WIV OAE
England

The *Inter-Governmental Maritime Consultative Organization* (IMCO) was established March 17, 1958. Its main focus is on providing machinery for cooperation and exchange of information affecting international shipping among governments, encouraging the adoption of high standards of maritime safety, efficiency of navigation and prevention and control of marine pollution from ships, and considering any matters concerning unfair restrictive practices by shipping concerns. IMCO also drafts international conventions and agreements and convenes international conferences on shipping matters within its competence, functioning in a consultative and advisory capacity.

International Civil Aviation Organization
Headquarters:
International Aviation
   Square
P.O. Box 400,
   1000 Sherbrooke Street
   West
Montreal, Quebec
Canada H3A
   2R2

The convention providing for the establishment of the *International Civil Aviation Organization* (ICAO) was drawn up by the International Civil Aviation Conference held in Chicago in 1944. The President of the United States ratified the Convention on International Civil Aviation on August 6, 1946, and ICAO was formally organized in April 1947.

The purposes of ICAO are: to establish international standards and regulations for civil aviation; to foster the development and planning of international air transport; and to study the problems of international civil aviation. Through technical assistance programs, ICAO helps developing countries build up air transport services and train required personnel.

Since its organization, ICAO has secured significant simplification of government customs, immigration and public health regulations as they apply to international air transport.

International Fund for Agricultural Development

Headquarters:
Via del Serafico 107
00142, Rome, Italy

Liaison Office with the UN:
Room 3255
United Nations
New York, New York 10017
Tel. (212) 754-5506

One of the World Food Conference's most notable achievements has been the creation of the *International Fund for Agricultural Development* (IFAD) to marshall additional resources for food production. The agreement establishing IFAD entered into force on November 30, 1977, and, shortly thereafter, the 114-member fund began operations as the 13th specialized UN agency.

An initiative of the Organization of Petroleum Exporting Countries (OPEC), the fund received widespread support because national governments recognized the importance of increasing agricultural production among developing countries. IFAD was proposed as a new means of providing concessional financing for viable projects aimed at both increasing food production and improving nutrition in food-deficit countries. Major emphasis was placed on ensuring that it would rely on existing international financial institutions to identify projects and administer loans.

With respect to the IFADs lending operations, several degrees of concessionality are to be employed, based primarily on the economic and financial condition and the capacity of the countries to be assisted. The largest portion of its resources are expected to go to the poorest food deficit countries on highly concessional terms.

The initial capital resources of IFAD are over one billion dollars, consisting of pledges from developed member countries, the OPEC developing countries and recipient developing nations. As of October 31, 1978, total paid-in contributions against these pledges amounted to $434 million. The U.S. commitment of $200 million was authorized and appropriated by Congress.

Unlike most other multilateral aid institutions, IFAD was conceived as a joint undertaking bringing together the traditional foreign aid donors and the newer OPEC donors.

International Labor Organization

Headquarters:
4, route des Morillons
CH-1211 Geneva 22
Switzerland

ILO Branch Office in Washington:
Suite 330
1750 New York Avenue, N.W.
Washington, D.C. 20006
Tel. (202) 634-6335

Formerly established in 1919 as part of the League of Nations, the *International Labor Organization* (ILO) is a tripartite organization in which governments, employers and workers are represented. In 1946, the United Nations and the ILO concluded an agreement under which the ILO was recognized as the specialized agency responsible for international action to improve labor conditions, raise living standards and promote economic and social stability.

In bringing government, labor and management together, ILO recommends international minimum standards and drafts international labor conventions on such subjects as human rights, freedom of association, wages, hours of work, minimum wages for employment, conditions of work for various classes of workers, workmen's compensation, social insurance, etc.

By a joint resolution effective August 20, 1934, the Congress authorized the President on behalf of the United States to accept an invitation for membership. Employees and workers are represented by the U.S. Council of the International Chamber of Commerce and the AFL-CIO respectively. However, on November 5, 1975, the United States notified the ILO of its intent to withdraw from the organization within two years unless changes were made to rectify the following conditions: the erosion of tripartite representation; the selectivity with which the ILO expresses concern about human rights; the lack of due process in ILO proceedings and the organizations' increasing politicization. On November 6, 1977, the United States ceased to be a member of the ILO.

Although the ILO has not fully resolved all of the issues that led to U.S. withdrawal, a presidential commission noted that the organization made significant progress and recommended that the United States rejoin the ILO, which it did in early 1980.

International Telecommunication Union

Headquarters:
Place des Nations
1211 Geneva 20
Switzerland

The International Telegraph Union and the International Radiotelegraph Union were merged in 1932 to form the *International Telecommunication Union* (ITU). Its functions are to: allocate radio frequencies and register radio frequency assignments; seek to establish the lowest rates possible, consistent with efficient service and sound economy; promote the adoption of measures for ensuring the safety of life through telecommunication; foster the improvement, extension and rational use of telecommunication services (i.e., telephone, telegraph, space, aeronautical and maritime radio-communication, broadcasting and television) with a view to making them generally available to all countries; and encourage standardization in telecommunications, prevent interference in radio-communication and cooperate with requesting countries in developing telecommunication facilities.

ITU works to attain these objectives through international conferences and meetings, publications of technical information and technical cooperation.

United Nations Educational, Scientific and Cultural Organization

Headquarters:
7 Place de Fontenoy
75700 Paris, France

Liaison Office:
918 16th Street, N.W.
Suite 201
Washington, D.C. 20006
Tel. (202) 457-0770

The *United Nations Educational, Scientific and Cultural Organization* (UNESCO) came into being on November 4, 1946.

The purpose of UNESCO is to contribute to peace and security by promoting collaboration among the nations through education, science and culture in order to further universal respect for justice, for the rule of law and for the human rights and fundamental freedoms which are affirmed for the peoples of the world, without distinction of race, sex, language or religion, by the charter of the United Nations. To realize these aims, UNESCO pursues two parallel and complementary avenues of action: international intellectual cooperation in the fields of its competence and operational activities for development, embracing social, cultural and economic dimensions.

National commissions, composed chiefly of representatives of nongovernmental organizations, are set up in most of the member states to act as liaison groups between UNESCO and the educational, scientific and cultural communities of their own countries.

A joint resolution approved July 30, 1946, provided for membership and participation by the United States in UNESCO and authorized the establishment of a *U.S. National Commission for UNESCO*. The Department of State is the U.S. agency charged with primary responsibility in relation to UNESCO.

United Nations Environment Programme

Liaison Office:
UN Headquarters
Room A - 3630

In December 1972, the UN General Assembly, acting on a recommendation of the Stockholm Conference, established the *United Nations Environment Programme* (UNEP) to encourage and help coordinate the development of sound environmental practices, both in and outside the UN system. Its work program is carried out by:

• A 58-member Governing Council which determines UNEP's

Tel. (212) 754-8138

priorities and guidelines, subject to approval by the ECO-SOC and the General Assembly.
- A small secretariat under an executive director, located in Nairobi, Kenya, the first headquarters of a UN body to be located in a developing country.
- An Environment Fund, made up of voluntary contributions from governments, to provide partial assistance or seed money—now about $30 million a year—for projects designed to fill gaps in information or action or to develop new techniques suitable for adaptation on a global basis. More than 500 projects have been approved so far. A target of $150 million in contributions has been set for the four-year period 1978-82.

Responsibility for action within the UN system is usually divided among the specialized agencies according to their areas of expertise, such as food and agriculture (FAO), health (WHO) and training and education (UNESCO). Environmental issues cut across these traditional lines. The main function of UNEP is to act as a focal point for environmental action and coordinate within—and even beyond—the UN system.

The executive director is authorized to draw attention to possible threats to the world environment. His annual State of the Environment Report has dealt with such problems as toxic chemicals, the environmental causes of cancer and malaria, threats to the earth's ozone layer, damage caused by cutting down of trees, soil loss through erosion, increased use of nitrogen fertilizers and the use of agricultural waste.

In 1982, 10 years after the Stockholm Conference, and every five years after that, a comprehensive State of the Environment Report will be issued to review progress and determine new tasks.

Universal Postal Union
Headquarters:
Weltpostrasse 4
3000 Berne 15
Switzerland

The *Universal Postal Union* (UPU) was formally established in 1875, with the coming into force of the Universal Postal Convention adopted by the Postal Congress of Berne in 1874. The UPU was known at first as the General Postal Union, its name being changed at the Congress of Paris in 1878.

UPU's objective is to assure the organization and perfection of the various postal services, to promote the development of international collaboration and to develop procedures concerning the details of handling international mail.

The United States approved the treaty of 1874 and has continued to participate in the UPU from that date under subsequent conventions.

World Food Council
Liaison Office:
Suite 3255
UN Headquarters
New York, New York
10017
Tel. (212) 754-5506

The *World Food Council* (WFC) was created by a UN General Assembly resolution in December 1974, on the recommendation of the 1974 World Food Conference. It is a UN organ and reports to the General Assembly through the Economic and Social Council.

WFC promotes the implementation of World Food Conference and UN General Assembly resolutions concerned with food. It monitors the world food situation, mobilizes support and strives to ensure the coherence of overall efforts of governments and agencies to alleviate hunger and malnutrition. Its main objectives are to increase food production in countries where it is most needed, to broaden the effective distribution of food through measures for improving trade, consumption and nutrition and to provide a better system of world food security. WFC does not itself carry out any programs or projects of technical, financial or food assistance, unlike other UN bodies concerned with food. Rather, it acts as an advocate, catalyst and coordinator.

Its membership consists of 36 countries, from all continents, represented by their ministers or other high-ranking government officials. Members are elected by the UN General Assembly on a three-year rotating basis after nomination by the Economic and Social Council.

The Council meets periodically to review and propose action to improve the world food situation. It is assisted by a small export secretariat headed by an executive director appointed by the UN Secretary-General. Through its secretariat, the Council maintains contact with governments and agencies to stimulate political action for overcoming food problems.

World Health Organization

Headquarters:
20 Avenue Appia
1211 Geneva, 27
Switzerland

Regional Office:
Pan American Sanitary
Bureau
525 23rd Street, N.W.
Washington, D.C. 20037
Tel. (202) 861-3200

The *World Health Organization* (WHO) was established on April 7, 1948, with participation authorized by a joint congressional resolution approved by the President on June 14, 1948.

The objective of WHO is the attainment by all peoples of the highest possible levels of health. WHO acts as the directing and coordinating authority on international health work, promotes research in the field of health and promotes international standards with respect to food, biological, pharmaceutical and similar products. Regional organizations have been established for Africa, the Americas, Southeast Asia, Europe, the Western Pacific and the Eastern Mediterranean.

WHO's services, which benefit all countries, include: a day-to-day information service on the occurrence of internationally important diseases; publication of the international list of causes of disease, injury and death; monitoring adverse reaction to drugs; and establishing global standards for antibiotics, vaccines and other medications.

World Intellectual Property Organization

Headquarters:
32 Chemin des
Colombettes
12, Geneva
Switzerland

Liaison Office:
Permanent Representative
of WIPO to the United
Nations
Room 821
U.N. Plaza, 6th Floor
New York, New York
10017
Tel. (212) 867-0029

Established by a convention in 1967, the *World Intellectual Property Organization* (WIPO) succeeded the United International Bureau for the Protection of Intellectual Property, representing the combined secretariats of the Paris Union (for protection of industrial property) and the Berne Union (for protection of literary and artistic work) which orginated in 1883 and 1896 respectively.

Among its purposes are those designed to promote the protection of intellectual property throughout the world, through cooperation among states and in collaboration with other international organizations and to ensure administrative cooperation among states in the enforcement of various international agreements on such matters as trademarks, industrial designs, the classification of goods and services, the protection of appellations of origin, of literary and artistic works and, among other agreements, the Patent Cooperation Treaty. To achieve its objectives, WIPO encourages the conclusion of new international treaties and the harmonization of national legislation and provides legal and technical assistance to developing countries to promote their industrialization through modernization of their industrial property and copyright systems. In addition, WIPO assembles and disseminates information and maintains services for international registration or other administrative cooperation among member states.

World Meteorological Organization

Headquarters:
41 avenue Giuseppe-Motta
Geneva
Switzerland

A Conference of Directors of the International Meteorological Organization, set up in 1878, met in Washington, D.C., in 1947, and adopted a convention creating the *World Meteorological Organization* (WMO). WMO was formally established on March 19, 1951, when its congress first convened in Paris.

Its functions are: to promote international cooperation in the field of meteorology and the quick exchange of weather data; to establish worldwide networks of meteorological stations and facilitate the publication and standardization of their observations; to further the application of meteorology to aviation, shipping, water problems, agriculture and other activities; and to encourage research and training in the field of meteorology.

WMO has implemented the establishment of a "World Weather Watch," based on meteorological satellites and a system of world and regional meteorological centers operated by national weather services of members, and also has initiated an international program for research in meteorology in the light of developments in outer space.

c. Organizations/Bodies/Conferences of the United Nations

General Agreement on Tariffs and Trade

Centre William Rappard
154 Rue de Lausanne
1211 Geneva, 21
Switzerland

The *General Agreement on Tariffs and Trade* (GATT) is the only multilateral agreement that sets out agreed rules for world trade. GATT entered into force on January 1, 1948, with 23 contracting parties. There are now 87 GATT signatories, while an additional 24 nations apply its rules in their trade practices. GATT's basic objectives are to expand world trade by limiting trade barriers.

Besides being a code of rules for international commerce, GATT is also an institution that provides a forum for negotiating further liberalization of world trade and for conciliating trade disputes between member countries. It is the main instrument through which the United States works with other countries—between them accounting for more than four-fifths of world commerce—to reduce tariffs and nontariff barriers to trade. From the U.S. point of view, GATT rules are contractual obligations rather than codified laws.

GATT is not a formal part of the United Nations. However, it has always had a close working relationship and is treated as a *de facto* specialized agency.

The basic GATT principles are: that trade should be conducted on the basis of nondiscrimination ("most-favored-nation" treatment is the cornerstone of GATT); that domestic industry should be protected only through the customs tariff and not through quantitative restrictions or other measures; that tariffs should be reduced through multilateral negotiations and be "bound" against subsequent increase; and that member countries should consult together to overcome trade problems.

Past GATT trade negotiations (including the "Kennedy Round" of 1964-1967) have brought about far-reaching reductions in tariffs and other trade barriers. The most recent of the seven rounds of multilateral trade negotiations (MTN), held under the auspices of GATT, opened in Tokyo in September 1973, but did not begin in earnest until February 1975, after the adoption of the Trade Act of 1974, through which the United States finally acquired its negotiating mandate. After more than four years of intensive negotiations, involving some 98 governments, a set of major new international trade agreements was concluded in Geneva in 1979.

The purpose of this "Tokyo Round" was to further reduce tariff and nontariff barriers to trade in agricultural and industrial products and to work out updated rules for the future conduct of world trade. Another important element in this round was to establish a framework for better surveillance of the international trade system and improved mechanisms for settlement of disputes.

International Trade Centre (UNCTAD/ GATT)
4, Route des Morillons
CH-1211, Geneva 22
Switzerland

The *International Trade Centre* (ITC), established by the General Agreement on Tariffs and Trade (GATT) in 1964 to help developing countries promote their exports, has been jointly operated by GATT and the United Nations Conference on Trade and Development (UNCTAD) since 1968. ITC activities include training of developing country government trade officials and business executives in all aspects of trade promotion and international marketing, identifying export possibilities for selected products in world markets and exploiting these opportunities through export marketing and sales promotion activities.

United Nations Centre on Transnational Corporations
United Nations Plaza
New York, New York 10017
Tel. (212) 754-8452

The *United Nations Centre on Transnational Corporations* (UNCTC) was established by a General Assembly Resolution in December 1974, and began operations in November 1975. The Centre's functions include:
- Providing necessary support to the General Assembly, the Economic and Social Council and the Commission on Transnational Corporations on the full range of issues related to transnational corporations.
- Developing and maintaining a comprehensive information system by gathering, analyzing and disseminating information on transnational corporations.
- Conducting research on political, legal, economic and social aspects relating to transnational corporations, including work on the elaboration of a code of conduct and specific international arrangements and agreements.
- Organizing and coordinating programs of technical cooperation on the above matters.

The Centre also has endeavored to involve other relevant organizations and institutions outside the UN in its work and to gain inputs from them. The Centre has held seminars and discussions on research and information projects with participants from academic and business circles as well as from trade union and consumer organizations.

The Centre's work program has five priorities:
- The formulation of a code of conduct dealing with transnational corporations (TNCs). This is the Centre's most visible priority.
- The establishment of a comprehensive information system about TNCs. The Centre is developing information on individual transnationals and on contracts and agreements between transnational corporations and host countries.
- Research regarding the social, political, economic and legal effects of TNCs.
- Technical assistance related to issues involving transnationals. The area of technical assistance is one of the most important priorities because it offers a chance to improve dealings between TNCs and host countries. Most countries will call upon the Centre for assistance, for example, in evaluating a contract, providing information on a trans-

national corporation, advising on national legislation and training specialists at workshops.
• The elaboration of a definition of transnational corporation.

The last item involves the important political question of whether or not state enterprises should be described as transnationals. The socialist countries contend that TNCs are solely a free-market phenomenon and state enterprises therefore should not be classified in the same category.

Transnational business activity has significant effects on the international economy as well as on host and home countries' economies. There are an estimated 15,000 transnational corporations in the world, with 60,000 to 70,000 foreign affiliates, representing a book value of about $200 billion. The total production of these foreign subsidiaries is higher than the total volume of exports of market economies. In the United States, the volume of production of American TNCs abroad is four times higher than the volume of American exports. Therefore, transnational corporations and their foreign subsidiaries have become important vehicles for delivering goods to foreign markets.

United Nations Conference on the Law of the Sea
United Nations Plaza
Room 2727
New York, New York
10017
Tel. (212) 754-5757

Delegates to the *United Nations Conference on the Law of the Sea* (UNCLOS) have undertaken the monumental task of defining international rules to govern use of the oceans and ocean resources.

While concern with this issue dates back centuries, the major impetus came in 1958 and 1960 with the organization of the first and second United Nations Conferences on the Law of the Sea. These initiatives produced three treaties, to which the United States remains a signatory: the *Convention on the High Seas,* providing for freedom of navigation on the high seas; the *Convention on the Territorial Sea and the Contiguous Zone,* outlining rules by which a coastal state may exercise jurisdiction within its territorial sea; and the *Convention on the Continental Shelf,* providing exclusive rights to coastal states over the exploitation of mineral and non-living resources on the continental shelf. Both conferences, however, failed to resolve the question of the extent of the territorial sea and differences over fisheries jurisdiction.

In 1974, the third UNCLOS convened in Caracas, Venezuela, to begin consideration of the gamut of remaining ocean issues. Sessions have been held in Geneva (1975), New York (1976) and most recently in Geneva (1979), producing several draft negotiating texts subject to ratification by the conference as a whole. While consensus and compromise have been achieved on approximately 75 percent of the issues—such as the declaration by most coastal states of 200-mile fisheries or resource zones—control of the deep seabed remains the major impasse to concluding the negotiations. Lines are sharply drawn as to the type of regime that should be instituted to cover access, exploration, exploitation, production, marketing strategy and control over mineral resources. In essence, the "Group of 77," (now representing approximately 114 developing countries) desires a strong system of international control, under the auspices of an International Seabed Authority, with redistribution of profits to the poorer nations. Against this, the developed, industrialized countries at the conference favor a looser system of control and freedom of operation commensurate with a competitive free market system. However, the requirement that a percentage of profits be placed in an international fund for the benefit of the developing world has been accepted by the industrialized countries.

In the United States there has been considerable congressional support for unilateral action to permit American firms with the necessary technological capabilities to initiate deep seabed mining operations. The legislation would protect such operations from any retrograde actions that might arise from an eventual unilateral agreement.

Harmonization of national goals, particularly on the deep seabed issue, has yet to be accomplished. Yet most delegates to the third UNCLOS are determined to ratify an international regime for the oceans, which will at least promote a modicum of global security and increased economic welfare and set a precedent for international cooperation and interdependence.

United Nations Conference on Science and Technology for Development
United Nations Plaza
Room 3161A
New York, New York
11017
Tel. (212) 754-6893

The *United Nations Conference on Science and Technology for Development* (UNCSTD), held in Vienna, August 1979, was the last of this decade's major world economic conferences. Its basic objectives were to secure agreement on a plan to bring the benefits of modern science and technology to all countries, particularly those in the Third World. Specifically, the conference was an effort to develop the scientific and technological components of the New International Economic Order (NIEO) identified in a 1974 UN resolution.

Against this background, UNCSTD 1979 took a very different approach than the United Nations Conference on the Application of Science and Technology for the Benefit of the Less Developed Areas, held in Geneva in 1973, which was essentially a scientific conference which resulted in a useful exchange of scientific and technological information. In contrast, UNCSTD 1979 dealt mainly with the identification and removal of social, political, economic, institutional and cultural obstacles to the application of science and technology to development.

The UNCSTD conference was intergovernmental, with delegates serving as official representatives of their governments. In addition, certain organizations and representatives of liberation movements which have standing invitations from the General Assembly to send observers to conferences held under its auspices were invited to attend.

The conference followed two main approaches: one, to explore the application of science in all its aspects to the development needs of the poorer countries; and two, to establish standards for international technology transfer transactions together with rules governing major aspects of direct investment, industrial property rights, licensing and so on.

One hundred forty-one nations participated in the session in which the proposals of the less developed countries, the so-called "Group of 77," were essentially pitted against those of the Group B, or developed countries. The Group C category of developed socialized states generally supported the Group of 77.

Little substantial agreement on the core issues emerged from the discussions. Group of 77 proposals focused heavily on demands for special concessions on the terms and conditions for acquiring technology. Group B positions were essentially opposed to these claims, stating instead that technology flows would tend to taper off if the climate in developing countries were too restrictive. To this extent, much of the discussions at Vienna echoed those already underway in the UNCTAD and other organizations.

Specific subject areas on which agreement was not reached included maintenance of property rights, disclosure of proprietary information, access to private technology, code of conduct for transfer of technology and unbundling.

A renewed effort is expected within the UN to take up again the issues covered at Vienna with the probability of much moderated positions on the part of the Group of 77.

United Nations Conference on Trade and Development

Headquarters:
Palais des Nations
1211 Geneva, 10
Switzerland

Liaison Office:
UNCTAD
United Nations
Rooms 927
New York, New York
10017
Tel. (212) 754-6893

The *United Nations Conference on Trade and Development* (UNCTAD) was established as a permanent organ of the General Assembly on December 30, 1964. Among its principal aims is to be a forum for discussion between developed and developing nations in order to promote trade between countries with different economic and social systems and to speed the economic development of the developing countries.

UNCTAD's work includes the consideration of ways to increase the flow of financial resources to the developing countries, particularly official development assistance.

In recent years, one of the major concerns under UNCTAD's auspices has been the "Integrated Program for Commodities." The goal of this program is to ensure remunerative, equitable and stable prices for the primary products of developing countries and to improve these products' access to the markets of industrialized countries. A pivotal part of the program calls for the establishment of a common fund for financing buffer stocks.

As an executing agency of the United Nations Development Program (UNDP), UNCTAD is responsible for technical assistance activities in all matters related to trade.

Presently, total membership in UNCTAD is 159 countries. The fifth General Session was held in Manila, the Philippines, May 7-June 3, 1979. Consensus was reached on several items from a broad agenda of development issues.

The conference decided without dissent to launch a comprehensive new program for action for the least developed countries and called for the provision of "much larger flows" of assistance to such countries.

On development assistance generally, it urged all donor countries "to increase effectively and substantially" their official aid flow towards the United Nations target of 0.7 percent of gross national income and called for a doubling of this target "as soon as possible" with respect to the least developed countries.

The conference called on all countries to reduce and eliminate protectionist practices, in particular limits on developed country imports from developing countries. However, the developing countries said this resolution fell far short of their expectations.

UNCTAD V agreed to lines of action for a possible international strategy to boost the technological capacity of the Third World, and 13 countries pledged a total of $87 million to a commodity development facility—the "second window"—of the Common Fund for commodities.

However, agreement could not be reached in Manila on the main issues that have so far blocked completion of a code of conduct for the transfer of technology. A second session of the conference on this issue was convened in Geneva in February 1980 but failed to resolve outstanding differences.

United Nations Development Programme

The *United Nations Development Programme* (UNDP) was established by a General Assembly Resolution No. 2029 on November 22, 1965, and now operates in 150 countries and territories

1 United Nations Plaza
New York, New York
10017
Tel. (212) 754-1234

and with two dozen international agencies to promote faster economic growth and improve standards of living throughout Asia, Africa, Latin America, the Middle East and parts of Europe. The UNDP supports numerous projects in agriculture, industry, transport, trade and related fields. These projects form part of three-to-five year "country programs" which are closely linked with overall national development plans. About two-thirds of UNDP's assistance goes to countries where annual per capita GNPs are under $300.

Most projects are designed to be self-continuing, with local personnel taking over operations as UNDP support phases out. The goal is to integrate UNDP assistance into coordinated national or regional development efforts. As of year-end 1978, the total cost on completion of all current projects will exceed $6.2 billion. Approximately 40 percent of this amount is furnished by UNDP. The remaining 60 percent is supplied by the recipient countries, in the form of personnel, buildings, facilities and supplies.

Operating policies are established by a governing council, which meets twice a year. The council is composed of representatives of 48 states—21 developed, 27 developing—and reports to the General Assembly through ECOSOC. The United States has been a member of the governing council since UNDP's establishment.

UNDP executes directly only a small percentage of the projects it funds. The remainder of UNDP assistance is channeled through 26 other UN agencies. These executing agencies perform two major functions for UNDP. They serve as data banks for development techniques in their respective specialities and they recruit international experts, purchase equipment and procure specialized contract services needed for project execution.

United Nations Industrial Development Organization

Headquarters:
P.O. Box 707
1011 Vienna, Austria

Liaison Office:
United Nations Plaza
Room 900
New York, New York
10017
Tel. (212) 754-6890

The General Assembly established the *United Nations Industrial Development Organization* (UNIDO) on January 1, 1967, in order to promote industrial development generally and to help accelerate the industrialization of developing countries.

In providing assistance to developing countries wishing to formulate industrial policies, more than 2,100 projects in over 100 countries were being carried out under the auspices of UNIDO as of 1978. Operational activities include the Special Industrial Services (SIS) program, designed to supplement other assistance by helping to solve urgent industrial problems at short notice and on flexible terms. Over a thousand requests for assistance of this type have been made.

In addition, considerable effort is being made by UNIDO to give developing countries access to current industrial and technical information by conducting symposia, seminars and training programs dealing with specific industries and industrial techniques.

At the UNIDO's second General Conference, held in Lima, Peru, in March 1975, a declaration and a plan of action were approved by the members, setting the goal that the share of developing countries in world industrial production should be increased from 7 percent to 25 percent by the year 2000. Also at that conference, a move to transform UNIDO into a specialized agency was begun.

UNIDO adopted a constitution on April 8, 1979, in Vienna, clearing the way for the organization to become the UN's sixteenth specialized agency with headquarters in Vienna. At least 80 states must ratify the constitution before it will enter into force.

2. International Intergovernmental Organizations

The United States participates in one way or another in a number of other international intergovernmental organizations with functions that bear on trade and investment. Among these are the following:

African Development Bank and Fund
B.P. No. 1387
Abidjan, Ivory Coast

The *African Development Bank and Fund* (ADBF) was established in 1964. It has 48 members, all of which are African states. As of June 30, 1978, the bank had approved 172 loans to 36 countries (and 4 regional or subregional organizations) totalling $622 million.

ADBF's resources are derived from equity subscriptions of its members. Subscriptions are 50 percent paid-in and 50 percent callable. Callable capital is used by the bank as backing for its borrowings in international capital markets. The proceeds from these borrowings, along with the proceeds from paid-in subscriptions, are lent, at near-market terms, to members for development projects.

As of this writing, only African countries belong to the bank, but negotiations have been completed to clear the way for others to join; however, entry has not yet taken place. This should result in a significant expansion of the bank's capital stock, from a current level of almost $1.2 billion to cover $6 billion by the mid-1980's.

The United States and 19 other aid donors (mostly Western countries) do belong to the African Development Fund, the bank's "soft loan" affiliate. The fund was established in 1973. Its capital is raised by direct contributions by donors and is lent by the fund to the poorest countries in Africa at highly concessional rates. A major replenishment agreement was concluded in 1978. The fund had committed $547 million for 113 projects in 32 countries through December 31, 1978.

Most bank- or fund-financed projects require the procurement of goods and services for the project through international competitive bid procedures.

Asian Development Bank
Roxas Boulevard
P.O. Box 789
Manila, Philippines

The *Asian Development Bank* (ADB) was established in 1966 to further economic growth by lending money and providing technical assistance to Asian developing member countries. It has 43 members, including 29 Asian countries, the United States, Canada and 12 European countries.

The bank's resources are derived from two sources, equity subscriptions and direct contributions. Members' subscriptions have averaged 17 percent paid-in over the life of the bank, although recent subscriptions have been only 10 percent paid-in. The balance is callable capital, which is used by the bank as backing for its borrowings in international capital markets. The proceeds from the borrowings, along with the proceeds from the paid-in portion of subscriptions, are lent, at near-market terms, to developing country members for development projects. These are called ordinary loans.

Direct contributions by ADB-developed country members to the bank's special funds, primarily the Asian Development Fund, are lent by the bank on highly concessional terms to the bank's poorest developing country members.

Most bank-financed projects require the procurement of goods and services for the project through international competitive bid procedures.

At the end of 1978, the bank had approved 359 loans totalling $5.4 billion for 23 countries. Of this total, special fund loans amounted to $1.5 billion.

Caribbean Development Bank

P.O. Box 408 Wildey
St. Michael, Barbados
W.I.

The *Caribbean Development Bank* (CDB) was established in 1970 "to contribute to the harmonious growth and development of the member countries in the Caribbean and promote economic co-operation and integration among them, having special regard to the needs of the less developed member countries."

Bank membership is open to "states and territories of the region" and to nonregional members of the United Nations, its specialized agencies and the Atomic Energy Commission (AEC). Admission requires the concurrence of two-thirds of the governors representing at least three-fourths of the voting power.

Present membership of the CDB consists of 16 regional members (Bahamas, Barbados, Dominica, Grenada, Guyana, Jamaica, St. Lucia, St. Vincent, Trinidad and Tobago, and seven Commonwealth Caribbean Territories) and four nonregional members (Canada, Colombia, the United Kingdom and Venezuela).

Total loan approvals rose in 1978 by some 60 percent to U.S. $49 million, compared with an increase of 20 percent in 1977. An important factor in expanded operations was the extension for the first time of program loans from resources channeled through the CDB by the newly created Caribbean Development Facility for onlending to Jamaica (U.S. $12 million), Guyana (U.S. $4.5 million), Barbados (U.S. $1.5 million) and the less developed member countries of the Caribbean Common Market, CARICOM (U.S. $2 million).

At the end of 1978, total resources of the bank amounted to U.S. $259 million, compared with U.S. $210 million a year earlier.

In 1978, a Technical Assistance Fund was established to simplify the administration of technical assistance activities and eventually replace the numerous funds that have been contributed by donor countries for that purpose.

European Community

Commission Headquarters:
200 Rue de la Loi
1049 Brussels
Belgium

European Community
  Information Service
2100 M Street, N.W.,
  Suite 707
Washington, D.C. 20037
Tel. (202) 862-9500

One Dag Hammarskjold
  Plaza
245 East 47th Street

The *European Community* (EC) is an economic association originally composed of Belgium, France, Italy, Luxembourg, The Netherlands and West Germany. The EC now unites the economies of nine nations, with the accession of Denmark, Ireland and the United Kingdom and will be joined by Greece in 1981. Spain and Portugal are expected to join the Community in the mid-1980s.

The EC actually embraces three "communities:"

1. The *European Coal and Steel Community* (ECSC), created by the Paris Treaty of April 18, 1951. It paved the way for further economic unity by joining the coal and steel industries in a single "common market."

2. The *European Economic Community* (EEC), the official name for the Common Market, created by the Rome Treaty of March 25, 1957. On January 1, 1958, the EEC began to remove trade and economic barriers between its member countries, adopt common import duties on goods from other countries and provide

New York, New York
10017
Tel. (212) 371-3804

a framework for harmonizing their economic policies. The Community, for example, negotiates as a unit with the GATT.

3. The *European Atomic Energy Community* (Euratom), created by a second Rome Treaty of March 25, 1957. Euratom promotes peaceful uses of nuclear energy.

The Community's purposes are:

- To put an end to national prejudice, discrimination and armed conflict which has culminated in two world wars.
- To open up the economic frontiers which formerly divided Western Europe into small, protected markets.
- To harness the constructive energies of the European peoples to improve the quality of life.
- To make the Community a single economic area, promoting social and technological progress and the efficient use of resources in both agriculture and industry.
- To recover together some of the world influence that Western Europe's separate nations can no longer command alone.
- To become a strong force for peace and a generous provider of aid to the world's poorer nations.
- To contribute to world stability and the beginning of international law and order.

The Community differs from traditional international organizations in that it provides for an ''ever closer union'' of unlimited duration between member states. Its permanent institutions not only apply and administer the treaties, which are the Community's ''constitution,'' but also engage in a continuous process of legislation, making and revising policy as the integration process advances. In 1979, the European Community adopted the European Monetary System (EMS). EMS was created to promote exchange-rate stability within the Community by bringing eight of its members (the United Kingdom is the exception) as well as ''associate'' members into a system in which the exchange rates of their currencies will be more or less fixed in relation to each other. EMS thus provides a structure of fixed but adjustable exchange rates, as in the Bretton Woods System, under which members may from time to time devalue or revalue their currencies relative to others in the system.

The European Parliament until June 1979 consisted of 198 members nominated by the nine national parliaments. The Community's first direct elections (June 7-10, 1979) sent 410 directly elected representatives to the European parliamentary assembly. (There will be 435 when Greece takes part in 1981.)

The new Parliament's daily responsibilities will be the same as the previous assembly's—approval of the budget, advising on legislation and exercising political control. The directly elected Parliament takes on a new importance, however, in the advancement of the Community beyond its formerly largely economic role to one that is at the same time economic, social and political.

Information and publications on the European Community can be obtained from the Delegation of the Commission of the European Communities, 2100 M Street, N.W., Suite 707, Washington, D.C. 20037. Note especially, *Europe,* published bimonthly, available by subscription for $6 per year; $10 per two years; $14 per three years.

**Inter-American
Development Bank**

The *Inter-American Development Bank* (IDB) became operational in 1961. Its original membership comprised 20 countries—19

308 17th Street, N.W.
Washington, D.C. 20557
Tel. (202) 634-8152

Latin American republics and the United States. By 1977, the bank's membership had increased to 41 countries—26 countries in the Western Hemisphere and 15 from Europe, Asia and the Middle East.

The purpose of IDB is to promote the economic and social development of its regional developing member countries, both individually and collectively. The bank may make loans to both governmental and private entities. Loans are made for specific projects and are also granted to development banks and institutions in member countries for relending on projects not large enough to warrant direct credits from the bank. In addition, technical advice and assistance in preparing, financing and executing development plans and projects is administered by IDB, including the consideration of priorities and the formulation of loan proposals on specific national or regional development projects.

As of December 31, 1978, IDB had subscribed capital resources totaling $9.66 billion, of which $1.16 billion was paid-in and $8.5 billion was callable capital. The bank has approved loans totaling almost $4 billion to help finance development projects and programs in its Latin American member countries.

The 1978 $9.75 billion replenishment of the bank's resources, the fifth in the bank's history, will enable the bank to increase the growth of its real lending between 5 and 7 percent a year. In voting for the recommended replenishments, the bank's board of governors approved a report which outlines new guidelines for the bank's future actions. Approximately one-half of the proposed lending program for the 1979-82 period would be directed toward projects which create productive employment in rural and urban areas to help low-income groups.

About 20 to 25 percent would be devoted to financing energy projects, including the support of conventional and nonconventional sources of energy. Between 20 and 25 percent would be assigned to projects which, by directly increasing exports or substituting imports, would reduce the relative burden of servicing external debts. A small portion would go to projects in other sectors considered essential to eliminating existing development bottlenecks in specific countries.

International Monetary Fund
700 19th Street, N.W.
Washington, D.C. 20431
Tel. (202) 477-7000

The *International Monetary Fund* (IMF) was created with the signing of the Final Act of the United Nations Monetary and Financial Conference, at Bretton Woods, New Hampshire, on July 22, 1944. U.S. membership was authorized by an act of Congress approved July 31, 1945.

Its purposes are: to promote international monetary cooperation and the expansion of international trade; to promote exchange stability, maintain orderly exchange arrangements and avoid competitive exchange depreciations; and to assist in the establishment of a multilateral system of payments in respect to currency transactions between members and in the elimination of foreign exchange restrictions which hamper foreign trade.

The fund meets these objectives by selling foreign exchange to members to help them meet balance-of-payments difficulties, advising governments on financial problems and recommending anti-inflationary measures with respect to investment and bank credit, government spending and taxation.

In 1976, the fund's board of governors adopted a resolution approving a comprehensive international monetary reform amendment designed to adapt the fund and its operations to present-day conditions. In April 1978, a *second amendment* to the IMF Articles of Agreement entered into force. The second amendment makes possible further alteration of the articles as future conditions warrant.

Among the important features of the second amendment are new provisions dealing with exchange arrangements and a gradual reduction in the role of gold within the international monetary system. It also provides that the status of the Special Drawing Right (SDR) be enhanced as an international reserve asset.

Drawings on the fund during 1978 totalled $4.725 billion (SDR 3.774 billion) and net drawings outstanding totalled $14.813 billion (SDR 11.831 billion).

Organization of American States
1889 F St., N.W.
Washington, D.C. 20006
Tel. (202) 789-3000

The *Organization of American States* (OAS) is the oldest regional society of nations in the world, dating back to the First International Conference of American States, which established the International Union of American Republics on April 14, 1890, in Washington, D.C. When the United Nations was established, the OAS joined it as a regional organization. The charter governing the OAS was signed in Bogota in 1948 and amended by the Protocol of Buenos Aires, which entered into force in February 1970. Today the OAS is made up of 28 member states.

The purposes of the OAS are to strengthen peace and security in the Western Hemisphere; to prevent possible causes of difficulties and to ensure the pacific settlement of disputes that may arise among the member states; to provide for common action on the part of those states in the event of aggression; to seek the solution of political, juridical and economic problems that may arise among them; and to promote, by cooperative action, their economic, social and cultural development.

The supreme authority of the OAS is the General Assembly. Economic and social questions are dealt with by the Inter-American Economic and Social Council, which has as one of its subsidiary bodies the Special Committee for Consultation and Negotiation to handle specific problems of trade relations between the United States and the other member countries.

Organization for Economic Cooperation and Development
Headquarters:
2, rue Andre-Pascal
75775 Paris Cedex 16
France

Washington, D.C., Center:
1750 Pennsylvania
   Avenue, N.W.
Washington, D.C. 20006
Tel. (202) 724-1857

The *Organization for Economic Cooperation and Development* (OECD), was established on September 30, 1961, replacing the Organization for European Economic Cooperation (OEEC), created in 1948 to implement the Marshall Plan for European Recovery.

The change in title reflected the organization's altered status and functions—ceasing to be a purely European body with the accession of Canada and the United States as full members and the addition of development aid to its list of activities. Since September 1961, Japan, Finland, Australia and New Zealand have also become full OECD members.

The OECD convention specified that the organization shall promote policies designed to achieve the highest sustainable economic growth and employment and a rising standard of living in member countries, while maintaining financial stability, and thus to contribute to the development of the world economy. In addition, the OECD shall contribute to the expansion of world trade on a multilateral, nondiscriminatory basis in accordance with international obligations.

The OECD conducts research, makes recommendations and issues publications relating to the economic problems of its 24 member countries: Austria, Australia, Belgium, Canada, Denmark, Finland, France, Germany, Greece, Iceland, Ireland, Italy, Japan, Luxembourg, New Zealand, the Netherlands, Norway, Portugal, Spain, Sweden, Switzerland, Turkey, the United Kingdom and the United States. Yugoslavia participates in certain OECD activities and has been given special status for this participation. The Washington Center has a complete library of all OECD publications, some of which are available for purchase from the sales office.

3. World Bank Group

The *World Bank Group* consists of three international financial institutions: the *International Bank for Reconstruction and Development* (IBRD), the *International Development Association* (IDA) and the *International Finance Corporation* (IFC). Each of these institutions was established to fulfill a distinct function but all are devoted to the provision of financial and technical assistance for economic development. A fourth affiliate of the World Bank Group is the *International Centre for Settlement of Investment Disputes* (ICSID).

International Bank for Reconstruction and Development (World Bank)
1818 H Street, N.W.
Washington, D.C. 20433
Tel. (202) 477-1234

Conceived at the Bretton Woods Conference in 1944 along with the complementary institution, the International Monetary Fund, the *World Bank* began operation in June 1946.

The World Bank was designed to promote the international flow of capital for productive purposes and to promote the long-term growth of international trade. Recently, attention has been focused on increasing the proportion of World Bank projects which directly assist the poorest peoples in the developing countries. As of July 1979, effective loans totalled $51.1 billion (total loans 1946 to present). The authorized capital stock of the World Bank, formerly $10 billion, was increased to $32.6 billion in 1976. Outstanding borrowing totalled $42.5 billion as of July 1979.

The World Bank functions either by making loans out of its own funds or out of funds raised by it in the private market. The loans may be made to member countries, to their political subdivisions or to private business enterprises in their territories. It also promotes private foreign investment by guarantees of, and participation in, loans and investments made by private investors.

Technical assistance is provided by the World Bank to its members in various ways. The most important method is to send general survey missions to study a country's resources and formulate recommendations to serve as a basis for a long-term development program.

U.S. membership in the World Bank was authorized by an act of Congress approved July 31, 1945.

International Centre for Settlement of Investment Disputes
1818 H Street, N.W.
Washington, D.C. 20433
Tel. (202) 676-1438

The *International Centre for Settlement of Investment Disputes* (ICSID) was established in 1966, following entry into force of the 1965 Convention on the Settlement of Investment Disputes between States and Nationals of Other States. Seventy-five states, including the United States, are parties to the convention, while an additional five states have signed the convention but not ratified it.

The Centre is governed by an administrative council consisting of the representatives of contracting states under the chairmanship *ex officio* of the President of the World Bank. The Secretary-General of the Centre is elected by the administrative council.

The Centre administers conciliation and arbitration proceedings between parties, one of which must be a contracting state (or state agency) and the other a national of another contracting state. The dispute must arise directly from an investment and the parties must have consented to submit the dispute to the centre. The convention provides that neither party may unilaterally withdraw consent given by it, whether with respect to an existing dispute or future disputes. The arbitral awards are final and binding and must be recognized by all contracting states. These states are also required to enforce the pecuniary obligations imposed by awards, subject, however, to state immunity from execution which may be recognized by the country in which enforcement is sought.

In 1978, the Centre was also authorized to administer certain proceedings outside the scope of the convention and therefore not governed by its provisions (the so-called additional facility).

The convention, the rules of the Centre, the additional facility rules and the Centre's annual reports may be obtained from the centre.

International Development Association
1818 H Street, N.W.
Washington, D.C. 20433
Tel. (202) 477-1234

An affiliate of the World Bank, the *International Development Association* (IDA) came into existence on September 24, 1960, in order to promote economic development, increase productivity and raise standards of living in the least developed areas of the world. IDA seeks to meet this objective by providing financing to less developed countries within its membership, on terms which are more flexible than conventional loans. These credits may be long-term, provide for extended grace periods and carry no interest rate, except for a .75 percent service charge. IDA thus supplements developmental objectives of the World Bank, although it remains a separate legal entity. By July 31, 1979, IDA had committed $16.9 billion for development projects.

International Finance Corporation
Headquarters: 1818 H Street, N.W.
Washington, D.C. 20433
Tel. (202) 477-1234

The *International Finance Corporation* (IFC) was formed in July 1956 to further economic development by encouraging the growth of private enterprise in its member countries, particularly in less developed regions of the world. It achieves its purpose by investing in, or lending to productive private enterprises, with private investors, where private capital is not available on reasonable terms. In this manner, IFC serves as a clearinghouse, bringing together investment opportunities, foreign and domestic private capital and experienced management.

While IFC is an affiliate of the World Bank, similar to IDA, it remains a separate legal entity. As of June 30, 1979, IFC had made commitments of $2.5 billion.

---

4. Private Organizations in the United States

a. U.S. International Business and Trade Organizations

In the United States, numerous private sector organizations work to promote U.S. foreign commerce, serve specific and general interests of foreign traders and study many aspects of foreign conditions and affairs.

Some are national in scope, devoted principally to investigation and analysis of questions of vital interest to the entire foreign trading community. Their membership represents large segments of foreign commerce and related interests and brings into focus experience and opinion which figure prominently in national policy formulation, as well as invaluable service to members.

Others are national or local bodies which represent separate divisions of the international trading service field or the interests of individual industries in exporting and importing. Still others are local or regional, serving international traders in one way or another within given areas. Business organizations, which publish guides and magazines and provide foreign trade services of various kinds, contribute valuable information for specialized services and for public education.

The large number of business organizations in the United States makes a complete listing impractical. The following, therefore, is limited to better-known business organizations having interests and functions in the general field of foreign commerce, or devoted principally to specialized fields of foreign trade or foreign policy.

AFL-CIO (American Federation of Labor-Congress of Industrial Organizations)
815 16th Street, N.W.
Washington, D.C. 20006
Tel. (202) 637-5000

The *AFL-CIO*, born in 1955 with the merger of the American Federation of Labor and the Congress of Industrial Organizations, is a federation of 104 national and international trade unions. These, in turn, are made up of some 63,000 local unions with a total membership of about 13.6 million working men and women.

The federation plays no part in labor-management relations, which is the province of its affiliated unions. It serves as a national forum in which its affiliates can discuss mutual problems and goals, as a national coordinating center through which they can pool their strength in pursuit of those goals and as a spokesman for labor's point of view on national issues—especially legislative issues—to the Administration, the Congress and the public.

Specialized functions are carried out by the federation's nine trade and industrial departments: *Building and Construction, Food and Beverage, Industrial Unions, Maritime Trade, Metal Trade, Professional Employees, Public Employees, Railway Employees* and *Union Label and Service Trades*.

The headquarters departments include *Civil Rights, Community Services, Education, International Affairs, Legislation, Occupational Safety and Health, Organization and Field Services, Publications, Public Relations, Research* and *Urban Affairs*.

The federation's national functions are matched on the state and local level by its 51 state federations (including Puerto Rico) and its 743 local central labor councils.

Except for the work of its Committee on Political Education, which is funded by voluntary donations, AFL-CIO activities are financed by a per capita tax of 16 cents per month, paid by its affiliated unions on behalf of each employed member.

As a part of its functions as the U.S. labor center, the AFL-CIO maintains fraternal relations with the labor centers of other countries, assists with the work of a number of International Trade Secretariates and conducts extensive training programs for trade unionists in developing countries in Latin America, the Caribbean, Africa, Asia and Indonesia.

American Arbitration Association
140 West 51st Street
New York, New York 10020
Tel. (212) 977-2000

The *American Arbitration Association* (AAA) provides various services to parties seeking to resolve their disputes through the use of arbitration, mediation, fact-finding, elections and other non-judicial methods. Any party to a dispute may use the administrative services of the association.

In the area of foreign commerce, the AAA functions as an administering organization for disputes in foreign trade that are to be arbitrated under its auspices and represents the U.S. point of view in meetings concerned with international commercial arbitration. Within the United States, the AAA administers cases not only under its own rules, but also under the new rules developed by the United Nations Commission on International Trade Law (UNCITRAL) and the rules of the International American Commercial Arbitration Commission (IACAC). It has also made arrangements for the resolution, through arbitration or mediation, of disputes between U.S. corporations and the Soviet Union, certain Eastern European countries and the People's Republic of China. In this regard, the AAA administers international conciliation procedures on behalf of the U.S. Chamber of Commerce pursuant to agreements with Poland, Romania, Hungary and Bulgaria.

The association offers advice on arbitration clauses in contracts; provides technical information on international arbitration; publishes a quarterly, *The Arbitration Journal;* and issues numerous other periodicals, pamphlets and books on specialized and timely subjects within its field. Several committees of the association are actively engaged in studying the use of international arbitration, both as to the application of foreign laws and as to procedural matters.

The Eastman Library of the AAA publishes selected bibliographies on international arbitration and a current international arbitration kit which includes the texts of various conventions and international arbitration rules.

American Enterprise Institute for Public Policy Research
1150 17th Street, N.W.
Suite 1200
Washington, D.C. 20036
Tel. (202) 862-5800

The *American Enterprise Institute* (AEI), established in 1943, is a publicly supported, nonprofit, nonpartisan research and educational organization whose purpose is to assist policymakers, scholars, business executives, the press and the public by providing objective analysis of national and international policy issues. AEI fosters innovative research, identifies and presents varying points of view on issues, develops practical options and analyzes public policy proposals. Areas of concentration are economics, government regulation, foreign policy, energy, health policy, defense policy, legal policy, social security and retirement policy, political and social processes and tax policy. The institute itself does not take positions on policy issues.

AEI works to place scholarly studies on public issues into the mainstream of political and academic debate. It pursues this objective by commissioning scholars to undertake original research and publishing their findings and by sponsoring conferences and debates, roundtables and other forums and making the proceedings available for wide public dissemination on television and radio, in newspapers, periodicals and scholarly journals. The institute publishes some 130 titles per year, including four periodicals: *Regulation* magazine; *Public Opinion* magazine; the *AEI Economist;* and the *AEI Foreign Policy & Defense Review.*

American Importers Association
11 West 42nd Street
New York, New York 10036
Tel. (212) 944-2230

The *American Importers Association* (AIA), formerly the National Council of American Importers, is a nonprofit commercial body organized in 1921 for group action on behalf of import trade. It represents the import industry and focuses concern on every major development affecting U.S. imports and the solution of import problems. AIA seminars keep importers up-to-date on changes in laws, regulations and practices.

The association is financed solely by membership dues. Members are drawn from all segments of import trade and include banks, custom house brokers, steamship lines, insurers and other import-related services.

Committees study import problems and make recommendations for corrective action. Issues addressed by the AIA include problems of customs administration, trade agreements, import regulations, import insurance, import financing, international transportation and communications, international agreements, currency conversion problems and foreign and domestic trade proposals affecting unencumbered reciprocal trade across international boundaries.

American Institute of Marine Underwriters
14 Wall Street, 21st. Floor
New York, New York 10005
Tel. (212) 233-0550

The *American Institute of Marine Underwriters* (AIMU), founded in 1898, has a membership representing nearly the entire American ocean marine insurance market. Membership is composed of U.S. companies as well as foreign companies admitted to do marine insurance business in this country.

Its functions are confined largely to advice and information. It keeps underwriters informed of legislation, both at home and abroad, which affects their business; provides a medium for the exchange of information relating to marine insurance; and handles public relations. AIMU maintains correspondence throughout the world to obtain the earliest possible news of maritime casualties and provides surveyors to protect the interests of its members in the event of loss or damage to vessels and cargoes insured by its members.

Association of American Chambers of Commerce in Latin America
1615 H Street, N.W.
Washington, D.C. 20062
Tel. (202) 659-3055

The *Association of American Chambers of Commerce in Latin America* (AACCLA) was founded in 1967 by business representatives from five American chambers of commerce (AmChams) in Latin America (Argentina, Brazil, Colombia, Mexico and Venezuela).

Today, AACCLA has become a broadly based, close-knit organization of 15 AmChams with six branches, representing approximately 17,000 firms and individuals of American, host country and third country nationalities, dedicated to the free enterprise system as the most viable way of advancing social and economic progress in the Western Hemisphere.

AACCLA's growth during the past ten years has been as dramatic as the increase in U.S. direct investment in Latin America—which has grown from $10.3 billion in 1967 to over $28 billion today. Also, U.S.-Latin American trade has risen significantly, now totaling over $40 billion. The significance of these economic flows to U.S. and Latin American development has prompted AACCLA to adopt and articulate policy positions on critical issues that affect inter-American trade and investment.

Association of Marine Underwriters of the United States

The *Association of Marine Underwriters of the United States* was founded in 1918, its membership being limited to domestic marine insurance companies. Its functions are confined largely to advice

66

14 Wall Street, 21st. Floor
New York, New York
10005
Tel. (212) 233-0300

and information, keeping its members informed of federal legislative matters and international affairs which affect their business.

The Brookings Institution
1775 Massachusetts
  Avenue, N.W.
Washington, D.C. 20036
Tel. (202) 797-6000

Founded in 1927, *The Brookings Institution* is an independent, nonpartisan organization whose purposes are threefold: to conduct research on significant issues of public policy within the general fields of economics, government, foreign relations and national security; to publish its findings for the benefit of policymakers and the public; and to help leaders in the public and private sectors to develop informed insights into public problems.

Brookings' activities are carried out through three research programs (economic studies, governmental studies and foreign policy studies); an Advanced Study Program, which conducts educational conferences and seminars for senior executives; a Social Science Computation Center; and a Publications Program. The institution publishes approximately 25 books and monographs each year, together with an annual report and the quarterly *Brookings' Bulletin.* Each Brookings' study is offered as a competent scholarly treatment of a subject worthy of public consideration; the institution itself does not take positions on policy issues.

The Business Roundtable
200 Park Avenue, Suite
  2222
New York, New York
  10017
Tel. (212) 682-6370

Washington Office:
1801 K Street, N.W.
Washington, D.C. 20006
Tel. (202) 872-1260

The Business Roundtable is an association of business executives who examine public issues that affect the economy, develop positions which seek to reflect sound economic and social principles and make these positions known to the public and its representatives in government. Established in 1972, the Roundtable was founded in the belief that business executives should take an increased role in the continuing debates about public policy. The Roundtable draws on the resources of major corporations for the talented and expert personnel who formulate recommendations on specific issues.

The Roundtable believes that the basic interests of business closely parallel the interests of the U.S. public, who are directly involved as employees, investors, suppliers and consumers. Thus, business leaders, although they speak as individuals, have responsibilities for the economic well-being of millions of Americans.

A principal strength of the Roundtable is the extent of participation by the chief executive officers of the member firms. Working in task forces on specific issues, they direct research, supervise preparation of position papers, recommend policy and speak out publicly on the issues. The activities of these task forces are reviewed by the Roundtable Policy Committee and position papers are issued for circulation among members and for public use.

In an effort to insure a broad base in information for the decision-making process, membership of the Roundtable is diversified. Member selection reflects the goal of having representation varied by category of business and by geographic location. Thus, the members, some 190 chief executive officers of companies in all fields, can present a cross section of thinking on national issues.

**Chamber of Commerce
of the United States**

The *Chamber of Commerce of the United States* was established in 1912 on the recommendation of President William Taft, who

1615 H Street, N.W.
Washington, D.C. 20062
Tel. (202) 659-6000

saw the need for a "central organization to provide Congress with the benefit of the thinking of the business community on national problems and issues affecting the economy." In its first year, U.S. Chamber membership totaled 82 local and state chambers of commerce and trade associations. The organization has grown steadily ever since in size, stature, prestige and in the scope and effectiveness of its work. Presently, U.S. Chamber membership includes over 93,000 corporations and individuals, 1,300 trade and professional organizations, 2,700 local and state chambers of commerce and 44 American chambers of commerce (AmChams) in 42 countries.

As the world's largest voluntary business federation, the U.S. Chamber's broad purpose is to advance human progress through an economic, political and social system based on individual freedom, incentive, initiative, opportunity and responsibility. Policies of the U.S. Chamber reflect diverse interests in the United States and must be "national in character, timely in importance and of significance to business and industry," as prescribed by its bylaws.

To represent and serve its membership interests, the U.S. Chamber maintains staff specialists who are experts on major issues of concern to the business community. Staff work is guided by committees composed of business and professional representatives, experts in their respective fields. In addition, the U.S. Chamber has divided the country into six geographical regions and maintains regional offices in six principal cities to render prompt and efficient service and to promote grass roots action on national issues.

The U.S. Chamber's international activities are carried out by its International Division, serving members interested in international economic, political and social affairs. Three subcommittees, specializing in international trade, international investment and international economic development, as well as the International Insurance Advisory Council and the International Service Industry Committee, report through the International Policy Committee to the board of directors on matters of international policy development and implementation.

Economic and commercial problems which mutually affect the United States and its major trading partners are handled by joint business councils cosponsored by the U.S. Chamber and foreign counterpart organizations. These bilateral councils include business representatives from the United States and—the ASEAN countries, Brazil, Bulgaria, Czechoslovakia, Egypt, the European Community, Hungary, India, Iran, Israel, Japan, Poland, Romania and the Sudan. The International Division also staffs the Association of American Chambers of Commerce in Latin America, the Committee on Canada-United States Relations and the United States-European Community Conference on Agriculture. (see Part 1, Section 2 D for descriptions of U.S. Chamber international committees and councils)

Through this system of committees, subcommittees, councils and task forces as well as its member AmChams overseas, the International Division provides the basis for policy and program recommendations to the administration and to the Congress. In addition, the division maintains the U.S. Chamber's relations with several international organizations, produces a variety of reports, surveys and other publications on international economic issues and organizes conferences, seminars and symposia to publicize topical trade and investment issues.

Committee for Economic Development

1700 K Street, N.W.
Washington, D.C. 20006
Tel. (202) 296-5860

477 Madison Avenue
Avenue
New York, New York
10022
Tel. (212) 688-2063

The *Committee for Economic Development* (CED) is an independent, nonpartisan, nonprofit research and educational organization whose approximately 200 trustees develop specific recommendations for business and public policy. Most of these trustees are board chairmen, presidents of major corporations or presidents of universities.

Working with economists and social scientists, CED's trustees develop findings and make recommendations on national and international economies; the management of federal, state and local government; and education and urban development. These recommendations, published by CED's Research and Policy Committee, are designed to contribute to the continued strength of U.S. free society through high employment, increased productivity, rising living standards, greater economic stability and greater opportunity for all Americans.

At CED, business leaders actively engage in the policy process, drawing on their practical operating experience and the fruits of academic research to formulate policy positions from the standpoint of the general welfare, rather than from the point of view of any special interest group.

The Conference Board

845 Third Avenue
New York, New York
10022
Tel. (212) 759-0900

The Conference Board is an independent, nonprofit research institution with facilities in the United States, Canada and Europe. Its scientific studies of management and economics produce a continuing flow of timely and practical information to assist leaders of business, government, labor and other institutions in arriving at sound decisions. The Conference Board's research is also made available to the news media in order to contribute to public understanding of economic and management issues in market economies.

Worldwide, the organization is supported financially by more than 4,000 associates, comprised of corporations, national and regional governments, labor unions, universities, associations, public libraries and individuals. Research reports, access to a variety of meetings and personalized information services are among the direct benefits that associates receive from their support of the Conference Board.

Council of the Americas

684 Park Avenue
New York, New York
10021
Tel. (212) 628-3200

The *Council of the Americas* (CoA) is a nonprofit business association supported by more than 200 member corporations. Its programs are carried out through active participation by representatives on member companies.

Founded in New York City in 1958 as the United States Inter-American Council, Inc., the mission of the CoA is to further understanding and acceptance of the role of private enterprise as a positive force for the development of the Americas.

Council on Foreign Relations, Inc.

58 East 68th Street
New York, New York
10021
Tel. (212) 734-0400

The *Council on Foreign Relations, Inc.* is a noncommercial, nonpolitical and nonprofit educational organization established in 1921 to study foreign policy and international aspects of economics, politics and military strategy.

A private, nonpartisan research institution, the council acts also as a forum—with several hundred meetings and seminars annually—for approximately 1900 individual members drawn from the public and private sectors.

69

Approximately 180 major multinational firms subscribe annually to the council's Corporation Service, participating in conferences and meetings on issues relevant to the international business community.

The organization is affiliated with 37 committees on foreign relations across the United States, which maintain their own membership of over 3,000 persons.

Since 1922, the council has published the quarterly journal *Foreign Affairs* and continues to publish scholarly books and monographs.

East-West Trade Council
1700 Pennsylvania
  Avenue, N.W.
Suite 670
Washington, D.C. 20006
Tel. (202) 393-6240

The *East-West Trade Council* is a nonprofit organization composed solely of U.S. businesses, financial institutions, associations, academicians and other interested individuals. Its members are involved in trade with the communist countries including the U.S.S.R., Eastern Europe, the People's Republic of China and Cuba. The council is financed solely from its U.S. membership.

The council was established in 1972 and is the oldest U.S. trade association specializing in East-West trade. The council works closely with officials of the executive branch, Congress, officials of foreign countries both in Washington and abroad, business leaders and others interested in the area of East-West trade. With the support of its membership, the council has been able to promote its goal of expanding East-West trade and at the same time provide many vital services to its membership.

In addition to its newsletter issued every two weeks, the council sponsors frequent symposia on East-West trade and exerts a concentrated effort to gain increased trade opportunities for American business in the communist countries. The council is active in promoting legislation which would expand East-West trade.

Through close relations wtih committees of Congress, as well as with federal agencies involved in East-West trade and representatives of communist countries, the council assists members in all facets of East-West trade.

**Emergency Committee
  for American Trade**
1211 Connecticut
  Avenue—Suite 801
Washington, D.C. 20036
Tel. (202) 659-5147

**Michael Moynihan and
  Associates**
730 Fifth Avenue, Rm.
  607
New York, New York
  10019
Tel. (212) 541-4040

The *Emergency Committee for American Trade* (ECAT) is a nonprofit membership organization of leaders of 64 major American multinational corporations. Organized in 1967, its purpose is to influence public policy in the direction of an open and equitable international trading, investment and monetary system, through contacts with the Congress and the executive branch.

ECAT operates in three basic ways: (1) through its members, either individually or as a group; (2) through its staff and consultants; and (3) through action with other groups.

Because all members of ECAT share the view that liberal foreign trade and investment policies are in the national interest, ECAT is able to support measures that would expand international trade and investment and to oppose measures that would curtail them.

**FCIB (Foreign Credit
  Interchange Bureau-
  National Association of**

The *FCIB* (formerly known as the Foreign Credit Interchange Bureau) is the international department of the *National Association of Credit Management*. It was established in 1919 to provide

Credit Management Corporation)
475 Park Avenue South
New York, New York
10016
Tel. (212) 725-1700

service to those of its 44,000 members engaged in foreign trade. Its activities cover the entire spectrum of export credit and collections.

The association seeks to promote sound credit techniques and ethics throughout the world. It works closely with credit and financial associations in other countries for the purpose of promoting sound credit administration and improving the free flow of credit information.

The FCIB provides to its members credit reports on overseas buyers, worldwide collection of delinquent accounts, biweekly and monthly roundtable conferences on export credit, collection and exchange problems, the minutes of which are available on an annual subscription basis.

Foreign Credit Insurance Association
Ninth Floor
One World Trade Center
New York, New York
10048
Tel. (212) 432-6200

The *Foreign Credit Insurance Association* (FCIA), founded in 1961, operates in cooperation with the Export-Import Bank of the United States to provide export credit insurance to U.S. exporters. This insurance protects the exporter against commercial and political loss, thereby allowing the exporter to offer competitive credit terms within overseas markets and facilitate the financing of these foreign receivables. Membership in the association is open to any qualified insurance company. Currently, there are 49 marine, property and casualty insurance companies participating.

Foreign Policy Association
205 Lexington Avenue
New York, New York
10016
Tel. (212) 481-8450

The *Foreign Policy Association* is a nonpartisan educational organization, working with voluntary organizations and communities throughout the United States to encourage discussion of foreign policy problems and informed activity in world affairs. Its purpose is to carry on research and educational activities to aid in the understanding and constructive development of U.S. foreign policy.

The association is supported by contributions from foundations, corporations and individuals.

International Advertising Association, Inc.
475 Fifth Avenue
New York, New York
10017
Tel. (212) 684-1583

The *International Advertising Association, Inc.* (IAA) is the only worldwide association of persons in advertising, marketing and related business. With a membership of more than 2,500 individual members in more than 75 countries, it is a unique body representing advertising companies, advertising agencies and media on an international scale.

IAA informs its members around the world of trends and developments affecting their interests. Its world advertising congresses and chapter and regional meetings provide members with the opportunity to share ideas, experiences and skills and contribute to the advancement of the level of advertising and marketing proficiency, with strict adherence to codes of ethics and the interests of the consuming public.

International Centre for Industry and the Environment
c/o General Mills, Inc.
P.O. Box 1113

Before the 1972 Stockholm Conference on Man and Environment, a major characteristic of the many international environment programs was their lack of coherence within any overall structure. This was recognized by the General Assembly of the United Nations which established a secretariat for a United Nations Environment Programme (UNEP) mandated to develop an integrated

Minneapolis, Minnesota
55440
Tel. (612) 540-2473

Registered Office:
Nairobi, Kenya

Administrative Offices:
26, rue de Tourville, B1
78100 St-Germain-en-Laye
France

and coordinated approach to environment by the UN system within an overall set of global, regional and sectoral objectives.

The value of industrial experience in environmental protection and improvement was recognized from the beginning by the Executive Director of UNEP. To facilitate communication and consultation on environment, the *International Centre for Industry and the Environment* (ICIE) was formed in 1973 in order to: make industrial experience on environment known early in the development of international programs; make better known industrial achievements and policy in respect of environment; and make known to industry developments in international programs.

In February, 1974, the ICIE was incorporated in Kenya.

UN Environment Programmes are generally formulated and implemented with the advice of expert groups. Industrial experts have from time to time been members of these groups, but more normally the groups have been formed by governmental and academic experts. A principal function of ICIE is to facilitate contribution of industrial expertise to relevant expert groups in aspects of programs where industry has practical experience to contribute and where industry could benefit from a greater and more systematic involvement in international developments in environment. ICIE itself has no policy formulation role.

The International Economic Policy Association
1625 Eye Street, N.W.
Washington, D.C. 20006
Tel. (202) 331-1974

Founded in 1957, *The International Economic Policy Association* (IEPA) is a Washington-based nonprofit research group with a diverse but representative membership of American companies. It offers its members factual analyses of U.S. and foreign government policies affecting international trade, aid, investment, finance, taxation and related economic and monetary developments. IEPA advocates policies and practices by business concerns and governments that will keep American trade and investments abroad in good health and repute. The association has made a specialty of analyzing U.S. balance of payments and foreign investment and raw materials problems. Their affiliated Center for Multinational Studies conducts a research program in conjunction with academic scholars. The center's *Occasional Paper* series and some IEPA books and studies are available to the public at cost.

International Executives Association, Inc.
Suite 1014
122 East 42nd Street
New York, New York
10017
Tel. (212) 661-4610

The *International Executives Association, Inc.* (IEA) is a national service organization whose membership includes executives of U.S. companies and institutions which are dedicated to the development of overseas trade or services dealing with international trade promotion.

The association's primary purpose is to facilitate the exchange among its members of experience, information and opinion on all aspects of international trade. It conducts surveys concerning trading techniques and problems, the results of which are assimilated for the use of members.

The IEA conducts monthly professional programs with top international speakers and publishes the monthly *International Communicator* and *Trade Highlights* which are distributed to its entire membership.

National Association of Export Management Companies, Inc.

The *National Association of Export Management Companies, Inc.* (NEXCO) was organized in 1965 at the suggestion of the U.S. Department of Commerce. Its members, representing manufac-

65 Liberty Street
New York, New York
10005
Tel. (212) 766-1343

turers from most states, are responsible for a total of $1-2 billion of U.S. exports of manufactured products.

NEXCO's primary objective is to promote the reputation and standing of export management companies both in this country and overseas and to publicize the advantages to manufacturers and buyers of doing business through qualified Export Management Companies (EMCs). Special articles on the important role played by EMCs in developing and maintaining U.S. export sales are provided for the press and trade publications. NEXCO representatives are frequent speakers at trade association meetings and trade shows to explain the functions and services of export management companies.

NEXCO members are professional international marketing specialists experienced in all phases of export sales. Each firm specializes in particular fields assuring the manufacturer that his products will receive effective sales promotion and customer acceptance.

EMCs provide the same services the manufacturer should expect from an efficient export department within his company, with the added benefits of eliminating fixed overhead and reduced sales development time at no financial risk to the manufacturer.

Successful salesmanship, advertising, exporting and after-sales service in overseas markets involve greater expenses than in domestic markets because of distance, language, customs and competition. Many manufacturers, large and small, have found it more advantageous to have an export management firm handle their export sales, especially when wide dispersal of markets or a large volume of small orders is involved. In other cases, producers of diverse lines have found it more effective to use an exporter or exporters for specialized products.

Because export management companies have established sales organizations overseas familiar with the markets for their specialties, they can reduce to a minimum the time and cost of developing sales for the manufacturers they represent. Since neither the exporter nor his overseas distributors receive compensation until sales are concluded, EMC will make every effort to promote sales.

The EMC, acting as principal (booking orders in its own name) relieves the manufacturer of foreign credit risk and the overhead involved in checking credits and setting up a reserve for bad debts.

Acting as agent (booking orders in the manufacturer's name), the EMC is qualified to guide the manufacturer in establishing realistic payment terms as a result of its experience in international trade.

National Association of Manufacturers
1776 F Street, N.W.
Washington, D.C. 20006
Tel. (202) 331-3700

The *National Association of Manufacturers* (NAM) is a nonprofit voluntary association of approximately 13,000 companies located in every state and industrial center in the United States. Organized in 1895, its broad purposes are to promote the industrial interests of the United States; to foster domestic and foreign trade; to improve relations between employers and employees, government and industry, the public and business; and in general, to foster the principle of individual liberty.

The NAM aims to assist manufacturers in appraising the significance of social, legislative and economic trends as they affect business, the community and the nation, and especially as they point to opportunities to win the respect and support of the American public.

With seven divisional offices, the NAM maintains policy committees to consider numerous subjects affecting the interest of manufacturers and makes recommendations on specific international economic matters of a major character through its International Economic Affairs Policy Committee and standing subcommittees on international trade, investment and monetary issues.

National Association of State Development Agencies
Suite 213
One Skyline Place
5205 Leesburg Pike
Falls Church, Virginia 22041
Tel. (703) 820-0404

The *National Association of State Development Agencies* (NASDA) was founded in 1946 to assist the various states and territories in their efforts to attract business investments to their particular jurisdiction.

NASDA performs a liaison role with federal government agencies involved in economic development and provides information that will assist state development offices to implement their economic development program. NASDA also conducts seminars to inform foreign investors about direct investment opportunities in the United States and the type of services states make available to investors.

National Cargo Bureau, Inc.
Suite 2757
One World Trade Center
New York, New York 10048
Tel. (212) 432-1280

The *National Cargo Bureau, Inc.* is a nonprofit membership organization incorporated May 15, 1952, under the laws of the state of New York. It was created to formulate recommendations to the government on regulations for the safe handling and stowage of dangerous goods, other cargoes and cargo containers. It also works at the industry level in the national and international fields to achieve uniformity of safety standards and regulations and to remove obstacles resulting from the lack of uniformity in cargo stowage methods.

The bureau also is a central information agency specializing in mobilizing data on commodities transported by water; offering low-cost cargo loading inspection service, whether aboard vessels or in containers; making available inspection service of cargo, containers and cargo handling gear; and generally promoting the security of life and property on the seas.

The National Committee on International Trade Documentation
30 East 42nd Street - Suite 1406
New York, New York 10017
Tel. (212) 587-6261

The National Committee on International Trade Documentation (NCITD) is a nonprofit, privately financed membership organization dedicated to simplifying and improving international trade documentation and procedures, including information exchange by either paper or electronic methods.

Working through individuals and companies, members and nonmembers, U.S. and overseas governmental departments and agencies and duly constituted national and international committees and organizations, it serves as a coordinator and as a central source of information, reference and recommendations on problems of international trade information exchange and procedures.

Through continuing technical research, combining intermodal and intercompany experiences of all parties to international transactions, specific programs and all-inclusive systems to eliminate international paperwork, simplify documentation and improve information exchange methods are being recommended. The goal—to eliminate the major paperwork barriers and to encourage the automated exchange of the necessary trade data.

National Customs Brokers and Forwarders Association of America, Inc.
Suite 1109
One World Trade Center
New York, New York 10048
Tel. (212) 432-0050

The *National Customs Brokers and Forwarders Association of America, Inc.* (NCBFAA) is a nonprofit national organization founded to protect the business interests of customs brokers and foreign freight forwarders, to maintain the standards of efficiency within the industry and to protect the interests of both clients and governments, by aiding in the fair, reasonable and equitable administration of tariff and maritime laws and regulations.

Regular membership is restricted to persons, firms or corporations regularly engaged in business as licensed customs brokers and/or licensed foreign freight forwarders located within the United States. Associate membership, without a vote or the right to hold office, is available to persons, firms or corporations so engaged outside the United States.

National Foreign Trade Council, Inc.
10 Rockefeller Plaza
Room 530
New York, New York 10020
Tel. (212) 581-6420

The *National Foreign Trade Council, Inc.* (NFTC), founded in 1914, is a private nonprofit, nonpartisan organization of U.S. companies engaged in international trade and investment.

Its continuing purpose is: to promote and expand American foreign trade and investment through private initiative; to preserve and protect the effective role of free, private, competitive enterprise in international trade and investment; to serve as an authoritative voice of the broad cross section of U.S. international interests, large and small, represented by the membership of the council; and to develop in consultation with industry and government measures to achieve the foregoing.

The council's membership comprises U.S. companies representing broad and highly diversified interests from all parts of the nation and includes manufacturers, banks, exporters and importers and members of the shipping, airlines, insurance, communications, publishing, advertising, engineering and construction industries.

Activities of NFTC committees and groups relate principally to the following technical subjects: balance-of-payments, foreign property, industrial property, international compensation, international finance, international trade and investment policy, management resources and organization, multinational corporations, public relations and taxation of foreign source income.

Geographical committees are concerned with Europe, Eastern Europe, Latin America, the Middle East and Pacific-Asia.

The NFTC publishes two weekly news digests, *Noticias* and *Breve*, covering Latin America and Europe respectively, and periodic editions of *Pacific-Asia Report* and *Middle East Notes*.

The annual Policy Declaration of the National Foreign Trade Council, adopted by the board of directors on the basis of recommendations by several council committees, contains recommendations on a wide range of current economic problems affecting U.S. foreign trade and investment.

The National Foreign Trade Convention has been sponsored annually by the council since 1914.

National Planning Association
1606 New Hampshire Avenue, N.W.
Washington, D.C. 20009
Tel. (202) 265-7685

The *National Planning Association* (NPA) is an independent, private, nonprofit, nonpolitical organization that carries on research and policy formulation in the public interest. NPA was founded during the 1930's when conflicts among the major economic groups—business, farmers, labor—threatened to paralyze national decision making on critical issues confronting American society. It was dedicated, in the words of its statement of purpose, to the task "of getting (these) diverse groups to work together . . . to narrow areas of controversy and broaden areas of agreement . . . (and) to provide on specific problems concrete programs for action planned in the best traditions of a functioning democracy." Such democratic planning, NPA believes, involves the development of effective governmental and private policies and programs not only by official agencies but also through the independent initiative and cooperation of the main private-sector groups concerned.

NPA brings together influential and knowledgeable leaders from business, labor, agriculture and the applied and academic professions to serve on policy committees. These committees identify emerging problems confronting the nation at home and abroad and seek to develop and agree upon policies and programs for coping with them. The research and writing for these committees are provided by NPA's professional staff and, as required, by outside experts.

In addition, NPA's professional staff undertakes research designed to provide data and ideas for policymakers and planners in government and the private sector. These activities include the preparation on a regular basis of economic and demographic projections for the national economy, regions, states and metropolitan areas; the development of program planning and evaluation techniques; research on national goals and priorities; planning studies for welfare and dependency problems, employment and manpower needs, education, medical care, environmental protection, energy and other economic and social problems confronting American society; and analyses and forecasts of changing national and international realities and their implications for U.S. policies.

Overseas Development Council
1717 Massachusetts Avenue, N.W. Ste. 501
Washington, D.C. 20036
Tel. (202) 234-8701

The *Overseas Development Council* (ODC) is an independent, nonprofit organization established in 1969 to increase American understanding of the economic and social problems confronting the developing countries and of the importance of these countries to the United States in an increasingly interdependent world. The ODC seeks to promote consideration of development issues of the American public, policymakers, specialists, businessmen, laborers, educators and the media through its research, conferences, publications and liaison with U.S. mass membership organizations interested in U.S. relationships with the developing world. The ODC's program is funded by foundations, corporations and private individuals. Its policies are determined by its board of directors.

The council's research and publications programs focus attention on international economic issues, particularly trade, international finance and investment. The council annually publishes an assessment of U.S. relations with the developing world entitled *The United States and World Development: Agenda*. In addition to substantive essays on a variety of key issues, this publication includes extensive statistical annexes on U.S. trade and other economic relations with the developing countries.

Private Export Funding Corporation
280 Park Avenue
New York, N.Y. 10017
10017

Private Export Funding Corporation (PEFCO), owned by 54 commercial banks, seven industrial companies and one investment banking firm, was established in 1971 to help mobilize nonbank funds for the financing of U.S. exports. PEFCO provides medium- and long-term loans to borrowers outside the United States for the

Tel. (212) 557-3100

purchase of U.S. goods and services. All PEFCO loans carry the unconditional guarantee of the Export-Import Bank of the United States (Eximbank).

PEFCO generally makes its loans jointly with and upon referral from a commercial bank, Eximbank or both.

Trade Relations Council of the United States, Inc.
1001 Connecticut Avenue, N.W.
Room 901
Washington, D.C. 20036
Tel. (202) 785-4194

The *Trade Relations Council of the United States, Inc.* (TRC), according to its bylaws, carries on:

"continuous research into all the facts and forces brought into play in trade between nations; and to make these facts available in an educational effort designed to provide a better understanding of the effect of these forces on the prosperity of American labor, agriculture and industry."

TRC is a nonprofit corporation, with an ancestry dating back to 1885. Membership consists of manufacturing firms and trade associations.

In 1978, TRC released its sixth edition of *Employment, Output and Foreign Trade of U.S. Manufacturing Industries,* a massive study examining import, export and U.S. industry data at the two-, four-, and five-digit SIC (Standard Industrial Classification) level. The purpose of the study is to provide those concerned with foreign economic policy in government and industry with unique data by which the impact of foreign economic policy on individual industries and the national industrial economy can be judged.

In addition, TRC in 1978 began a series of special industry studies, with each study focusing in greater detail on one four-digit SIC industry.

TRC also answers inquiries, provides consulting and reference services, conducts seminars and distributes data compilations.

United States Council of the International Chamber of Commerce
1212 Avenue of the Americas
New York, New York 10036
Tel. (212) 354-4480

International Chamber of Commerce
38 Cours Albert 1er
75008 Paris, France

The *International Chamber of Commerce* (ICC) is an association of 54 national councils or committees, each embracing the larger, more successful internationally operating businesses in the 54 nations represented. In another 30 countries, individual enterprises are members.

A central secretariat in Paris coordinates the viewpoints of these councils on matters of international economic policy and on the standardization of procedures, terms and practices in international banking, commerce and transportation. This is accomplished through meetings of specialized ICC commissions.

The ICC also has special consultative status with a number of international organizations—i.e., the United Nations, the General Agreement on Tariffs and Trade (GATT) and through the Business and Industry Advisory Committee in the Organization for Economic Cooperation and Development (OECD). This privileged position affords the international business community an opportunity to participate in the important decisions taken by these organizations.

United States Council

The *United States Council* represents the ICC in the United States and carries the American viewpoint into ICC commission meetings and consultations with other organizations. These meetings enable business executives and specialists from various countries to discuss matters of common interest and reach mutually satisfactory conclusions or decisions.

One of the primary responsibilities of the United States Council is to maintain close and open lines of communication with various branches of the U.S. government. Not only does it present to government the concerns of the American business community on a broad range of issues, but it provides government representatives with a forum in which to explain their positions. Some of the topics which have recently been under consideration include North-South relations, ethical business practices, foreign investment and international commercial policy.

Commercial Services

The International Chamber of Commerce offers a broad range of commercial services to the worldwide business community in order to facilitate the freer flow of goods among countries. These services are developed, updated and supervised by some 40 specialized ICC technical commissions. They are constantly being revised so as to reflect technological and organizational changes in international trade and banking. In each case the United States Council participates actively and assists in administering these programs in the United States. Some of the most important commercial services include the ATA Carnet System, allowing for the temporary export/import of merchandise into one or more countries, the ICC Court of Arbitration and a variety of publications dealing with banking, finance and the legal aspects of commerce.

United States of America Business and Industry Advisory Committee
1212 Avenue of the Americas
New York, New York 10036
Tel. (212) 354-4480

The *United States of America Business and Industry Advisory Committee* (USA-BIAC) to the Organization for Economic Cooperation and Development (OECD) was established in 1962. It is composed of representatives of major business organizations in the United States, namely the Chamber of Commerce of the United States, the National Association of Manufacturers and the United States Council of the International Chamber of Commerce. The purpose of USA-BIAC is to represent U.S. business interests to the OECD both through the Business and Industry Advisory Committee (BIAC) and through the U.S. government on those economic issues considered by the OECD which may affect the private enterprise system.

The Business and Industry Advisory Committee, with headquarters at 38, Cours Albert, Paris 75008, France, represents business and industry of all 24 OECD member countries.

See subject heading: Organization for Economic Cooperation and Development.

b. Other Private Organizations

Other private organizations serving the interests of foreign traders in one way or another are numerous. Their number and diversity of purpose preclude mention of all of them here. They embrace such types of organizations as: regional or local organizations of foreign traders, shippers and other interests for the promotion of the foreign trade of their areas or communities; national or local associations of firms engaged in exporting or importing in individual lines of industry or trade; national or regional associations of foreign trade service industries, such as shipping, banking, insurance, forwarding and the like; regional or national associations of industry or trade, commonly referred to as trade associations, many of them having special bureaus which serve their membership engaged in exporting or importing; foreign trade or world trade bureaus of local chambers of commerce; foreign trade or world trade clubs in various parts of the country, American chambers of commerce abroad and foreign chambers in the United States; and private business firms specializing in the publication of market, credit, shipping or other services adapted particularly to the needs of exporters and importers. Still other organizations deal in influencing national policy and public understanding of international trade and economic development.

International business organizations with varying purposes and objectives are described in the *Yearbook of International Organizations,* governmental and nongovernmental, published by the Union of International Associations in Brussels, Belgium. (see Bibliography)

---

c. Chambers of Commerce

Among the many types of organizations contributing to foreign trade promotion and servicing, *chambers of commerce* are among the most visible and active. This is true not only of local chambers of commerce throughout the United States, but also of American chambers of commerce abroad and foreign chambers of commerce in the United States.

Local Chambers of Commerce in the United States

Chambers of commerce and similar organizations in many cities or metropolitan areas of the United States promote the foreign trade of their communities and offer services of various kinds to members engaged in exporting or importing.

Some chambers of commerce have highly organized programs for their communities, involving the association of all foreign trade interests and the maintenance of committees and special departments for consideration of the foreign commerce of the area. Many issue bulletins, newsletters, directory material and other aids.

A list, given in the Appendix, includes the principal chambers of commerce of the United States which have special arrangements for promotion and service in connection with foreign trade matters. Arrangements have been made also with some 570 chambers of commerce and similar groups to serve as official Cooperative Offices of the Department of Commerce in the dissemination of reports and publications of the Department.

American Chambers of Commerce Abroad

American chambers of commerce abroad (AmChams) are independent, private, nonprofit associations of business executives supported principally by local membership dues. They are members, but not branches of the U.S. Chamber. In cooperation with host country individuals, private groups and governments, AmChams work to (a) develop mutually beneficial economic, social and commercial relations between the U.S. business community and their respective host countries; (b) foster goodwill for U.S. private enterprises abroad; and (c) promote local economic and social interests for the benefit of host countries to bring about a better understanding of the private enterprise system. AmChams represent their members before the governments, business communities and the general public of host countries. Their membership is drawn from firms and individuals of American and other nationalities, both resident and nonresident.

AmChams throughout the world are united into three regional groupings: the Association of American Chambers of Commerce in Latin America (AACCLA), the Asia-Pacific Council of American Chambers of Commerce (APCAC) and the Council of American Chambers of Commerce—Europe and Mediterranean (EuroMed).

The 44 AmChams operate in the following 42 countries:

Argentina	Japan (Tokyo & Okinawa)
Australia	Korea
Austria	Malaysia
Belgium	Mexico
Bolivia	Morocco
Brazil (Rio de Janeiro &	Netherlands
Sao Paulo)	New Zealand
Chile	Nicaragua
Colombia	Panama
Costa Rica	Peru
Dominican Republic	Philippines
Ecuador	Portugal
El Salvador	Singapore
France	South Africa
Germany	Spain
Guatemala	Switzerland
Haiti	Taiwan
Hong Kong	Thailand
Indonesia	United Kingdom
Iran	Uruguay
Ireland	Venezuela
Italy	

Many chambers publish weekly, fortnightly or monthly bulletins, with subscription information available from the individual AmChams. A number of these are listed under Periodicals in the Bibliography.

See also: *Activities of American Chambers of Commerce Abroad.*

Foreign Chambers of Commerce and Associations in the United States

The activities of foreign chambers of commerce and associations in the United States are directed toward fostering friendly commercial relationships between the countries they represent and U.S. trading interests; furnishing information regarding the resources and industries of their countries; and disseminating general information about the country they represent.

Considerable diversity exists in the kinds of organizations, types of membership and the official position, if any, they hold with the countries they represent. Most such chambers follow the policy of admitting American concerns to membership.

A list given in the appendix contains the principal foreign chambers and associations now established in the United States.

Local Chambers of Commerce in Foreign Countries

Chambers of commerce, or other organizations having functions similar to local chambers of commerce in the United States, exist in the more important commercial centers of foreign countries. Many countries have national federations of the local organizations.

A list of chambers of commerce in principal cities throughout the world can be found in *Johnson's Worldwide Chamber of Commerce Directory*. Information about foreign chambers may be obtained by inquiry of foreign embassies or legations in the United States. Also, a letter addressed to Chamber of Commerce, (city), (country), usually reaches the appropriate organization.

---

d. Joint Business/Economic Councils and Committees

Joint Business/Economic Councils and Committees are uniquely equipped to develop innovative approaches to trade expansion. Such private sector councils develop for government consideration policy and program recommendations designed to establish a climate for the successful pursuit of U.S. economic interests *vis-a-vis* counterpart countries, focusing particularly on areas of concern to U.S. firms interested in or actually doing business with those countries.

The Chamber of Commerce of the United States currently sponsors 17 bilateral business councils and committees with selected countries or regions, bringing together on a regular basis more than 500 U.S. senior corporate officials with their counterparts from Asia, Africa, Latin America, Canada, the Middle East and Eastern and Western Europe.

The U.S. members of these councils, including several hundred corporate board chairmen, presidents and other senior executives, work regularly with their foreign counterparts to build a consensus on key trade, investment, monetary and economic development issues. As they seek freer international flows of goods, services, capital and technology, these business diplomats work to find solutions to pressing international economic problems. The insights gained by business leaders of different nationalities working on common problems allow the U.S. Chamber to make a significant private sector contribution to the formulation of U.S. international economic policy.

Advisory Council on Japan-U.S. Economic Relations (U.S. Section)
Chamber of Commerce of the United States
International Division
1615 H Street, N.W.
Washington, D.C. 20062
Tel. (202) 659-3054

The *Advisory Council on Japan-U.S. Economic Relations* is composed of approximately 50 top management leaders of companies engaged in a wide range of business activities involving the United States and Japan. It was formed at the request of the U.S. government in 1971. At that time, U.S. Cabinet officials, concerned about certain deteriorating trends in Japan-U.S. economic relations, perceived a need for a representative cross section of American business leaders to advise them on the means of bringing about a mutually beneficial level of economic interchange and greater overall communication between Japan and the United States.

The Advisory Council meets annually with its counterpart organization in Japan—the Japan-U.S. Economic Council. It has examined both short-term and long-term solutions to the imbalances in U.S.-Japan trade and has contributed to a major study designed to encourage additional U.S. investment in Japan called "United States' Manufacturing Investment in Japan," which can be obtained through the American Chamber of Commerce in Japan.

The Advisory Council also serves as the U.S. sponsoring organization for other conferences involving the business leadership of Japan, the European Community and the United States. This arrangement has made possible the consideration of international economic policy deliberations in a multilateral context. Four "quadrilateral" conferences have taken place with the participation of individuals from Middle East and North African countries.

ASEAN-U.S. Business Council (U.S. Section)

Chamber of Commerce of
the United States
International Division
1615 H Street, N.W.
Washington, D.C. 20062
Tel. (202) 659-6117

The *ASEAN-U.S. Business Council* was established in 1979 at the request of the respective governments to enable ASEAN and U.S. business leaders to conduct an effective and continuing dialogue on bilateral economic relations, to provide a mechanism for identifying policies which would strengthen commercial ties and to stimulate two-way trade and investment.

The U.S. Section of the Council—consisting of more than 60 companies of differing size—was formed in February, 1979. The first ASEAN-U.S. Business Conference took place in Manila in July 1979, under the sponsorship of the ASEAN Chambers of Commerce and Industry (ASEAN CCI) and the Chamber of Commerce of the United States.

The Association of Southeast Asian Nations (ASEAN)—composed of Indonesia, Malaysia, the Philippines, Singapore and Thailand—has made particularly significant progress in economic cooperation over the last three years. The five member nations of ASEAN are achieving growth rates averaging 7 percent per annum and represent the fifth largest U.S. trading partner, with U.S. investment in the region almost $4 billion and two-way trade over $16 billion in 1979.

The joint council is carrying out a number of projects including (1) an investment identification project to assess investment opportunities in the ASEAN region for which American capital, technology and management skills are particularly well suited; (2) a program to bring the 15 ASEAN industry and commodity clubs into closer contact with U.S. trade associations in parallel fields of interest; (3) the establishment of a joint study group on trade, investment and technology transfer; and (4) the creation of a joint study group on energy to examine opportunities for the development of alternatives to conventional energy sources and to exchange information on energy conservation.

The Council convened a joint executive committee meeting in the United States in May 1980 and held a full council meeting in Singapore, October 10-11, 1980.

Brazil-U.S. Business Council (U.S. Section)

Chamber of Commerce of
the United States
International Division
1615 H Street, N.W.
Washington, D.C. 20062
Tel. (202) 659-3055

The *Brazil-U.S. Business Council* was established in 1976 to provide a channel for discussion of trade, investment and economic relations between Brazil and the United States by business leaders from both countries. The Council is sponsored jointly by the Chamber of Commerce of the United States and by a Brazilian Joint Commission representing the National Confederation of Industry, the National Confederation of Commerce, the Brazilian Exporters Association and the Confederation of Commercial Associations of Brazil. The National Board of the American Chambers of Commerce for Brazil provides advisory assistance to the Council's U.S. Section.

The Council's membership comprises a cross section of U.S. and Brazilian business leadership, assuring representation of major business sectors and geographical areas within each country.

The Council meets annually in joint plenary sessions, alternating between locations in Brazil and in the United States. The executive committees of the two national sections provide direct and continuous channels of communication with government leaders of both countries to discuss those issues which affect matters of mutual interest.

Through its meetings, publications and trade missions, the Council seeks to: (1) stimulate and facilitate business relations and contacts between the two business communities; and (2) provide a forum to propose solutions to problems within the Brazil-U.S. economic relationship which may limit trade and investment between the two countries.

The Council has sponsored a number of studies on technology transfer, subsidies and countervailing duties, agribusiness, capital markets and doing business in Brazil.

Bulgarian-U.S. Economic Council (U.S. Section)
Chamber of Commerce of the United States
International Division
1615 H Street, N.W.
Washington, D.C. 20062
Tel. (202) 659-2024

The *Bulgarian-U.S. Economic Council* was created by an agreement signed by the presidents of the Chamber of Commerce of the United States and the Bulgarian Chamber of Commerce and Industry on September 24, 1974. The Council is designed to provide a channel for regular communication on bilateral business and economic problems and opportunities between U.S. business leaders and key Bulgarian commercial decision makers. Ranking government officials from both countries witnessed the signing of the agreement—one of the first between national institutions of Bulgaria and the United States.

As in other bilateral economic councils sponsored by the Chamber of Commerce of the United States with Eastern European countries, the American membership in this Council comprises firms and organizations with significant current and potential involvement in Bulgarian-U.S. business relations. They vary widely in size, geographic location and type of business, with agriculture and related industries prominently represented.

At the first bilateral meeting, held in September 1975 in Sofia, discussions centered on such issues of mutual concern as streamlining contractual negotiations and eliminating bottlenecks in government export and import authorizations.

The third session of the Council took place in March 1979, in Sofia, Bulgaria. Discussions at the session centered on new oportunities for commercial cooperation and changes within the Bulgarian economic structure.

Committee on Canada-United States Relations (U.S. Section)
Chamber of Commerce of the United States
International Division
1615 H Street, N.W.
Washington, D.C. 20062
Tel. (202) 659-3054

The *U.S. Section, Committee on Canada-United States Relations* has worked since 1933 to strengthen close, friendly relations between Canada and the United States. Established by joint action of the Chambers of Commerce of Canada and the United States, the Committee alternates its semi-annual meetings between the two countries. Its membership of selected corporate officers, established by invitation, represents a cross section of the Canadian and U.S. business leadership. The Committee is the first bilateral businessmen's group in which the Chamber of Commerce of the United States participated and is the precursor of the 17 bilateral committees and councils in which the U.S. Chamber participates at present.

The Committee was formed in recognition of the unique relationship existing between the United States and Canada. Each is the other's major trading partner and main source of outside investment. The scale of this mutual business activity brings problems with it as well as benefits. Maximizing the benefits and minimizing the areas of friction are the Committee's predominant concerns.

The Committee was the catalyst in bringing about the 1935 Trade Agreement between Canada and the United States based upon the Reciprocal Trade Agreements passed by the U.S. Congress the previous year. This was the mainspring of the tremendous subsequent growth in Canada-U.S. trade and investment. Several years afterward, the Committee produced the first set of guidelines for international corporate conduct and, in so doing, held one of the first discussions on the role of the multinational corporation.

These are two early accomplishments in the long list of Committee actions. Over the years, the Committee has brought its influence to bear upon most Canadian and U.S. issues of importance. These include problems associated with economic policy, trade and trade procedures, industry and commodity problems and investment, as well as items such as defense sharing, Great Lakes pollution and offshore boundaries. On several occasions, *ad hoc* subcommittees have been created to study specific problems. Representations, based on Committee recommendations, are made regularly by the two national Chambers to their respective governments.

The U.S. Section of the Committee is currently involved in a research project on North American interdependence (Canada, the United States and Mexico) in an attempt to identity complementary areas of economic interest.

Czechoslovak-U.S. Economic Council (U.S. Section)
Chamber of Commerce of the United States
International Division
1615 H Street, N.W.
Washington, D.C. 20062
Tel. (202) 659-2024

The *Czechoslovak-U.S. Economic Council* was created by an agreement signed by the presidents of the Chambers of Commerce of the United States and Czechoslovakia on October 17, 1975. The Council's aim is to open channels of direct dialogue between key commercial decision makers of the two countries and to work for the resolution of those problems impeding an expansion of trade and commercial cooperation. To this end, the Council has received the support of the U.S. and Czechoslovak governments.

As a matter of principle, the Council supports a final and equitable resolution of outstanding financial claims between the United States and Czechoslovakia and the conclusion of a bilateral commercial agreement between the two countries which would grant nondiscriminatory tariff treatment to Czechoslovak goods entering the United States in return for a satisfactory balance of commercial concessions.

The Council's two national sections meet annually, alternately in Czechoslovakia and in the United States. The Czechoslovak Section of the Council includes more than 30 principal executives of leading Czechoslovak producing enterprises and foreign trade organizations. The U.S. Section is composed of companies representing key commercial sectors and various geographic regions, all having significant actual or potential involvement in U.S.-Czechoslovak trade.

Egypt-U.S. Business Council (U.S. Section)
Chamber of Commerce of the United States
International Division
1615 H Street, N.W.
Washington, D.C. 20062
Tel. (202) 659-3058

In response to the growing importance of the Middle East in the global economy and to the liberalization of the Egyptian economy, the *Egypt-U.S. Business Council* was established at the request of the two governments to enable Egyptian and American business decision makers to maintain an effective and continuing dialogue on bilateral economic relations and to provide a means for stimulating two-way flows of trade and investment.

The Council has two national sections composed of key business leaders from both countries to discuss Egyptian-American commercial and investment issues and to develop policy positions designed to promote increased economic relations between the two countries. Council positions and recommendations are submitted to the appropriate authorities of the two governments for policy action.

84

The membership of the U.S. Section is made up of firms of differing size and geographical location in the United States, drawn from sectors which are of particular relevance to Egypt's economic development priorities. The members share an interest in advancing Egypt's economic development and in establishing strong commercial ties between the two countries. The Egyptian Section membership includes representatives of the Egyptian private sector as well as leaders of the principal state enterprises.

Since its inception in August 1975, the Council has made a major contribution to increased economic cooperation between the two countries and has advised officials of both governments concerning policies which would permit the establishment of increased commercial ties. Since the signing of the Egypt/Israel peace treaty in 1979, the Council has worked closely with the U.S. government in developing Egypt's economic potential as part of the peace program.

In addition to the preparation of a report on foreign investment in Egypt presented to the Egyptian government for use in its revisions of the foreign investment laws, the Council has sponsored: a workshop on doing business in Egypt; a seminar which brought Egyptian government officials to the United States for a series of meetings to familiarize them with American corporate priorities concerning foreign investment; the preparation of abstracts of a variety of projects in Egypt of potential interest to foreign investors; a program to assist the Egyptian government in stimulating American foreign investment in Egypt; and a study to assist Egyptian exporters to expand their activities in U.S. markets. The Council operates through a series of joint action committees which deal with specific trade, investment and other economic issues of particular concern to Council members.

**European Community-
United States
Businessmen's Council
(U.S. Section)**
Chamber of Commerce of
the United States
International Division
1615 H Street, N.W.
Washington, D.C. 20062
Tel. (202) 659-6116

The *European Community-United States Businessmen's Council* occupies a unique position within the network of communication that presently links the U.S. and European business communities. It is the only nongovernmental forum in which businessmen from both sides can discuss outstanding economic issues in a framework which focuses on relations between the United States and the European Community as a whole. Therefore, the Council provides a distinctive vehicle through which E.C. and U.S. business leaders can contribute to action on policy issues of mutual concern.

The origins of the Council stem from a major effort in 1972 by the Chamber of Commerce of the United States to bring together top business executives of the United States and the six nations which were at that time forming an enlarged European Community. The dialogue began in March 1972 with the convening of a wide-ranging conference on E.C.-U.S. relations in Versailles and culminated in 1974 in the formation of a permanent E.C.-U.S. Businessmen's Council.

The Council's membership includes chairmen and presidents of corporations and business organizations which represent a broad cross section, with respect to both character and geographical distribution, of the European and American business communities. The Council meets annually and, in addition, creates joint task forces to deal with specific issues of current importance.

The Council was founded upon the conviction that closer business contacts permit the greatest possible reciprocal awareness of E.C. and U.S. problems and preoccupations, thereby promoting the emergence of common attitudes. It operates on the assumption that common problems discussed in an open and candid atmosphere at the private sector level can lead to tangible conclusions and provide useful guidance to the governments of the countries concerned.

A number of major European and American business organizations lend support to the work of the Council. The European secretariat is based in Brussels at the Union of Industrial Federations of the European Community (UNICE) and involves the industry organizations in each E.C. member country. The U.S. Section of the Council is sponsored by the Chamber of Commerce of the United States, where the U.S. secretariat is located, and by the National Association of Manufacturers. American chambers of commerce abroad operating in Europe serve in an advisory capacity to the Council's U.S. Section.

The Council's first joint plenary meeting in October 1974 in Brussels focused on trade, investment and monetary issues in light of a dramatically changing world energy picture. Since then, the Council has worked to develop concrete recommendations on energy policy, on questions of raw materials investment and supply and on the implications of the Geneva multilateral trade negotiations.

Hungarian-U.S. Economic Council (U.S. Section)

Chamber of Commerce of the United States
International Division
1615 H Street, N.W.
Washington, D.C. 20062
Tel. (202) 659-2024

The *Hungarian-U.S. Economic Council* was established by an agreement signed by the Chamber of the Commerce of the United States and the Hungarian Chamber of Commerce on March 14, 1975. Ranking U.S. and Hungarian government officials at the signing ceremony indicated their firm support for the Council, which is designed to promote cooperation and contacts between key commercial decision makers in each country. It also works to develop solutions to problems encountered by either country in doing business with the other.

The Hungarian Section of the Council includes principal executives of the Hungarian producing enterprises, as well as foreign trade organizations and other commercial institutions. U.S. Section members comprise a cross section of leading businessmen, representing key commercial sectors and various geographic regions—all with significant actual or potential involvement in U.S.-Hungarian trade.

The two national sections meet annually, alternately in Hungary and the United States. The fifth joint session took place on October 15-16, 1979, in Budapest. Attending the session were some 60 American industry and trade leaders, making this the largest U.S. commercial delegation to travel to Hungary. Among the specific areas discussed were cooperation in the fields of food processing, machine tools, packaging, irrigation and land reclamation and wines and beverages.

The U.S. Section of the Council has played an active role in the pursuit of improved and expanded commercial relations between the United States and Hungary. The U.S. Section, moreover, consistently supported the conclusion of a trade agreement between the United States and Hungary. This support culminated in the signing of an agreement on March 17, 1978. Included in the trade agreement is a provision for the reciprocal extension of most-favored-nation tariff status, a major step in the normalization of trade relations between the two countries.

India-U.S. Business Council (U.S. Section)
Chamber of Commerce of the United States
International Division
1615 H Street, N.W.
Washington, D.C. 20062
Tel. (202) 659-3058

In view of India's urgent need for the increased employment and income which could be generated by expanded trade with and investment from the United States, and considering India's potential as a commercial partner of the United States, the *India-U.S. Business Council* was established in 1976 at the request of the two governments to enable Indian and American business decision makers to conduct a continuing dialogue on bilateral economic relations.

The Council has two national sections composed of key business leaders from both countries. They meet annually, alternating between India and the United States, to discuss Indian-American commercial and investment issues and to develop policy positions designed to promote increased economic relations between the two countries. Council positions and recommendations are submitted to the appropriate authorities of the two governments for policy action. The members of the U.S. Section, over 30 in number, include firms of differing size and geographic location in the United States which share a common interest in developing stronger commercial ties with India and are of particular relevance to India's development priorities. The Council's Indian Section includes more than 50 leaders from the private and public business communities.

The Council has sought to stimulate a constructive discussion of Indian-American commercial and economic policy issues and recommendations on a variety of subjects which have been developed for consideration by the appropriate government authorities. In addition, the Council has sponsored research and information programs designed to better equip the members of each business community to understand the factors which shape the other country's commercial environment and to assist in identifying and developing specific trade and investment opportunities.

Subjects which are regularly reviewed by the Council include: economic conditions in India and in the United States; the role of foreign investment in Indian development and the conditions under which such investments are made; transfer of technology; ways to strengthen Indian-American trade, in particular through the identification of opportunities for India's manufactured products contained in the U.S. Generalized System of Preferences; and the prospects for Indian-American commercial collaboration in third countries.

International Insurance Advisory Council
Chamber of Commerce of the United States
International Division
1615 H Street, N.W.
Washington, D.C. 20062
Tel. (202) 659-6114

The *International Insurance Advisory Council* (IIAC) is composed of U.S. insurance and reinsurance companies that operate in international markets. Its secretariat is headquartered in the International Division of the Chamber of Commerce of the United States.

Founded in 1967, the Council has the primary objective of representing, speaking for and coordinating the noncommercial activities of the U.S. overseas insurance industry. It has no tariff-making powers or functions.

The Council's activities include the following:
- Provides a forum for coordinating international, noncommercial activities of the U.S. insurance industry.
- Generates information on international developments affecting the insurance and reinsurance industry and carries out specialized studies.
- Interprets and explains the functions, modus operandi and contributions of insurance and reinsurance at the international level.

87

- Represents the industry before the U.S. government.
- Represents the industry at all international meetings, public and private, that concern the insurance and reinsurance industry. In the governmental sphere these include multinational meetings such as those falling under the aegis of the United Nations—the United Nations Conference on Trade and Development (UNCTAD), the Economic and Social Council (ECOSOC), as well as the Organization for Economic Cooperation and Development (OECD). In the private sphere, its representation includes organizations like the Inter-American Federation of Insurance Companies and the European Insurance Committee.
- Maintains liaison with insurance associations throughout the world. This includes exchanging information with foreign insurance associations on insurance developments in the United States and within the associations' host countries.

Iran-U.S. Business Council (U.S. Section)
Chamber of Commerce of the United States
International Division
1615 H Street, N.W.
Washington, D.C. 20062
Tel. (202) 659-3058

In July 1975, the *Iran-U.S. Business Council* was formed at the request of the two governments. The purpose of such a council is to enable Iranian and American business leaders to create an effective and ongoing dialogue on bilateral economic relations and to provide a mechanism to stimulate two-way flows of trade and investment.

From 1975 until late 1978 the council was organized into two national sections represented by key business leaders from both countries. They met periodically to discuss Iranian-American commercial and investment issues and to develop policy positions designed to promote increased economic relations between the two countries. With the change in government in Iran and the resulting change in the role of the private sector in that country, the direction of the council has shifted accordingly. Until such time as Iranian-U.S. government relations improve and there is a redefinition of commercial relations between the two countries, the major focus of the council will be on activities of the U.S. Section. The U.S. Section will meet as needed to assess economic and commercial developments in Iran as they occur and to assess the impact of such developments on U.S. business interests.

Members of the U.S. Section include a variety of firms having interests and investment in Iran and a commitment to stabilizing commercial relations between the two countries.

During its meetings the council has dealt with a number of pressing issues including: the possible use of surety bonds as substitutes for bank guarantees in Iranian construction projects; the role of agents in Iranian-American commerce; Iran's foreign investment regulations; the share distribution program; extension of the U.S. Generalized System of Preferences to Iran; the negotiation of a double taxation treaty and a bilateral social security agreement; arbitration and conciliation procedures; Iran's price control policy and the implications of Iranian assets control regulations on letters of credit raised by American corporations.

Israel-U.S. Business Council (U.S. Section)
Chamber of Commerce of the United States
International Division

In July 1974, the governments of Israel and the United States established a joint U.S.-Israel Committee for Investment and Trade, believing that a closer and sounder economic relationship between the two countries would benefit both nations and would have a stabilizing influence on the political climate in the Middle East. At this time, the two governments also agreed to encourage,

1615 H Street, N.W.
Washington, D.C. 20062
Tel. (202) 659-6116

as a corollary to the Committee, the formation of a joint *Israel-U.S. Business Council,* composed of top business leaders from each country, which could provide a private sector complement to official government-to-government deliberations on trade and investment issues.

At the request of the U.S. government, the board of directors of the Chamber of Commerce of the United States in November 1975 authorized the U.S. Chamber to participate in the establishment and staffing of this entity. The Council's U.S. membership includes senior corporate representatives from companies of varied size and different geographical regions.

The Council, in its membership and program of work, is designed to broaden contacts between the business sectors of the two countries and, in that way, fulfill both a commercial and a diplomatic function. It operates on the assumption that increased investment flows to Israel, the reduction or removal of trade barriers, expanded technological cooperation and the acceleration of Israel's economic growth in other ways are in the interest of both nations. Through a continuing series of bilateral meetings between the U.S. and Israeli sections, the Council provides a forum for discussion of outstanding problems in Israel-U.S. economic relations and seeks to assist governments in eliminating irritants and solving those problems that are identified.

In 1978, the U.S. Section played a significant advisory role when the government of Israel carried out a major revision of laws and regulations applicable to foreign investment in Israel. The recommendations presented by the U.S. Section emerged from a comprehensive study of obstacles to U.S. investment in Israel.

Removal of hindrances to increased U.S. investment continues to be a major goal of the Council. The U.S. Section also cooperates with various organizations to broaden the awareness among U.S. businessmen of Israel's investment opportunities. In addition, the Council seeks to promote cooperation in the areas of trade, research and development and taxation.

Polish-U.S. Economic Council (U.S. Section)
Chamber of Commerce of the United States
International Division
1615 H Street, N.W.
Washington, D.C. 20062
Tel. (202) 659-2024

The *Polish-U.S. Economic Council* was created by an agreement signed by the presidents of the Chamber of Commerce of the United States and the Polish Chamber of Foreign Trade on October 8, 1974. The signing was witnessed by Edward Gierek, First Secretary of the Polish United Workers' Party, on his first visit to the United States.

The Council's aim is to provide a channel for direct dialogue between key commercial decision makers and to encourage the broadest possible interface between enterprises of both countries. The Council also advises the governments of Poland and the United States on matters of concern to their respective business communities. As an example, it submits regular reports to meetings of the intergovernmental Joint American-Polish Trade Commission and consults with officials of both governments.

The Council meets annually, alternately in Poland and in the United States. The most recent plenum was held in Chicago in May, 1980. Discussion at this session centered around a number of major issues in U.S.-Polish commercial relations including trade financing, joint ventures and industrial cooperation and market access.

In addition to the annual plenum, the Council also conducts two intersessional working groups on industrial cooperation and market access.

Romanian-U.S. Economic Council (U.S. Section)
Chamber of Commerce of the United States
International Division
1615 H Street, N.W.
Washington, D.C. 20062
Tel. (202) 659-2026

The *Romanian-U.S. Economic Council* was created by an agreement signed by the presidents of the Chambers of Commerce of the United States and of Romania on December 4, 1973. Romanian President Nicolae Ceausescu and high-ranking officials of the governments of the two countries witnessed the ceremony.

The Council has two national sections composed of more than 60 key commercial decision makers from both countries. They meet annually, alternately in Romania and in the United States, to discuss Romanian-U.S. trade and investment issues and to formulate policy positions designed to promote and expand economic relations between the two countries. U.S. Section member organizations represent a broad cross section of industries with significant active and potential involvement in U.S.-Romanian trade, varying in size and geographic location.

The Council was able to play an active role in the chain of events that led to congressional approval of the Romanian-U.S. Agreement on Trade in July 1975. This agreement provides for the extension of nondiscriminatory tariff status (MFN) and the reopening of Eximbank credits for Romania. The Council has been active since then in all congressional review proceedings regarding the trade agreement.

The Council held its sixth plenum in Washington, D.C., in July 1979. During the session, the U.S. Section learned of new opportunities for commercial cooperation under Romania's 1981-1985 Five-Year Plan. Established during the plenum was an intersessional working group on finance and services.

Sudan-U.S. Business Council (U.S. Section)
Chamber of Commerce of the United States
International Division
1615 H Street, N.W.
Washington, D.C. 20062
Tel. (202 659-3057

The *Sudan-U.S. Business Council* was organized in 1977 at the request of President Gaafar Nimeiri to enable Sudanese and American business leaders to conduct effective and continuing discussions on bilateral economic relations, to provide a mechanism for identifying policies which would strengthen commercial ties and to stimulate trade and investment.

The Council has two national sections composed of key business leaders from both countries. They meet annually to discuss Sudanese-American commercial and investment issues and to develop policy positions designed to promote increased economic relations between the two countries. Council positions and recommendations are submitted to the appropriate authorities of the two governments for policy action. The membership of the U.S. Section includes approximately 40 companies of differing size and geographic location in the United States that are interested in developing stronger commercial ties with the Sudan and whose business activities are particularly well-suited to Sudan's development priorities. The Sudanese Section of the Council includes 70 prominent business executives from the public and private sectors.

The Council, during its meetings and through the projects it sponsors, seeks to promote a better understanding in each business community of the factors which shape the business environment in the other. In addition, the Council identifies aspects of government policy which constitute barriers to expanded investment or trade relationships and develops recommendations to alleviate these problems. The Council, at the request of the Sudanese authorities, prepared detailed recommendations on legal changes which would improve the Sudan's foreign investment environment. In addition, at the Council's request, OPIC financed a study of policies and procedures used by other developing countries to promote foreign investment. The study, *Foreign Investment in the Third World: A Comparative Study of Selected Developing Country Investment Promotion Programs,* has recently been published by the International Division of the Chamber of Commerce of the United States. Also, the Council sponsored a study to identify joint venture investment opportunities for American companies and has developed processes to provide continued follow-up as new opportunities arise. The Council is structured around several task forces, each dealing with specific economic and commercial issues of interest to the membership.

United States-European Community Conference on Agriculture
Chamber of Commerce of the United States
International Division
1615 H Street, N.W.
Washington, D.C. 20062
Tel. (202) 659-2022

The *United States-European Community Conference on Agriculture,* held every year since 1972, forms the agricultural leg of a wider U.S.-E.C. businessmen's dialogue designed to help the private sector contribute to bilateral and multilateral solutions of transatlantic economic problems. These separate agricultural meetings have taken place in Brussels (twice), Washington, Savannah, Minneapolis, Reims (France), San Francisco and Copenhagen.

Delegates to this conference series include influential representatives from European and American farm organizations and associations, in addition to representatives of particular commodity interests. The meetings, featuring open discussion on broad issues as well as commodity-by-commodity analyses, afford delegates an opportunity to explain each other's national and regional agricultural policies, to air grievances and, most important, to gain a better understanding of each other's point of view. Outside agricultural excursions provide a stimulating supplement to the formal discussions. Between meetings, delegates pursue contacts, on a private basis, in various commodity areas.

The participating agricultural representatives and the co-sponsoring organizations—the Chamber of Commerce of the United States, the Committee of Professional Agricultural Organizations (COPA) and the General Committee for Agricultural Cooperation of the European Community (COGECA)—feel that this series of meetings improves mutual understanding of U.S. and E.C. agricultural policies.

Other

Other joint councils not under the auspices of the U.S. Chamber are similarly suited to promote U.S. business interests. They are as follows:

Committee for the Caribbean
1333 New Hampshire Avenue, N.W.
Washington, D.C. 20036
Tel. (202) 466-7464

The *Committee for the Caribbean,* a nonprofit, nongovernment organization was founded in 1978 with the support of about 30 major U.S. firms interested in and concerned about the future of the Caribbean and this region's relationship with the United States.

The committee's purposes are to harness U.S. private sector resources for Caribbean development, to increase U.S. public and government sensitivity, to foster goodwill toward private enterprise in the Caribbean and to strengthen relations between the U.S. and Caribbean societies. The committee also works closely with Caribbean private sector organizations to sponsor conferences, exchanges and research.

The committee points out that U.S. firms have invested over $3 billion in the Caribbean. U.S. industry and consumers depend on the region for key raw materials and Caribbean markets account for more than $6 billion a year in trade for U.S. commerce. The committee seeks to assist the U.S. business community in preserving Caribbean economic health and protecting the private enterprise system in this region.

The National Council for U.S.-China Trade
Suite 350
1050 17th Street, N.W.
Washington, D.C. 20036
Tel. (202) 828-8300

The National Council for U.S.-China Trade was formally established on May 31, 1973, following resumption of Sino-American trade in 1971 and the subsequent rapid growth of U.S. commercial relations with the People's Republic of China. The National Council provides American companies, large and small, importers and exporters, with up-to-date information, representation and other practical assistance for developing and continuing their trade with China.

The Council acts as host to Chinese trade officials visiting the United States, sponsors visits of commercial groups from China to U.S. firms and vice versa, represents the interests of companies involved in trade with the People's Republic of China to both American and Chinese authorities, is the contact point for reciprocal exhibitions in the two countries and provides an extensive range of services related specifically to the special features of doing buiness with China.

The National Council is a private, nonprofit membership organization of more than 400 firms, financed by membership dues. Its main office is in Washington, D.C., and staff representatives are available to assist members in Hong Kong and New York.

The U.S.A.-Republic of China Economic Council
200 Main Street
Crystal Lake, Illinois 60014
Tel. (815) 459-5875

The *U.S.A.-Republic of China Economic Council* was founded in 1976. Its purpose is to strengthen economic ties with Taiwan. The Council's membership of some 230 encompasses the spectrum of manufacturing, construction, engineering, banking, shipping, legal services, port authorities and export-import activities.

The Council's contacts and communication facilities assist members in resolving questions, problems and disputes with government offices and corporations and with private firms about Taiwan. It makes available to members numerous reports on sales opportunities, new laws and regulations and other developments affecting business relations with Taiwan.

The Council also facilitates business and government contacts in both Taiwan and the United States, analyzes investment prospects, reports on trade opportunities and disseminates major Taiwan business and government reports and information on Taiwan business and banking regulations.

The U.S.-German Democratic Republic Trade and Economic Council
40 Westminister Street, 19th Floor

The U.S.-G.D.R. Trade & Economic Council and its counterpart council, the *German Democratic Republic-United States Trade and Economic Council,* held their first joint plenary session in Washington, D.C., in June 1977. It is composed of about twenty leading U.S. firms and other private sector organizations actively engaged in trade with the German Democratic Republic (GDR). A purpose of the Council is to ''promote economic, scientific and

Providence, Rhode Island
02903
Tel. (401) 331-2400

technological cooperation between institutions and companies of the United States and the GDR on a long-term basis . . . and to work toward broadening trade opportunities in the two countries." The two councils meet once a year, alternately in each country.

**The U.S.-Korea
Economic Council**
88 Morningside Drive
New York, New York
10027
Tel. (212) 749-4200

The *U.S.-Korea Economic Council* was established to foster mutually beneficial economic relations between the two countries and to serve as an information and conference center on Korean economic affairs. Its main objectives are to stimulate U.S. investment in Korea's rapidly developing economy and to increase the flow of trade between the two countries. It was incorporated in 1962 as the Korea-American Commerce and Industry Association and changed to its present name in 1973.

The Council is a nonprofit association organized under the membership corporation laws of the State of New York. It is supported by the dues and contributions of its corporate membership. Annual dues for corporate members are based on a sliding scale related to annual sales.

The program of the U.S.-Korea Economic Council is designed to acquaint the American business community with opportunities for trade and investment in Korea and to mobilize the support of American business for their economic development plans.

Specifically, the Council:
- Represents the views of American business before the Congress and appropriate departments and agencies of the executive branch on important problems of U.S.-Korean economic relations.
- Provides a reference and information service on doing business in Korea.
- Facilitates contacts with Korean government officials and businessmen.
- Publishes a monthly *Economic Newsletter* on Korean economic affairs and other occasional publications.
- Conducts studies and conferences with its Korean counterpart organization, the Korea-U.S. Economic Council.
- Arranges lunches, seminars, and other meetings (all open to the representatives of corporate members) for leading Korean and American officials and businessmen to discuss problems of mutual concern.
- Sponsors receptions, press conferences and other hospitality services for visiting dignitaries.
- Commissions research on important problems in U.S.-Korean economic relations.

**The U.S.-U.S.S.R. Trade
and Economic Council**
1211 Ave. of the Americas
New York, N.Y. 10036
Tel. (212) 840-5500

Washington, D.C., Office:
2550 M St., N.W.

The *U.S.-U.S.S.R. Trade and Economic Council* is a binational organization of U.S. and Soviet business-related enterprises devoted to facilitating trade expansion between the two countries.

Established in 1973, the Council has a membership of over 250 U.S. firms and 114 Soviet organizations. It has a binational staff of about 40 persons (approximately half U.S. and half Soviet) evenly divided between the New York and Moscow offices. There are 30 U.S. citizens and 30 Soviets on the board of directors, which holds annual meetings alternating between the United States and the Soviet Union.

Washington, D.C. 20037
(202) 223-8533

The Council's ten committees, each of which is binational and has a U.S. and a Soviet cochairman, are responsible for the development of policy and the initiation of programs in their areas. The committees are: Executive, Science and Technology, Finance, New Forms of Economic Cooperation, Tourism, Legal, Membership, Nominating, Small Business and Program and Planning.

The objectives of the Council are to create a business and governmental environment in both countries conducive to the expansion of trade, to facilitate the exploration of opportunities for expanded trade, to conduct research on trade issues, to assist Council members in the execution of commercial agreements and to work with the U.S. and Soviet governments on expanding trade. Its Moscow office organizes seminars and symposia to acquaint Soviet ministries, foreign trade organizations and enterprises with the products and technologies of American companies. The Council also arranges visits to U.S. companies for commercial and technical delegations from the Soviet Union.

The Council has catalogued the products of its member companies by Standard Industrial Classification (SIC) numbers to facilitate responses to trade opportunities, has accumulated a file of member company literature for distribution in Moscow and has formed a library of U.S. and Soviet trade periodicals and reference works in its New York office.

The U.S.-Yugoslav Economic Council, Inc.
51 East 42nd Street
New York, New York 10017
Tel. (212) 687-7797

The U.S.-Yugoslav Economic Council, Inc. is a nonprofit organization with members having a current or potential interest in selling to, buying from or investing in Yugoslavia. Among the services the Council offers its members are: an annual off-the-record briefing with representatives of key U.S. government agencies and top Yugoslav officials on the current situation and prospects for growth in U.S.-Yugoslav trade; an annual joint meeting in Yugoslavia with counterpart organizations; and special seminars on such questions as joint ventures, countertrade, licensing of technology, foreign investment and foreign exchange.

The Council also distributes assorted publications and translations of legislation, arranges meetings and appointments, identifies trade leads and sources of financing and makes representations to governmental agencies on procedures or regulations impeding trade.

Part II. The Daily Language of Foreign Commerce

The following alphabetical guide of key subjects and frequently used terms in international trade serves both as a primer on issues, practices and procedures for the beginner in international trade, and as a quick reference and glossary for the seasoned international trader.

Advertising Abroad

Advertising and promotion are key aspects of export marketing. Although *advertising abroad* may be channelled through many of the same media as in the United States, there are variations in circumstances which require special treatment. The effectiveness of any program rests upon full knowledge and consideration of the peculiarities of each market, population characteristics, language variations and many other factors.

Because of its highly individualized nature, foreign trading interests generally seek the advice or the services of experienced international advertising specialists. Advertising agencies which specialize in business abroad may be contacted through professional advertising associations such as: the International Advertising Association, Inc., 475 Fifth Avenue, New York, New York 10017; and the American Association of Advertising Agencies, 200 Park Avenue, New York, New York 10017.

Also, service departments of U.S. trade and technical journals can be helpful in handling advertising problems. Their names and addresses may be obtained from the Magazine Publishers Association, Inc., 575 Lexington Avenue, New York, New York 10022. Besides approaching the advertising agency or the service department of trade journals, information may be obtained from publications, e.g.: (also see Bibliography)

- *Advertising: A New Approach.*
- *Advertising Agency Business Around the World.*
- *Comparison Advertising.*
- *Concise Guide to International Markets.*

Samples and Advertising Matter

An important element in promoting sales in many export lines is the use of samples and distribution of various forms of advertising matter. Samples are defined as articles imported solely for the purpose of being demonstrated in the territory of importation for the soliciting of orders for merchandise to be supplied from abroad.

Carrying commercial samples and professional equipment to foreign markets has become much easier for U.S. business executives now that the United States has joined the international customs carnet system (see page 101). The carnet system is designed to permit duty-free entry of certain goods temporarily imported into another country.

U.S. business executives can purchase ahead of time in the United States a carnet which can be used to pass samples, professional equipment and certain other articles through customs at the borders of several countries during a single trip. By using the carnet, the commercial traveler reduces the expense and time-consuming inconvenience of posting bonds or cash deposits at each border for the goods accompanying him or those sent unaccompanied.

Two international customs conventions that establish temporary importation privileges for specified goods and provide for the use of carnets to facilitate such importation are: *The International Convention to Facilitate the Importation of Commercial Samples and Advertising Material* which provides for duty-free admission of advertising material including such things as catalogues, price lists and trade notices relating to goods and services, under specified conditions, and the *ECS carnet convention.*

The ECS carnet convention makes available to U.S. business executives carnets guaranteeing payment of customs duties which would be due on commercial samples (including advertising films up to 16 mm.) temporarily imported into member countries. Each carnet is valid for a period not to exceed one year. The items temporarily imported must be reexported within the period of validity of the carnet and may not be leased or sold while in the territory of importation.

Carnets for commercial samples and professional equipment can be used in countries which have signed the related conventions and designated local carnet-issuing and guaranteeing associations. These countries, which include most major U.S. trading partners except the Latin American countries, are: Australia, Austria, Belgium, Luxembourg, Bulgaria (for professional equipment only), Canada, Czechoslovakia, Denmark, Finland, France (including Guadeloupe, Guiana, Martinque, Reunion), Germany (Federal Republic of), Hungary, Iceland, Ireland, Israel, Italy, Ivory Coast, Japan, the Netherlands, Norway, Poland, Portugal, Romania, Spain, Sweden, Switzerland, the United Kingdom (including Gibraltar), and Yugoslavia.

(See also subject headings: Carnets; Postal Service, International; Exchange and Trade Controls, Foreign.)

Air Transport

Air transport service is routinely available to and from all major trading areas of the world and is of exceptional value to export and import interests.

Regulation of air services to and from the United States (rates, routes, condition of service, etc.) is vested in or carried on by the *Civil Aeronautics Board*. The *Federal Aviation Administration* is responsible for regulation of flight safety and related aspects of civil aviation.

The *International Civil Aviation Organization,* a specialized agency of the United Nations, has the function of studying the problems of international civil aviation and the establishment of standards for safety and operation.

Scheduled airlines of the United States are associated with the *Air Transport Association of America,* 1709 New York Avenue, N.W., Washington, D.C. 20006.

Most U.S. scheduled airlines with international services also are members of the *International Air Transport Association,* 1000 Sherbrooke Street, W. Montreal, Quebec, Canada H3A 2R4. Most U.S. nonscheduled (chartered) airlines are associated with the *National Air Carriers Association,* 1730 M Street, N.W., Washington, D.C. 20003.

Most foreign freight forwarders and specialized air freight forwarders will act as shippers' agents in the same manner as on ocean-freight shipments and will prepare the required shipping documents. Many forwarders maintain offices at airports in order to expedite overseas air shipments for their customers.

Among publications and periodicals which contain data of various kinds pertaining to airlines and international air transport in general, the following are suggested: *American Aviation; Air Forwarder; Air Freight Weekly; Air Freight World; Aviation Daily; Aviation Weekly; Brandon's Shipper and Forwarder; Custom House Guide; Exporters' Encyclopedia; Shipping Digest; Space Research and Technology;* and *World Aviation Directory.*

On specific questions, consult individual airlines; the International Trade Administration, U.S. Department of Commerce; foreign trade bureaus of local chambers of commerce; air freight forwarders; and custom house brokers.

See also subject headings: Foreign Freight Forwarders; Postal Service, International.

Antiboycott Laws, United States

Antiboycott laws prohibit U.S. persons from furnishing information about business relationships with boycotted countries when that information is furnished with intent to comply with an unsanctioned foreign boycott. The law also prohibits U.S. persons from refusing, or agreeing to refuse, to do business with a boycotted country, blacklisted companies or anyone else with intent to comply with an unsanctioned foreign boycott.

Antiboycott provisions of the Export Administration Act of 1969, as amended, are administered by the U.S. Department of Commerce. Violators of the act face a range of stiff civil sanctions, including the suspension or revocation of outstanding validated export licenses or denial of export privileges as well as fines of up to $10,000 per violation.

Antiboycott provisions of the Tax Reform Act of 1976 are administered by the U.S. Department of the Treasury. Violators of this act are denied favorable tax treatment of foreign income.

Antitrust Laws

America's *antitrust laws* are based on a national commitment to competition.

Antitrust laws are different in focus and technique from many other legal rules businessmen deal with in international transactions. Antitrust statutes do not provide a checklist of specific, detailed statutory requirements, but instead set forth principles of almost constitutional breadth.

International transactions which raise possible antitrust issues can include: overseas distribution arrangements; overseas joint ventures for research, manufacturing, construction and distribution; patent, trademark and know-how licenses; distributorship contracts; mergers with foreign firms; and raw material procurement agreements and concessions. Likewise, U.S. businesses frequently operate as foreign firms' distributors, licensees and joint venture partners in the United States.

The most relevant and best known provisions of antitrust law are Sections 1 and 2 of the *Sherman Act,* enacted in 1890, in which are found the primary legal prohibitions against restraints on international trade.

Sherman Act, Section 1: prohibits any conspiracy, contract or combination in restraint of trade. The Department of Justice's Antitrust Division brings civil suits under this law against such actions as price-fixing, boycotts or any anticompetitive agreement among competitors. The Antitrust Division may also seek felony indictments under this law.

Sherman Act, Section 2: prohibits monopolization, attempts to monopolize or conspiracy to monopolize. The Antitrust Division of the Justice Department brings civil suits under this law for using a substantial market power against competitors in an effort to monopolize the market or succeeding in doing so. The essence of the offense is conduct—being a monopoly is no violation in itself. The Antitrust Division also has criminal authority under this law.

A special antitrust exemption is provided under the *Webb-Pomerene Act* for acts of a collective export association of American producers, provided that the association does not (a) artificially or intentionally restrain U.S. domestic trade or affect U.S. domestic prices, or (b) restrain the export trade of any U.S. competitor of the association. The Webb-Pomerene Act applies solely to the export of "goods, wares or merchandise" and, therefore, does not explicitly extend to service and licensing transactions. An association must be limited to domestic firms. (For a more detailed discussion of Webb-Pomerene, see following section.)

Clayton Act, Section 7. This law prohibits anticompetitive mergers or acquisitions. Under this law, the Justice Department's Antitrust Division may bring civil suits, seeking divestiture, and the Federal Trade Commission (FTC) can bring administrative actions, even long after the merger occurs. Under the pre-merger notification requirements enacted in the late 1970's, prior notice of mergers over a certain size must be made to both the FTC and Justice, after which authorities have 30 days to sue.

Wilson Tariff Act. The act's antitrust provisions (Sections 73 and 74) prohibit restraints affecting imports into the United States, providing one of the parties to the trade is an actual importer. The Antitrust Division may bring civil suits or misdemeanor criminal charges for violation.

All antitrust statutes enforced by the Justice Department can be enforced through private civil suits by injured parties as well, regardless of federal action.

The Federal Trade Act, Section 5. This prohibits unfair trade actions, is broader than Section 1 of the Sherman Act and is enforced solely by FTC. *The Robinson-Patman Act* prohibits price discrimination by a manufacturer or supplier. This act is also enforced solely by FTC. For more information, contact the Federal Trade Commission, (Bureau of Competition), Washington, D.C. 20580.

For more information on antitrust law, see the *Antitrust Guide for International Operations,* United States Department of Justice, (Antitrust Division), January 26, 1977 (revised March 1977).

Webb-Pomerene Act

The *Webb-Pomerene Act* provides export trade associations with qualified exemptions from the prohibitions of the Sherman Antitrust Act of 1890 and the Federal Trade Commission (FTC) and Clayton Acts of 1914.

The purpose of the Webb-Pomerene Act is to encourage the export of U.S. products. The association serves as export agent for the member companies, takes orders, negotiates prices and terms of trade for sale of the members' merchandise abroad and arranges transportation for members' goods. An association may also purchase the members' products for resale in foreign markets, under terms and conditions agreed upon by the members, and arrange for distribution of products in these markets.

Legal formalities for setting up a Webb-Pomerene association are not complicated. The act requires only that the association file with the FTC within 30 days after its organization:

- A verified written statement setting forth the location of its offices or places of business.
- Names and addresses of all its officers, stockholders and members.
- If incorporated, a copy of the certificate or articles of incorporation and bylaws, or if unincorporated, a copy of the articles or contract of association.

Some associations employ agents and maintain offices abroad. The expense of developing the sale of members' products through advertising and introducing them in new markets may thus be shared by all the members. The association may bid on and secure large orders for shipments over a long period, which a single company could not handle. It can fill orders for a variety of grades, styles and dimensions by allocating the business among members. Price-fixing, allocating quotas for export, setting agreed terms of sale and adopting uniform sales contracts are other association functions. Through the association's power to make joint shipping arrangements, important savings may be effected.

Practically all of the associations perform informational services for the members. They collect and disseminate trade information on market conditions abroad, foreign credits, stocks available for export by the members, the foreign exchange situation of certain foreign countries, tariff requirements, shipping rules and regulations, foreign laws affecting foreign trade and other data of value to U.S. firms seeking export business.

A Webb-Pomerene association may occupy the same status as an independent exporter so far as some government programs and assistance are concerned. Webb-Pomerene law associations may avail themselves of opportunities offered by the financial aids of the Export-Import Bank—loans, guarantees and export credit insurance.

In addition to receiving the antitrust exemption provided by the Webb-Pomerene Act, associations may also qualify for the special tax benefits provided by the *Domestic International Sales Corporation* (DISC) provisions of the Revenue Act of 1971. A Webb-Pomerene association can qualify for special DISC tax treatment if it is organized as a corporation. If an association is not incorporated, it may reorganize as a corporation and readily qualify as a DISC. A Webb-Pomerene association which qualified as a DISC would have one-half of the federal income tax on its export earnings deferred and could make "producer's loans" of the income thus deferred to its member companies or other export producers.

For more information on the Webb-Pomerene Act, contact the Office of International Finance and Investment, Department of Commerce, Washington, D.C. 20230 or the Federal Trade Commission, Bureau of Competition, Washington, D.C. 20580.

The publication, *Webb-Pomerene Association: A 50-Year Review,* can be obtained from the Government Printing Office.

Arbitration, International Commercial

Commercial arbitration is playing an increasingly important role in the settlement of foreign trade controversies. Standard arbitration clauses have been prepared for inclusion in written contracts with a view to settling disputes effectively and quickly at low cost. They refer to rules of established agencies that administer arbitration under their respective rules on behalf of parties submitting disputes to arbitration.

The principal arbitration agency in the United States is the American Arbitration Association (AAA), which maintains a nationwide system of arbitration tribunals and panels and has bilateral agreements with the major foreign arbitration organizations and chambers of commerce throughout the world. The AAA administers international conciliation procedures on behalf of the U.S. Chamber of Commerce pursuant to agreements with such countries as Poland, Romania, Hungary and Bulgaria. Through its corporate council committee, the AAA maintains an active and current overview of developments in international arbitration. Besides its 24 regional offices, the AAA has an Office of General Counsel and a library for dissemination of information and literature on private dispute settlement.

For Western Hemisphere commercial arbitration, the facilities of the *Inter-American Commercial Arbitration Commission* and of the *Canadian-American Commercial Arbitration Commission,* both at 140 West 51st Street, New York, New York 10020, are also available.

For standard arbitration clauses, rules and other information concerning arbitration in foreign trade, consult the aforementioned organizations and the *U.S. Council of the International Chamber of Commerce,* 1212 Avenue of the Americas, New York, New York 10036.

For the conciliation procedures adopted with Poland, Romania, Hungary and Bulgaria, contact the AAA or the Chamber of Commerce of the United States.

On December 29, 1970, the United States adhered to the *1958 United Nations Convention on the Recognition and Enforcement of Foreign Arbitral Awards.* This international agreement provides uniform rules under which arbitral awards issued in foreign countries may be recognized and judicially enforced in other participating member countries. An article on the subject appeared in the November 1975 issue of the Commerce Department publication, *Foreign Business Practices.*

Among publications providing instructive material and current information on arbitration in foreign trade, the following are suggested:
- *The Arbitration Journal.*
- *Commercial Arbitration and the Law Throughout the World.*
- *Foreign Business Practices.*
- *Guide to ICC Arbitration.*
- *How to Use Arbitration in Foreign Trade.*
- *The International Trader and International Commercial Arbitration.*

Balance of International Payments, United States

The *balance of payments* is a system of accounts covering a particular period of time that is intended to record systematically a flow of economic transactions between U.S. residents and non-U.S. residents, plus certain transactions or accounts which are joined or grouped together as selected individual balances within the overall presentation. The purpose of drawing such balances is to determine whether there is a surplus or deficit.

Periodic statements of the balance of international payments of the United States, often referred to as international transactions of the United States, are prepared and published by the Bureau of Economic Analysis, U.S. Department of Commerce.

Current quarterly statements, giving detailed data for the various elements involved, with like data for earlier periods, are published in *Survey of Current Business*, a monthly statistical publication of the Department of Commerce.

See: *Balance of Payments Reports; Balance of Payments Yearbook.*

Carnets

The ATA *carnet* is an international customs document designed to simplify customs procedures for business and professional people taking commercial samples, advertising materials or film or medical or professional equipment into specified countries for a short period. More than 30 countries participate in the carnet system, including all of Western Europe, Japan, Canada and certain countries in Eastern Europe and Africa.

A carnet eliminates extensive customs procedures and delays at borders for temporary imports. Without a carnet, these procedures would include the payment of tariffs and excise taxes that cannot be refunded until departure, or the purchase of a bond for these tariffs and taxes at every customs station. Carnets generally are valid for 12 months, although those covering professional equipment are limited by international convention to six months.

The carnet also allows the commercial traveler to: make customs arrangements in advance; make those arrangements in the United States quickly and at a predetermined cost; use a single document for goods which will pass through the customs of several countries; and make as many trips as desired within the period of the one-year validity of the document.

The *U.S. Council of the International Chamber of Commerce*, 1212 Avenue of the Americas, New York, New York 10036, has been designated by the U.S. Bureau of Customs as the U.S. issuing and guaranteeing organization. U.S. firms or their designated representatives should apply for carnets to the U.S. Council at its New York address.

A fee is charged for the carnet to cover services rendered by the U.S. Council. This fee is based on the value of the goods covered and runs from a minimum of $60 to a maximum of $150.

Completed applications, with fee, should be accompanied by a bank letter of credit (or a cash deposit, bank guarantee or a similar security in favor of the U.S. Council), to remain in force for 30 months from the date of issuance of the carnet. The amount of the guarantee will be 40 percent of the value of the goods covered by the carnet. This is required in order that the Council may have recourse should duties not be paid on goods exported under a carnet and actually sold overseas. The security is released when the used carnet is returned to the Council, indicating that all foreign customs requirements have been met.

It should be noted that carnets in no way substitute for the usual U.S. export control procedures required under the Export Administration Act of 1969.

The carnet system has worked successfully in Europe for a number of years and more than 100,000 are issued annually worldwide. U.S. business representatives have found the carnet particularly useful when displaying goods at overseas exhibits or sending technicians with tools of trade to repair equipment installed abroad.

The TIR (see below) convention makes TIR carnets available to U.S. exporters so that their shipments under the convention en route to an interior destination shall not be subjected to the payment or deposit of import or export duties and taxes at customs offices en route. As a general rule, such shipments would not be subject to customs inspection until arrival at the final destination. The *Equipment Interchange Association* (EIA) has been designated by the U.S. Customs Service as the official U.S. TIR carnet issuing and guaranteeing association. Inquiries concerning the TIR carnet should be addressed to the EIA, at 1616 P Street, N.W., Washington, D.C. 20036.

What the letters mean

The letter designations for the different types of carnet stand for:

ATA—the combined French and English words Admission Temporaire/Temporary Admission;

ECS—the combined French and English words Echantillons Commerciaux/Commercial Samples; (see section on samples and advertising matter, page 95)

TIR—Transport International Routier (international road transport).

Copyrights

An author may be automatically protected by *copyright* in about 65 countries on the basis of a copyright on his work first obtained in the United States. Such protection is afforded under the Universal Copyright Convention, to which the United States and other countries are parties. Under this Convention, all that the owner of a copyright need do to secure protection in these countries is to show in his work his name, year of first publication and the symbol ''c'' in a circle. The United States, together with 17 Latin American countries, is also party to the Buenos Aires Copyright Convention of 1910. This agreement specifies that authors of any member country who have secured copyright in their own country will enjoy in each of the other countries the rights it accords its own works, if the work contains ''a statement indicating the reservation of the property rights.'' The United States also has bilateral arrangements with a number of countries for reciprocal protection of copyrights of nationals of the other country.

The other major international copyright convention is the Berne Convention for the Protection of Literary and Artistic Works. The United States is not a member but U.S. authors can receive automatic protection of their works in the other member countries by publishing them in a Berne country simultaneously with their first publication in the United States.

For further information on copyright protection in the United States and through international conventions, consult the United States Copyright Office, Library of Congress, Washington, D.C., 20559. Also see:

- *Copyright Laws and Treaties of the World,* compiled by UNESCO, World Intellectual Property Organization, published by the Bureau of National Affairs, Inc., Washington, D.C. (Looseleaf—updated yearly.)
- ''Copyright,'' Monthly Review published by the World Intellectual Property Organization, Geneva, Switzerland.
- United States Copyright Office ''Circular R 38'' (addenda and supplements) on international copyright relations and treaties of the United States.

Countertrade

Countertrade (CT) in its broadest sense is a worldwide phenomenon of exchange systems and other arrangements in various forms, all designed to permit mutually beneficial transactions without aggravating existing trade deficits and hard currency shortages or causing other economic inconvenience or hardship. Japan, France and Germany, for example, have concluded reciprocal economic agreements with energy-producing countries under which exports, technological aid or credits are offered in exchange for badly needed oil.

Countertrade, however, is a more prevalent, and more highly promoted practice in the East European arena than in other trading regions. In this context, CT is the practice of linking Western suppliers' sales to Eastern Europe and the Soviet Union to purchases of Eastern goods by these suppliers. Rapid industrial growth in the communist countries has derived significantly from increased business with Western suppliers, but also has led to trade and payment deficits in the communist countries. These nations' exports, in turn, have not captured the needed market shares in the West to restore their trade balances. Because CT helps reduce trade imbalances, fosters exports and minimizes the outflow of limited hard currency resources, it has become an important element of long-range planning in the communist countries.

CT transactions can take many forms, which are known by various names (e.g., barter, buyback, swap). The three basic forms of CT commonly encountered in East-West trade are *counterpurchase, compensation* and *barter and switch.*

Counterpurchase involves Eastern counterdeliveries of goods not derived from or related to Western exports of technology, plant or equipment, so-called "nonresultant products." The value of these goods (manufactured, semimanufactured, raw materials, machinery, etc.) generally is less than 100 percent of the original Western sales contract value and the exchange of goods usually takes place over a 1-5 year period.

Compensation ("buyback") transactions differ from counterpurchase arrangements in that the dollar values are generally greater, the time frame is longer (e.g., 10-20 years), the Western participant usually buys products derived directly from or produced by the Western-supplied technology, plant or equipment and the cumulative value of Western purchases often is equal to or greater than the value of the Western export contract.

Barter and Switch. Barter is the direct exchange of goods with off setting values, no money changing hands. It is used far less frequently than counterpurchase or compensation. Switch trade transactions, through the multilateral use of bilateral clearing accounts and other complex international transactions, enable the Eastern countries to sidestep financial difficulties resulting from the nonconvertibility of their currencies and lessen some of the problems related to the shortage of hard currencies. Switch trading occurs more often in trade between less developed countries and communist countries than in trade with the West.

For further information contact the Department of Commerce, Bureau of East-West Trade; also consult the Department's publication, *East-West Countertrade Practices: An Introductory Guide for Business,* August 1978.

Credit Information

A matter of vital importance to direct exporting and importing interests is complete and reliable information on the financial and ethical responsibility of prospective foreign customers, representatives, agents or distributors and foreign producing, manufacturing and exporting firms.

The foreign departments of banks usually are in a good position to supply valuable *credit information* to customers. Credit files, which it is in their interest to maintain, are as a rule, sources of comprehensive data obtained largely from their offices or correspondents abroad and in the regular course of their foreign business.

Various sources in the United States exist for gathering information on the credit risks of foreign firms. Among outstanding organizations operating in this field are:

- Foreign Credit Interchange Bureau, National Association of Credit Management, 475 Park Avenue South, New York, New York 10016. Service to members includes credit reports based on actual ledger experience of members and consultation services. See also *Minutes of Monthly Roundtable Conference*.
- U.S. Department of Commerce, Bureau of Export Development (BED)—Export Information Division. Although the division does not supply technical credit reports, it provides valuable information on the general standing of concerns in foreign markets through its World Trade Directory Reports (U.S. Department of Commerce, BED—Export Division, World Traders Data Reports, Room 1313, Washington, D.C. 20230).
- Dun and Bradstreet, Inc., 99 Church Street, New York, New York 10007, makes individual investigations of foreign credit risks on a fee basis, renders complete service through foreign branches and affiliates and has extensive files in its New York office.
- Export-Import Bank, 811 Vermont Avenue, N.W., Washington, D.C. 20571. The Export-Import Bank has on file detailed credit information on several thousand foreign firms.
- Publishers of certain export magazines intended for circulation in foreign markets often are in a position to furnish their advertisers credit information concerning actual and prospective customers and also to render other related services.

Other sources of information are agents or traveling representatives abroad, customers' own reports, branches of foreign banks in the United States and other foreign traders by exchange of experience through foreign trade clubs or other trade groups.

An enlightened and practical discussion of the whole field of credit in foreign trade is contained in the book, *International Trade Handbook*. See also: *World Trade Directory Reports*.

For listing of banks with special facilities for the collection of shippers' drafts see: *Exporters' Encyclopedia* and *Custom House Guide*.

(See also subject headings: Foreign Marketing and Financing Foreign Trade.)

Custom House Brokers

Clearing imported goods through U.S. customs requires thorough training and accuracy. The complexities involved, in many cases, make necessary the employment of specialists in this field, known as custom house brokers. In the entry of a shipment, the custom house broker is prepared to undertake a sequence of detail which, ordinarily, importing interests find it difficult to perform themselves unless an office or a trained employee is maintained at the port of entry.

Custom house brokers are familiar with all phases of importing, including the special and administrative provisions of customs laws and regulations, rates of duty, trucking, warehousing, insurance, foreign exchange, foreign consular invoices, railroad and steamship rates and many other details.

No person, firm, corporation or association may transact business as a custom house broker without license from the Treasury Department's U.S. Customs Service, whose regulations are contained in Part 11.1, Section 19 of the Code of Federal Regulations. Frequently, custom house brokers also conduct a freight forwarding business.

Among convenient sources for names, addresses and information on custom house brokers, the following are suggested:
- American Importers Association (Membership Directory).
- *American Shipper*.
  Customs Bulletin and Decisions, Vol. 13, No. 27, July 4, 1979 (List of Licensed Custom House Brokers).
  Custom House Guide.
- National Customs Brokers and Forwarders Association of America (Membership Roster).
  Pacific Shipper.

Consult also foreign trade bureaus of local chambers of commerce, banks in foreign trade and port authorities.

The names of principal organizations of custom house brokers and foreign freight forwarders are mentioned under subject heading: Foreign Freight Forwarders.

Diplomatic and Consular Services

For lists of United States diplomatic and consular officials abroad and foreign diplomatic representatives and consular offices in the United States, the following are recommended:
- *Diplomatic List*. Foreign diplomatic representatives in Washington, D.C.
- *Exporters' Encyclopedia*. Foreign consulates in the United States and American consular offices abroad.
- *Foreign Consular Offices in the United States*.
- *Key Officers of Foreign Service Posts—Guide for Business Representatives*. (U.S. embassies, missions, consulates general and consulates abroad)

For information concerning the Foreign Service of the United States, see the following:
- *Department of State Bulletin*.
- *Foreign Service Journal*.

Contact also Foreign Service, Department of State; and Foreign Commercial Service, Department of Commerce, Washington, D.C.

(Note: It is best not to address business letters to U.S. consular officers by name, because communications so addressed are frequently forwarded to them in the event they are transferred to another post.)

Directories and Trade Lists

Classified directory material of service to foreign traders is available in great variety and from numerous sources. It includes formal directories, published both in the United States and abroad, listings of many kinds in yearbooks, foreign trade reference works and trade publications and special files of credit agencies, banks, publishers and other foreign trade service organizations.

Many directories and other directory materials are mentioned in connection with individual subjects in various chapters of this *Handbook*. They are also listed in the Bibliography.

Widely used by foreign traders is *An Index to Trade Lists* of the U.S. Department of Commerce. These are listings of foreign firms and individuals in the usual channels of distribution abroad, and principal industries, processors and service organizations. *World Trade Directory Reports* provide additional data on such points as relative size of firm, lines handled, method of operation, territory covered and sales data.

Many commonly used directories and reference works containing directory material are kept on file in field offices of the Department of Commerce and often with foreign trade bureaus of local chambers of commerce. Some of the latter issue specialized directory material covering their areas.

See especially: *American Register of Exporters and Importers; Export Directory; Exporters Directory/U.S. Buying Guide; Guide to American Directories; Johnson's Worldwide Chamber of Commerce Directory;* and *The Encyclopedia of Associations;* and *World Trade Data Yearbook.*

Other good sources of information on documents and documentation include banks in foreign trade and foreign freight forwarders. See section on Documents in Foreign Trade.

For United States tariff law and customs regulations respecting documents in import, see the *Custom House Guide.*

Documents in Foreign Trade

Care in the documentation of export shipments is essential to avoid delay, fines or penalties. The number and kind of documents needed vary according to the type of goods and regulations of the country of destination.

Ordinarily, they include a commercial invoice with packing list, shipper's export declaration, bill of lading and marine insurance certificate. In other cases, a visaed consular invoice, a sanitary certificate and often a certificate of origin are required. Many local chambers of commerce certify origin of export shipments for their members when required.

A new system called "U.S. Standard Master for International Trade" has standardized international shipping and collection forms so that all necessary documents required to process a specific shipment can be reproduced from a single master. This has resulted in considerable savings. Further, efforts are underway to eliminate documents requiring preparation in the language of the destination country.

Many firms are taking advantage of a reporting procedure whereby information regarding all export orders beyond a 30-day period is filed with the government only once a month instead of on a separate Shipper's Export Declaration each time a shipment is made.

To simplify and speed the preparation and processing of all documents and facilitate the use of data transmission systems and equipment, standard universal transportation and commodity descriptions and code systems are being developed.

Finally, there is some relief in sight for U.S. firms burdened by international documentation. To reduce the volume of paperwork, the U.S. government has been cooperating with the National Committee on International Trade Documentation (NCITD) and other private organizations. A number of documents have been eliminated entirely or their contents have been incorporated in other required documents. For further details and implementation instructions, contact:

Office of Facilitation
Department of Transportation
400 Seventh Street, S.W.
Washington, D.C. 20590.

or

The National Committee on
  International Trade Documentation (NCITD)
Suite 1406, 30 East 42nd Street
New York, New York 10017.

Information regarding required documents and assistance in their preparation may also be obtained from any Department of Commerce district office (see page 221).

The two U.S. government agencies with the most direct involvement in trade transactions are the *Bureau of the Census* and the *United States Customs Service*. The former obtains accurate, detailed trade statistics on exports and imports. Customs' responsibility lies in the assessment and collection of duties and the enforcement of import regulations. Coordination among the many agencies engaged in documentation is provided by the *Department of Transportation* and its *Office of Facilitation*.

Other good sources of information on documents and documentation include banks active in foreign trade, foreign freight forwarders and foreign trade bureaus of local chambers of commerce.

Note also the following publications:
  • ''Standard Documentation for United States Domestic and International Trade and Transport.'' (NCITD).
  • *Exporters' Encyclopedia.*

For U.S. tariff law and customs regulations regarding documents for imports, see *Custom House Guide.*

Following is a list of U.S. international trade documents used by exporters and importers. These documents can be divided into three classes:
  • *Government Documents*
    Shipper's Export Declaration
    Drawback-Notice of Exportation of Articles with Benefit of Drawback
    General Services Administration Export Shipping Instructions, GSA Form No. 472
    Special Customs Invoice, Customs Form No. 5515
    Customs Consumption Entry Form, Customs Form No. 7501
    Supplier's Certificate and Agreement of the Agency for International Development, AID Form No. 282
    Phytosanitary Certificate
  • *Transaction-Related (Commercial) Documents*
    Commercial Invoice
    Consular Invoice
    Letter of Credit
    Marine Insurance
  • *Transport-Related Documents*
    Bills of Lading
    Shipper's Letter of Instruction to Airlines

Special Cargo Insurance Policy
Certificate of Origin
Delivery Instructions
Dock Receipt
Terminal and Handling Documents
Dangerous Goods/Hazardous Materials Documents

Government Documents

Many departments and agencies of the U.S. government are involved in enforcing statutes, regulations and administrative procedures that affect the conduct of trade transactions. The government responsibility for creating documents and related procedures varies from transaction to transaction and depends on the type of commodity, the destination and many other factors.

Shipper's Export Declaration. This document is used by the Bureau of the Census to record all the necessary U.S. export trade statistical data. It may also be identified as Commerce Form 7525-V. For specific regulations concerning use, contact the Foreign Trade Statistics Regulations, Bureau of the Census, Department of Commerce.

The form is required for statistical purposes and, where applicable, for monitoring compliance with export licensing or control regulations. Filing of this form is required, unless specific exemptions apply, for shipments by vessel, air, rail, vehicle, pipeline, parcel post and ferry, for merchandise shipped to all foreign countries, to the Virgin Islands and from the United States to Puerto Rico or from Puerto Rico to the United States.

When a declaration is required, it shall be presented to the exporting carrier, the customs office or to the postmaster at the post office from which the shipment is mailed, generally in the number of copies specified below.

(1) *Exports by means other than by mail.* Two copies of the declaration are required for shipments valued at more than $500, except for shipments to Canada and shipments between the United States and its territories and possessions, where only one copy is required.

(2) *Mail shipments.* For a mail shipment, present one copy of the declaration to the postmaster at the place of mailing when the shipment: (i) is under a validated license, or (ii) is of a commercial nature and its value is more than $500.

The commodity description items of the SED call for "Schedule B" numbers, units and descriptions. The Schedule B is a taxonomy of export commodities prepared for statistical record-keeping and monitoring by the Bureau of the Census, and is found in: "Schedule B: Statistical Classification of Domestic and Foreign Commerce Exported from the United States."

Drawback-Notice of Exportation of Articles with Benefit of Drawback. By definition, a drawback is a refund of duties paid upon imported materials used in the manufacture of products which are later exported from the United States. In addition to providing a refund of duties paid on imported material which is directly used in the products, drawback also permits a refund if domestic material of the same kind and quality is substituted for such imported material in the manufacture of the exported products. Also, imported merchandise which does not conform to sample of specifications is entitled to drawback if it is re-exported under customs supervision. Drawback is a privilege, rather than a right.

The drawback form is completed and submitted by a claimant to substantiate the export of articles against which drawback is to be claimed. The claimant certifies on the form that the drawback articles described are to be exported and not relanded in the United States; and, further, that the articles have not been used and are entitled, on exportation, to a drawback of duties paid on the imported materials used in their manufacture or of the internal revenue tax paid on the domestic material used.

Provision is made for certification by customs at the port of export that its records show the drawback articles described were exported by the exporter named.

General Services Administration Export Shipping Instructions, GSA Form No. 472. The General Services Administration (GSA) uses this document as a shipper would use a shipper-provided bill of lading. It provides carriers and forwarders with details of the shipment.

This form is widely used by the GSA, which is the government's second largest international shipper after the Department of Defense. On other than defense shipments, it serves the major needs of government shipments.

Special Customs Invoice. This document, identified as Customs Form No. 5515, is well known throughout the world, since it must be prepared for each shipment to the United States containing dutiable goods worth more than $500. The form may be obtained free of charge from the United States consular and customs offices. The purpose of the form is to provide customs with full goods descriptions, values and other pertinent statistical information for the assessment of duty and for validation for entry into U.S. domestic commerce. In some cases, where exemptions from the use of the special customs invoice have been granted, a commercial invoice, aligned and prepared in the same manner, may be substituted.

Customs Consumption Entry Form. The consumption entry form is identified as Customs Form No. 7501. It is the single most important document in the entry cycle of the duty assessment process.

Supplier's Certificate and Agreement of the Agency for International Development (AID), AID Form No. 282. This form contains most of the trade information required for AID transactions and replaces many separate forms that were formerly used.

Phytosanitary Certificate. This certificate is required by the 1951 Rome International Plant Protection Convention. This convention stipulates that each government shall arrange for the issuance of phytosanitary certificates to certify compliance with the plant protection regulations of other contracting governments.

The data content of the certificate includes all informational material about plants, vegetables and vegetable or plant products intended for planting or propagation.

Most foreign countries require that shipments of plants and unmanufactured plant products be accompanied by phytosanitary certificates certifying conformity with their plant quarantine import regulations.

Phytosanitary export certification is not a requirement of the United States but is provided as a service at the request of a shipper. The certificates are issued based upon inspection and the determination that the commodity is substantially free from injurious pests and plant diseases considered as harmful by the destination country. Phytosanitary certificates are not issued to satisfy letters of credit or other commercial contract terms and are not certifications of grade or quality. Information on phytosanitary certification may be obtained by contacting Plant Protection and

Quarantine Programs, Animal and Plant Health Inspection Service, U.S. Department of Agriculture; at ports of export; or by writing to PPQ, APHIS, USDA, Regulatory Support Staff, Room 637, Federal Building, Hyattsville, Maryland 20782.

Transaction-Related (Commercial) Documents

This group of documents consists of those that are primarily related to details of the transaction, rather than to transportation. Transaction-related documents contain the key data needed by seller, buyer, their forwarders or agents and banks. This same type of data is often necessary to meet government regulations and information requirements. In the transaction-related list of documents, the following are of major importance and in most common usage:

Commercial Invoice. The commercial invoice is recognized as the basic document between buyer and seller. The information that this document contains is just as important to commercial parties as the bill of lading is to carriers. The invoice is also of interest to banks to support letters of credit and to insurance companies because of their interest in shipment valuation. This same information is of interest to governments, particularly as the basis for customs entry and consular data.

Consular Invoice. A few foreign countries require a special form of invoice in addition to the commercial invoice. These documents must be prepared in the language of their country and on official forms sold by the respective consulates. They are then visaed by the resident consul, thereby certifying their accuracy and authenticity. It is recommended that the shipper's forwarder prepare these documents at time of shipment.

Letter of Credit. For centuries, commercial letters of credit have been used by exporters and importers throughout the world to finance the exchange of goods and services. Commercial letters of credit remain a foremost banking service designed to meet the financing needs of both buyers and sellers.

In the financing of export shipments, U.S. sellers make extensive use of export letters of credit because they afford the highest degree of protection, with the exception of cash in advance, especially if credits are issued in irrevocable form. Importers of many types of commodities and merchandise likewise have found this method of financing of particular advantage.

A letter of credit is an instrument issued by a bank to a seller, in which the bank undertakes to pay the seller for purchases made by a foreign buyer. It describes the terms and conditions under which payment will be made.

Until recently, the parties applying to banks for letters of credit were met with different types of "application" forms, varying considerably from bank to bank in detail and configuration. In the United States, under the leadership of the three regional committees on international banking and the National Council of Committees on International Banking, a standardized application form has been adopted. While not aligned with documents based on the United States Master, this standardization of the letter of credit application form is compatible with the standard letter of credit instrument adopted by the Banking Commission of the International Chamber of Commerce (ICC).

Marine Insurance. In international trade, the carrier of merchandise is freed from many responsibilities for loss and damage to cargo, under the U.S. Carriage of Goods by Sea Act (1936 Merchant Marine Act, as amended) and similar legislation abroad. It is advisable, therefore, that the shipper employ shipper-purchased cargo insurance for protection against certain perils to which his goods may be exposed during a voyage, liability for which the carrier or others in possession of the cargo are relieved by terms of the bill of lading or by law.

A marine cargo insurance policy is a contract insuring the goods against specified perils named in the contract, but not necessarily against all cause of loss. Additional risks may be covered, depending upon the special requirements of the assured, the class of merchandise and the voyage or the type of vessel.

This policy, a document with long evolution and language drawn from maritime case law, is viewed as arcane and hard to understand. It is therefore prudent for a cargo owner or shipper to consult an experienced international marine insurance broker or freight forwarder before engaging in overseas transactions

Most U.S. companies writing marine cargo insurance are members of the American Institute of Marine Underwriters (AIMU) with offices at 14 Wall Street, New York, New York 10005. AIMU includes in its membership many foreign companies admitted to do marine insurance business in this country. (see page 66)

Marine insurance may be placed directly with insurance companies or through brokers or freight forwarders. Wide experience with desirable forms of policies for given voyages and types of merchandise makes the service brokers or forwarders of particular advantage. Brokers are organized nationally in the National Association of Insurance Brokers, Wall Street Plaza, 88 Pine Street, New York, New York 10005, and are listed in various directories, such as the *New York Port Handbook*.

Among other publications containing helpful information on marine insurance are the following:
- *Custom House Guide.*
- *Exporters' Encyclopedia,* Section VIII.
- *Exporters' Guide to Cargo Insurance.*
- *International Trade Handbook.*
- *Marine Insurance Claims: American Law and Practice.*
- *Marine Insurance Digest* (H. Mullins).

Consult also: International Trade Administration (ITA), U.S. Department of Commerce; American Importers Association; the National Foreign Trade Council; U.S. Council of the International Chamber of Commerce; banks in foreign trade; and local chapters of the Foreign Traders Association.

Transport-Related Documents

Bills of Lading. This category of documents contains the key information required by carriers.

The importance of the bill of lading as a commercial document cannot be overstated. It serves three distinct purposes in connection with the carriage of goods: (1) as a receipt for the goods; (2) to represent the contract of carriage; and (3) as a document of title, i.e., taking the place of the goods themselves for the purpose of sale, pledge, etc.

These commercial documents may be ocean or overland (truck or rail) bills of lading or air waybills, depending on the mode of transportation or terms of sale. As in a domestic shipment, there are two basic types—"straight," or nonnegotiable, and negotiable or "shipper's order" bills of lading. The latter is used for sight draft or letter of credit shipments. The shipper must endorse the original copy of the "order" bill of lading before it is presented to the bank for collection. The endorsement may either be "in blank" or "to the order of" a third party such as the negotiating bank. The letter of credit will stipulate which endorsement to use. With the exception of ocean shipments, only one original bill of lading is issued by the carrier. Any number of original ocean bills of lading may be issued, depending upon the requirements of the buyer. Normally all original copies are endorsed and submitted to the bank. Efforts are currently underway to eliminate or at least substantially reduce the use of multiple bills of lading. This undertaking, led by the National Committee on International Trade Documentation (NCITD), seeks to encourage the adoption by all parties of a "sole original" bill of lading for ocean shipping.

According to the rules set forth by the International Chamber of Commerce governing foreign trade terms, documents, etc., on draft or letter of credit shipments, the only acceptable bill of lading is one marked "clean on board," meaning that the carrier has taken no exception to the condition of the cargo or packing and that the merchandise has actually been loaded aboard the carrying vessel.

Shipper's Letter of Instruction to Airlines. The shipper's use of this document has the effect of shifting from the shipper or his agent the responsibility of preparing the actual air waybill to the air carrier or its agent.

The document may be used for domestic or international air transportation, and it constitutes a shipper's letter of instruction to the carrier. The document, which has been approved by the Civil Aeronautics Board, is subject to the tariffs on file with that body and to the terms and conditions of the Warsaw Convention governing international air cargo shipments.

Special Cargo Insurance Policy. This document is an important form for insurance purposes. Referred to both as a "certificate of insurance" and as a "special cargo insurance policy," it contains much of the information used on ocean bills of lading. Forms are available through the headquarters of the American Institute of Marine Underwriters in New York or individual insurance underwriters and brokers.

Certificate of Origin. To meet statistical or licensing requirements, many countries require specific information as to the origin of the goods, the transaction or both. Statements of origin are often required to establish possible preferential rates of import duties under a most-favored-nation arrangement. The certificate of origin contains this data and is usually "certified or authenticated" by a neutral party, trade association or local chamber of commerce.

Delivery Instructions. This document, which also is known as a "shipping delivery order," is limited to a few major port areas. It is issued by an exporter or his forwarder, with instructions to his trucker to pick up the goods at an in-transit (temporary) terminal position and deliver them to a pier or pier terminal. The same instructions may be issued to a railroad for completion of delivery by land or water to the pier. Usually, at U.S. ports where this document is separately prepared, it is issued simultaneously with the dock receipt.

Dock Receipt. This document is a steamship company form, evidencing receipt of the goods at a pier. Copies of this form are made available to shippers (or their agents) as a means of expediting handling at piers.

The dock receipt controls the ownership of the goods until the ocean bill of lading is issued.

Because all pertinent shipping information must be included in the dock receipt, extra copies of this form are useful for the shipper, the forwarder, dock forces and the steamship company office.

The dock receipt and the extra form for delivery instructions are usually presented by the shipper or his agent simultaneously when delivering freight to the dock.

Terminal and Handling Documents. In addition to delivery instructions and dock receipts, there are several documents used in intermediate services and handling which have similar functions and include related data.

This group of documents includes those involving: handling and storage of goods; port charges; receipts, such as goods receipt and mate's receipts, but excluding dock receipts; handling orders; and gate and terminal passes.

Dangerous Goods/Hazardous Cargo Documentation. To insure the safe and efficient international transport of increasing volumes of hazardous cargo, a standardized way of showing the essential information on an aligned form has now been developed.

This recognizes the varying requirements of different modes of transport and of combined transport. It aims to: (1) decrease complexity and increase safety; (2) reduce delays; (3) reduce paperwork and administrative costs; and (4) improve accuracy and efficiency.

The Inter-Governmental Maritime Consultative Organization (IMCO) has developed the International Maritime Dangerous Goods Code for shipments by sea.

The International Air Transport Association (IATA) is working on measures for effective identification of dangerous goods on the air waybill.

The International Federation of Forwarding Agents Association (FIATA) has developed the so-called FDT standard to govern movements of dangerous goods by rail, highway and water.

Employment Abroad

Increased interest on the part of younger men and women in international affairs has led them to seek employment in one branch or another of foreign trade.

Employment in foreign trade may take any of a number of forms. Various positions may be sought with U.S. businesses well established in trading abroad, such as: exporting or importing manufacturers; export or import merchants and houses conducting related foreign trade businesses; firms engaged in activities serving foreign traders in the fields of transportation, forwarding, banking, insurance and the like; and government departments or agencies and private organizations with functions in the fields of foreign trade or international affairs.

Usually, interest centers on employment with U.S. companies with overseas operations, providing opportunity for residence or extensive travel in foreign countries. It should be emphasized, however, that chances for inexperienced persons in this respect are exceedingly limited. A considerable portion of these firms' overseas personnel consists of foreign nationals. Furthermore, those manufacturers who maintain their own organizations abroad generally require substantial periods of employment in the United States first, for requisite training and experience before serving abroad. Large numbers of manufacturers rely almost entirely on established foreign outlets for the distribution of their products and many utilize export merchants or other specialized exporting facilities located in the United States.

Many colleges and universities in the United States conduct formal courses of study in foreign trade subjects or basic studies in merchandising, shipping and other subjects as they relate to trade abroad.

For additional information consult: *Career Opportunities in the International Field; Federal Jobs Overseas; How to Get the Job You Want Overseas; International Jobs: Where They Are, How to Get Them;* and *Employment Abroad: Facts and Fallacies.*

Exchange and Trade Controls, Foreign

Among nontariff laws and regulations which restrict trading of many classes of goods, *foreign exchange control* is one of the most serious problems with which the international trader has to deal today.

Banks doing international business necessarily are up to date on existing controls and adjustments in them. Many banks issue periodic bulletins indicating changes as they occur and some publish annual surveys summarizing existing exchange controls, import and export restrictions or regulations and other data affecting trade in given areas.

Reports on foreign exchange rates and controls and other nontariff trade regulations are compiled by specialists in the Office of Country Marketing, Bureau of Export Development, U.S. Department of Commerce, from data submitted on a regular basis by Foreign Service Officers in American Embassies and Consulates abroad. Information on individual country regulations is published in the Department's *Overseas Business Reports* (OBR) series. Changes in existing regulations are reported as they occur in *Business America,* the Commerce Department's biweekly journal of industry and trade.

Other announcements on exchange and trade regulations are made available through the Department of the Treasury and through published services, such as: *Exporters' Encyclopedia,* current supplements; *International Trade Reporter's Export Shipping Manual;* and *World Trade Data Yearbook.*

Study of foreign controls and barriers to a freer flow of trade is made continuously by private organizations of foreign traders. Some keep members informed through periodic bulletins. The Association of Executives in Finance, Credit and International Business of the National Association of Credit Management issues, on subscription, minutes of roundtable conferences on exchange problems and other matters relating to foreign credit and finance. See: *Minutes of Monthly Roundtable Conferences.*

Export Controls, United States

The policy of the U.S. government is to encourage exports in nonstrategic goods with all nations with which we have diplomatic relations. The authority over the control of exports from the United States is presently divided among a number of federal agencies, although this responsibility was significantly consolidated in early 1980, when portions of the Departments of State and Treasury were moved into the Commerce Department's International Trade Administration.

The Office of Export Administration (OEA), Commerce Department, has responsibility under the Export Administration Act of 1979 (for more information on the act see below) to control the export of most commercial commodities and technical data. Most shipments may be made under "general license," a standing authorization to export. Certain commodities and technical data, specified in the *Export Administration Regulations,* require an individual validated license. These are generally high-technology goods or goods going to restricted destinations such as communist nations or nations with which there are diplomatic exigencies. Technical data controls include patent applications. In making determinations on applications, OEA confers with other agencies, including the Departments of Defense, State and Energy, among others.

The Commerce Department has licensing jurisdiction over all commodities and unclassified technical data exported from the United States except certain specialized items handled by other government agencies (arms, ammunition and implements of war are licensed by the U.S. Department of State, Office of Munitions Control; atomic energy material and facilities by the U.S. Nuclear Regulatory Commission or the U.S. Department of Energy; narcotics and dangerous drugs by the U.S. Department of Justice). The Departments of State and Energy have further responsibilities for control of exports of classified and unclassified data relating to commodities under their jurisdiction. The Department of Treasury, Office of Foreign Assets Control, has responsibility for particular countries' assets.

Export Administration Act of 1979 (Public Law 96-72)

Effective October 1, 1979, through September 30, 1983, the act is the latest chapter in a legislative evolution with origins in World War II government regulation of exports. It is the enabling legislation for the Commerce Department's Office of Export Administration, which is thereby authorized to exert validated export licensing requirements only to the extent necessary:

- To restrict the export of goods and technology which would make a significant contribution to the military potential of any other country or combination of countries which would prove detrimental to the national security of the United States.
- To restrict the export of goods and technology where necessary to further significantly the foreign policy of the United States or to fulfill its declared international obligations.
- To restrict the export of goods where necessary to protect the domestic economy from the excessive drain of scarce materials and to reduce the serious inflationary impact of foreign demand.

The act is intended by its authors to provide reforms in U.S. export control policies and practices and to address U.S. exporters' concerns about alleged inadequacies in the export controls system.

These reforms fall into the following primary areas: congressional findings, national security and foreign policy controls, license applications processing and public participation.

The act also contains a summary of policy findings on government regulation of exports and on foreign boycott compliance guidelines, which were instituted primarily in response to the Arab nations' commercial boycott of Israel. The new act goes into greater detail than ever before about internal licensing review procedures and deadlines and sets criteria for controlling commodities. Also included are enforcement and appeals provisions and confidentiality standards.

Exports, Importance of

Exports are important both to manufacturers and to workers. They are also of great importance to the American public. Increased exports mean more profits and more jobs, providing a broader marketing base and stimulating greater company growth. In addition, however, exporting contributes to a healthier economy and strengthens the U.S. international trade position.

The United States has experienced record trade deficits in recent years. Not long ago Americans were able to rely solely on abundant U.S. natural resources and huge internal markets to maintain a high standard of living. Today soaring energy needs and a growing taste for imported goods have increased dependence on outside sources. The relatively slow growth of American exports has been a major contributing factor as well.

In September 1978, President Carter announced a National Export Policy (NEP) that elevated export expansion to a national priority. Based on the belief that increasing U.S. exports should be the principal means of reducing trade deficits, the policy underscores the importance of exports and the role they play in making the United States a stronger, more competitive force in the world economy.

The Commerce Department is coordinating and directing follow-through on the diverse elements of the NEP throughout the government. Among many government efforts being undertaken in connection with NEP are:

- A comprehensive study of export disincentives covering known major direct disincentives.
- A detailed analysis by regulatory agencies of how the U.S. foreign trade position would be affected by significant regulations which they propose.
- A review of proposed regulatory actions to assess their export impact.
- Expedited treatment by the Justice Department to requests by business firms for guidance on international antitrust issues.
- Up to $100 million in Small Business Administration loan guarantees to provide seed money for small business exporters to enter into foreign markets.
- Day-to-day decision-making on export license matters is being influenced by the President's instruction to weigh foreign availability and adverse export consequences in reaching those decisions.
- New procedures governing export license denials for foreign policy purposes will require an assessment to be made with respect to whether the item in question is available from foreign sources as well as the overall export consequences of a denial. Before imposing export controls for

foreign policy purposes, this assessment will be considered by any agency recommending a denial.

- A computerized information system which will provide exporters with prompt access to international marketing opportunities abroad and will expose American products to foreign buyers.
- Greater accessibility to Eximbank programs for smaller exporters through a new short-term insurance program for small businesses and through special treatment for smaller firms with respect to medium-term commercial bank guarantees.
- A Presidential Executive Order on environmental effects abroad of major federal actions, exempting export licenses from its coverage, clarifying the kinds of environmental reviews required for U.S. actions abroad and reducing uncertainties faced by agencies and exporters.
- Increased guidance to the business community as to the scope and meaning of the Foreign Corrupt Practices Act.

The President's Export Council also was reconstituted in 1979 to enable representatives from all sectors of the U.S. economy to advise the President on export policy. (see page 3)

See: *Policies and Programs for Expanding U.S. Exports,* Recommendations of the Chamber of Commerce of the United States, International Division, Chamber of Commerce of the United States, 1979.

Export Management Companies

A U.S. firm can take two basic approaches to selling internationally. It can deal directly with a foreign firm or indirectly through another U.S. firm which acts as a sales intermediary and normally will assume responsibility for selling the firm's products overseas.

Most small companies that decide to use a U.S. company as an intermediary find that *export management companies* (EMCs), acting as "export departments," do the best job of soliciting and attracting overseas buyers.

EMCs work simultaneously for a number of exporters for a commission, salary, or retainer plus commission. Often products of an EMCs client are related, although the items usually are noncompetitive.

The advantage of an EMC is the availability of resources that would take many years for a smaller firm to develop marketing its own exports individually. EMCs work through their own network of overseas distributors. They are in a good position to enlist the services of foreign representatives because of the broad range and large volume of related products they carry. Since most EMCs specialize in a particular product area, they remain current on developments in many markets. Many also assume financing of sales and extend credit, thus facilitating prompt payment to an exporter.

Most EMCs provide a multitude of services, including market research, appointing overseas distributors or commission representatives, exhibiting a client's products at international trade shows, advertising, shipping, and documentation. In short, the EMC takes full responsibility for the export end of the business, relieving the manufacturer of all the details except filling orders.

Before choosing an export management company, it is important to obtain a list of EMCs specializing in the product range involved; there are about 1,000 EMCs in the United States. Most are located in the larger seaport or inland lakeport cities, though some are found in other major cities and in smaller manufacturing centers.

For assistance in locating and selecting the proper EMC, contact:

- U.S. Department of Commerce district offices.
- The National Federation of Export Management Companies, P.O. Box 7612, Washington, D.C. 20044.
- District Export Councils and local foreign trade clubs.
- Agency for International Development, Washington, D.C. 20523.
- Field Offices of the Small Business Administration.
- State departments of commerce or industrial development.
- Port authorities.
- Export trade magazines.
- Foreign trade departments of local chambers of commerce.
- Foreign trade executives in banks.
- The National Association of Export Management Companies, Inc., 65 Liberty Street, New York, N.Y. 10005.
- Foreign freight forwarders and foreign trade consultants.
- Industry trade associations.

The following publications also may be utilized in selecting an EMC:

Government Publications:

The EMC—Your Export Department.

A Directory of U.S. Export Management Companies.

Using the Services of an Export Management Company.

Commercial Publishers:

The Foreign Trade Market Place.

Check the list with members of the business community in your area who use EMCs and find out what their experience has been. Also, talk with the various EMCs, find out what they have to say and compare them.

After selecting an EMC, review its proposal with your business advisers.

Most contracts between EMCs and manufacturers are for at least three to five years. Because of the wide physical separation of markets, it sometimes takes a year or longer to develop a volume of overseas business satisfactory to both parties. Contracts usually carry a 60- to 90-day termination clause as well as automatic renewal.

Financing Foreign Trade

Although the basic principles underlying the financing of foreign business are similar to those which apply in domestic trading, there are many factors which are peculiar to the foreign transaction and which require special consideration.

The difference arises principally from the distance of markets and the fact that transactions are extended to territories which have differing monetary systems, laws, regulations and customs. Those unacquainted with the methods and special characteristics of financing foreign business should seek the advice and guidance of banks or other financing institutions.

Many leading banks of the United States maintain foreign departments especially for financing overseas shipments and otherwise serving foreign traders. They have either their own branches in foreign countries or well-established correspondent relationships with foreign banks. Local banks of the United States without direct foreign connections usually have connections with American banks which do.

Among books or pamphlets which discuss the general nature of export or import financing, the functions of banks, methods, instruments used and related matters, the following are suggested: *A Guide to Financing Exports; A Handbook on Financing U.S. Exports; Export-Import Financing—A Practical Guide; Financing Imports and Exports; The Financing of Exports and Imports;* and *Sources of Aid and Information for U.S. Exporters.*

Helpful advice on many points of financing may be obtained also from foreign freight forwarders, custom house brokers, local chambers of commerce with foreign trade services and the International Trade Administration, Office of Export Development, U.S. Department of Commerce.

Banks in Foreign Trade

Many commercial banks in the United States have specialized foreign trade departments as well as international banking relationships which enable them to perform a variety of financing services in connection with export trade and foreign investment. Some maintain branches abroad or have well-established correspondent relationships with banks in foreign countries. Local American banks without direct foreign connections generally have correspondent connections with international banking institutions or with other larger financial centers. Many foreign banks also maintain agencies or offices in the United States.

Banks play an indispensable role in the conduct of foreign trade. Their functions include financing of exports and imports, acceptance financing, collection of drafts on foreign countries, purchase and sale of foreign exchange, remittances to foreign countries and related services.

Aside from their direct financing function, banks are important sources of many kinds of information which the foreign trader needs, such as reports on economic and exchange conditions abroad, the credit status of foreign firms, collection of market survey data, advice on representatives or agents abroad and information on many points of trading technique.

Many banks in foreign trade issue periodic bulletins of value to foreign traders in keeping them abreast of conditions and developments in foreign countries. They vary in type and coverage, but generally deal with control and exchange developments, market conditions and related matters.

Readings on the varied functions of banks in the conduct of foreign trade may be found in *International Bankers Directory.*

An outstanding directory of banks in the United States and foreign countries, with branches, correspondents and other information is: *Polk's Bank Directory.*

See also:

Custom House Guide. Banks with foreign trade departments in each port of the United States.

Exporters' Encyclopedia, Section VII. Banks with special facilities for the collection of shippers' drafts, and other data.

Principal national associations of bankers of the United States are: American Bankers Association, 1120 Connecticut Avenue, N.W., Washington, D.C. 20036; and Bankers Association for Foreign Trade, c/o The Bank of New York, 48 Wall Street, New York, New York 10005.

Exchange Rates

Foreign departments of banks are of primary importance as sources of information on current rates of foreign exchange, as well as other data on conditions in the exchange field, including the controls and regulations of foreign countries in respect thereto.

Published statements of prevailing rates of exchange in foreign currencies may be found daily in many of the leading commercial and financial newspapers, such as the *Journal of Commerce;* the *American Banker;* and *Financial Times of London.*

Past records of rates, which give indications of trends, are carried in weekly and monthly periodicals of general interest to foreign traders such as: *Business International Money Report; International Financial Statistics;* and *International Reports.*

Conversion rates for the purpose of assessment and collection of duties on merchandise imported into the United States are certified daily to the Department of the Treasury by the Federal Reserve Bank of New York. They are published in the *Journal of Commerce.*

It is the function of the International Monetary Fund to promote exchange stability and orderly exchange arrangements among its members, principally through establishment and maintenance of par values of member currencies.

For inquiry on special points pertaining to exchange rates and exchange conditions and problems, consult: International Monetary Fund; Federal Reserve Bank of New York; and International Trade Administration, Office of International Finance and Investment, U.S. Department of Commerce.

For discussions of the general aspects of foreign exchange practices and policy, the following are suggested: *About Foreign Exchange; Foreign Exchange Markets in the United States; Guide to Foreign Exchange;* and *World Trade Data Yearbook.*

Letters of Credit

In the financing of export shipments, American sellers make extensive use of export letters of credit as affording the highest degree of protection, with the exception of cash in advance (prepayment from the foreign buyer), especially if credits are issued in irrevocable form. United States importers of many types of commodities and merchandise likewise have found this method of financing of particular advantage.

A letter of credit is an instrument issued by a bank to a seller, in which the bank undertakes to pay the seller for purchases made by a foreign buyer. It describes the terms and conditions under which payment will be made.

Basically, there are three forms of the letter of credit:

1. *A revocable letter of credit* is a form in less use because it can be revoked or cancelled by the issuing bank and the exporter cannot rely on it with certainty as a source of payment.

2. *An irrevocable L/C,* even if unconfirmed, cannot be cancelled or amended before expiration without the consent of all parties concerned and it enables the exporter to rely upon the payment promise by the foreign bank which issued it even though the correspondent "advising" bank has no *legal* obligation to honor it.

3. *An irrevocable confirmed L/C,* confirmed to the exporter by his bank as correspondent, allows the exporter to rely upon his bank as the source of payment because it has assumed the irrevocable obligation jointly with the issuing bank and payment is now not contingent upon the foreign bank's ability to pay.

Financing Aspects of L/C's. Besides assurance of payment, an exporter can also use a letter of credit advantageously to carry any part of the financing that he may bear or to arrange complete financing for the manufacture and sale of the merchandise without using any of his own operating capital.

Discounting L/C's for Immediate Cash. The exporter, for example, can obtain immediate cash payment even on a time draft on a letter of credit if, upon shipment of the goods after prior arrangements with the importer to have the letter of credit issued in favor of the correspondent bank, his draft and documents are "accepted" by his bank and he discounts the acceptance with the bank for payment (rather than holding it to maturity). The seller may take this "financing" cost into account in establishing his price for the merchandise to the foreign buyer.

Export Financing

In a world where comparable products, services, and technologies are widely available, the terms of financing may be the persuasive factor in securing an export market. Adequate financing for international transactions—at competitive credit terms—is so crucial to exporting that even the best marketing efforts fail without it. Thus, government and private financing sources have, with varying degrees of involvement, made financing programs available to the U.S. exporter.

Financial Services to Exporters

Official export credit and insurance programs in the United States are administered by the Export-Import Bank of the United States (Eximbank) in conjunction with the Foreign Credit Insurance Association (FCIA) (see pages 29 and 71). Eximbank is an independent government agency, while FCIA is a group of more than fifty of the nation's leading, private marine and casualty insurance firms. Eximbank extends financing and guarantees for medium- and long-term export transactions. FCIA, in cooperation with Eximbank, insures short- and medium-term export transactions against certain political and commercial risks. The Private Export Funding Corporation (PEFCO) (see page 76), a private corporation owned by fifty-four commercial banks, seven industrial firms and one investment banking firm, is a further source of private capital which participates in export financing with Eximbank. PEFCO generally supports medium- and long-term transactions.

The basic programs available through Eximbank and FCIA are:

- Long-term fixed rate financing and financial guarantees of commercial bank and PEFCO loans.
- Medium-term discount financing for fixed rate U.S. commercial bank export obligations and medium-term lines of credit for foreign financial institutions.
- Medium-term credit insurance and guarantees for commercial and political risk.
- Short-term credit insurance (FCIA only).

Long-Term. Export transactions whose contract value exceeds $5 million and which involve long fabrication or construction periods are eligible for Eximbank's direct or "buyer" credit program. Long-term, fixed-rate loans are extended directly to the foreign buyer for the purchase of U.S. manufactured goods and services. The foreign buyer must submit an application for a loan directly to Eximbank with sufficient information to support the technical, economic and financial feasibility of the export project. Frequently, Eximbank requests that the foreign buyer secure the loan with a public (Ministry of Finance or Central Bank) or acceptable private (foreign commercial bank) guarantee in order to establish a reasonable assurance of repayment.

Eximbank requires at least a 15 percent cash down payment by the foreign buyer, after which the Bank will cover from 45 to 85 percent of the financed portion of the export contract. This percentage depends on the transaction's total term, competition in the product market, credit offers from other official export financing agencies and the extent to which U.S. commercial banks are willing to participate in the financing.

Eximbank encourages private credit institutions to share in the financing of large export transactions and may guarantee all or a portion of the private loan. These so-called "financial guarantees" will cover a commercial bank's outstanding balance for an export loan against both commercial and political risk for a yearly fee of from 0.5 to 1 percent.

In periods of tight credit, Eximbank also encourages PEFCO to participate with commercial banks in export loans. Eximbank unconditionally guarantees PEFCO loans and therefore maintains a broad measure of supervision over PEFCO's loan commitments as well as borrowings. PEFCO raises funds through the public sale of its debt obligations which are secured through pledges of the Eximbank guarantees. Interest on the PEFCO obligations is guaranteed directly by Eximbank.

PEFCO's credits are generally made at fixed rates of interest calculated in accordance with the cost of PEFCO's funds at the time of the offering. During the report period the rates ranged from 7.75 to 9.5 percent. PEFCO traditionally lends in conjunction with one or more commercial banks and will cover from 10 to 45 percent of each transaction. Loan commitments have ranged from $1 million to $116 million with an average of $14.6 million. Repayment terms are generally over five years although PEFCO will also participate in medium-term transactions.

Eximbank's direct loans carry a fixed interest rate ranging from 7.75 to 8.75 percent, depending on the transaction's total repayment term and the rates being offered by other public export financing institutions for the same project. During this report period the average weighted interest rate on all direct credit authorizations was 8.28 percent. Eximbank interest cannot be capitalized, nor can it be included in the direct loan financing.

Commercial bank financing extended in conjunction with an Eximbank direct credit is provided at a floating rate, typically one or two percent above the prevailing prime rate. At the end of this report period the U.S. prime rate was 9.75 percent.

Eximbank charges a commitment fee of 0.5 percent per annum on the undisbursed portion of a direct credit as well as a commitment fee of 0.125 percent on the undisbursed guaranteed portion of a commercial bank loan.

Repayment of principal and interest on direct loans begins six months after project completion and is made in equal semiannual installments. If private sector financing is participating with Eximbank, it is usually repaid in the earlier installments. As with all Eximbank transactions, repayment must be denominated in U.S. dollars and paid in the United States.

Medium-Term. Export transactions whose contract value is below $5 million and which require less than five years construction or fabrication are eligible for Eximbank's two medium-term financing programs: the discount loan program or the Cooperative Financing Facility. The choice would depend on the type of transaction and the exporters, foreign buyers and commercial banks involved.

The discount loan program provides U.S. commercial banks with a standby re-discount assurance for eligible fixed rate medium-term export obligations. Eximbank issues an advance commitment to buy a fixed rate note that a U.S. commercial bank has extended to either a U.S. exporter or a foreign buyer to finance export sales. Repayment terms may run from 180 days to five years depending upon the export. Eximbank's commitment covers 100 percent of the financed portion of the export transaction, but—until the commercial bank draws on the discount loan—the bank retains the full credit risk unless the financed portion is also insured or guaranteed by Eximbank.

Eximbank charges the commercial bank an interest rate which is one percent below the yield on the bank's note, but not lower than Eximbank's minimum discount loan rate (MDLR) in effect on the day of Eximbank's authorization. Because of this relationship between commercial export paper rates and the MDLR, the latter is reviewed frequently by Eximbank and changed in accordance with private market trends. During this report period the MDLR was raised from 8 percent to 8.25 percent in May and again to 8.5 percent in July where it remained through September.

Eximbank also charges the commercial bank a commitment fee which ranges from $0.15 to $0.55 per $100 of the authorized amount, depending on the length of the repayment term of the underlying loan. The fee is payable on a one-time, front-end basis. Thus, the effective cost to the foreign borrower is never less than one percent above the MDLR plus Eximbank's fee and any commercial bank fees. (The cost of Eximbank insurance or a guarantee must also be added where such protection is sought.)

The Cooperative Financing Facility (CFF) is a medium-term direct credit program. Eximbank provides lines of credit to eligible *foreign* financial institutions to help finance the purchase of U.S. exports by small- and medium-sized foreign buyers who have not developed an international credit rating but who are known locally. Under the credit line, Eximbank approves a loan to the foreign bank equal to 50 percent of the financed portion of each export sale and the foreign bank provides the remaining 50 percent. In turn, the foreign bank may borrow the remaining 50 percent from a U.S. commercial bank with an Eximbank guarantee. However, the foreign bank assumes the *full* commercial risk for each credit. As with the direct credit program, the foreign buyer must provide a 15 percent cash payment on each transaction.

Repayment terms are generally three to five years, although they can be as little as one year. Eximbank's interest rate for CFF loans remains fixed at 7.75 percent. A commitment fee of 0.5 percent is charged on the undisbursed balance of each sub-loan extended under the line. Foreign banks may charge the foreign borrower any rate above 7.75 percent that they deem appropriate.

Short-term. Export transactions whose contract value is small and which require no more than 180 days for fabrication or shipment are eligible for short-term FCIA insurance. See section on Insurance and Guarantee. There are no short-term credit programs.

Foreign Currency Financing. Eximbank does not offer foreign currency financing.

Other *Export Financing Sources* available to the U.S. exporter are:

Small Business Administration (SBA). Up to $100 million of current (FY 1980) authorizations will be reserved for smaller exporters wishing to enter foreign markets. Individual loan guarantees will be allowed up to $500,000. Requests for the SBA to participate in financing are initiated by the bank or lending institution.

SBA can offer financial assistance by providing guarantees for bank loans to qualified small businesses interested in exporting. For example, SBA's guarantee can help a small firm to expand its production facilities to meet foreign demand, or to finance overseas market development costs.

For more details about the Small Business Administration's Financial Assistance Programs, contact the SBA Office of Public Information. (see page 35)

The *Overseas Private Investment Corporation* (OPIC), which offers investment insurance, guaranties, and financing, is the U.S. government's principal catalyst for encouraging investments of U.S. private capital in developing countries. Although its incentive programs concern capital investments, OPIC's loan guaranties provide eligible parties with the necessary support to obtain private loans for the purchase of U.S. goods and services, and the proceeds of its dollar loans for investments may be used for the same purpose. For more information on OPIC, see page 38.

The *U.S. Agency for International Development's* (AID) loans and other support for economic development programs and projects abroad also are directed largely to procurement of U.S. goods and services. Although American exporters have no direct role in initiating such financing, as they do under Eximbank and FCIA programs, they can be the indirect "beneficiaries" of AID credits in expanding their overseas marketing. (see page 38)

Commodity Credit Corporation (CCC). The U.S. Department of Agriculture's Commodity Credit Corporation operates an Export Credit Sales Program under which U.S. exporters may apply for export financing of eligible U.S. commodities in large exportable supply. (see page 7)

Publications: *Export-Import Bank of the U.S.-Annual Report and Supplement* (EXIM); *A Businessman's Guide to the Cooperative Financing Facility* (EXIM); *Active CCF Cooperating Institutions* (EXIM); *Eximbank: What It is, What It Does, What It Can Do For You* (EXIM); *Glossary of Services* (EXIM); *A Guide to Financing Exports* (USDOC/EXP); *Obtain Tax Deferral Through a Domestic International Sales Corporation* (DISC) (USDOC/EXP); *How to Work With PEFCO* (PEFCO).

Insurance and Guarantees

INSURANCE. Post-shipment credit insurance covering default, political risks such as war, expropriation, confiscation and currency inconvertibility, and commercial risks such as the foreign buyer's insolvency or protracted default, is provided by the Foreign Credit Insurance Association (FCIA) in cooperation with Eximbank. Although Eximbank and FCIA share the credit risks of the insurance programs, FCIA operates with a high degree of independence due to its extensive delegated authority covering a wide range of transactions and circumstances. Eximbank, however, restricts this authority where it deems appropriate (types of buyers, types of products, etc.). The insurance provided by FCIA is useful to exporters who self-finance their own foreign receivables and to exporters who discount foreign receivables with U.S. commercial banks. Several types of Eximbank/FCIA insurance policies are available, the appropriate policy being determined by the product mix, terms of repayment, volume of the exporter's business and type of buyer (end user, dealer, etc.).

Short-term whole turnover policies (to 180 days)—usually issued for a one year period, provide blanket coverage for all or a reasonable spread of an exporter's overseas sales. The overseas sales may include products with "foreign content" as defined in each policy. This comprehensive policy covers both commercial and political risk for up to 90 percent of each loss. Insurance for political risks only is available and covers 95 percent of each loss. Short-term policies often have a moderate per buyer discretionary credit limit which allows the exporter to obtain insurance automatically for individual buyers based on the exporter's own credit decision. No cash payment is required on short-term transactions. Repayment terms are generally 180 days; however, for certain commodities and for "initial inventory" longer terms may be authorized.

Master policies—provide whole turnover coverage for both political and commercial credit risks for all of an exporter's eligible short- and medium-term credit sales with repayment terms up to five years. Again, sole political risk coverage is available. The U.S. exporter may determine the amount of insured credit extended to individual buyers within the overall discretionary limit assigned to the policy. The extent of the coverage provided is the same as under the short-term policy—90 percent for comprehensive and 95 percent for political risks only.

Medium-term policies (181 days to five years)—cover credit sales of U.S. manufactured capital and quasi-capital goods on a buyer-by-buyer basis. The exporter can request selective coverage either on a single sale or a credit line basis for repetitive sales to specific foreign buyers. Most medium-term policies cover both commercial and political risks for up to 90 percent of each transaction. FCIA will also issue a policy covering selective political risks only. Medium-term policies require that the foreign buyer make a cash payment of at least 15 percent of the contract value and obtain a promissory note detailing a uniform repayment schedule. Repayment terms are based on the contract price with various exceptions for specific exports.

Combination policies—of short- and medium-term insurance are available to protect U.S. exporters in transactions with overseas dealers and distributors. These policies afford protection in two principal areas: 1) inventory financing (repayment terms up to 270 days) where the exporter may ship goods under a "floor plan" arrangement with no cash payment required and 2) receivables financing (repayment terms up to 3 years) with the required minimum cash payment of 15 percent.

Various special policies—are provided to cover inventory held overseas in the U.S. exporter's name, the export of U.S. services (engineering, advertising, etc.), and the risks incurred by small enterprises that are exporting for the first time.

Premium rates for all insurance policies vary by type of buyer, repayment term and by the percentage of cover and security arrangements. They are payable by the exporter on a one time basis except for multibuyer policies which may be paid on an installment basis. For short-term cover, premiums generally range from 0.98 to 2.4 percent annually and, for medium-term cover, from 1.1 to 2.0 percent annually.

GUARANTEES. Eximbank provides guarantees to U.S. commercial banks covering up to 90 percent of the bank's commercial and political risk on purchases of foreign buyer medium-term (i.e., repayment terms of six months to five years) promissory notes which specify the terms and conditions of a specific export sale. The requirements, guidelines, and fees for Eximbank's guarantee are similar to those of FCIA's medium-term, individual buyer insurance.

Commercial banks participating in the medium-term guarantee program execute a Master Guarantee Agreement with Eximbank which specifies the terms and conditions of Eximbank's guarantee. Each guarantee is authorized in accordance with these stated terms and conditions. Prospective export deals requiring financing are first evaluated by the commercial bank. If the transaction is acceptable and if Eximbank's guarantee is desired then a formal application is submitted to Eximbank which will approve the request if there is a reasonable assurance of repayment.

The fee for the medium-term guarantee is paid by the U.S. bank and is based upon the term of the obligation as well as the exporter's retention requirement for the particular purchasing country. The commercial bank may retain up to 25 percent of the fee charges as payment for its own costs in executing each transaction. Generally, the exporter must retain 10 percent of the total credit risk (it may be higher for certain countries) and the foreign buyer must provide a cash payment of no less than 15 percent.

The bank guarantee and the FCIA insurance programs are mutually exclusive. If an exporter obtains FCIA insurance, Eximbank will not entertain a guarantee application from a bank for the same transaction.

Eximbank also guarantees repayment to U.S. commercial banks of medium-term revolving lines of credit that the banks have extended to financial institutions in developing countries. The lines of credit must be used by the foreign banks only for financing purchases of U.S. capital goods. The requirements, fees, and guidelines for these "bank-to-bank" guarantees are similar to those of the regular bank guarantee program.

Eximbank does not have a short-term guarantee program.

Foreign Freight Forwarders

The shipper of goods in foreign trade may book transportation through a *foreign freight forwarder,* who provides expert attention to details of shipping procedures, including documentation at origin and destination. The forwarder acts as an agent for the exporter in moving the cargo to the overseas destination. With few exceptions (air shipments, overland shipments to Canada, or shipments to Hawaii and Puerto Rico), it is recommended that a freight forwarder, licensed by the Federal Maritime Administration, move the cargo from the U.S. port of export. These agents are familiar with the import rules and regulations of foreign countries, methods of shipping, U.S. government export regulations, and foreign trade documents.

Besides handling paperwork such as the export declaration, dock receipts, ocean bill of lading, and delivery orders, the full service foreign freight forwarder also provides the shipper with routing and scheduling information, booked ocean cargo or air freight space, rates and related charges quoted in advance, advice on consular and licensing requirements, warehouse storage, and complete arrangements for smooth, safe delivery of goods to the overseas buyer. Further, the agent can arrange to have the merchandise packed at the export port or have it containerized. Agents may also consolidate shipments from different shippers in containers in order to lower the freight costs. Both large and small shippers find freight forwarders' services useful and well worth the fees normally charged.

Depending on the exporter's needs, a freight forwarder is also prepared to handle inland transportation of goods, both in this country and abroad, and forward banking collection papers. Some will even help arrange financing, check on potential markets, and assist in finding agents and customers. The fees charged are usually on a per shipment basis or are based on the value of the shipment and the services performed. An annual retainer arrangement is not uncommon. Many freight forwarders also act as custom house brokers.

Although most forwarders' rates and services will be competitive, some even regulated by federal law, it is recommended that several different bids be obtained as there may be some variations in price. (For a fair rate comparison, make certain that all of the services being compared are equal.)

Freight forwarders also may represent shippers on air freight shipments and perform many of the same services as they do for an ocean shipment because the procedures and documents involved in both modes of shipment are quite similar.

More than 1,500 freight forwarders, licensed by the Federal Maritime Commission and/or the Civil Aeronautics Board, are located throughout the country to serve exporters, as are the *estimated 3,000 custom house brokers,* who, licensed by the *Treasury Department,* serve as importers' agents in clearing goods through entry into this country.

Names, addresses, and advertising of freight forwarding concerns are obtainable from the following published sources, among others: *American Import/Export Bulletin; Brandon's Shipper and Forwarder; Custom House Guide*—listing forwarders in each U.S. port and forwarding agents in foreign countries; *Exporters' Encyclopedia*—listing freight forwarders and custom house brokers in leading cities; *Foreign Trade Marketplace;* and *Pacific Shipper.*

Consult also foreign trade bureaus of local chambers of commerce, banks in foreign trade, port authorities, and the National Customs Brokers and Forwarders Association of America.

See also subject heading: Custom House Brokers.

Foreign Marketing

Foreign marketing information helps determine which particular foreign markets offer an export potential and how it can be exploited. This includes, for example, information on foreign economic conditions and prospects; product and industry trends abroad; business customs and practices and trade laws and regulations in the various countries; the foreign government's overall trade policy and attitudes; and the sources and extent of market competition. While most such information is provided in published form, it can also be obtained in person from U.S. government country specialists or by writing the appropriate agency.

Although most intimate and effective knowledge of sales potential of particular types of goods may be gained through direct personal contact with conditions in foreign countries, there are many valuable sources of information available in the United States which may be utilized to great advantage in connection with analyses of markets for export.

Under this heading the aim is to point out certain sources of basic data which may be taken into consideration profitably in market analyses, covering such aspects as economic structure and conditions of foreign countries, general market characteristics, population and geographic peculiarities, standards of living, government and political structure, industry, finance, trade, etc.

Government contacts on this topic are the following: Foreign Agricultural Service, U.S. Department of Agriculture and the Foreign Commercial Service, U.S. Department of Commerce.

Information on foreign market conditions and trends is available from literally thousands of individual sources in the United States and abroad. In general, these can be grouped into five types of sources:

- Organizations providing specialized international business information services as their principal activity.
- The publishing industry—including the daily press, wire services, and periodicals covering international business developments generally, specific foreign countries or regions, or specific industry sectors.
- Commercial Services—banks, accounting firms, shipping and airline companies—which provide marketing information primarily as a sideline to increase use of the mainline export services.
- Business associations—such as chambers of commerce, trade and industry associations, world trade clubs and similar groups—whose membership services include newsletters or publications containing international business information.
- Foreign governments and international organizations issuing publications in the United States.

Among important general sources of published data in these fields, the following are of special value. Sources of more detailed information will be found elsewhere in this handbook.

- *Business America.*
- *Overseas Business Reports.*
- *Foreign Economic Trends.*
- *Country Sectoral Studies.*
- *Foreign Market Report Service.*
- *International Marketing Newsmemo Service.*

See also subject headings: Directories and Trade Lists; Exchange and Trade Controls, Foreign; Government Assistance; Trade Opportunities and Leads.

Foreign Trade Definitions and Commercial Abbreviations

The definition of terms used in foreign trade and their acceptance by both buyer and seller are vitally important if subsequent misunderstandings and disputes are to be avoided.

To help promote the necessary uniformity and standard practice in the use of trade terms, two sets of definitions have traditionally been used by traders. The *Revised American Foreign Trade Definitions—1941* were adopted that year by a U.S. Chamber of Commerce committee, the National Foreign Trade Council and the predecessor of the American Importers Association. An alternative, more up-to-date set known as INCOTERMS, was introduced in 1953 by the International Chamber of Commerce.

Confusion caused by the existence of two sets of terms and the need for further updating led to the adoption of a revised, consolidated set of trade terms, *INCOTERMS, 1980.* This set now is sponsored by a wide selection of business organizations, including the sponsors of the sets that it replaced:

- American Importers Association.
- Chamber of Commerce of the United States.
- National Association of Councils on International Banking.
- National Committee on International Trade Documentation.
- National Foreign Trade Council.
- U.S. Council of the International Chamber of Commerce.

Copies of *INCOTERMS, 1980* are available from the U.S. Council of the International Chamber of Commerce. Future editions of the

Dun & Bradstreet *Exporters' Encyclopedia* will also carry the new definitions.

Another area of trade procedures requiring uniformity in practice and understanding pertains to *documentary credits*. Since 1951, rules have been standardized and frequently updated by the International Chamber of Commerce. For the U.S. version, contact the U.S. Council of the International Chamber of Commerce for ICC publication No. 305, "Guide to Documentary Operations." A related publication, "Standard Forms for Issuing Documentary Credits," also is available as ICC document No. 323.

Sources of information on trade definitions, documentary credits, and on the numerous abbreviations used in international trade documentation include: *Exporters' Encyclopedia, Shippers' Digest* and *Custom House Guide*.

Among sources of information on interpretation of trade definitions, documentary credits and abbreviations are: field offices of the U.S. Department of Commerce, foreign trade departments of local and state chambers of commerce, foreign chambers of commerce in the United States, freight forwarders and custom house brokers and the international departments of banks.

Free Trade Areas, Customs Unions, Common Markets and Other Regional Groupings

Regional groupings differ in their economic organization and motivation. There are three basic kinds of organization for economic integration: free trade areas, customs unions and common markets.

Free Trade Areas

In a *free trade area* member countries agree to have free movement of goods among themselves, that is, no tariffs or quotas against goods coming from other members. The European Free Trade Association (EFTA), the Latin American Free Trade Area (LAFTA) and the New Zealand-Australia Free Trade Agreement (NAFTA) are the major examples in existence today.

European Free Trade Association (EFTA)

The *European Free Trade Association* is only partly a free trade area, as the members have agreed to free trade primarily in industrial goods. Agricultural products are still subject to many restrictions in trade among member countries. On the other hand, EFTA is somewhat more than a simple free trade area as members cooperate on other regulations and policies affecting trade, such as government procurement and antitrust policy.

EFTA was established in 1960 by the Stockholm Convention and provides for the gradual elimination of customs duties and other trade barriers among its members. Its membership declined from nine to seven on January 1, 1973, when the United Kingdom and Denmark joined the European Community. The remaining full members are Austria, Iceland, Norway, Portugal, Sweden, Switzerland, and one associate member, Finland, whose status is, for all practical purposes, the same as full membership.

Unlike the European Community (EC), members of EFTA retain their own individual tariffs against outside countries. On December 31, 1966, EFTA made the final internal tariff reduction on manufactured goods originating in EFTA countries. However, Portugal and Iceland are still gradually reducing tariffs on industrial goods. As part of an economic aid package to Portugal, the period of tariff elimination for some products has been extended for five years to December 31, 1984.

Selected EFTA publications: *Annual Report; EFTA Bulletin* (nine issues per year); *EFTA Trade* (annual statistical review); and *The European Free Trade Association—Structure, Rules and Operation*. EFTA publications are distributed free of charge. They can be obtained from EFTA Information Service, 9-11, rue de Varembe, CH-1211 Geneva 20/Switzerland.

Latin American Free Trade Area (LAFTA)

The *Latin American Free Trade Area* was established in 1961 by the Montevideo Treaty. Its primary goals were to reduce most tariff and trade barriers among the signatory countries by 1973. Indeed some expected it to become a full-fledged common market. In 1969, however, LAFTA members reassessed their association and drew up the Caracas Protocol, extending LAFTA's transitional period to 1980 when barriers to free trade among the member countries are to be dismantled. The agreement also slowed the tariff-reduction timetable and temporarily suspended certain aspects of the tariff-reduction program, once it became clear that member countries were unwilling to make the economic and political sacrifices necessary for further liberalization.

The Caracas Protocol was ratified and put into effect in late 1973. It called for negotiating a "new stage" of LAFTA integration, and meetings began in 1974 to deal with the trade liberalization program and reform of LAFTA's institutional structure. Today, LAFTA's principal activity, through a large staff and office complex in Montevideo, is the publication of trade information and the organization of meetings of various distinct industrial sectors to conclude complementation agreements. These agreements, which currently form the main area of movement in LAFTA, are first worked out by private industry to cut tariffs in a single field and only in those LAFTA countries which ratify them. There are 23 such agreements. LAFTA is composed of Argentina, Bolivia, Brazil, Chile, Colombia, Ecuador, Mexico, Paraguay, Peru, Uruguay and Venezuela. The official source of information on LAFTA is: the Comite Ejecutivo Permanante, Asociacion Latinoamericana de Libre Comercio, Cebollati 1461, Montevideo, Uruguay.

New Zealand-Australia Free Trade Agreement (NAFTA)

The *New Zealand-Australia Free Trade Agreement* was established in 1965-66 and was extended in 1976 for another ten years. The pact provides for the successive reduction and elimination of tariffs between the two countries and covers a wide variety of traded items.

Tariffs were reduced in five stages over an eight-year period with 20 percent of the tariff lifted at each stage.

Extensions of NAFTA schedules are made under an annual review system. Tariff reductions on these goods are also proceeding in five stages of 20 percent each. Currently, about 30 percent of trade between the two countries is covered by NAFTA, and two-way trade has increased from some $200 million in 1964-65 to in excess of $1 billion in 1979.

At a ministerial meeting in the spring of 1979, Australian and New Zealand leaders confirmed their faith in NAFTA's value in promoting expansion of trade between the two countries. Ministers agreed, however, that in today's circumstances the NAFTA agreement may have to be reviewed and new techniques of commercial cooperation established if the free trade area is to be significantly expanded. Business associations and others are being urged to probe and study how commercial activity between the two countries could be further extended.

Customs Unions

A *customs union* is similar to a free trade area in that it has no tariffs on trade among members. It goes beyond a free trade area, however, in its more ambitious requirement that members also have a uniform tariff on trade with nonmembers. Thus a customs union is like a single nation for trading purposes; it presents a united front—in effect yields commercial sovereignty—to the rest of the world with its common external tariff, rather than just reducing internal tariffs among a small number of member nations. A customs union is therefore more difficult to create than a free trade area, but its advantage lies in making the economic integration stronger and avoiding the administrative problems of a free trade area.

The leading example of a customs union is the European Community (EC). In July 1968, the EC achieved full customs union status, a goal it had been seeking since January 1, 1958. The Community endeavor has been slower but more far reaching than EFTA's, because it includes not only a free trade area among members but also a common external tariff and many other common policies. In addition, it covers agricultural products, which are omitted by EFTA. For more detailed information on the EC, see page 58.

Common Markets

A true *common market* includes a customs union but goes significantly beyond it. A common market seeks to standardize or harmonize all governmental regulations affecting trade. These include all aspects of government policy toward business—for example, corporation and excise taxes, labor laws, fringe benefits and social security programs, incorporation laws and antitrust laws. In such an economic union, business and trade decisions are based on geographic, cultural and market factors but would be unaffected by the national laws of different members because they would be uniform. The EC, besides its successful customs union, has established a common market with a common agricultural policy and made progress toward common policies for labor, antitrust law, excise taxes and transportation. Other examples of common markets include:

The Andean Common Market (ANCOM)

In 1967, six Andean countries—Bolivia, Chile, Colombia, Ecuador, Peru and Venezuela—agreed to the basic proposals for a subregional common market to accelerate their integration within the broader context of LAFTA. The plans were approved in principle by LAFTA and the Cartagena Agreement forming the *Andean Common Market* was signed by all of the six except Venezuela on May 26, 1969. Opposition by protectionist Venezuelan business groups held up that country's entry until December 1973. Chile withdrew from ANCOM in October 1976 in a disagreement over the group's foreign investment code and common outer tariff.

ANCOM is committed to reducing intra-regional tariffs on many products and to achieving a common external tariff. While intra-regional nontariff barriers have been theoretically eliminated, intra-regional tariff restraints on most goods remain in effect.

The ANCOM agreement emphasizes other aspects of integration besides trade. It calls for joint planning of major infrastructure and industrial investment, harmonization of economic policies and investment incentives, creation of multinational enterprises and common treatment of foreign capital and technology.

The principal source of information on ANCOM is the Junta de Acuerdo de Cartagena, Esquina Avenidas Paseo de la Republica y Andres Aramburu, Casilla 3237, Lima, Peru.

131

Caribbean Common Market (CARICOM)

The *Caribbean Common Market* was formed with the signing of the Treaty of Chaguaramas in 1973. The original signatories were Barbados, Guyana, Jamaica and Trinidad and Tobago. In 1974, eight smaller Caribbean nations signed the treaty, bringing the total membership to 12. The eight less developed countries of the region are Antigua, Belize, Dominica, Grenada, Montserrat, St. Kitts-Nevis-Anguilla, St. Lucia and St. Vincent.

CARICOM's stated objectives include: strengthening regional trade and economic relations; achieving increased, balanced development of the members; bolstering the members' economic independence of outside governments and institutions; coordinating foreign policy initiatives; and promoting functional cooperation among the region's institutions.

CARICOM is an outgrowth of the Caribbean Free Trade Association (CARIFTA) established in 1968. CARIFTA laid the groundwork for CARICOM by proposing such region-wide measures as a common outer tariff (COT) and the harmonization of fiscal incentives. CARICOM also has its roots in the East Caribbean Common Market (ECCM) created in 1968 by the less developed countries (LDCs). This agreement called for the establishment of a COT by mid-1971; harmonization of taxes, fiscal incentives and development plans; coordination of currency, financial and agricultural policies; cooperation in establishing improved transportation and communications; and elimination of customs duties and other restrictions among the signatories.

For more information write: CARICOM Secretariat, Bank of Guyana Building, P.O. Box 607, Georgetown, Guyana, South America.

Central American Common Market (CACM)

The *Central American Common Market* was established by the General Treaty of Central American Economic Integration, effective June 4, 1961. Its members are: Guatemala, El Salvador, Honduras, Nicaragua and Costa Rica. The CACM holds to ten bilateral agreements which exclude a number of commodities of Central American origin from immediate participation in the free arrangement. Provisions for a common external tariff are included.

During the early 1960s, CACM members had made notable progress toward their goal of achieving a customs union by substantially establishing a common external tariff. Integration within this economic area has been hampered, however, by slowdowns in growth rates, a serious border dispute between El Salvador and Honduras, conflict between Costa Rica and Nicaragua, and internal tensions in Nicaragua itself. Notwithstanding these difficulties, intra-regional trade continues to grow and makes up about one-fifth of the region's total world trade. For information contact: Secretaria Permanente de Tratado General de Integracion Economica Centro America, 4 Avenida 10-25, P.O. Box 1237, Guatemala City, Guatemala.

Other Regional Groupings

Council For Mutual Economic Assistance (CMEA)

The *Council for Mutual Economic Assistance* was founded in Moscow in January 1949, as a rival grouping to the Organization for European Economic Cooperation. The Soviets had rejected Marshall Plan aid, claiming the Anglo-American bloc opposed true East-West collaboration and discriminated against their former allies, and it was therefore necessary to "establish wider economic cooperation between the countries of people's democracy and the USSR," in the words of CMEA's inaugural communique. CMEA's original members were Bulgaria, Czechoslovakia, Hungary, Poland, Romania and the USSR. Albania and the German Democratic Republic joined soon after. In 1956, Yugoslovia and China assumed "observer" status, but since the early 1960s China (and Albania) have been inactive in CMEA.

Latin American Economic System (SELA)

The 1973–75 recession in the industrialized countries brought in its train a considerable reduction in exports from Latin America, thus revealing the region's vulnerability to the foreign trade sector and its dependency on the outside. The negative effects of this dependency dramatized the need for vigorous regional action toward third countries and in international forums, as well as common, coordinated positions and greater economic cooperation within the area.

Thus, Latin America's search for new mechanisms to permit joint development of their economies and maximize the rational exploitation of the region's vast human, natural, financial and technological resources, led to the creation of the *Latin American Economic System* in October 1975, with the signing of the Panama Convention by the 25 independent countries existing in Latin America at that time. In April 1978, Surinam announced its intention to adhere to the Panama Convention. The Convention established an organizational structure through which a wide range of cooperative activities can be pursued, provided there is the political will to do so and concrete projects have been identified. One of the SELA's innovations is that for cooperative work, unanimous agreement by member countries is not required. A joint program may be undertaken if three member countries agree.

SELA's work covers two main aspects. The first is consultation and coordination among the countries of Latin America, for the formulation of common strategies and positions on economic and social matters *vis-a-vis* third countries, groups of countries and in international forums. Second is the promotion of regional cooperation in all fields, including support for regional economic integration. These two aspects are closely intertwined, since much cooperative action implies the adoption of a position in international relations and, in turn, the success of such action calls for joint support strategies. One example is the creation of mechanisms and forms of partnership in defense of the prices and markets of raw materials.

One of SELA's more significant efforts is the promotion of Latin American Multinational Enterprises, which can be constituted with government, quasi-government, private or mixed capital with the sole condition that each state shall guarantee the national nature of such capital. This structure makes it possible to obtain private national capital and allows the member states to participate in accordance with the peculiarities of their own social and economic organization and in keeping with the policies they are pursuing as regards the treatment of national capital.

Association of Southeast Asian Nations (ASEAN)

The *Association of Southeast Asian Nations* was established in Bangkok in 1967 at a meeting of the foreign ministers of the five member nations—Thailand, Indonesia, Malaysia, the Philippines and Singapore. ASEAN's goal is to accelerate economic growth, social progress and cultural development and to promote peace, prosperity and stability in the Southeast Asian region. ASEAN projects concern economic cooperation and development; the intensification of regional trade, both internal and with the rest of the world; joint research and technological programs; educational exchanges; cooperation in transport and communications;

the promotion of tourism and Southeast Asian studies; maintaining close and beneficial cooperation with existing international and regional organizations; and cultural, scientific and administrative exchanges. General publication: *ASEAN Journal*.

Government Assistance

As a major component of the policy to alleviate the country's trade deficits, the U.S. government is making a concerted effort to help American business expand exports. All government agencies provide assistance to U.S. business. In particular, the Department of Commerce provides a wide variety of services to inform exporters about foreign markets and sales opportunities overseas and to assist them in achieving their marketing goals abroad:

Information Services—
- Agent/Distributor Service.
- Business Counseling.
- Export Mailing List Service.
- Office of Country Marketing.
- Trade Complaints Assistance.
- Trade Opportunities Program.
- Minority Business Export Assistance Program.
- World Traders Data Reports.

Marketing Services—
- Trade Fairs.
- Business Sponsored Promotions.
- Catalog Exhibitions.
- Video/Catalog Exhibitions.
- East-West Business Assistance.
- Export Development Center Exhibitions.
- Foreign Buyer Program.
- Major Export Projects.
- New Product Information Service.
- Product Marketing Service.
- Tailored Export Marketing Plan Service.
- Trade Missions/Seminar Missions.

Following are detailed a few of the above-mentioned services provided by the Department of Commerce.

Office of Country Marketing

The *Office of Country Marketing* (OCM) develops expertise on commercial matters for the free world countries, counsels and assists U.S. business with commercial and marketing information on these countries, develops Country Commercial Programs governing the U.S. government's utilization of its commercial resources; programs and plans overseas trade promotion activities; and coordinates all ITA activity on the Near East.

The Office of Country Marketing consists of the following units: Office of the Director; European Division; Latin America Division; Asia/Africa Division; and Commerce Action Group for the Near East (CAGNE).

The Office of the Director plans and formulates the execution of OCM's programs, directs the collection and analysis of foreign market information, and guides and coordinates scheduling of overseas trade promotion events to be implemented by the Office of Export Promotion.

Each regional division facilitates trade between the United States and its specified countries and areas:
- Monitoring information on marketing developments/commercial information, and maintaining in-depth marketing expertise on individual countries.

- Providing counseling to U.S. firms on overseas business opportunities and assisting them in expanding their sales to specific markets abroad. Responding to specific letter, visit, and telephone inquiries for country marketing information.
- Preparing a broad range of publications on foreign commercial conditions, laws, regulations, tariff structures, etc.; best prospects for export sales; trade outlooks and other appropriate country data.
- For each major trading partner, preparing an annual Country Commercial Program which plans the utilization of State/Commerce resources in each country.
- Participating in exporting seminars and supporting other domestic export stimulation activities.
- In support of ITA's overseas trade promotion responsibility, identifying and recommending the most suitable product/industry themes to be promoted in a particular market; in consultation with other offices, selecting and scheduling overseas trade promotion events; and preparing market plans for these events.
- Providing support for recommendations on Foreign Service economic/commercial staffing levels and other Foreign Service-related issues.
- Serving as liaison with the regional and country desk officers at State, Treasury and other U.S. government agencies on ITA activities related to specific geographic areas.

The Commerce Action Group for the Near East (CAGNE) supports U.S. business efforts to take advantage of the commercial opportunities in the Near East and North Africa. In addition to the above activities of the regional divisions, CAGNE is responsible for developing information on upcoming major development projects in the Near East and North Africa and bringing these projects to the attention of American firms. The staff works with U.S. bidders to assist them in developing their marketing strategies and to maximize their chances of winning the contract awards for these projects. CAGNE also serves as the Commerce coordinator for the Department's participation in the bilateral joint commissions which the United States has established with six Near East/North African countries.

Office of Export Marketing Assistance

1. *Minority Business Export Assistance Program*

As part of the National Export Policy, the Minority Business Export Assistance Program (MBEAP) is designed to provide assistance to export-capable minority firms interested in selling products and services abroad.

In addition to providing general assistance to minority firms, conducting seminars geared to minority business, etc., the MBEAP, with funding from the Minority Business Development Agency, offers a total assistance plan to qualified export-capable minority firms. This plan includes:
- Preparing a Tailored Export Marketing Plan that determines the country markets which are the major users of the company's products or services.
- Familiarizing company with basic mechanics of exporting.
- Performing initial market testing in target countries.
- Initiating identification and evaluation of prospective representation in target countries.
- Allowing company to travel to one or more target market countries and to participate in an international trade show.

- Providing for subscriptions to various Department of Commerce publications and services.
- Designating a trade specialist from the Commerce District Office nearest a participating company, along with a carefully selected "pilot" firm experiment in the same field, to give personal counseling on a continuing basis.

Tailored Export Marketing Plan Service

The Tailored Export Marketing Plan Service (TEMPS) provides custom prepared and documented marketing plans designed for specific companies or industry groups identified as particularly motivated and capable of exporting but which either are not exporting or exporting at less than their full potential. Prospective users of this service are generally identified by District Office trade specialists working within and familiar with their local business communities.

TEMPS provides the company with a basic strategy for exporting: market identification for the company's products and fundamental management guidance in the planning of a foreign marketing program and in its implementation, through education, preparatory work and follow-through.

Once the Export Marketing Plan has been accepted by the client company, TEMPS and U.S. Department of Commerce District Office personnel follow up on a regular basis to offer encouragement and assistance. This consultation is continued until the client company feels it is sufficiently established to continue exporting on a regular basis without further specialized assistance. The cost of this service is $350.

New Product Information Service

The New Product Information Service (NPIS) is a free export promotion program offered by the U.S. Department of Commerce to help American companies publicize the availability of new U.S. products in foreign markets and to test market interest in a particular new product. Specifically, this service is designed to encourage foreign companies to contact American manufacturers regarding new products, thus providing trade leads which result in the American supplier exporting foreign buyer interest and frequently making sales and establishing overseas agents.

Through NPIS, promotional descriptions (with selected photographs) of new products are obtained for publication in *Commercial News USA*, a Department of Commerce publication which is distributed to 240 U.S. diplomatic and consular posts around the world. The posts then excerpt items on products relevant to the local foreign market and reprint them in the post "commercial newsletters" in a format and language appropriate to the local business community.

NPIS participation criteria are available upon request.

Business Counseling

The Business Counseling service provides U.S. industry with information and counseling on a wide range of export services available both from the public and private sectors. Like Department of Commerce District Offices located throughout the country, the Counseling unit is designed to serve as a point for first contact for businesses which are interested in exporting, but which are not sure if or where assistance can be obtained. Further, it acts as a conduit through which District Offices can direct inquirers to appropriate specialists in Washington. The Counseling service also includes the Export Information Reference Room (EIRR), and shortly will also maintain the International Marketing Information Center (IMIC).

The major purpose of the business counseling service is to respond expeditiously to telephone, visitor or letter inquiries about available export assistance and to match services with each particular need. Counselors can provide literature describing U.S. government export services and the advantages of exporting; can discuss a company's particular export-related needs; and, based on these discussions, can refer inquirers to officials providing particular services. Whenever possible, appointments with appropriate international trade specialists are arranged for those inquiring in person.

The Export Information Reference Room is a centralized source of information on major foreign projects. It embraces the most timely data available on proposed and ongoing projects, drawing upon reports from Foreign Service posts, multilateral development banks and other sources. The International Marketing Information Center will be an archive of market research sponsored by the Commerce Department on export opportunities for various U.S. industries in the most promising foreign markets. Materials in both the EIRR and the IMIC are available for review on a personal visit basis only; visitors interested in purchasing specific documents will be referred to the appropriate office.

Trade Complaints Assistance

The Trade Complaints Assistance program works to resolve disputes between U.S. sellers and foreign purchasers. U.S. firms experiencing trade problems should bring supporting materials to their area District Office; after screening and transmittal by officials in Washington, the appropriate U.S. embassy or consulate then investigates the dispute in an effort to restore amicable business relations. Assistance is limited to friendly representation. No judgement is rendered and no legal authority can be applied.

Types of trade complaints handled include alleged noncompliance with specifications; merchandise quality; payment and/or delivery terms; nonlegal questions on contractual obligations; misrepresentation or misunderstanding of facts; and claims of agents, distributors or dealers against principals (and vice versa), etc. The service is not available for noncommercial disputes, strict collection problems, complaints involving transactions of minor cash value and for any dispute that is already being handled through legal channels.

This program also offers a trade facilitation service, designed to foster better communications between trading partners. Through Foreign Service commercial officers, prospective foreign customers may request, for example, the name of a U.S. manufacturer of a specific product or the holder of a particular patent. Both American and foreign firms may also use this service to restore direct communications with their trading partners.

For more information on the above program services contact the nearest U.S. Department of Commerce District Office or write the Deputy Assistant Secretary for Export Development, International Trade Administration; the Assistant Secretary for Trade Development or Foreign Commercial Service, U.S. Department of Commerce, Washington, D.C. 20230.

See also: *15 Ways the U.S. Department of Commerce Can Help Make Your Business More Profitable Through Ex-*

ports published by the Commerce Department.

Trading Channels

Differing methods are employed by American manufacturing exporters and by importing manufacturers, wholesalers and retailers in the sale or purchase of goods abroad.

Many U.S. manufacturers prefer to sell directly through their own established export departments or companies, dealing firsthand with customers or other outlets abroad. Others conduct their business less directly, dealing through export merchants, commission houses or purchasing agencies or make arrangements for export with combination export managers or through export trade associations.

Importing manufacturers or wholesale and retail merchants also generally have the choice of purchasing directly or employing differing types of intermediaries.

Discussions of principal channels for the conduct of foreign trade may be found in *International Trade Handbook*.

Among listings of the various types of exporting and importing intermediaries in the United States, with data concerning their businesses, the following is suggested: *American Register of Exporters and Importers*.

For information concerning the Webb-Pomerene Act or export trade associations operating under the Export Trade Act of 1918, apply to the Federal Trade Commission, Washington, D.C. See: *Foreign Commerce and the Antitrust Laws* and *Practice and Procedure Under the Webb-Pomerene Export Trade Act*. See also subject headings: Webb-Pomerene Act, page 98; Trade Opportunities and Leads; and Directories and Trade Lists.

Trade Opportunities and Leads

Notices of foreign *trade opportunities,* both in export and import, are carried regularly in many periodic publications. They give general information regarding firms or individuals in foreign countries expressing an interest in buying or selling in the United States, business interests abroad wishing to represent American firms in their countries, and foreign business representatives visiting the United States seeking purchases in this country or markets here for their own goods.

The Department of Commerce's *Trade Opportunities Program* furnishes U.S. business firms with detailed opportunities for direct sales to overseas buyers—private and governmental—and notices of foreign companies offering to represent U.S. firms overseas. Firms subscribing to the program are automatically sent sales leads as they are telexed to the Trade Opportunities Program computer in Washington from more than 200 overseas American embassies and consulates. In addition, a firm can also subscribe to a weekly bulletin compiling all trade opportunities received from overseas posts called the *Weekly Trade Opportunities Bulletin,* which publishes all trade opportunities processed during the week. The Bulletin sells for $100 per year and presently has over 1,500 subscribers. Also, a computer tape containing all trade opportunities received is prepared biweekly.

Among other outstanding sources of information of this kind, the following are suggested: *American Import and Export Bulletin; Business America; Country Market Sectoral Surveys; Foreign Economic Trends Reports; Global Market Surveys: Index to Foreign Market Reports; Index to Trade Lists; Journal of Commerce; Overseas Business Reports;* and *Overseas Export Promotion Calendar.*

Consult also Bureau of Export Development district offices of the Department of Commerce; foreign departments of banks;

foreign trade bureaus of local chambers of commerce; foreign chambers of commerce in the United States; American chambers of commerce abroad; and publishers of export business magazines.

See also subject headings: Trading Channels; Directories and Trade Lists; and Foreign Marketing.

International sales *leads* are unsolicited business proposals or inquiries received by a U.S. supplier from a prospective foreign purchaser. These leads may enable the U.S. fiirm to make an export sale to a customer not previously known.

Almost all manufacturing organizations with international involvement receive sales leads from their connections overseas. If the lead is of specific interest to the receiving firm, it will be followed. If not, it may be passed on to another interested firm.

Many nonmanufacturing organizations with international interests also receive and disseminate sales leads. They include banks, foreign embassies, port authorities, state organizations, chambers of commerce, trade associations, export management companies, international financial institutions, mercantile agencies and commercial carriers. These organizations, for the most part, distribute the leads to their customers or associates free of charge, in the hopes of obtaining recognition which will benefit their principal commercial activity. No known organization has, as its primary function, the development and distribution of international sales leads.

See publication: "A Survey of Business Needs and Export Marketing (Federal and Nonfederal Sources of Assistance)," published by the office of Export Planning and Evaluation, Bureau of Export Development, U.S. Department of Commerce.

Imports, Entry of

Shipments of merchandise from foreign countries to persons or businesses in the United States, by sea or air or across continental boundaries, and whether subject to duty or free of duty, come under control of the United States Customs Service and are released only after compliance with certain procedures.

The powers and duties vested in the Secretary of the Treasury pertaining to U.S. import regulations and the entry of merchandise procedures are administered by the U.S. Customs Service, Office of Regulations and Rulings. The service cooperates with other agencies in enforcing the preventive, sanitary, and other laws relating to merchandise brought into the country.

The process of making proper clearance of imported goods in many cases are detailed and complex, involving technicalities which require expert knowledge. Most importing concerns which do not maintain offices or experienced personnel at ports of entry find it advisable to utilize customs house brokers.

Various kinds of information helpful in understanding customs organization and procedures are found in the following publications:

- *Customs Bulletin.* Weekly pamphlet containing current amendments to Customs Regulations and decisions of U.S. Customs Court and U.S. Court of Customs and Patent Appeals. Price: $65 a year; foreign mailing $16.25 additional. Single copy: $1.30 each.
- *Customs Regulations of the United States.* Looseleaf volume (over 500 pages) of regulations for carrying out customs, navigation, and other laws administered by the United States Customs Service. 1976 reprint includes amended text

in Revised Pages Nos. 1 through 159. Price: $37 which includes subscription to Revised Pages; foreign mailing $9 additional. Renewal subscription to revised pages only beginning with 159, $29; foreign mailing $7 additional.

- *Customs Rulings on Imports.* Explains how importers may obtain a binding U.S. Customs duty ruling on items before importation.
- *Exporting to the United States.* A 100-page booklet for foreign exporters planning to ship goods to the U.S. Price: $2.50.
- *Import Quota.* Summary of information on import quotas administered by the United States Customs Service.
- *Marking of Country of Origin.* Customs requirements for marking imported merchandise with name of country of origin. Price: 40 cents.
- *Tariff Schedules of the United States.* Available from the International Trade Commission or the Superintendent of Documents, U.S. Government Printing Office.
- *U.S. Import Requirements.* General information of U.S. Customs requirements for imported merchandise. Available from Customs. Free.
- *807 Guide.* General information for importers/exporters on use of Item 807.00 TSUS which permits a reduced duty treatment for the value of components manufactured in the United States and assembled abroad.

A valuable compendium of information of many types regarding U.S. Customs and matters related to import is *Custom House Guide.* The *American Import and Export Bulletin,* issued monthly, supplements the *Guide* and keeps it up to date.

On questions relating to entry, consult: U.S. Customs Service, 1301 Constitution Avenue, N.W., Washington, D.C. 20229; American Importers Association, 11 West 42nd Street, New York, New York 10036; U.S. International Trade Commission; and International Trade Administration, U.S. Department of Commerce.

See also subject headings: Custom House Brokers; Tariffs, United States; Foreign Trade Zones; and other Import headings.

Imports, Importance of

Imports by the United States of numerous raw materials and semi-manufactures from foreign sources are essential to fill its needs for goods not produced domestically or produced in insufficient quantity. Many other types of goods requiring special craftsmanship or other foreign methods of production find extensive markets in the United States.

Imports also help to control price pressures by introducing an additional element of competition into the market place. Imports, therefore, help to provide consumers with the broadest possible range of goods at competitive prices. In the process, imports also provide workers with significant job opportunities in distribution, sales and service.

U.S. purchases from the many foreign countries that buy American exports enable them to earn the foreign exchange necessary to continue purchasing American goods. In this way imports help the U.S. to export a growing amount of domestic products and, thereby, provide jobs for millions of American workers. It is estimated that in 1976 at least six million U.S. jobs were directly or indirectly related to import and export trade.

Among publications with data on the significance of U.S. import trade, the following are suggested: *American Imports; Im-*

port Bulletin; and *The Annual Report of the President of the United States on Trade Agreements Programs.*

The International Trade Administration, U.S. Department of Commerce, maintains special facilities for fostering and promoting U.S. import trade through direct services to importers; close co-operative relations with diplomatic posts abroad, chambers of commerce, and domestic importers' organizations; publishing trade opportunities; and assisting foreign visitors and other foreign interests in understanding U.S. markets.

Private organizations for foreign trade are active in the study of balance of trade matters and improvements in customs proce-dures and technicalities which affect the volume of import trade.

The principal association of importers in the United States is the American Importers Association.

See also subject headings: Balance of International Payments, United States; Tariffs, United States; and other Import headings.

Imports, Sources of

The United States imports merchandise from all parts of the world. *Imports* consist principally of raw materials, crude foodstuffs and semi-manufactured goods, generally for further fabrication, al-though manufactured goods of numerous kinds also find a ready market in this country.

Among publications indicating countries of origin for U.S. imports or potential sources for supply of foreign goods, the fol-lowing are suggested: *American Register of Exporters and Im-porters, Import Bulletin* and *Index to Trade Lists.*

Many references to information on foreign countries given under the major heading Foreign Marketing will be helpful also in understanding their potentialities as suppliers of import goods.

Data concerning fairs, exhibitions and trade missions in for-eign countries and foreign products exhibitions in the United States may be obtained from the Office of Export Promotion, U.S. De-partment of Commerce.

Consult also: U.S. International Trade Commission; Bureau of International Economic Policy and Research, U.S. Department of Commerce; American Importers Association; American cham-bers of commerce abroad; and foreign chambers of commerce in the United States.

See subject headings: Directories and Trade Lists; Trade Opportunities and Leads; and other Import headings.

Investment Abroad, Private Capital

Investment of U.S. capital abroad is related to the level and pattern of U.S. trade and often supplements or complements U.S. exports. One of the major reasons for U.S. *investment abroad* traditionally has been to preserve access to foreign markets from which U.S. companies would otherwise have been excluded by the import restrictions of foreign governments or by a disparity in product costs. In establishing operations abroad, U.S. investors boost pro-duction, exports and employment in the United States and make positive contributions to our balance-of-payments.

International investment also contributes to economic effi-ciency by transferring productive resources from places where they are relatively plentiful to places where they are scarce. Not only is U.S. private investment (now totaling $180 billion) the world's largest single source of capital for development, but it also brings technology and managerial expertise that may be un-available from other capital sources. Therefore, it serves as a vital addition to other forms of resource transfer, including government-sponsored capital development and technical assistance programs.

In order to respond to increased concerns regarding multinational enterprises and to create a framework that recognizes and fosters foreign direct investment's positive contribution to economic growth, the OECD countries in 1976 promulgated an *International Investment Declaration,* which incorporates guidelines for multinational corporations and two intergovernmental agreements dealing with national treatment and the use of investment incentives and disincentives. In November 1977, the International Labor Organization approved a declaration of principles on industrial relations and social policy. In addition, various other UN organizations are formulating a variety of agreements, including a code of conduct relating to transnational corporations, principles relating to the transfer of technology, a code covering restrictive business practices and a treaty banning illicit payments. The U.S. government is also contemplating negotiating bilateral investment protection agreements that delineate the rights and obligations of both host countries and foreign investors.

For information on the character and extent of American private investment in foreign countries, and consideration of the problems and opportunities involved, see the following:

- *Directory of American Firms Operating in Foreign Countries.*
- *Foreign Investment in The Third World: A Comparative Study of Selected Developing Country Investment Promotion Programs,* U.S. Chamber of Commerce, 1980.
- *Investment Incentive Programs in Western Europe,* published by the International Division of the Chamber of Commerce of the United States, 1978.
- "Coping with New Challenges to Investment Ventures Abroad," *Commerce America,* July 3, 17, 1978.
- *The Multinational Corporation: Studies in U.S. Foreign Investment, Volumes 1 & 2,* March 1972, U.S. Department of Commerce.
- *Survey of Current Business* (various issues).
- "U.S. Foreign Direct Investment: Shifting Patterns of the Seventies," *The International Essays for Business Decision Makers,* Vol. IV, October, 1979.

Sources of Assistance and Information. Information for potential investors and licensors is available from the Department of Commerce. A wide range of current and periodically updated information is provided by the Department's publications, including the biweekly *Business America, Overseas Business Reports, Trade Lists* and *World Trade Directory Reports.*

American companies considering overseas investment may find helpful U.S.-based organizations representing foreign countries. They are able to provide a wide range of services to facilitate investment in their countries. Current information on the economy, sources of finance, taxes, and investment incentives is available from these offices. In addition, they can identify potential local participants and assist business executives planning visits to their countries by making referrals to appropriate government and industry officials.

Organizations dealing on a multinational basis, such as the Overseas Private Investment Corporation (OPIC), can provide finance, legal and technical assistance and, in the case of OPIC, investment insurance for certain ventures. OPIC also deals with less developed countries on a worldwide basis. Companies with well-developed potential investment projects may wish to discuss them with these organizations. Consult also the International Finance Corporation (IFC), whose activities are limited to member countries. For investment information on specific countries, inquiries should be directed to the country's embassy in Washington, D.C., or its consular offices. Also contact: U.S. embassies, consulates general and consulates during exploratory visits in countries of investment or licensing interests; chambers of commerce, trade associations and industry organizations; foreign departments of private banking institutions; private foreign investment counseling entities; international marketing research and advertising agencies; and other U.S. investors or licensors in the foreign area of interest.

Investment, Foreign Direct in the United States

U.S. companies and land have become increasingly attractive to foreign investors for a variety of reasons, especially the depreciation of the dollar *vis-a-vis* other major currencies and a decline in U.S. production costs relative to those other industrial countries. Consequently, *foreign direct investment in the United States* has undergone rapid expansion over the past several years, and is now valued at some $34 billion. According to the Department of Commerce's definition, foreign direct investment includes ownership of 10 percent or more of the voting securities of a U.S. concern.

Investment from abroad is an important source of needed capital and technology; it creates additional jobs for Americans and contributes to a favorable U.S. balance-of-payments position. The basic U.S. policy toward foreign investors in the United States is "national treatment," that is, to admit them freely and to treat them on the basis of equality with domestic investors in their U.S. operations. Foreign investors consequently are offered no special incentives to attract them to the United States and, with few exceptions, they are confronted with no special barriers. This policy, which has prevailed since the nation's inception, is consistent with the overall dedication of the United States to free and fair competition from all sources.

There are certain exceptions to this open-door policy. Federal legislation imposes limited restrictions on foreign investment in certain sectors of the economy which have a fiduciary character, relate to the national interest or involve the exploitation of natural resources. Important sectors affected include radio communications, nuclear energy, hydroelectric power, mining on federal lands, domestic air transport and coastal and inland shipping. These restrictions are generally accepted internationally as appropriate exceptions to national treatment. In addition, some states impose restrictions on foreign investment, particularly in banking, insurance and land ownership.

After entry, foreign-owned firms generally have the same rights and responsibilities under the law as U.S. firms. Federal and state laws, regulations and programs include such fields as general corporate law, federal securities and antitrust law, transportation, communications, energy and natural resources, banking and insurance, taxation and land law. State and local investment incentives are equally available to foreign and domestic firms. Foreign companies producing in the United States are permitted to compete for procurement by U.S. government agencies, subject to clearance procedures involving classified contract activity. Environmental requirements also are enforced on a nondiscriminatory basis.

In recent years, questions have been raised nationally whether foreign investments are sufficiently monitored and whether some may be adverse to the national interest. A number of events have contributed to this trend, including a substantially increased rate of growth in foreign investment in the United States, the emergence of new countries as actual or potential sources of such investment, the acquisition by foreign firms of a number of U.S. companies, the enormous increase in dollars held abroad that are available for foreign investment and increased foreign interest in acquiring U.S. natural resources, especially land.

Heightened concern about foreign investment in the United States began in 1972 and 1973 when West European and Japanese investors turned to U.S. agriculture, seeking a stable country and a means of diversifying their investment holdings. This concern increased in 1974 as petroleum prices rose rapidly and countries producing and exporting oil began to accumulate substantial amounts of additional funds that could be used to purchase goods and services, as well as to make investments in other countries. Numerous proposals were introduced in the Congress to study and monitor the flow of foreign investment in the United States.

In 1974, an act focusing directly on foreign investment, the *Foreign Investment Study Act of 1974,* called for identification, investigation and analysis by the Commerce and Treasury Departments of foreign direct investment and foreign portfolio investment in the United States. In 1976, the *International Investment Survey Act of 1976* continued the benchmark survey that had been conducted in the late 1960s and expanded the scope of data collection by paying greater attention to inward flows of investment into the United States, as well as to U.S. direct investment abroad.

The Commerce and Treasury reports to the Congress, in eleven volumes, are available from the U.S. Government Printing Office. Because the reports are extensive and cover various topics, readers will probably desire to be selective. The following is a listing of volume titles and highlights of the contents.

- *Foreign Direct Investment in the United States Report to the Congress of the United States,* prepared by the U.S. Department of Commerce, *April 1976.*

    Volume I: Report of the Secretary of Commerce to the Congress Summary Volume and Recommendations (by the Department of Commerce Staff)

    Investment Perspectives

    Benchmark Survey of Foreign Direct Investment in the United States, 1974

    Industrial and Geographic Concentration of Foreign Investment

    Reasons for Foreign Direct Investment

    Financing, Accounting and Financial Reporting

    Management and Employment Practices

    U.S. Policies, Laws and Regulations Concerning Inward Investment

    Taxation and Foreign Direct Investment

    Policies, Laws and Regulations of Other Major Industrialized Nations Concerning Inward Investment

    Foreign Investment in Land

    Technology Transfers Associated with Inward Foreign Investment

    Economic Effects

    Data Collection of Foreign Direct Investment

    Conclusions and Recommendations

The Foreign Investment Study Act of 1974
Volume II: Report of the Secretary of Commerce: Bench-
mark Survey, 1974 (by the Bureau of Economic
Analysis, U.S. Department of Commerce)
Classification of Data
Table 1 List of Countries and Selected Data
by Country
Table 2 List of Industries and Selected Data
by Industry

As it does each year between major surveys, the Department of Commerce is now updating its nine-volume 1976 study of foreign direct investment in the United States. The survey consists of aggregate statistical data only—there is no disclosure on a company-by-company or country-by-country basis.

Over 40 pieces of legislation have been introduced since 1976, with the predominant concern being foreign purchases of U.S. farmland and, to a lesser extent, foreign interest in U.S. banking activities. The special task of gauging the level of this farmland investment has been left to the Department of Agriculture under the Agriculture Investment Disclosure Act of 1978. For the foreseeable future, foreign investment in the United States probably will become subject to more elaborate reporting requirements and certain restrictions could be placed on foreign acquisitions in banking and farmland. However, the enormous size and strength of the U.S. economy should enable it to absorb large amounts of foreign investment without any harmful effects on the nation's economic, political or social structure. U.S. legislation and policy pertaining to foreign investment in America therefore should remain relatively unrestrictive in the coming years.

For additional information to foreign direct investment see: Bibliography.

Marking

In export trade, special attention should be given to regulations regarding the *marking* or *labeling* of merchandise and also to approved methods of marking external shipping containers.

Most countries, including the United States, have strict regulations requiring that imported merchandise bear an indication of the country of origin. Failure to comply with such regulations may subject the importer to fines or to detention of the goods until proper marking has been made.

On this point, country requirements are carried also in *Exporters' Encyclopedia* and current supplements.

Approved methods of marking symbols, weights, numbers, cautions, etc., on outside shipping cases or containers also should be followed for protection and to prevent unnecessary delay or loss. Consult *Exporters' Encyclopedia* and foreign freight forwarders, steamship companies or airlines for more information.

Marking requirements of U.S. customs in respect to imported goods are contained in the *Federal Code of Regulations,* Section 19, Part 134, "Country of Origin Marking;" the *Customs Regulations of the U.S.* in *Custom House Guide,* also describes required marking procedures.

Specific information can also be obtained from U.S. customs attaches or representatives stationed abroad, from American consular offices, or from the Commissioner of Customs, Washington, D.C. 20229.

Publications on marking include:
* *Exporting to the United States* (U.S. Customs Service).
* *Marking Digest* (U.S. Customs Service).
* *Marking of Country of Origin on U.S. Imports.*

See also subject headings: Packing; Ocean Shipping.

Ocean Shipping

Ocean transportation is an integral part of the whole system of international trade. By far the largest proportion of the export and import trade of the United States is handled by ocean-going vessels.

Among publications dealing with principles, practices and technicalities of *ocean shipping,* the following are suggested: *American Shipper; Brandon's Shipper & Forwarder; Fairplay Shipper Weekly; Lloyd's Shipping Economist; Marine Digest; Marine Engineering/Log; Marine Week; Maritime Reporter; Pacific Shipper; Seatrade;* and *Traffic World.*

The principal associations of American shipowners and operators in the United States foreign trade are: American Institute of Merchant Shipping, 1625 K Street, N.W., Suite 1000, Washington, D.C. 20006; American Maritime Association, 17 Battery Place North, Room 944-952, New York, New York 10004; Council of American-Flag Ship Operators, 1625 K Street, Suite 1200, Washington, D.C. 20006; and Federation of American-Controlled Shipping, 25 Broadway, New York, New York 10004.

Chief agencies of the U.S. government with regulatory or other functions relating to ships, ocean shipping and marine matters are: Maritime Administration; U.S. Department of Commerce; U.S. Coast Guard and Office of Maritime Affairs, Federal Maritime Commission; Department of Transportation; the Customs Service, Department of the Treasury; and Office of Maritime Affairs, Department of State.

An international agency associated with the United Nations, the Inter-Governmental Maritime Consultative Organization (IMCO), has as its purpose the promotion of international cooperation in maritime navigation, encouragement of the maximum use of safety measures, environmental protection and the removal of governmental restrictions and discriminations.

For current news and developments in the ocean shipping field, consult leading maritime and shipping journals listed in the bibliography under periodicals. An annual American Merchant Marine Conference is sponsored by the Propeller Club of the United States, 1730 M Street, N.W., Washington, D.C. 20036, proceedings of which are available in leading libraries.

See also subject headings: Steamship Services; Chartering; Foreign Freight Forwarders; Ports and Port Facilities.

Chartering

Under certain circumstances where shipping is in large volume, producers, manufacturers, exporters and importers find it advantageous to charter steamships. The contract between the shipowner and the person or firm chartering it is known as a charter party. Usually contracts are for a specific number of voyages or for a definite period of time.

In chartering ships, traders frequently operate through ship brokers. Lists of ship brokers are summarized in the Port Section of the *Custom House Guide*. Principal U.S. associations of shipowners are listed under the subject heading Ocean Shipping.

For information on specific questions in chartering, consult the Maritime Administration, Department of Commerce; local chambers of commerce with foreign trade services; and the Association of Ship Brokers and Agents, 17 Battery Place, New York, New York 10004.

See also references under subject headings: Ocean Shipping; Steamship Services.

Ports and Port Facilities, United States

Chambers of commerce and port authorities of most U.S. port cities are in a position to supply data describing facilities and services for export and import business or are able to answer inquiries on specific points. Railroad traffic bureaus, foreign freight forwarders and local chambers of commerce with foreign trade services also are good sources of information.

Three of the most convenient published summaries of information on American ports and their facilities and services are contained in:

- *Ports of the World 1979*. Port authorities, facilities, accommodations, navigation approaches, ship repair, towage, pilotage, charges and bunkers.
- *Custom House Guide*. Activities, facilities, charges, customs officials, port authorities, chambers of commerce and directory of the shipping and allied trades.
- *Exporters' Encyclopedia*. Ports and facilities, steamship companies, freight forwarders and customs brokers.

News items and developments relating to ports of the United States are carried in many journals in the marine and ocean shipping fields.

See the Bibliography under periodicals.

Government agencies having special functions in connection with port activity, service or protection are: U.S. Customs Service, the United States Coast Guard and the Maritime Administration within the Department of Commerce.

Port authorities are organized nationally in the American Association of Port Authorities, 1612 K Street, N.W., Washington, D.C. 20006.

See also subject headings: Foreign-Trade Zones; Ocean Shipping; and Air Transport.

Steamship Services

A number of periodicals and yearbooks used generally by foreign traders carry directories or special departments which give the names of steamship companies and their agents, steamship company advertising and in many cases schedules of sailings with information as to dates of departure, types of cargo, destinations, ports of call and other pertinent data. Among these the following are suggested:

- *Brandon's Shipper and Forwarder*. Advance sailing schedules.
- *Custom House Guide*. Steamship lines and agents by U.S. ports.
- *Exporters' Encyclopedia*. Steamship companies by ports of U.S.
- *N.Y. Journal of Commerce*. Sailings, arrivals, etc.
- *Official Steamship Guide*.
- *Pacific Shipper*. Schedules, sailings, etc.
- *Shipping Digest*. Steamship companies, agents, sailing, etc.

The names of dailies or other periodicals published in port cities may be obtained from chambers of commerce at respective ports. Consult also local chambers of commerce with foreign trade services (page 235); foreign freight forwarders; and custom house brokers.

See subject headings: Ocean Shipping; Ports and Port Facilities, U.S.

Packing

In overseas shipments special consideration must be given to proper *packing,* to protect against loss in handling, possible damage by sea water, cargo shifting, entrance of vermin, pilferage and often excessive heat or moisture.

The risks inherent in ocean shipping and the repeated handling of goods in transit require packages of sturdier construction than those used for domestic transportation.

Packing instructions should be requested from the customer. This individual is familiar with conditions in his country and the type of packaging best suited to his needs. Foreign freight forwarders and marine insurance brokers also can supply details on the special packing requirements of any country of destination.

The U.S. Customs Service of the Treasury Department is one of the best central sources of information on overseas packing questions and developments.

For information on packaging surveys and approved type of containers, consult the Maritime Association of the Port of New York, 80 Broad Street, New York, New York 10005; the Society of Packing and Handling Engineers, 14 East Jackson Boulevard, Chicago, Illinois 60604; and the Bulk Packaging and Containerization Institute, P.O. Box 3444, Grand Central Station, New York, New York 10017.

Current developments in the field of packing are carried in leading export and shipping magazines, such as *Brandon's Shipper and Forwarder,* and *Shipping Digest.*

Consult also: *Coast Marine & Transportation Directory; Exporters' Encyclopedia, Section IX;* and *Export Documentation and Shipment Preparation.*

Patents

The ability of firms to penetrate foreign markets and expand exports will be considerably enhanced by acquisition of *patents* abroad for their inventions and innovations. Also, a foreign patent program, by establishing protection against piracy or infringement of new products and processes, will encourage capital investments by firms in research and development and provide a sound basis for the licensing and sale of technology and related know-how. Firms seeking patents abroad must file an appropriate application in each country where patent protection is desired. This country is not party to any agreement whereby a U.S. patent is automatically recognized and protected in a foreign country or vice versa. Because of differing formalities and technicalities in securing rights abroad, competent legal counsel is usually employed for this purpose.

The United States does adhere to various treaties with about 95 countries under which exporters and other businesses can now receive the same treatment under patent laws as those countries extend to their own citizens (national treatment). The most important of these is the Paris Union International Convention for the Protection of Industrial Property to which 88 other countries also belong. This country also adheres to the Inter-American Convention of 1910 on Inventions, Patents, Designs and Models, which includes 12 Latin American countries. These conventions embody the national treatment principle, as well as other special advantages for U.S. businesses seeking patent protection abroad.

The United States and about 25 other countries belong to a Patent Cooperation Treaty, which entered into force in January 1978. This Treaty simplifies international filing procedures by allowing a patent applicant to file one application at a central source, with the effect of a filing in every member country where the applicant desires protection. Each member country then processes the application in accordance with its own procedures. There is also a European Patent Convention under which U.S. nationals may file a single application with the European Patent Office in Munich, Germany, and designate those member European countries in which a so-called European patent is sought. The European patent is granted, in effect, as a national patent is sought. It is granted as a national patent in the designated countries.

The United States also has concluded a number of bilateral arrangements with countries, some of which are not members of the above conventions, under which our exporters receive national treatment and other protection against discriminatory practices in acquiring and maintaining patent rights.

For information on the general subject of foreign patent protection, laws and conventions, consult the Foreign Business Practices Division, Office of International Finance and Investment, Bureau of International Economic Policy and Research, Industry and Trade Administration, United States Department of Commerce. Official journals of foreign patent offices and copies of foreign patents are maintained by the United States Patent and Trademark Office, Crystal Plaza, 2021 Jefferson Davis Highway, Arlington, Virginia. For digests of foreign patent laws and regulations and general information on foreign practices, consult the following publications:

- *Foreign Business Practices.*
- *Overseas Business Reports* on Marketing in ____ , or Trading with ____ .
- *Industrial Property.*
- *General Information Concerning Patents.*
- *Patents Throughout the World.*
- *Manual for the Handling of Applications for Patents, Designs and Trademarks Throughout the World.*

Postal Service, International

Postal services play an important part in foreign trade, as a means both of communication and transfer for goods. Air mail is of particular value to the exporter and importer, for it is a rapid and inexpensive method of communication, particularly in the dispatch of correspondence, quotations, orders, documents, etc.

Parcel post is a convenient and widely used method for the shipment of certain types of articles in export and import, both by surface and by air.

The Universal Postal Union, organized in 1874, is responsible for agreement by governments on the present-day, worldwide postal interchange. It unites member countries in a single postal territory for the reciprocal exchange of mail.

Information on mail facilities and rates to and from foreign countries is contained in United States Postal Service (USPS) Publication No. 42, "International Mail." Inquiry on special points may be made of local postmasters or the USPS, Washington, D.C. 20260.

In the international movement of goods by mail, certain formalities of individual countries must be respected. Among important sources of information or service, their types, requirements, rates, foreign country formalities, etc., the following references are suggested: *International Mail* (USPS Publication No. 42); *Exporters' Encyclopedia; Foreign Air Mail Guide, Official; International Trade Reporter; Leonard's Guide* (foreign section); and *Postal Bulletins*.

For U.S. customs regulations concerning importations by mail, see Customs Regulations of the United States, in the *Custom House Guide*.

See also subject headings: Air Transport; Telecommunications; Documents in Foreign Trade.

Product Liability

For the past several years, U.S. manufacturers and retailers have experienced a *product liability* explosion. Lawsuits based on product-related injury have become numerous, courts have eased the path to recovery for injured persons and awards have increased. Foreign companies exporting to the United States also have felt the impact of this rapidly expanding exposure to product liability.

U.S. exporters to Europe and other developed countries therefore may find themselves obliged to consider questions of product liability more seriously than in the past. Lately these countries have created increasingly strict rules for holding both foreign and domestic manufacturers liable for product-related injuries. Despite significant variations in rules from one country to another, the evolution toward higher standards of liability is taking place everywhere and the rate of change accelerating. Moreover, the European Community and the Council of Europe are now considering international agreements on rules for product liability which are significantly tougher than most existing national laws.

In the case of products exported by U.S. manufacturers, they may be primarily liable if product injury occurs abroad. Foreign importers, wholesalers, and retailers will be eager to see the U.S. manufacturer brought before the foreign court, if for no other reason than to reduce the likelihood of their being held liable. U.S. companies and trade associations have devoted increasing time and attention to the dangers of liability for injuries caused by exported products.

In a case of product injury caused in a foreign country by an exported U.S. product, those potentially liable include: the retailer in the foreign country, the foreign importer—who may be an independent business executive or a subsidiary of the U.S. manufacturer-exporter—and the U.S. manufacturer.

Thus, legal problems may arise for the exporter and importer because goods have crossed some international boundary. Hence, unfamiliar rules of jurisdiction, conflict of laws and foreign legal rules of liability are becoming of increasing concern to the U.S. business.

For the last 25 years, conflict of laws rules in torts and product liability cases have been controversial and courts have adopted several new legal theories. Some commentators see a unifying thread in these decisions—adoption by courts of the theory most favorable to plaintiff. Conflict of law problems between national legal systems are likely to increase as the level of international travel and commerce increases. To contribute order and predictability to resolution of international conflict of laws problems, the Hague Conference on Private International Law sponsored drafting of "A Convention on the Law Applicable to Product Liability," which entered into force October 1, 1977. The United States has not signed.

In the United States, rules for recovery are warranty, tort and strict liability in tort—which is the theory most favorable to plaintiffs. In general, foreign countries have not adopted strict liability but rely on tort and warranty. In some countries, however, especially France and Luxembourg, the results approximate strict liability. Britain, Ireland, West Germany and Belgium are somewhat less favorable to plaintiffs than France; Denmark, the Netherlands, Italy and Japan are much less favorable. If strict liability is adopted in Europe, it will probably be by approval of a proposed EC draft directive on product liability, which the EC Council is now evaluating.

If a foreign defendant has no assets in the United States, a plaintiff must seek recognition and enforcement of the judgment abroad. Most countries have rules for evaluating foreign judgments before recognizing and enforcing them, although most foreign companies intending to do business in the United States would not dare refuse to pay a valid court judgment. Finally, damage awards abroad are usually smaller than those in the United States, in part because abroad the contingent fee system is not used, pain and suffering enjoys limited recognition and comparative negligence is widely used.

For information on product liability, consult the Department of State, Office of Treaty Affairs or the Office of Legal Advisors; also the Department of Commerce Foreign Business Practices Division, Office of International Finance and Investment. The publication *Current Developments in Product Liability Affecting International Commerce, U.S.* (Department of Commerce, August 1978) also may be helpful.

Public Law 480 Program

The *Public Law 480 Program* has served many purposes during its 25-year history, from its original emphasis as an outlet for the disposal of surplus commodities to the current emphasis on economic development in the less developed countries (LDC's). Structurally, Public Law 480 (the Agricultural Trade Development and Assistance Act of 1954) is organized into three major parts or titles, each concerned with a separate authority. *Title I* authorizes the *Commodity Credit Corporation,* or CCC, to finance agricultural exports over credit periods of up to 40 years at low rates of interest, with payment for those exports made mostly in dollars. In financing exports under Title I, commercial practices are followed insofar as possible. That is, the importing countries make the purchases from U.S. suppliers, arrange their own shipping and generally operate an import program as close as possible to normal commercial practices within the legislative and regulatory requirements of the PL 480 Program.

A central strategy of PL 480, which is administered by the U.S. Department of Agriculture and other agencies, is to assist the evolution of developing countries from recipients of humanitarian and economic aid to participants in the international marketplace.

Under most Title I agreements, importing countries resell their commodities either directly to consumers or to domestic processors who sell their products in the local economies. The local currencies generated by importing governments from such sales must be used for programs designed to foster economic development in the importing countries. Thus, a single Title I program provides the multiple benefits of increasing U.S. agricultural exports, increasing food supplies in the recipient countries and contributing toward increased economic development.

Further information on Title I program operations can be obtained from the U.S. Department of Agriculture, Office of the General Sales Manager, Program Operations Division.

Title II authorizes the donation of commodities and associated shipping costs. These donated commodities are distributed primarily through U.S. private voluntary agencies such as CARE, Church World Services, etc., and through the U.N. World Food Program. Title II commodities are used for emergencies, but their major impact is through maternal health programs, school lunch programs and food-for-work projects where the commodities are provided as a form of payment.

Contacts for information on this program are the Department of Agriculture, Agricultural Stabilization and Conservation Service, Procurement and Sales Division.

As a market development tool, Public Law 480 gives the United States a competitive edge by establishing contacts and product familiarity (quality and dependable supply) that can be tapped once the country has achieved economic viability. An ideal evolutionary process for a PL 480 Program recipient is to move from assistance under Title II, to assistance under Title I, to CCC credit. Depending on financial status, a country can enter the program at any one of these stages.

The third authority, *Title III*, was established by Congress in October of 1977, with the major purpose of providing assistance for economic development in low-income countries. Under Title III, the poorest countries are provided the additional incentives of multi-year commodity commitments and loan forgiveness under Title I agreements *if* mutually-agreed-upon policy and project activities to increase the incomes of their poor people are included in the agreement. Under Title III, countries with approved development proposals deposit in a special account the proceeds they generate from selling on their domestic markets the commodities they import under a Title I agreement. Then, as they spend the currencies from this account on the approved development activities, the dollar equivalent of the Title I loan is forgiven.

During fiscal year 1978, a total of about 4.3 million metric tons of agricultural commodities with a market value of $732 million were sold under Title I to 27 countries. Of the commodities being shipped under Title I in 1978, wheat accounts for 79 percent, rice 9 percent and feedgrains 10 percent.

State and Territory International Business Offices

State governments, like the federal government, encourage international trade. Many states have trade development offices overseas that sponsor export seminars and obtain trade leads from U.S. Foreign Service posts.

Several state agriculture departments have formed regional groups to promote exports from the states. The Mid-America International Agri-Trade Council in Chicago, an association of twelve midwest state departments of agriculture, serves as a source of marketing information and assistance to its members.

The council publishes a free *Export Handbook*. This handbook contains chapters on trade assistance from the private sector, international terms, foreign trade abbreviations, revised foreign trade definitions and conversion tables. The council's address is:

Mid-America International Agri-Trade Council
300 West Washington Street
Chicago, Illinois 60606
Tel. (312) 368-4448

The state departments of agriculture also have a national association that monitors federal legislation affecting the agricultural industry and coordinates state agricultural programs with those of the U.S. Department of Agriculture. The national headquarters is:

National Association of State Departments of Agriculture
1616 H Street, N.W., Suite 401
Washington, D.C. 20006
Tel. (202) 628-1566

The National Governors Association is another association which tries to improve state government work requiring interstate cooperation including programs to expand foreign trade and investment. The association's address is:

National Governors Association
4444 North Capitol Street
Washington, D.C. 20001
Tel. (202) 624-5300

See appendix for list of state, territory and the District of Columbia international business offices, page 248.
See also subject headings: Trade Opportunities and Leads; National Association of State Development Agencies.

Statistics, Foreign Trade

A variety of reports on U.S. foreign trade are prepared monthly and annually by the Commerce Department's Census Bureau (see page 17) from mandatory documents filed with Bureau of Customs (Treasury) officials. They are of great value to foreign traders in analyzing the volume and character of exports and imports and the importance of various countries as markets and as sources.

The basic trade reports cover some 4,000 export commodities and 10,000 import commodities, by quantity and value, by country of destination and origin, monthly and cumulative for one year. Import statistics are available based on three different methods of valuation: f.a.s. (free alongside ship at foreign port); c.i.f. (includes insurance and freight to U.S. port); and customs value (as defined by law). Export data are valued f.a.s. and are available by mode of transportation—sea and air—and by customs region and district.

Summary monthly reports are issued also on total export and import value, total trade in given commodities and total trade with individual countries and areas. They are compiled in several different classifications: *Tariff Schedules of the United States (imports)* and *Schedule B (exports); Standard International Trade Classification,* the UN's international classification called Schedule E (exports) and A (imports); and the *U.S. Standard Industrial Classification* (SIC)—industry codes.

Summary commodity and country data for analytical purposes, monthly and cumulative, are generally published three to four weeks after the total monthly trade values are released. Also, a series of annual *Overseas Business Reports,* published by the

Department of Commerce, provide U.S. trade data for a series of seven years by commodity, country, commodity-by-area and commodity-by-major-trading-partners.

Current census data are available to the public on microfilm, microfiche and in printed form from the Government Printing Office or the Bureau of the Census. They are also available for use in the *U.S. Trade Reference Room* in the Department of Commerce and in Department of Commerce district offices around the country. The Department of Commerce also maintains a *Foreign Trade Reference Room* with annual foreign trade publications for each country in the world. These are available for public use, with assistance provided in translation, commodity classification and exchange rate conversion. Limited help can also be provided by letter and by telephone.

Data on U.S. exports and imports classified by end use commodity categories, quarterly by commodity and annually commodity-by-country are published from time to time as a supplement to the Department of Commerce's *Survey of Current Business.* Current data are available in that publication and in the FT-990. Also, the Department of Agriculture publishes monthly trade in farm products, commodity-by-country, in "Foreign Agricultural Trade of the United States."

The Corps of Engineers, Department of the Army, publishes annually "Waterborne Commerce of the United States" (five volumes, by U.S. area) which includes freight traffic by individual port; by commodity; and foreign, coastwise and internal in quantity terms.

The Department of Commerce publishes every few years a series of *State Export Reports*—one for each state—showing exports of manufactured goods, farm products, fish, minerals and metals. These reports are based on data collected by the Bureau of the Census and Departments of Agriculture, Interior and Energy.

Other useful publications related to U.S. trade statistics are:
- *U.S. Foreign Trade Statistics*—Classifications and Cross-Classifications (Census Bureau).
- *Guide to Foreign Trade Statistics* (Census Bureau).
- *Schedule B—Statistical Classification of Domestic and Foreign Commodities Exported from the United States* (Census Bureau).
- *Tariff Schedules of the U.S. Annotated* (International Trade Commission).

Some of the publications listed by organization available from the Department of Commerce's *Foreign Trade Reference Room* for the international market researcher on foreign trade statistics include:

United Nations

Foreign trade data for 24 individual developed countries in five-digit Standard International Trade Classification (SITC) categories, by quantity and dollar value, by major country of destination and origin, are published annually in a series of installments, *Commodity Trade Statistics.* Quarterly (and annual) data are available on microfiche.

Similar data are published for several of the developing countries annually in the same series, with a considerable time lag.

The *World Trade Annual* (five volumes) provides trade data organized by commodity, for the 24 developed countries on a one, two, three, four and five-digit SITC commodity-by-country of origin/destination-by-partner-country basis for one year.

The *Yearbook of International Trade Statistics* (two volumes) shows for 156 countries trade with partner countries and trade by major SITC commodities, by quantity and dollar value, for a series of years (Volume 1). Volume 2 presents world trade, commodity-by-country, for three-digit and selected four and five-digit SITC products.

Monthly Bulletin of Statistics includes the monthly value of exports and imports in dollar and national currency and quantity and unit value indexes of trade for about 150 countries. There also are from time to time special summary tables showing world trade matrixes, exports of manufactured goods, etc.

Organization for Economic Cooperation and Development (OECD)

Statistics on Foreign Trade

Series A (Monthly Bulletin) shows for the 23 member countries and Yugoslavia the monthly value of trade in dollars with partner countries and of trade in broad one-digit sections.

Series B (Trade by Commodities: Country Summaries) provides for each member country, quarterly for one year, the quantity and value of principal SITC commodity trade in dollars with regions and OECD member countries of origin and destination, and the trade of various combinations of countries.

Series C (Trade by Commodities: Market Summaries—two volumes) includes for each member country quarterly trade by quantity and value in dollars of five-digit SITC commodity categories with a full list of countries of origin and destination.

OECD trade statistics are available in printed form and on magnetic tape and microfiche.

European Community (EC)

Analytical Tables of Foreign Trade present annual export and import data for about 6,500 products traded by the nine EC members, in quantity and value, by partner country. These data in 13 volumes are based on a six-digit NIMEXE classification, a breakdown of the EC's Common Customs Tariff, which is correlated to Brussels Tariff Nomenclature used by the individual countries.

Values are in European unit of account. Data are available in book form and on microfiche.

A second series of five volumes provides data by quantity and value for each of the EC countries by SITC (CST) categories at various levels of detail.

International Monetary Fund

Direction of Trade presents in monthly and annual publications the dollar value of trade with partner countries for 151 countries.

International Financial Statistics shows the monthly, quarterly and annual value of total exports and imports in national currencies for all member countries. For many, the values of principal food and crude material exports are shown. A summary table of free-world exports and imports by years and quarters is included, as are tabulations of export and import unit values by country.

Food and Agriculture Organization (FAO)

Annual data on exports and imports of major agricultural products, in quantity and dollar value, are shown in the *Trade Yearbook* of the FAO for three years by country of destination and origin. Tabulations of broad categories of farm products traded are provided for six years for each of about 175 foreign countries.

155

Tax

DISC (Domestic International Sales Corporation)

A DISC is a special type of United States corporation engaged in the business of export sales. DISC was added to the tax code by the Revenue Act of 1971. The DISC itself is not taxed on its income, although each year its shareholders are treated as receiving certain amounts of the DISC's taxable income and are taxed currently on this amount. American exporters may defer taxes on the remaining DISC income so long as the corporation continues to qualify as a DISC and this income is not distributed to the shareholders.

To qualify for DISC treatment, at least 95 percent of a corporation's gross receipts must arise from export activities. In addition, at least 95 percent of the corporation's assets must be export-related. The Tax Reduction Act of 1975 denied DISC benefits to income from export sales of certain natural resources such as gas and depletable minerals.

The Tax Reform Act of 1976 substantially cut back DISC benefits. For tax years beginning after December 31, 1975, the tax deferral on DISC profits is limited to the amount by which its export gross receipts exceed 67 percent of the DISC's average gross receipts in a four-year base period. Until 1980, the base period years are 1972 through 1975. The base period for taxable years beginning in 1980 moves forward each year. DISCs with incomes of $100,000 or less are exempt from this rule, with the exemption phased out for incomes between $100,000 and $150,000. In addition, the 1976 Act limits DISC treatment to 50 percent of the profits from products sold for use as military equipment. Finally, DISC benefits are not available for those export sales from operations in connection with which there was an agreement to participate in or cooperate with an international boycott, or which result from illegal payments to foreign officials.

Any company exporting or interested in exporting can form a DISC to handle its export sales. There is no limit on the number of shareholders. In addition, a DISC can handle the exports of any number of U.S. producers, whether or not their products are related. For example, several small companies might jointly own a DISC to sell their complementary products in a full product line.

A corporation seeking treatment as a DISC must file a statement of election (IRS Form 4876) with the Internal Revenue Service within 90 days preceding the beginning of the year for which it seeks DISC status, or if newly formed, within 90 days after the date of incorporation.

For further information contact the Department of Treasury Office of International Tax Affairs.

Foreign Tax Credit

Since 1918, the United States has used the *foreign tax credit* to protect businesses and individuals from the severe burden of multiple taxation on foreign income. Unlike countries that tax income only from domestic sources, the United States has always asserted the right to tax the worldwide income of its citizens and domestic corporations. Such worldwide income, however, is often subject to tax in the country in which it is earned as well as in the United States. By allowing U.S. businesses and individuals a credit against their U.S. taxes for "income, war profits and excess profits taxes" paid or accrued during the tax year to any foreign country, the risks of multiple taxation are reduced.

Under present law, taxpayers subject to U.S. tax on their foreign source income may claim a tax credit for foreign taxes paid directly on this income. The Internal Revenue Code also allows a U.S. corporate taxpayer to take a foreign tax credit for the foreign taxes it pays indirectly (the so-called deemed-paid credit). Thus, when a foreign subsidiary of a U.S. corporation pays a dividend, the parent company can take a credit against its U.S. tax liability both for the direct foreign taxes the parent pays on the dividend and for the foreign taxes paid by the foreign subsidiary on its earnings from which the dividend was paid.

The Tax Reduction Act of 1975 substantially modified the foreign tax credit available to petroleum companies. The Act limited creditable foreign tax to a percentage of oil and extraction income and defined such income to exclude foreign extraction losses. The Tax Reform Act of 1976 placed the percentage at the highest U.S. corporate tax rate.

Originally there was no limit on the foreign tax credits which taxpayers could claim to offset U.S. tax liability on domestic income. Since 1921, however, the foreign tax credit has not been allowed to reduce U.S. tax on U.S. income. The "overall" limitation provided that the total foreign taxes used as a credit in any year could not exceed the U.S. tax attributable to foreign source income for the same year. In 1932, a "per country" limitation was added whereby the foreign tax credit on taxes paid to any one country in a year could not exceed the U.S. tax liability on the income earned in that country in that year. After vacillating for many years between these two limitations, the Tax Reform Act of 1976 required taxpayers to use the "overall" limitation.

See: *Proceedings of a Conference on the Foreign Tax Credit,* John Volpe and John Sarpa, eds., International Division, Chamber of Commerce of the United States, 1979.

"Tax Deferral" of Foreign Corporate Income

Foreign corporations, including subsidiaries of U.S. companies, generally are taxed by the United States only to the extent they are engaged in business in the United States or derive investment income here. As a result, the United States usually does not impose a tax on the foreign source income of a foreign corporation. Instead, the foreign source earnings of a foreign corporation generally are subject to U.S. income taxes only when they are actually remitted to U.S. shareholders as dividends. The tax in this case is imposed on the U.S. shareholder and not the foreign corporation. The fact that no U.S. tax is imposed until, and unless, the income is distributed to the U.S. shareholders is referred to by some as "tax deferral."

In 1962, the concept of taxing the shareholders of a controlled foreign corporation on certain items of current income was introduced into the federal tax laws, as Subpart F of the Internal Revenue Code. A controlled foreign corporation is defined as a foreign corporation in which U.S. shareholders own, directly or indirectly, more than 50 percent of the voting power. Subpart F provides that the profits derived from certain categories of foreign income (so-called Subpart F income) would be included in the income of the controlled foreign corporation's U.S. shareholders on a pro rata basis, even though these profits are not distributed as dividends. Subpart F income initially included personal holding company income and certain foreign base company income derived from sales and services. In adopting Subpart F, Congress specifically rejected a general proposal to tax the undistributed income of foreign corporations to their U.S. shareholders.

The Tax Reduction Act of 1975 widened the reach of Subpart F. The Act repealed the minimum distribution exception, imposed a tax on shipping income except to the extent that the profits are reinvested in shipping operations and eliminated the exception for dividends reinvested in less-developed countries.

Taxation of Foreign Earnings of U.S. Citizens, Sections 911-913 of the Internal Revenue Code

The *Foreign Earned Income Act of 1978* substantially revised the rules for taxation of U.S. citizens working abroad. Relief is provided through a variety of complex provisions which for most Americans replace the earned income exclusion with a series of deductions to reflect the excess cost of living in a foreign country. Also provided are liberalizations of the moving expense deduction limitations for foreign moves and special rules allowing employees working in "camps" and foreign locations with adverse living conditions to exclude up to $20,000 per year. The Act is effective for tax years beginning in 1978. It also repeals the changes made by the 1976 Act for taxable years beginning before 1978.

To provide relief where needed most, the excess foreign living cost deductions provided in the Act are open-ended and apply to the actual living expenses incurred by most individuals. These include a cost of living differential, housing expenses, school expenses, home leave travel expenses and a special hardship area deduction. In addition, the problem areas of moving expenses and residence replacement have been liberalized. An expanded record-keeping burden is imposed on individuals claiming the new deductions, however, because they are based on the actual costs incurred. Detailed records of virtually all expenses of living abroad, as well as specific dates of all arrivals and departures from foreign locations, will be necessary to support the deductions.

Value-Added Tax (VAT)

Value-Added Tax (VAT) is a tax levied on the value added to a good or service at each level of the production and distribution process, that is on the difference between the selling price and the cost of goods used. VAT is an across-the-board tax on the increase in a product's value which is attributable to a company's productive activities.

VAT is part of the price of each good—capital goods, materials used in the production of other goods, and consumer goods and services. VAT may be stated separately on each invoice, or included in the price without being shown. While companies pay VAT when purchasing goods used in production, they may receive rebates against tax owed on sales. Only the final consumer cannot receive rebates.

The nine European Community countries and more than a dozen other nations have adopted VATs. The State of Michigan uses a form of VAT called the single business tax, but it has not been tried in other states or at the national level in the United States.

Because VAT is imposed on imports but rebated on exports, proponents contend it is more advantageous to trade than the nonrebatable taxes used in the United States. Advocates also say that VAT is more beneficial to capital formation than the corporate or personal income tax and that as a revenue source it is relatively stable, easy to administer and difficult to evade.

Telecommunications, International

Telegraph, telephone and radio play an extremely important role in the conduct of foreign trade in permitting rapid communication between buyers and sellers. By these means, immediate contact may be made with almost any part of the world.

Much of the business of foreign traders is done by means of radio and cable code. Communications companies offer various services which range in cost according to speed of delivery and whether plain or code language is used.

Information on telecommunication services may be obtained from the well-known communication companies, with branches in most communities such as: International Telephone and Telegraph Company; American Telephone and Telegraph Company; RCA Communications, Inc.; and Western Union International, Inc.

The Office of Commercial Affairs and Telecommunications of the Department of State has charge of formulation and coordination of policy and action with respect to the international aspects of telegraph, telephone, cable and radio.

The International Telecommunication Union, established in 1932 and now associated with the United Nations as a specialized agency, has as its purpose the establishment of international regulations for radio, telegraph and telephone service (see page 48).

Radio and cable rates to foreign countries on various types of messages, regulations, conditions of acceptance and other data on telecommunications are published in *Exporters' Encyclopedia.* Similar information is furnished by the *International Trade Reporter. Marconi's International Register* lists cable addresses and codes of registered firms of the world.

U.S. Department of Commerce field offices are in a position to furnish information and advice on telecommunications.

See also: *International Telex Directory; Transportation Telephone Tickler;* and *World Telex—International Telex Directory.*

See also subject heading Postal Service, International.

Trade and Professional Associations

Producers, manufacturers and merchants of the United States having similar business interests are organized in national, regional, state or local *trade and professional associations* for the purpose generally of protecting and serving the collective interests of their members.

Many are only indirectly concerned with foreign trade, but others whose members make, sell or buy products that figure prominently in foreign commerce, maintain separate departments, bureaus, committees or other facilities for consideration of, or action upon, international trade matters and for serving the common interests of their members in this respect.

On the other hand, there are associations composed solely of exporting manufacturers, producers or merchants in given lines, and of importing manufacturers, wholesalers, retailers or import merchants. Their activities generally are concerned wholly with export and import matters.

For listings of trade associations and related organizations with data as to purposes and activities, see: *Encyclopedia of Associations,* Gale Research Co., Detroit, Michigan; *Associations Registered Under the Webb-Pomerene Export Trade Act;* NTPA (National Trade and Professional Associations of the United States and Canada), Columbia Books, Inc., Washington, D.C.

World Trade Clubs in the United States

A type of voluntary association of foreign trade interests found in many of the larger cities or trade centers of the United States is the *world trade* or foreign trade club, export managers' club or international trade association or council.

Although differing somewhat in objectives, methods and scope of activity, they have the common aim of promoting the foreign trade interests of their communities or of their members;

of providing forums for open discussion of mutual problems in export or import business, or both; and of interchanging experience and opinion on selling, management, foreign trading techniques, credit and exchange conditions, and the like.

As a rule, membership is limited to executives of firms and corporations and other individuals directly interested in foreign trading, although no hard and fast rule obtains. Regular meetings are held, usually as luncheon, dinner or roundtable sessions.

A few of the leading clubs conduct formal lecture courses, forums or clinics, some in cooperation with educational institutions, records of which are made available to participants and often to other interested parties at nominal costs.

Some clubs are wholly independent organizations, but others are affiliated with chambers of commerce, trade associations or other organizations or cooperate closely with them.

For a list of world trade clubs, see Appendix.

Trade Barriers

Tariffs, United States

Numerous classes of goods imported into the United States enter free of duty—both generally and under the General System of Preferences (GSP), applied to many developing countries' products. However, a wide range of goods are subject to varying duties—*specific, ad valorem* or *compound* in nature. Beginning January 1, 1980, most U.S. tariffs were subject to reductions as a result of the tariff agreements reached during the multilateral trade negotiations (MTN) completed in 1979. In general, U.S. industrial tariffs subject to the MTN agreement will be reduced over an eight to ten year period with most final rates taking effect on January 1, 1987. This schedule of reductions means that U.S. tariff rates for most dutiable products will change annually over the staging period.

For detailed information on the implementing process of the MTN agreements or on expected test cases and their results, see the *Trade Policy Review* published by the International Division of the Chamber of Commerce of the United States.

Information on the structure of U.S. tariffs, tariff classifications and specific rates of duty may be obtained most conveniently from the United States Customs Service or from Commodity Analysts in the United States International Trade Commission. Information can also be obtained from the following publications.

- *Tariff Schedules of the United States, Annotated*, published by the United States International Trade Commission, Washington, D.C. 20436.
- *Special and Administrative Provisions of the Tariff Act of 1930,* published by the United States International Trade Commission, Washington, D.C. 20436.
- *Exporting to the United States,* published by the United States Customs Service, Washington, D.C. 20229.
- *The Annual Report of the President of the United States on Trade Agreements Program,* published by the Office of the United States Trade Representative (Executive Office of the President), Washington, D.C.

See subject headings: Imports, Entry of; and Tariffs, Foreign.

Tariffs, Foreign

Most foreign countries levy duties of one kind or another on merchandise imported from abroad. Foreign tariff systems are often complicated and subject to frequent change.

In the course of the multilateral trade negotiations (MTN) completed in 1979, most industrialized countries and a number of developing countries who are parties to the General Agreement on Tariffs and Trade (GATT) agreed to significant reductions in tariff rates. Overall, the industrial tariffs of the developed countries will be reduced by about 35 percent over an eight to ten year period beginning January 1, 1980. The MTN agreement on tariffs means that foreign tariff rates on thousands of specific products will be changing on an annual basis over the staging period until such time as the final rates are reached.

The Bureau of Export Development, U.S. Department of Commerce, maintains current records of foreign tariffs and customs regulations. The Bureau is a widely used source of information on tariff structures, tariff classifications, rates of duty and tariff developments in foreign countries. The Bureau also maintains schedules of tariff concessions made by foreign countries which indicate those rates which will be in effect at a given date as a result of the MTN tariff agreements.

Inquiries concerning tariffs in other countries can also be made at the office of the United States Trade Representative (USTR) located in the Executive Office of the President (see page 4).

Complete schedules of foreign customs tariffs are not always readily available; however, schedules of concessions on tariffs granted by countries party to the GATT may be obtained from the Secretariat of the General Agreement on Tariffs and Trade, Geneva, Switzerland. In addition, full customs tariffs of a wide range of countries (douanes) are published periodically by the International Customs Tariffs Bureau, located in Brussels.

See subject heading: Tariffs, United States.

Nontariff Barriers: Multilateral Codes of Conduct

As successive rounds of multilateral trade negotiations progressively reduced the average level of import duties in most countries, there has been an increasing reliance on the use of nontariff measures by governments seeking to protect their domestic industries against international competition. Among the nontariff measures most frequently employed are government procurement preferences, trade-blocking product standards, import licensing schemes, arbitrary methods of customs valuation and government subsidies. While it is often impossible to quantify the level of protection represented by these measures, nontariff barriers (NTBs) are frequently more restrictive than tariffs.

In recognition of the importance of NTBs, international discussions held in the Tokyo Round of Multilateral Trade Negotiations (MTN), which concluded in 1979, focused on the need for increased international discipline over the use of NTBs. The MTN resulted in a wide range of multilateral NTB codes of conduct designed to liberalize international trade significantly. A summary of each of the NTB codes is presented below.

- *Subsidies and Countervailing Duties.* A major objective of the "Subsidies Code" is to limit the impact of subsidies on trade flows in international commerce. Countries adhering to the code are flatly prohibited from using export subsidies for nonprimary (industrial) products and primary mineral products. In addition, the code strengthens international rules governing the use of agricultural export subsidies and, for the first time, attempts to regulate the use of internal domestic subsidies. Countries found to be in

161

violation of the code are liable to retaliatory countermeasures, if the offending practice is not withdrawn.

Parties who claim they are being injured by foreign subsidy practices, or who allege that their export interests are adversely affected by the payment of foreign subsidies, can take advantage of two routes of redress under the code. The first route provides for traditional countervailing duties where domestic action is necessary to remove or prevent injury to a domestic industry. The second route provides for a multilateral mechanism through which signatories can enforce their rights under the code.

- *Government Procurement*. This code provides for national treatment and nondiscrimination on government purchases covered by the code. The code's coverage extends to purchases of goods by specific U.S. and foreign entities listed in an appendix to the code text pursuant to contracts valued at $199,000 or more. The code does not apply to such things as service contracts, construction contracts, national security items, purchases by state or local governments (with or without the use of federal funds) or purchases by an entity not specified as being covered.

To ensure compliance with the code, there are enforcement provisions to deal with both individual contract violations and larger, more systemic violations. On an individual contract basis, a firm will have the right to be told why its bid lost and why the winner was selected.

- *Technical Barriers to Trade (Standards)*. The purpose of this code is to discourage discriminatory manipulation of product standards, product testing and product certification systems. A major principle of the code is that imported products are to be treated no less favorably than domestically produced products. The code does not delineate standards for individual products, but establishes international procedures by which signatories may complain of code violations by other signatories, may secure reviews of their complaints and may, if a valid complaint remains unsettled, ultimately take retaliatory action.

- *Customs Valuation*. This agreement is expected to bring major benefits to U.S. exporters by, among other things, providing for an end to the now common practice of arbitrarily increasing the dutiable value of goods. The primary method of valuation prescribed by the code is transaction value—the price actually paid or payable for the imported goods with specified additions for costs, charges and expenses incurred with respect to imported goods which are not reflected in the price. A hierarchy of fallback methods is provided for instances in which the transaction value cannot be used and there are provisions guaranteeing the right of importers to an impartial appeals procedure. The code establishes a strong dispute settlement mechanism to guard against breaches of the agreement's procedures.

- *Import Licensing*. The aim of the import licensing code is to reduce administrative impediments to trade by simplifying and harmonizing import licensing procedures. The code deals with procedures used to implement import licensing systems rather than with the existence or extent of such systems and restrictions themselves. Illustrative of the requirements set out in the code are rules governing the publication of procedures for obtaining licenses; simplification of application and renewal procedures and requirements for foreign exchange availability in the case of licenses approved for imports.

In addition to the codes described above, the MTN resulted in important agreements covering: trade in civil aircraft; the international trading framework; and special agreements relating to trade in meat and dairy products.

The texts of the MTN codes and the other nontariff agreements reached in the MTN are available from the U.S. Government Printing Office under the title: *Multilateral Trade Negotiations: International Codes Agreed to in Geneva, Switzerland, April 12, 1979* (Reference-WMCP: 96-18).

See also: *Results of the Tokyo Round: Proceedings of a Conference on the Multilateral Trade Negotiations*, Elizabeth Perkins, ed., International Division, Chamber of Commerce of the United States, 1979.

Countervailing and Antidumping Duties

International agreements and U.S. law provide for combatting certain unfair trade practices that injure domestic producers. Special *countervailing* duties may be imposed in addition to any regular levies on imports that are found to be either subsidized by a foreign government or ''dumped'' by a foreign producer. These duties are designed to offset the advantages imports would otherwise receive from the subsidy or dumping practices.

GATT rules forbid the use of export subsidies, and signatories of the new MTN subsidy code have agreed to seek to avoid using even domestic subsidies in a manner that harms foreign producers. Whenever a subsidy causes material injury, countries are allowed to impose countervailing duties against subsidized import to bring the price of the product up to the level that it would have reached without the subsidy.

GATT rules also provide a remedy for dumping—i.e., selling goods overseas for less than in the home market—when it causes material injury to foreign producers. U.S. law broadens the definition of dumping (or selling at ''less than the fair market value'') to cover cases where the merchandise is sold below the cost of production, even if the overseas price is not lower than the home market price. The remedy is an *antidumping* duty equal to the dumping margin.

In the United States, domestic producers may petition the government to impose countervailing duties on imports alleged to be subsidized, and antidumping duties on imports alleged to be dumped. The duties are imposed if the Commerce Department determines that a subsidy has been granted or that sales have occurred at less than the fair market value, *and* if the U.S. International Trade Commission determines that a domestic industry is being, or threatened with being, materially injured by the imports. The Trade Agreements Act of 1979 added the injury test to countervailing duty investigations and streamlined the procedures for countervailing duty and antidumping cases.

Quotas

An import *quota* is a quantity control on imported merchandise for a certain period of time. Quotas are established by legislation and Presidential proclamations issued pursuant to specific legislation, and provided for in the *Tariff Schedules of the United States*.

163

United States import quotas may be divided into two types: *absolute* and *tariff-rate*.

The majority of import quotas are administered by the U.S. Customs Service. The Commissioner of Customs has no authority to change or modify any quota, but he does control the importation of quota merchandise.

Quota merchandise is subject to the usual Customs procedures applicable to other imports. No import licenses or permits are required for quota purposes for quotas administered by the Commissioner of Customs.

Detailed information on quota quantities, quota periods and quota allocations for the commodities may be obtained from the Commissioner of Customs, Washington, D.C. 20229.

a. *Absolute Quotas.* Absolute quotas limit the quantity of goods that may enter the commerce of the United States in a specified period. When an absolute quota is filled, further entries are prohibited during the remainder of the quota period. Some quotas are global while others are allocated to specified foreign countries. Certain absolute quotas are invariably filled at or shortly after the opening of the quota period. For this reason, an absolute quota is usually officially opened at a specified time on the first workday of the quota period so all importers may have an equal opportunity for the simultaneous presentation of entries.

If the quantity of quota merchandise covered by entries presented at the opening of the quota period exceeds the quota, the commodity is released on a pro rata basis (i.e., the ratio between the quota quantity and the total quantity offered for entry).

If not filled at the official opening of the quota period, the quota is thereafter administered on a first-come, first-served basis, that is, in the order of time of presentation of each entry.

Imports in excess of a specified quota may be exported or detained for entry during the next quota period. No importer may offer for entry a quantity in excess of the quota.

b. *Tariff-Rate Quotas.* Tariff-rate quotas permit a specified quantity of imported merchandise to be entered at a reduced rate of customs duty during the quota period. There is no limitation on the amount of the quota product that may be imported into the United States at any time, but quantities entered during the quota period in excess of the quota for that period are subject to higher duty rates.

Most of the tariff-rate quotas were proclaimed by the President under agreements negotiated under the Trade Agreements Act.

The status of merchandise subject to a tariff-rate quota cannot be determined in advance of its customs entry.

Duties at the reduced rates provided for in the President's proclamation are assessed on shipments entered under the quota. When the Commissioner of Customs determines the quota is nearing fulfillment, he instructs Customs field officers to require the deposit of estimated duties at the over-quota duty rates as of a specified date and to report the time of official acceptance of each entry.

When an official determination is made of the date and time the quota is filled, Customs field officers are authorized to make the required adjustments in the duty rates on that portion of the merchandise entitled to quota preference.

See subject heading: Imports, Entry of.

Textile Articles. The U.S. Customs Service administers import controls on certain cotton, wool and man-made fiber articles

164

manufactured or produced in designated countries. These controls are imposed on the basis of directives issued to the Commissioner of Customs by the Chairman of the Committee for the Implementation of Textile Agreements.

Information concerning specific import controls in effect may be obtained from the Commissioner of Customs. Other information concerning the textile program may be obtained from the Chairman, Committee for the Implementation of Textile Agreements, U.S. Department of Commerce, Washington, D.C. 20230.

Television Receivers. The U.S. Customs Service administers import controls on certain color television receivers and subassemblies manufactured or produced in Japan. These controls are administered pursuant to directives issued by the Office of the United States Trade Representative (USTR). Detailed information on controls presently in effect may be obtained from the Commissioner of Customs. For other information, contact the Office of the USTR, Washington, D.C. 20506.

Quotas Administered by Other Agencies

Fuel Oil. The Department of Energy administers import quotas on fuel oil and certain oil products on a licensing basis. Information concerning the licensing requirements on such products may be obtained from the Director, Oil Imports, Department of Energy, Post Office Box 7414, Ben Franklin Station, Washington, D.C. 20461.

Watches & Watch Movements. The Departments of Interior and Commerce administer import quotas on watches and watch movements from insular possessions admissible free of duty under General Headnote 3(a), *TSUS,* on a licensing basis. Information concerning licenses may be obtained from the Office of Import Programs, Special Import Programs Division, U.S. Department of Commerce, Washington, D.C. 20230.

Dairy Products. Certain dairy products are subject to annual import quotas administered by the Department of Agriculture and may be imported only under import licenses issued by that Department. Detailed information on the licensing of these products, or the conditions under which limited quantities of the products may be imported without licenses, may be obtained from the Import Branch, Foreign Agricultural Service, U.S. Department of Agriculture, Washington, D.C. 20250. A list of the dairy products subject to quotas can also be obtained from this office.

For a list of all commodities subject to import quotas administered by the Commissioner of Customs see: *Tariff Schedules of the United States* (TSUS).

Also, the status of all U.S. import quotas is issued by the U.S. Customs Service in its weekly publication *Quota Information.*

See also publication: *Import Quotas.* This is available free from Custom's Office of Information and Publications.

Trade Fairs and Exhibitions: International

The U.S. government's *International Trade Fair and Exhibition Program* provides U.S. business executives with display facilities in markets selected for their export sales potential. It is based on the premise that actual examination of a product, in operation if appropriate, enhances the ability of the end-user to make a comparative judgement and facilitates sales.

Commercial Fairs

International trade fairs are events at which hundreds of firms from many countries display their products. They are marketplaces in which buyer and seller meet. Many of the long-established fairs, especially in Europe, have a history that goes back centuries. More than 800 general and specialized international trade fairs are held each year. Once a year, usually in the January edition of *Business America* magazine, the U.S. Department of Commerce identifies fairs abroad, by country, product and date, that are considered most likely to be of interest to U.S. business. Because the cost of exhibiting overseas on an individual basis prohibits this type of promotion by many firms, the Department of Commerce sponsors an official U.S. participation in selected major international exhibitions. In areas where there are no suitable trade fairs, Commerce sponsors special solo exhibitions of U.S. products. Such exhibitions are scheduled only when in-depth research reveals excellent sales potential for the products being displayed. U.S. firms participating in these Commerce-sponsored events receive a full range of promotional and display assistance, all for a moderate participation contribution. For more information contact the Department's Office of Export Promotion.

U.S. Export Development Offices

The U.S. government has established permanent facilities for exporters to display, promote and sell their products in major marketing centers with high potential for sales of U.S. goods and services. The Department of Commerce and the U.S. Foreign Service of the Department of State currently operate a worldwide network of trade centers, international marketing centers, trade development offices and East-West trade development facilities, including several in strategically located developing markets. A number of specialized exhibitions are held annually at each center—exhibitions built around a product theme that is selected on the basis of in-depth market research. Certain centers also send out staff to stage U.S. pavilions at international fairs or U.S. "solo" exhibitions in a number of countries in the surrounding geographic region. Centers for export development are found in Bonn, London, Mexico City, Milan, Paris, Sao Paulo, Seoul, Singapore, Sydney, Taipei and Tokyo. A satellite office is located in Osaka and a regional trade development office serving the Middle East is located in Athens. In addition, offices in Moscow, Vienna and Warsaw assist U.S. firms in doing business in non-market economies.

Catalog and Video Catalog Exhibits

Catalog exhibits feature displays of product catalogs, sales brochures and other graphic sales aids. They are scheduled in advance for a preselected product theme and held either at foreign service posts or U.S. trade centers abroad. Some of these shows are video catalog exhibits, industry-organized, government-approved exhibits, in which a trade association produces the video tape product presentation with guidance and assistance from the Commerce Department's International Trade Administration instead of the regular catalog.

Each catalog exhibit is supported by an industry technical representative, an expert in the industry theme, who explains the catalogs to participants and writes a report on that market for them. Fees for video catalog exhibits vary according to the degree of government support.

Non-ITA Exhibit Support Services

Assistance in exhibiting abroad is available from many non-ITA sources. Services that produce and manage overseas exhibitions are provided by official and quasi-official trade fair authorities in many foreign countries. In addition, there are a number of private U.S. and foreign firms that specialize in producing and

166

managing international exhibitions. Among the U.S. firms in this category are Clapp & Poliak Inc., Martin C. Dwyer, Inc., Industrial Scientific Conference Management Inc., International Exposition Co. and the National Expositions Company, Inc.

Through the combined efforts of all the exhibition producers, hundreds of individual trade fairs are held each year in more than 50 countries around the world, though the frequency of these shows in any one country varies enormously. Certain countries, such as Canada and several European nations, offer a large number of shows each year—most focusing on particular industry themes.

Trade Missions: International

The *trade mission program,* administered by the Office of Export Promotion, Bureau of Export Development, is an important part of the export expansion activity of the U.S. Department of Commerce. In prearranged meetings with industrial leaders and government planners overseas, U.S. business executives explore opportunities to increase trade, investment, joint ventures, licensing and other business relations.

Specialized U.S. Government Trade Missions

U.S. specialized trade missions are planned, organized and led by staff officers of the Department of Commerce. The primary objective of such a trade mission is the sale of U.S.-produced goods and services and the establishment of agencies or representation abroad. The Department of Commerce, assisted by the State Department's Foreign Service, provides detailed marketing information, advance planning, promotional services and trip coordination. As sponsor of the mission, the Commerce Department selects a product line and itinerary that appear to offer good potential for export sales. This selection is based on in-depth market research data and made after consultations with Foreign Service posts. Mission members pay their own expenses and a share of the overseas operating costs and conduct business on behalf of the firms they represent.

U.S. Government Seminar Missions

U.S. seminar missions are designed to facilitate the sale of sophisticated products and services overseas through the sharing of American technology. A seminar mission team usually consists of about seven industry representatives who travel as an official U.S. government-sponsored mission. Seminar missions combine discussions of a generic nature with private appointments to assist in attaining each company's market objectives. The key ingredient is the one-to-two day seminar forum featuring technical presentations by the members of the U.S. seminar team on the "state of the art" in the industry. The seminar adds high-level, mutually educational sessions to the sales-oriented private appointments scheduled for each seminar mission member by the Department of Commerce.

Industry-Organized Government-Approved (IOGA) Trade Missions

Industry-organized government-approved (IOGA) trade missions are organized by trade associations, chambers of commerce, state development agencies and similar groups with the advice and support of the U.S. Department of Commerce. To qualify for government sponsorship, such missions must meet established criteria. The Department of Commerce assists in planning the missions and coordinating the arrangements with the support of the respective U.S. Foreign Service posts. The Commerce Department's direct financial support for IOGA missions is limited, but the overseas operations of the IOGA trade missions are virtually identical to U.S. specialized trade missions.

167

Trademarks

Exporters generally regard adequate trademark protection abroad for their goods and services as essential to development of foreign markets. A *trademark* provides important identification for a firm's products and services in foreign markets as it does in the United States and also serves as the focal point around which that firm can develop its advertising and sales promotion campaigns. It also symbolizes to the buying public the good will, quality standards and reputation inherent in the firm's products and services.

Exclusive use and protection against infringement abroad may be had only through timely and proper registration in each country and compliance with certain other formalities. Usually the services of professional counsel are necessary for the purpose.

The United States adheres to several treaties under which exporters and other businesses are entitled to receive, in about 95 countries, the same treatment under trademark laws as those countries extend to their own nationals (national treatment). However, it is not party to any agreement whereby a U.S. trademark registration is automatically recognized and protected in a foreign country or vice versa. While U.S. nationals have rights to apply for and receive trademark registrations in countries with which the United States has treaty arrangements, they must proceed under the laws of each country to obtain these rights.

The basic multilateral agreement on trademark rights to which the United States is a party is the Paris Union International Convention for the Protection of Industrial Property, to which about 88 countries also belong. The United States also belongs to the General Inter-American Convention for Trademark and Commercial Protection of 1929, to which nine other Western Hemisphere countries are party. All of these conventions embody the national treatment principle, as well as certain special advantages for the United States business seeking trademark protection abroad.

The United States also has concluded a number of bilateral arrangements with countries—some of which are not members of the above conventions—under which our exporters receive national treatment and other protection against discriminatory practices in acquiring and maintaining trademark rights.

For further information on the subject of foreign trademark protection, laws and conventions, consult the Foreign Business Practices Division, Office of International Finance and Investment, Bureau of International Economic Policy and Research, Industry and Trade Administration, U.S. Department of Commerce.

Official journals of foreign patent offices providing trademark information are maintained by the United States Patent and Trademark Office, Crystal Plaza, 2021 Jefferson Davis Highway, Arlington, Virginia. For digests of foreign trademark laws and regulations, and general information on foreign practices, consult the following publications.

- *Foreign Business Practices,* Materials on Practical Aspects of Exporting, International Licensing and Investing, published by the U.S. Department of Commerce, Washington, D.C.
- *Overseas Business Reports,* on Marketing in_____ , or Trading with_____ , published by the U.S. Department of Commerce, Washington, D.C.
- *Industrial Property,* published monthly by the World Intellectual Property Organization, Geneva, Switzerland.

- *General Information Concerning Trademarks,* published by the United States Patent and Trademark Office, Arlington, Virginia.
- *Trademarks Throughout the World,* published by Trade Activities, Inc., New York, New York.
- *Manual for the Handling of Applications for Patents, Designs and Trademarks Throughout the World,* published by Octrooibureau Los En Stigter B.V., Amsterdam, the Netherlands.
- *The Trademark Reporter,* published monthly by the United States Trademark Association, New York, New York.

Travel

Information and advice on the many aspects of *travel* in foreign countries, both commercial and tourist, can be obtained from several government agencies. The Department of State can provide for passport, visa, health and general country information; the Department of Agriculture, for restrictions on plants and animals (Animal and Plant Health Inspection Service) (USDA, APHIS); U.S. Customs Service, for exemptions, taxes, duties and import/export information; the Department of Commerce for information on traveling with samples, visual aids and carnet information, also traveling to communist countries and setting up appointments with U.S. firms, trade associations, and government officials. They can also facilitate visits to U.S. trade shows. The Department of Justice can provide for information on the regulation of imports of narcotics and other substances under the Controlled Substances Act of 1970. For more information contact the Drug Enforcement Administration.

Specific *passport information* can be obtained from the *Washington Passport Agency,* 1425 K Street, N.W., Washington, D.C. 20524, or from passport agencies located in Boston, Chicago, Detroit, Honolulu, Houston, Los Angeles, Miami, New Orleans, New York City, Philadelphia, San Francisco, Seattle and Stamford. See publication: *You and Your Passport.*

Visa information. General information on visa requirements for U.S. citizens traveling or living abroad can also be obtained from the Washington Passport Agency. (For specific information, however, it is best to contact the Washington embassy of the foreign country involved. See Appendix. Address and telephone numbers of foreign embassies in Washington are also listed in *Foreign Consular Offices in the United States.*) See publication: *Visa Requirements of Foreign Governments.*

Immunizations. Under the International Health Regulations adopted by the World Health Organization, a country, under certain conditions, may require International Certificates of Vaccination against smallpox, yellow fever and cholera from international travelers. For return to the United States only an International Certificate of Vaccination against smallpox will be required if within the preceding 14 days a traveler has been in a country reporting smallpox. Certain immunizations and preventive measures are advisable for travelers to some countries. Specific information may be obtained from your local health department, physician, or private or public agency that advises international travelers.

Doctors assigned to the State Department's *Overseas Medical Program* can give up-to-date information on health conditions anywhere in the world. Also see: *Health Information for the International Traveler* (HEW).

For general information, consult international airlines, passenger ship companies, travel bureaus, foreign chambers of commerce in the United States, banks in foreign trade, foreign trade bureau of local chambers of commerce and field offices of the Department of Commerce.

Information on travel facilities and conditions in foreign countries will be found in references listed under other subjects in this chapter. See particularly subject headings: Steamship Services; Air Transport; Foreign Marketing; Diplomatic and Consular Services; and Exchange and Trade Controls, Foreign.

To provide international travelers, the general public and the importing community information about U.S. Customs requirements and regulations, a variety of pertinent publications are listed below.

Leaflets may be obtained free of charge at the U.S. Customs office nearest you or by writing U.S. Customs, P.O. Box 7118, Washington, D.C. 20044:

A Gift . . . Are You Sure?
Information and suggestions about gift parcels sent by persons overseas to friends and relatives in the United States so that they may qualify for entry as bona fide duty-free gifts.

Books, Copyrights & Customs
Information about copyright restrictions or prohibitions applying to importation of books.

Customs Guide For Private Flyers
Outlines principal customs requirements and procedures for private and corporate pilots making business or pleasure flights to and from foreign countries.
Price: $2.00

Customs Hints—Returning U.S. Residents
Explains customs privileges and lists prohibited and restricted imports. "Know Before You Go."
Price: $1.00.

Currency Reporting
A flyer advising that if you take into or out of the United States more than $5,000, a report must be filed with Customs.

GSP & The Traveler
Questions and answers regarding duty-free entry of certain articles brought in by travelers from beneficiary developing countries listed under the Generalized System of Preferences (GSP).
Price: 60 cents.

Importing a Car
Customs requirements for travelers importing automobiles.
Price: 90 cents.

Multinational Executive Travel Companion—Your International Travel Encyclopedia 1979

Pets, Wildlife, U.S. Customs
Summary of Customs requirements for importing cats, dogs, birds and wildlife.

Pleasure Boats
Information for owners of yachts and pleasure boats on Customs procedures for importing a boat, entry and reporting requirements.
Price: 45 cents.

Tourist Trademark Information
List of the most popular tourist items prohibited importation because the trademark owners have recorded their marks with the Treasury Department.
Price: $1.10.

Your Trip Abroad
Provides U.S. citizens traveling abroad with basic information on official documents, vaccinations, unusual travel requirements, dual nationality, drugs, modes of travel, customs, legal requirements abroad and other topics. Available through GPO.
Cat. No. S1.69:8872
Price: 45 cents.

Traveler's Tips on Bringing Food, Plant and Animal Products Into the United States, U.S. Department of Agriculture. Free. Program *Aide No. 1083, September 1979.*

Treaties and Trade Agreements

The United States enters into commercial treaties and agreements to guard and protect the commercial or other nonpolitical interests of its citizens. The formulation, negotiation and administration of commercial agreements is primarily the responsibility of the Department of State.

Commercial treaties and agreements serve many different purposes. Separate or bilateral agreements with single countries are the most common form, but the increasing interdependence of nations in recent years has given rise to more general or multilateral agreements to which many nations adhere simultaneously.

Commercial Treaties

The United States has 43 comprehensive commercial treaties now in force, ten with developing countries. The latest of these Treaties of Friendship, Commerce and Navigation (FCNs) was concluded in 1968. A 1977 General Accounting Office (GAO) report recommended that bilateral investment treaties be sought with developing countries with potential for U.S. investment and that these FCNs should emphasize protection of private foreign investment.

Bilateral Trade Agreements

The Trade Act of 1974 gives additional authority to the President to negotiate trade agreements with foreign countries for the reciprocal modification of tariffs and other barriers to trade, for the purpose of trade expansion. The Trade Act supplants the Trade Agreements Act of 1934 and the Trade Expansion Act of 1962.

Multilateral Trade Agreements

Multilateral trade agreements promote greater trade mobility among participating countries. The General Agreement on Tariffs and Trade (GATT) has sponsored a series of seven multilateral negotiations since 1947. The function of these meetings is to establish trade liberalizing rules and mechanisms. In the past, negotiations have focused on lowering tariffs, but the "Tokyo Round," concluded in Geneva in 1979, placed most emphasis on lowering nontariff barriers.

Social Security Totalization Agreements

The U.S. Social Security Administration has legislative authority to negotiate bilateral agreements with counterpart agencies in foreign countries usually covering old age, disability and survivors benefits, which would provide for:

Totalization Agreements. This type of arrangement is to reconcile problems where *different* periods of coverage are involved, as when individuals migrate from one country to another. Under

171

totalization, the credits deriving from Social Security coverage in the United States and in the foreign country may be combined to allow the individual, who has worked in both countries, to obtain benefits based on the total period of covered employment. These benefits would be calculated on a prorated basis relative to the years worked in each country with benefits based on a fair share basis. Totalization implies considerable economies to the United States, due to the large number of immigrants in the population.

Elimination of Dual Coverage. This arrangement covers situations where the *same* periods of coverage are involved, for example, during temporary foreign assignments of employees of multinational corporations. The dual coverage provision eliminates the waste involved in the obligation to continue coverage under the home country system at the same time that contributions must be made to the host country system.

International Social Security agreements are of obvious importance to the large number of people who have either emigrated from one country to another or who are on temporary foreign work assignments.

The United States has Social Security agreements in force with Italy and Germany. Several others are under active negotiation.

Further information on International Social Security agreements is available from:

Office of International Social Security Agreements
U.S. Social Security Administration
Universal North Building
Room 323D
1875 Connecticut Avenue, N.W.
Washington, D.C. 20009
Tel. (202) 673-5655

Tax Treaties

Tax treaties are negotiated by the Office of International Tax Affairs of the Treasury Department. The law requires the State Department to be consulted prior to the signing of any treaty, but its involvement is usually minimal. Foreign negotiators are ordinarily representatives of their country's tax authorities. Presently there are approximately 38 tax treaties in force.

Sources of information on trade, tax and investment treaties include:

- The Office of Treaty Affairs, Department of State.
- Office of Overseas Private Investment, Commerce Department.
- Treasury Department.
- *Treaties in Force.* Published by the State Department. Gives list of treaties and international agreements in force as of the beginning of 1980.
- *Department of State Bulletin.* Published weekly.
- United States Trade Representative, Executive Office of the President.
- Chamber of Commerce of the United States.
- American Importers Association.
- National Foreign Trade Council.

U.S. Foreign-Trade Zones

Foreign-trade zones are enclosed areas within U.S. borders but considered outside the customs territory of the United States. They are the U.S. version of what are known internationally as free trade zones and are located in or near U.S. Customs ports of entry.

Operated as public utilities by qualified corporations, these zones function under customs supervision.

Foreign and domestic merchandise may be moved into zones for operations (not otherwise prohibited by law) involving storage, exhibition, assembly, manufacture or other processing. The usual formal customs entry procedure and payment of duties are not required on the foreign merchandise unless and until it enters customs territory for domestic consumption, in which case the importer has a choice of paying duties either on the original foreign materials or the finished product. Quota restrictions do not normally apply to foreign goods in free trade zones.

U.S. free trade zones, located as they are in "doorway" port of entry communities of the world's largest market, are generally known for their service to firms using imported materials and components which are eventually sold here. By providing greater flexibility as to when and how customs duties are paid, the zones encourage these companies to use domestic facilities in distributing their foreign items and to receive them in a less-finished condition.

The use of zones for exports, on the other hand, is often overlooked (domestic goods moved into a zone for export are considered exported upon entering the zone for purposes of excise tax rebates and drawback).

Foreign trade zone exports fall into one of the following categories:

- Foreign goods transshipped through U.S. zones to third countries.
- Foreign goods processed in zones then transshipped abroad.
- Foreign goods processed or assembled in U.S. zones with some domestic materials and parts then reexported.
- Goods produced in zones wholly of foreign content and exported.
- Goods produced in zones from a combination of domestic and foreign materials and components then exported.
- Domestic goods moved into a zone to achieve export status prior to their actual exportation.

The advantage zones provide in the first five situations is basic to the zone concept. Any foreign goods or materials brought into a zone for any permissible activity and ultimately shipped to a third country, either in their original or a completely altered condition, are not subject to customs duties or federal excise taxes and usually are not chargeable against quotas. Such operations would also not normally be subject to state inventory taxes.

This makes a zone a suitable place for export processing or manufacturing operations in which high duty foreign components and materials are needed to make the end product competitive in overseas markets.

The last type of zone exports involves a means of obtaining "accelerated export status" on domestic goods before their actual shipment overseas. This benefit applies in situations where some kind of government credit accrues upon exportation.

The Foreign Trade Zones Act provides that zone export benefits may also be made available under other export programs where it is deemed advisable by the administering agency.

Typically, a foreign trade zone is a fenced-in area with a warehouse-type building or buildings and access to all modes of transportation. Space is available for leasing to firms for authorized zone activity. Some zones have industrial park characteristics or are located within such facilities and have lots on which zone users can construct their own facilities. Subzones are sites authorized by the board through zone grantees for operations by individual firms when zone procedures are vital for an operation that is in the public interest but cannot be accommodated within an existing zone.

It is estimated that there are presently over 260 customs free trade zones located in 66 countries throughout the world. In developing countries these zones provide a wide range of incentives including exemptions from internal taxes.

The regulations of the Foreign Trade Zones Board are published in the *Code of Federal Regulations* at Title 15, Part 400 (15 C.F.R. Part 400), and the *Regulations of the U.S. Customs Service* concerning zones at Title 19, Part 146 (19 C.F.R. Part 146).

The Department of Commerce Office of Import Programs has general information on U.S. Foreign Trade Zones. Also, the Department's Office of International Financial Investment collects data on foreign trade zones outside of the United States. Information on customs-privileged areas in foreign countries is available in a Department of Commerce publication entitled "Free Trade Zones and Related Facilities Abroad."

See also subject headings: Ports and Port Facilities, United States; and Imports, Entry of.

Weights and Measures, Foreign (Metric)

Because of differing national systems and designations of *weights and measures*, information as to their character and equivalents is essential. U.S. importers and exporters are becoming increasingly aware of U.S. trading partners' tendency to require products to be packaged, labeled and documented in metric units. Therefore, it is important for U.S. importers and exporters always to ascertain from their foreign importers the precise requirements of local regulation and current practices in markets of interest. (The global status of the metric system among U.S. trading partners can be seen in *Table 1*.)

The Metric Conversion Act of 1975 established the *United States Metric Board* to coordinate a process of voluntary conversion to the metric system. Its function is to devise and implement a broad program of planning, coordination and public education consistent with other national policies and interests. Due to the voluntary nature of the conversion process, no timetable has been established, nor has a date for completion been set.

The board itself is composed of 17 members appointed by the President and confirmed by the Senate. Members are nominated by organizations representing labor, small business, industry and other groups with varying national opinions on metric conversion. The U.S. Metric Board was established because the private sector created a need to coordinate a national program in all sectors.

Information on the applicability of foreign standards to U.S. products can be obtained from the American National Standards Institute (ANSI), 1430 Broadway, New York, New York 10018. If exporters do not know whether a foreign standard exists for a product in a given market or a group of markets, they may write for assistance to the Technical Help to Exporters (THE) Program, National Technical Information Service, U.S. Department of Commerce, 5285 Port Royal Road, Springfield, Virginia 22161; or to the Standards Information Service, National Bureau of Standards, Washington, D.C. 20234.

TABLE 1. U.S. TRADING PARTNERS AND THE METRIC SYSTEM

Now Use Metric System

Afghanistan	Federal Republic of Germany	Mozambique
Albania	Greece	Nepal
Algeria	Guatemala	the Netherlands
Andorra	Guinea	Nicaragua
Argentina	Guinea Bissau	Niger
Austria	Haiti	Norway
Belgium	Honduras	Panama
Benin	Hungary	Paraguay
Bolivia	Iceland	Peru
Brazil	India	Poland
Bulgaria	Indonesia	Portugal
Burundi	Iran	Romania
Cameroon	Iraq	Rwanda
Central African Republic	Israel	Saudi Arabia
Chad	Italy	Senegal
Chile	Ivory Coast	Somalia
China	Japan	Spain
Colombia	Jordan	Sudan
People's Republic of Congo	Korea	Surinam
Costa Rica	Kuwait	Sweden
Czechoslovakia	Laos	Switzerland
Denmark	Lebanon	Syria
Dominican Republic	Libya	Taiwan
Ecuador	Liechtenstein	Thailand
Egypt	Luxembourg	Togo
El Salvador	Madagascar	Tunisia
Equatorial Guinea	Mali	Turkey
Ethiopia	Mauritania	Union of Soviet Socialist
Finland	Mexico	Republics
France	Monaco	Upper Volta
Democratic Republic of	Morocco	Uruguay
Germany		Venezuela
		Yugoslavia
		Zaire

Plan to Convert to Metric System

Australia	Jamaica	Qatar
Bahamas	Kenya	Sierra Leone
Bahrain	Lesotho	Singapore
Bangladesh	Malawi	South Africa
Barbados	Malaysia	Sri Lanka
Botswana	Maldives	Swaziland
Canada	Malta	Tanzania
Cyprus	Mauritius	Tonga
Fiji	Nauru	Trinidad and Tobago
The Gambia	New Zealand	Uganda
Ghana	Nigeria	United Arab Emirates
Grenada	Oman	United Kingdom
Guyana	Pakistan	Western Samoa
Hong Kong	Papua New Guinea	Zambia
Republic of Ireland	the Philippines	

Countries not yet metric and which have not announced an intention to change

Brunei	Liberia	Yemen (People's Democratic
Burma	Yemen Arab Republic	Republic)

175

Among convenient sources of information in this field, the following are suggested: *Custom House Guide; Exporters' Encyclopedia; Managing Metrication in Business and Industry; Metric Laws and Practices in International Trade—A Handbook for U.S. Exporters* (Commerce Department); *Metric Reporter; Metric System Day-to-Day;* and *Realities of Metrication.*

For additional information, consult the Bureau of International Economic Policy and Research, Office of International Finance and Investment, Foreign Business Practices Division of the Department of Commerce; U.S. Metric Board, 1815 North Lynn Street, Arlington, Virginia 22209; National Bureau of Standards, Room B162, Technology Building, Washington, D.C. 20234; American National Metric Council, 1625 Massachusetts Avenue, N.W., Washington, D.C. 20036; foreign freight forwarders; custom house brokers; and banks in foreign trade.

Part III. Bibliography

This section lists current publications useful in gathering data pertaining to foreign commerce and allied subjects. The arrangement is alphabetical, by title, under each of four general types of material:
- Indexes to Current Publications and Periodicals.
- Reference Works, Books and Pamphlets.
- Periodicals.
- Export Business Magazines.

Additional sources can be identified through use of those which have been listed and through frequent reference to current book and periodical indexes. As an aid in this respect, several of the widely used indexes to new books and periodicals are listed preceding the section on Reference Works, Books and Pamphlets.

Selections of publications for inclusion in the bibliography have been made impartially and an effort has been made to include representative material of value.

Many of the larger reference works are available for use at public libraries and often at District offices of the U.S. Department of Commerce, local chambers of commerce and foreign departments of banks.

Most U.S. government publications for which a charge is made are obtainable from the Superintendent of Documents, Government Printing Office, Washington, D.C. 20402. When free, they usually are available directly from the department or agency issuing them or from the U.S. Department of Commerce District offices in leading cities when issued by that department.

In ordering from the Superintendent of Documents, remittances should be made in cash or by check or money order made payable to the Treasurer of the United States. Stamps are not accepted.

Indexes to Current Publications and Periodicals

Ayer's Directory of Publications. (Ayer Press, 210 West Washington Sq., Philadelphia, Pa. 10106.) Annually $56.89. Comprehensive roster of 22,700 newspapers and periodicals in over 8,000 cities and towns in the U.S. and its territories, Canada, Bermuda, Panama and the Philippine Islands.

Biographic Index. (The H.W. Wilson Co., 950 University Ave., Bronx, N.Y. 10452.) A quarterly index to biographical material appearing in periodicals and books.

Business Periodicals Index. (The H.W. Wilson Co., 950 University Ave., Bronx, N.Y. 10452.) Monthly and cumulative. An index to trade and business periodicals.

Cumulative Book Index. (The H.W. Wilson Co., 950 University Avenue, Bronx, N.Y. 10452.) Monthly and cumulative. A world list of books printed in English.

New York Times Index. (Microfilming Corp. of America, 21 Harnstown Rd., Glen Rock, N.J. 07452.) Semimonthly and annually. A classified index to *The New York Times*.

Readers' Guide to Periodical Literature. (The H.W. Wilson Co., 950 University Ave., Bronx, N.Y. 10452.) Semimonthly and cumulative. A cumulative author/subject index to 180 periodicals of general interest.

Vertical File Index. (The H.W. Wilson Co., 950 University Ave., Bronx, N.Y. 10452.) Monthly. Each issue contains a subject list of current available pamphlets, booklets, leaflets and mimeographed material arranged alphabetically by subject, with descriptive notes and conditions of availability.

Reference Works, Books and Pamphlets

The reference to sources of information and services given in this book is intended to serve the interests not only of persons with experience in the conduct of foreign trade, but also those of business persons not trading abroad but who contemplate doing so, and students of foreign commerce generally.

A Basic Guide to Exporting. (Superintendent of Documents, GPO, Wash., D.C. 20402.) 1979. $2.20. Topics covered in this book include getting started, assessing export potential, researching foreign markets, selecting sales and distribution channels, drawing up an agreement with a representative, pricing, quotations and terms of sale, financing and receiving payment for exports and shipping. It contains a bibliography of export reference materials. When ordering, cite stock number 003-009-00315-6.

ABC Europ Production. (Europ Export Edition (GMBH), P.O. Box 4034, 61 Darmstadt, Germany.) Annual. $62.00. Lists 500,000 names and addresses of exporting manufacturers under 10,000 article headings arranged by countries according to a uniform system. Indices listing 50,000 products. Six languages: English, French, Spanish, German, Italian and Portuguese.

About Foreign Exchange. (American Importers Association, 11 West 42nd St., New York, N.Y. 10036.) 1977. 32 pages. $3.25 plus postage. Easy to understand reading for importers or anyone obliged to protect himself from violent fluctuations in an era of floating currencies in foreign exchange.

A Business Guide to the Near East and North Africa. (Superintendent of Documents, GPO, Wash., D.C. 20402.) $3.50 single copy. The guide is designed to provide U.S. business with information on the nature of the market, how to do business in the area and how the Dept. of Commerce can assist in penetrating the market. When ordering, cite stock number 003-009-00330-0.

Addresses to AID Missions Overseas. (Office of Small Business, Agency for International Development, Dept. of State, Wash., D.C. 20523.) Free.

Advertising Agency Business. (Herbert S. Gardner, Jr., Crain Books, 740 Rush St., Chicago, Il. 60611.) $19.95.

Advertising World. (Directories International, Inc., 1718 Sherman Ave., Evanston, Il. 60201.) $18.00 per year. Annual. This contains international advertising news.

A Gift . . . Are You Sure? (U.S. Customs Service, U.S. Department of the Treasury, 1301 Constitution Avenue, N.W., Wash., D.C. 20229.) Free. Information and suggestions about gift parcels sent by persons overseas to friends and relatives in the United States so that they may qualify for entry as bona fide duty-free gifts.

A Guide to Financing Exports. (Office of Export Development, Industry and Trade Administration, Dept. of Commerce, Wash., D.C. 20230.) Free.

A Handbook on Financing U.S. Exports. (Machinery and Allied Products Institute, 1200 18th St., N.W., Wash., D.C. 20036.) Third edition, 1978. 187 pages. $8.00 per copy to members, $12.00 per copy to nonmembers.

AID Commodity Eligibility Listing. (Office of Small Business, Agency for International Development, Dept. of State, Wash., D.C. 20523.) Free. This 178-page document lists groups of commodities, presents the Agency for International Development commodity eligibility list, gives eligibility requirements for certain commodities and describes commodities that are not eligible for financing by the agency.

AID-Financed Export Opportunities. (Office of Small Business, Agency for International Development, Dept. of State, Wash., D.C. 20523.) Free. These are fact sheets also referred to as Small Business Circulars. They present procurement data about proposed foreign purchases.

AID Regulation 1. (Office of Small Business, Agency for International Development, Dept. of State, Wash., D.C. 20523.) Free. This tells what transactions are eligible for financing by the Agency for International Development, and the responsibilities of importers, as well as bid procedures.

AID Small Business Memo. (Office of Small Business, Agency for International Development, Dept. of State, Wash., D.C. 20523.) Free. These are issued occasionally to treat matters such as new Agency for International Development procurement policies, and amendments to the regulation which governs the agency.

American Association of Advertising Agencies—A.A.A.A. Roster and Organization. (American Association of Advertising Agencies, 200 Park Ave., New York, N.Y. 10017.) Annual. Free. Alphabetical listing of member agencies, operating offices in the United States and abroad; gives home office address, location of branches. Listed geographically, by state and city; also by foreign country. Includes committees and regional councils. Single copies available to firms and organizations by request on letterhead.

American Chambers of Commerce Abroad: What They Are, What They Do, Why Join (5517). (Chamber of Commerce of the U.S., 1615 H St., N.W., Wash., D.C. 20062.) 1977. $1.00. A comprehensive analysis of the purposes, activities and services of American chambers of commerce abroad.

American Register of Exporters and Importers. (American Register, 1 Penn Plaza, 250 N. 34th St., New York, N.Y. 10001.) 1979. $60.00. A listing of 25,000 firms, this book is designed for persons searching for U.S. suppliers, for foreign manufacturers seeking U.S. buyers or representatives and for foreign representatives looking for U.S. firms to represent. It contains product lists in four languages, an advertisers' index, information about and a list of U.S. chambers of commerce abroad, a list of banks with international services and shipping, finance and insurance information.

An Introduction to Contract Procedures in the Near East and North Africa. (Superintendent of Documents, GPO, Wash., D.C. 20402.) 1978. $2.20 single copy. The book alerts U.S. business persons to the potential dangers while contracts are being negotiated for work in 17 countries of the Near East and North Africa. The book answers questions commonly asked of the Dept. of Commerce by U.S. companies. When ordering, cite stock number 003-009-00252-4.

The Annual Report of the President of the United States on Trade Agreements Programs. Free. (Office of the United States Trade Representative, Executive Office of the President, Wash., D.C.).

Annual Report on Exchange Restrictions. (International Monetary Fund, 700 19th St., N.W., Wash., D.C. 20431.) First copy free, any additional copies $5.00 each. Reviews exchange controls and restrictions in the world and describes the exchange systems and related measures of all fund members, as well as several other countries.

Antitrust Guide for International Operations. (U.S. Dept. of Justice.) Jan. 26, 1977 (revised March 1977).

A Selective Study Guide to the European Community. (European Community Delegation, Information Service, Ste. 707, 2100 M St., N.W., Wash., D.C. 20037.) 1977. 24 pages. Free. Bibliography of selected official documents and literature on European integration and related subjects dealing with the European Community.

Association of American Chambers of Commerce in Latin America (5516). (Chamber of Commerce of the U.S., 1615 H Street, N.W., Wash., D.C. 20062.) 1977. Single copy free. Describes the Association of American Chambers of Commerce in Latin America—its origins, mission, objectives and policy positions—and lists addresses of its members.

Associations Registered Under the Webb-Pomerene Export Trade Act. (National Trade and Professional Associations of the U.S. and Canada, Columbia Books, Inc., Wash., D.C.).

A Survey of Business Needs and Export Marketing: Federal and Nonfederal Sources of Assistance. (Office of Export Development, International Trade Administration, U.S. Dept. of Commerce.) March, 1978. Free.

ATA Carnet. (U.S. Customs Service, U.S. Dept. of Treasury, Wash., D.C. 20229.) 1978. Free. An explanation as to the use of ATA carnets which simplify customs formalities for the temporary admission of certain goods.

Background Notes. (Superintendent of Documents, GPO, Wash., D.C. 20402.) $16.00 per year or 75 cents per copy. These are four- to 12-page summaries on the economy, people, history, culture and government of about 160 foreign countries.

Bankers Handbook for Asia: Guide to Banks and Finance Companies in Asia. (UNIPUB, 345 Park Ave., S., New York, N.Y. 10010.) 1977. $32.50. This provides profiles of banks and finance companies in Asia, and reports about 21 Asian national economies. When ordering, cite symbol UNIPUB: N16.

Bilateral Treaties for International Investment. (U.S. Council of the International Chamber of Commerce, 1212 Avenue of the Americas, New York, N.Y. 10036.) 1977. $2.50. A checklist of nearly 150 treaties concluded since 1945 is provided, and the report concludes with a selection of points from various treaties, chosen to illustrate interesting questions of principle and of law.

Brandon's Shipper and Forwarder. (Herbert A. Brandon, One World Trade Center, Ste. 3169, New York, N.Y. 10048.) $20.00 per year.

Brazilian Investment Policy: Priorities and Perspectives (6022). (Chamber of Commerce of the United States, 1615 H St., N.W., Wash., D.C. 20062.) 1979. $4.00.

Bulletin of the European Communities. (European Community Information Service, 2100 M St., N.W., Ste. 707, Wash., D.C. 20037.) Surface mail: $37.60. Airmail: $18.40 additional. Eleven issues and Index. *Supplements to the Bulletin.* Standing order available. Invoiced quarterly according to the number of pages in supplement.

Capital Markets in Asia's Developing Countries. (Business International, One Dag Hammarskjold Plaza, New York, N.Y. 10017.) 1978. $152.00. Overview of the developments of the region's capital and money markets and how the changing financial scene affects local and foreign private investors and bankers. Covers the role of central banks, government and local and foreign private commercial banks, the history and short-term outlooks for currencies, stock exchanges, Asia dollars, economic nationalism, regional roles of the IMF, World Bank, Asian Development Bank.

Career Opportunities in the International Field. (School of Foreign Service, Georgetown University, Wash., D.C. 20057.) 1977. $3.50.

Careers in Foreign Languages: A Handbook. (June L. Sherif, Regents Publishing Company, Inc., 2 Park Ave., New York, N.Y. 10016.) 1966. Revised edition 1975. 228 pages. $3.50.

CEPAL (Comision Economico Para America Latina) Review. (UNIPUB, 345 Park Ave. S., New York, N.Y. 10010.) Annual. $3.00 per copy. By the United Nations Economic Commission for Latin America, this magazine contains economic news and various articles about Latin America. When ordering, cite symbol UN 77/2G5.

Chase World Guide for Exporters. Export Credit Reports. (Chase World Information Corp., One World Trade Center, Ste. 4533, New York, N.Y. 10048.) The *Guide,* covering 180 countries, contains current export financing methods, collection experiences and charges, foreign import and exchange regulations and related subjects. Supplementary bulletins keep the *Guide* up to date throughout the year. Annual subscription: $175.00. The *Reports,* issued quarterly, specify credit terms granted for shipments to all the principal world markets. The reports are skillfully designed to show at a glance the credit terms offered by industry groups as a whole, thereby enabling the reader to determine whether his terms are more liberal or constrictive than the average for specific commodity groups. Annual subscription: $250.00. Combination subscription for both the *Guide* and the *Reports:* $320.00.

China's Economy and Foreign Trade. (Superintendent of Documents, GPO, Wash., D.C. 20402.) 1978. $2.30. This book is primarily of background value. The appendix, which shows U.S. exports to China for 1977, is useful as an indicator of U.S. goods that already have found a market in the People's Republic of China. When ordering, cite stock number 003-009-00262-1.

Classification Manual for the OAS Official Records Series: A Manual for the Maintenance of the Series. (Sales and Promotion Unit, Dept. of Publications, Organization of American States, Wash., D.C. 20006.) 1977. 119 pages. $3.00. Expands and updates the OAS documents classification system, in accordance with the changes introduced by the Protocol of Buenos Aires (1970). Classifies documents for the eight principal organs, provides information on the classification for multilateral treaties, agreements, conventions, bilateral and regional agreements deposited with the General Secretariat and indices to the Series and guides to its use.

Cost Marine & Transportation Directory. (Pacific Shipper, Inc., 1050 Sansome St., San Francisco, Ca. 94111.) $14.00. Annual directory of names, addresses, phones of all Pacific Coast maritime and transportation industry persons, organizations and firms.

Commodity Identification Studies. (Export Trade Services Division, Dept. of Agriculture, 14th & Independence Ave., S.W., Rm. 4945-S, Wash., D.C. 20250.) Free. This series of booklets describes food markets and market potential in several foreign countries, presenting background information about the poeple, geography, government, business and similar matters.

Commodity Year Book. (Commodity Research Bureau, Inc., One Liberty Plaza, New York, N.Y. 10006.) 1978. 386 pages. $25.95. Tables, charts and text showing world trends in basic raw materials, prices, supplies and consumption.

Comparison Advertising. (J. Boddewyn, Hastings House Publishers, 10 East 40th St., New York, N.Y. 10016.) 245 pages. $12.50. Worldwide study of the practice, use and legal and other problems related to the naming of competitors in advertisements. Includes analysis of recent research on effectiveness of such advertising, and discusses future trends. Contains specific examples from many countries.

Concise Guide to International Markets. (Leslie Stinton & Partners, 39 London Rd., Kingston-upon-Thames, Surrey KT2 6ND, England.) 1977/78 edition. 512 pages. £20 or U.S. $38.00. Contains concise data and vital statistics in advertising and marketing in 110 world markets, including population, literacy, languages, religions, climate, working hours, income, retail and wholesale structure, advertising agencies, commissions, associations, advertising controls, advertising expenditures, media categories, market research facilities and more than 100 maps.

The Congressional Directory. (Superintendent of Documents, GPO, Wash., D.C. 20402.) Hard cover, thumb index $13.00 (S/N 052-070-04811-5). Paperback, $7.25 (S/N 052-070-04809-3). Names, addresses, biographies and office phones of government officials and members of Congress. Also lists committee assignments of every member.

Container Transport and Developing Countries. (U.S. Council of the International Chamber of Commerce, 1212 Avenue of the Americas, New York, N.Y. 10036.) 1977. $2.50.

Copyright Laws and Treaties of the World. (The Bureau of National Affairs, Inc., 1231 25th St., N.W., Wash., D.C. 20037.) 1978. $450.00. Compilation of texts of copyright laws, orders, rules and regulations in effect in the United States, foreign countries and their territories. Supplements issued periodically at special price.

Countertrade Practices in Eastern Europe, the Soviet Union and China: An Introductory Guide for Business. (Superintendent of Documents, GPO, Wash., D.C. 20402.) $3.75. When ordering, cite stock number 003-009-00332-6.

Country Experts in the Federal Government. (Washington Researchers, 918 16th St., N.W., Wash., D.C. 20006.) 1978. $15.00. This is a listing of individuals in the federal government who study foreign countries or regions. The listing includes telephone numbers.

Currency Reporting. (U.S. Customs Service, Wash., D.C. 20229.) Free. A flyer advising that if you take into or out of the United States more than $5,000, a report must be filed with Customs.

Custom House Guide. (North American Publishing Co., 401 N. Broad St., Philadelphia, Pa. 19108.) $98.00. Directory presents listings of approximately 10,000 firms serving foreign trade in each American port; railroad, steamship and airline, custom brokers, foreign freight forwarders, banks, warehousemen, truckmen, etc. Contains complete tariff schedule; alphabetic index of some 35,000 different commodities with duty rates.

Customs Guide for Private Flyers. (Superintendent of Documents, GPO, Wash., D.C. 20402.) $2.00. Outlines principal customs requirements and procedures for private and corporate pilots making business or pleasure flights to and from foreign countries.

Customs Hints for Visitors (Nonresidents). U.S. Customs Service, U.S. Dept. of Treasury. (Superintendent of Documents, GPO, Wash., D.C. 20402.) 1976. $1.00 per copy, $10.00 for 100 copies. Customs exemptions for foreign visitors arriving in the United States. (English language only.)

181

Customs Hints—Returning U.S. Residents. U.S. Customs Service, U.S. Dept. of Treasury. (Superintendent of Documents, GPO, Wash., D.C. 20402.) 1977. $1.00 per copy. $7.00 per 50 copies. Explains customs privileges and lists prohibited and restricted imports. "Know Before You Go."

Customs Rulings on Imports. (U.S. Customs Service, U.S. Dept. of Treasury, Wash., D.C. 20229.) Free. Explains how importers may obtain a binding U.S. Customs duty ruling on items before importation.

Digest of Commercial Laws of the World. (Six volumes.) (National Association of Credit Management, George Kohlik, Editor. Oceana Publications, Inc., Dobbs Ferry, N.Y. 10522.) 1978. $300.00. Embracing 65 nations, provides instant, up-to-date digest of national laws, keyed to single classification system and format.

Directory of American Firms Operating in Foreign Countries, Ninth Edition. (J. L. Angel. World Trade Academy Press, 50 E. 42nd St., New York, N.Y. 10017.) 1979. 1600 pages. $125.00. Contains the most recent data on more than 4,200 American corporations controlling and operating over 16,500 foreign business enterprises. Lists every American firm under the country in which it has subsidiaries or branches, together with their home office address in the United States. Also gives names and addresses of each of their subsidiaries or branches, products manufactured or distributed.

Directory of Foreign Firms Operating in the United States, Fourth Edition. (World Trade Academy Press, 50 E. 42nd St., New York, N.Y. 10017.) 1979. 600 pages. $85.00. Pinpoints the activities of foreign competitors in the United States. Demonstrates the feasibility of engaging in operations similar to those already established and reveals the vast opportunities that exist for doing business with foreign corporations.

Directory of United States Importers. (The Journal of Commerce, 445 Marshall St., Phillipsburg, N.J. 08865.) $150.00. Contains alphabetical and categorical listings of over 25,000 U.S. importers and the commodities they import by SITC classification.

District Export Councils-Membership Directory. (President's Export Council, Dept. of Commerce Building, 14th & Constitution Ave., N.W., Rm. 3064, Wash., D.C. 20230.) May, 1978. Free. District Export Councils are local businesses working with the Dept. of Commerce to expand U.S. exporting. This book lists their names, addresses and telephone numbers.

Doing Business in the Federal Government. (General Services Administration, Office of Publications (XI), 18th & F St., N.W., Wash., D.C. 20405.) 1978. Free.

Dun & Bradstreet Exporters' Encyclopaedia—World Marketing Guide. (Dun & Bradstreet International, Ltd., 1 World Trade Center, Ste. 9069, New York, N.Y. 10048.) $250.00. Annual. This reference book describes the filing of an export order, from the time it is received to the preparation of merchandise for shipment. By country, it outlines regulations concerning import and exchange controls and provides general export information about matters including banking terms, collection of drafts and letters of credit. The book also provides information about airmail fees, air cargo charges and international associations, chambers of commerce and U.S. government offices that offer trade assistance. Purchase of the book includes *Export Documentation Digest,* which sells separately for $50.00, a twice-monthly supplementary bulletin and the twice-monthly *World Marketing* news publication.

Dunn & Bradstreet Principal International Businesses. (Dunn & Bradstreet, Inc., 99 Church St., New York, N.Y. 10007.) $395.00. Annual. This book describes about 50,000 leading companies in 136 countries. It is cross-referenced by Standard Industrial Classification code and by geographic location.

East-West Trade Report. (Council of the International Chamber of Commerce, 1212 Avenue of the Americas, New York, N.Y. 10036.) 1977. $5.00. Includes a study of East-West trade, statistical data and a structural and country-by-country analysis of trade development.

Economic Bulletin for Asia and the Pacific. (UNIPUB, 345 Park Ave., S., New York, N.Y. 10010.) 1979. $11.00 plus $1.00 handling. Annual. By the United Nations Economic and Social Commission for Asia and the Pacific, this covers economic news. When ordering, cite symbol UN 79/2F9.

Economic Survey of Europe. (UNIPUB, 345 Park Ave., S., New York, N.Y. 10010.) $10.00 for each volume. Annual in two volumes. These books, by the Economic Commission for Europe, provide European economic statistical data. To order, cite cymbol UN 78/2E1.

Economic Survey of Latin America. (UNIPUB, 345 Park Ave., S., New York, N.Y. 10010.) $20.00. Annual. By the Economic Commission for Latin America, this book provides economic statistical data on Latin America. When ordering, cite symbol UN 78/2G1.

The EMC—Your Export Department. (Office of Export Development, Dept. of Commerce, 14th & Constitution Ave., N.W., Rm. 1326 or 1617, Wash., D.C. 20230.) Free. This Dept. of Commerce brochure explains the ways an export management company can assist a U.S. manufacturer in exporting, freeing the manufacturer from having to set up an export department.

Employment Abroad: Facts and Fallacies (6145). (Chamber of Commerce of the United States, 1615 H St., N.W., Wash., D.C. 20062.) 1979. $2.50. Discusses some of the major points to be considered in looking for employment which may result in foreign travel or residence. Gives some indication of the criteria used by American business in choosing employees for foreign operations. Lists sources of additional information.

Employment Output and Foreign Trade of U.S. Manufacturing Industries (1963-1979). (Trade Relations Council of the United States, Inc., 1001 Connecticut Ave., N.W. Wash., D.C. 20036.) $250.00.

The Encyclopedia of Associations. (Gale Research Co., Book Tower, Detroit, Mi. 48226.) Volume 1: *National Organizations of the U.S.* 1,434 pages. $95.00. Standard reference guide to America's 13,274 national associations, professional societies and other nonprofit membership organizations. Volume 2: *Geographic and Executive Index.* 750 pages. $85.00 Volume 3: *New Associations and Projects.* Provides details on newly formed associations (updates Volume I). Published three times per year. $95.00 for subscription.

The European Community and ASEAN. (European Community Information Service, 2100 M St., N.W., Ste. 707, Wash., D.C. 20037.) Europe Information No. 16/79, Commission, Brussels, February 1979. 14 pages. Free. Note on the development of EC/ASEAN relations including trade, investment and industrial cooperation and development assistance.

The European Community and the Countries of the EFTA. (European Community Information Service, 2100 M St., N.W., Ste. 707, Wash., D.C. 20037.) Europe Information No. 12/79, Commission, Brussels, January 1979. 15 pages. Free. Description of the trade agreements between the Community and each of the members of the European Free Trade Association.

Europe's Rules of Competition. (Business International, One Dag Hammarskjold Plaza, New York, N.Y. 10017.) 1978. $150.00. Comprehensive analysis of new and differing legislation affecting business in individual European countries and the EEC. Explains the guidelines used by national and supra-national authorities in assessing whether a business practice is harmfully restrictive or not.

Eximbank. (Export-Import Bank of the United States, 811 Vermont Ave., N.W. Wash., D.C. 20571.) Free. This booklet describes financing programs by the Export-Import Bank.

EXIM Bank Information Kit. (Export-Import Bank of the United States, 811 Vermont Ave., N.W., Wash., D.C. 20571.) Free. Includes "Annual Report," describes EXIM Bank programs, also includes information on interest rates and the Foreign Credit Insurance Association, as well as the latest issue of "EXIM Bank Record."

Export Administration Regulations. (Superintendent of Documents, GPO, Wash., D.C. 20402.) 1979. $30.00 in the United States, $37.50 to foreign countries; copies of the supplement are 50 cents each, and can be purchased from: Publications Sales Branch, Dept. of Commerce, 14th & Constitution Ave., N.W., Rm. 1617, Wash., D.C. 20230. A book with supplements, this lists regulations that explain when a U.S. exporter must have a validated export license, required for certain types of goods, such as weapons, being shipped to certain countries. The book is prepared by the Bureau of East-West Trade at the Dept. of Commerce. The supplement is called *Export Administration Bulletin.*

Export Directory. (Foreign Agricultural Service Information Services Staff, Dept. of Agriculture, 14th & Independence Ave., S.W., Rm. 5918-S, Wash., D.C.) 1978/1979. Free. The directory describes principal functions of the Foreign Agricultural Service and lists agricultural attaches in about 60 United States embassies abroad. It lists Foreign Agricultural Service marketing directors and other specialists in the United States. The book also lists state departments of agriculture, some of the foreign embassies in the U.S. and government and private organizations of help to international traders.

Exporters Directory/U.S. Buying Guide. (Journal of Commerce, 445 Marshall St., Phillipsburg, N.J. 08865.) The 1979-80 edition is current, $150.00. New in November, 1980—1980-81 edition, $175.00. This directory lists and provides business details about 40,000 U.S. exporting firms by Standard Industrial Trade Classification and state. It includes an alphabetical list of the firms, a list of banks that provide international banking services and a branch name index.

Exporter's Guide to Cargo Insurance. (American Institute of Marine Underwriters, 14 Wall St., New York, N.Y. 10005.) 16 pages. $1.00.

Export Handbook. (Mid-America International Agri-Trade Council, 300 West Washington St., Chicago, Il. 60606.) Free. The handbook includes chapters on trade assistance from the private sector, international terms, foreign trade abbreviations, revised foreign trade definitions and conversion tables.

Export-Import Financing—A Practical Guide. (Gerhard W. Schneider, John Wiley & Sons, Inc., Box 092, Somerset, N.J. 08873.) 1974. $23.95. This book presents details of foreign trade financing, including customs, practices and procedures of financing and services available for making international payments.

Export-Import Traffic Management and Forwarding. (Alfred Murr, Cornell Maritime Press, Box 456, Centerville, Md. 21617.) 6th edition, 1979. 640 pages. $22.50. Presents the diverse functions and varied services concerned with the entire range of ocean traffic management.

Exporting to the European Community, Information for Foreign Exporters. (European Community Information Service, Ste. 707, 2100 M St., N.W., Wash., D.C. 20037.) 1977. 70 pages. $1.40.

Exporting to the United States. U.S. Customs Service, U.S. Dept. of Treasury. (Superintendent of Documents, GPO, Wash., D.C. 20402.) 1977. 100 pages. $4.00. Booklet for foreign exporters planning to ship goods to the United States.

Export Marketing for Smaller Firms. (Superintendent of Documents, GPO, Wash., D.C. 20402.) 1971. $2.20. The book discusses the evaluation of foreign markets and the selection of foreign representatives or distributors. It also describes U.S. and foreign organizations that can assist exporters, and outlines what to say in a first letter to a potential foreign distributor. It covers the advantages and disadvantages of doing business with a large foreign trading company, emphasizing the importance of international trade fairs and exhibits. When ordering, cite stock number 045-000-00158-0. 1979. This has sections on shipping, banking and other information useful to exporters.

FAO Production Yearbook. (UNIPUB, 345 Park Ave., S., New York, N.Y. 10010.) 1978. Volume 32. $18.50. The latest issue of the Food and Agricultural Organization's standard reference annual, this contains data about important aspects of world production of food. The yearbook also includes statistics on land use, livestock, prices, wages and means of production. When ordering, cite symbol UNIPUB: F1837.

The Far East and Australasia. (UNIPUB, 345 Park Ave., S., New York, N.Y. 1001). 1979-80. $84.00. This book by Europa is a survey and reference publication on South Asia, South East Asia, Australasia and the Pacific Islands. It includes essays by about 50 geographers, historians and economists of several nationalities. There are detailed surveys of about 30 countries, discussing history, geography, economy, government, political parties and similar matters. The book is concluded with a who's who of the Far East and Australasia.

Federal Jobs Overseas. (U.S. Civil Service Commission. Superintendent of Documents, GPO, Wash., D.C. 20402.) 1977. 80 cents.

Federal Regulatory Directory. (Congressional Quarterly, 1414 22nd St., N.W., Wash., D.C. 20037.) 786 pages. $22.50. Information on each regulatory agency, where it gets its authority, within what limits, and who's who in each office, plus other details.

184

15 Ways the U.S. Department of Commerce Can Help Make Your Business More Profitable Through Exports. (International Trade Administration, U.S. Department of Commerce, Wash., D.C. 20230.) Free. Lists the facilities and services of the Commerce Department for overseas marketing.

Financing Imports and Exports. (International Division, Chemical Bank, 20 Pine St., New York, N.Y. 10005.) 52 pages. Free. This book discusses export letters of credit and shows samples. It also explains foreign collections and shows sample sight and time drafts, and explains non-recourse export financing.

The Financing of Exports and Imports. (Morgan Guaranty Trust Co. of N.Y., 23 Wall St., New York, N.Y. 10015.) 1979. Free. A booklet which discusses export letters of credit, drafts and other methods of payment and regulations of exports and imports.

Foreign Business Practices. (Superintendent of Documents, GPO, Wash., D.C. 20402.) 1975. $3.75. In this book is information about the practical aspects of exporting, international licensing and investing. Important laws, such as the Webb-Pomerene Act and world trademark laws are covered. When ordering, cite stock number 003-009-00213-3.

Foreign Consular Offices in the U.S. (Superintendent of Documents, GPO, Wash., D.C. 20402.) $3.50. When ordering, cite stock number 044-000-01759-8.

Foreign Exchange Markets in the United States. (Roger M. Kubarych. Federal Reserve Bank of N.Y., N.Y.) August, 1978. A guide to foreign exchange markets, the mechanics of how they work and how banks operate in them.

Foreign Investment in the Third World: A Comparative Study of Selected Developing Country Investment Promotion Programs (6005). (Chamber of Commerce of the United States, 1615 H St., N.W., Wash., D.C. 20062.) 1980. $10.00.

Foreign Market Reports. (National Technical Information Service, 5285 Port Royal Rd., Springfield, Va. 22161.) Price varies, depending upon the length of the report. Series of reports compiled by the Dept. of Commerce and based on information collected by commercial officers of U.S. Foreign Service posts in more than 100 countries. Topics covered include the West German market for pollution control devices and Japanese demand for foreign timber in the first half of 1977.

Foreign Trade Marketplace. (George J. Schultz, Editor. Gale Research Co., Book Tower, Detroit, Mi. 48226.) 1977. 622 pages. $58.00. This reference book for exporters lists export management companies, foreign distributors, importing organizations in socialist countries, general trading companies overseas and similar items. It includes data about export and import procedures, financing institutions and sources of assistance for international licensing, franchising and transportation.

Freight Shipping Directory. (Port of Los Angeles, P.O. Box 151, San Pedro, Ca. 90733.) 1978. Free. The directory is a port-to-port guide showing which shipping lines travel from the Port of Los Angeles.

GATT Activities. (GATT Secretariat, Centre William Rappard, 154 rue de Lausanne, 1211 Geneva 21, Switzerland.) Annual, $5.00. Describes trade policy issues and other work before the GATT Contracting Parties and Secretariat during the previous year.

GATT Annual Reports on International Trade. (GATT Secretariat, Centre William Rappard, 154 rue de Lausanne, 1211 Geneva 21, Switzerland.) Annual, $11.00. Describes trends and developments in international trade during the previous year.

GATT, What It Is, What It Does. (GATT Secretariat, Centre William Rappard, 154 rue de Lausanne, 1211 Geneva 21, Switzerland.) 1977. Free. A leaflet describing GATT's origins, aims and functions.

General Information Concerning Trademarks. (United States Patent and Trademark Office, Commissioner of Patents, Wash., D.C. 20231.) 1978. Single copy free.

Geographical Index. (Office of Public Affairs, International Trade Administration, Dept. of Commerce, 14th & Constitution Ave., N.W., Wash., D.C. 20230.) 1979. Free, semi-annual. Geographical index to market reports.

Global Market Surveys. (Contact: Commerce Dept. district offices.) Free. Developed by the Dept. of Commerce Market Research Division and officers of U.S. Foreign Service posts, these studies evaluate market potential for products and industries in individual countries.

GSP & the Traveler. (U.S. Customs Service, U.S. Dept. of Treasury, Wash., D.C. 20229.) 60 cents. Annual. Questions and answers regarding duty-free entry of certain articles brought in by travelers from beneficiary developing countries listed under the Generalized System of Preferences (GSP).

Guide to American Directories. (B. Klein Publications, Inc., P. O. Box 8503, Coral Springs, Fla. 33065.) 10th edition. $45.00. Describes under 300 subject headings 4,500 major general and specialized business directories of United States.

Guide to Documentary Credit Operations. (United States Council, International Chamber of Commerce, 1212 Avenue of the Americas, New York, N.Y. 10036.) $6.25. This book explains the International Chamber of Commerce Uniform Customs and Practice for Documentary Credits.

Guide to Foreign Exchange. (Continental Illinois National Bank and Trust Co., 231 South La Salle St., Chicago, Il. 60693.) Free.

Guide to Incoterms. (ICC Publishing Corp., Inc., 1212 Avenue of the Americas, New York, N.Y. 10036.) March, 1980. $8.75. An explanation of the terms and examples of their use.

Guide to Legislation on Restrictive Business Practices, 4th edition. (OECD Publications Center, 1750 Pennsylvania Ave., N.W., Wash., D.C. 20006.) 1976. 2,000 pages. $250 for four bound volumes, which includes eight series of supplements. $15.00 for 9th series; $30.00 for 10th series; $30.00 for 11th (and current) series. Contains authoritative comments of expert government officials on enactments of 20 OECD countries. Each country's legislation is accompanied by a review of the historical background, a selection of administrative and court decisions and a bibliography.

Handbook of International Trade and Development Statistics. (UNIPUB, 345 Park Ave., S., New York, N.Y. 10010.) 1979. $44.00. Analytical data in this publication show the value of trade, commodity prices, imports and exports, development indicators, commodity classification of world trade, trade volume and consumption. Covered are the European Economic Community, the United States and Japan. When ordering, cite symbol UN 79/2D2.

Harbor Handbook. (Port of Long Beach, P.O. Box 570, Long Beach, Ca. 90801.) Free. Published quarterly. The handbook describes port facilities.

How To Find Information About Companies. (Washington Researchers, 918 16th St., N.W., Wash., D.C. 20006.) 1979. $45.00. This book gives sources in the state, federal and local governments, the courts and the private sector for finding information about companies. It includes a chapter about obtaining facts on foreign firms.

How To Get the Job You Want Overseas. (Arthur Liebers, Pilot Books, 347 Fifth Ave., New York, N.Y. 10016.) 1976. $2.50. Tells where the jobs are, who is offering them, salary scales and employment benefits. Covers private industry and government opportunities.

How To Get the Most From Overseas Promotions. (Office of Export Development, Dept. of Commerce, 14th & Constitution Ave., N.W., Rm. 1326 or 1617, Wash., D.C. 20230.) Free. An eight-page booklet, this outlines the steps an exporter should take to participate in overseas exhibitions organized by the Commerce Department.

How To Work With PEFCO. (Private Export Funding Corp., 280 Park Ave., New York, N.Y. 10017.) Free. This explains the operations of the Private Export Funding Corporations.

ICC Arbitration Guide: The International Solution to International Business Disputes. (United States Council, International Chamber of Commerce, 1212 Avenue of the Americas, New York, N.Y. 10036.) 1975. $16.50. This book explains how the Arbitration Court of the International Chamber of Commerce works, and includes the court rules.

Importer Listings. (Office of Small Business, Agency for International Development, Dept. of State, Wash., D.C. 20523.) 1974. Free. Includes information about importing firms from the Dept. of Commerce world trade reports and from records of the Agency for International Development.

Importing a Car. (Superintendent of Documents, GPO, Wash., D.C. 20402.) 90 cents. Customs requirements for travelers importing automobiles.

INCOTERMS. (ICC Publishing Corp., Inc., 1212 Avenue of the Americas, New York, N.Y. 10036.) March, 1980. $5.00. A revision of the terms used in *American Foreign Trade Definitions—Revised 1941.*

The Increased Export Opportunities Accorded to India by the U.S. Generalized System of Preferences (GSP) (5687). (Chamber of Commerce of the United States, 1615 H St., N.W., Wash., D.C. 20062.) 1977. $20.00 A survey, prepared for the India-U.S. Business Council, which identifies increased opportunities for Indian exports to the U.S. by product category.

Index to Trade Lists. (Commerce Dept. district offices or: Dept. of Commerce, 14th & Constitution Ave., N.W., Rm. 1312, Wash., D.C. 20230.) Free. This is a list of trade lists available from the Dept. of Commerce. Revised every two to three months.

Information Guide for Doing Business in (Name of Country). (Price Waterhouse & Co., 1251 Avenue of the Americas, New York, N.Y. 10020.) Free. More than 80 countries are covered by this series. The publications include information about tax systems, business environment, exchange controls, regulations affecting foreign companies and similar matters. Each guide has a chapter on exporting. Updates periodically.

International Advertising Association Annual Membership Directory. (International Advertising Association, 475 Fifth Ave., New York, N.Y. 10017.) Free to members; $50.00 for nonmembers. Annual. This lists association members in 80 countries.

International Bankers Directory. (Rand McNally & Company, Bank Publishing Division, P.O. Box 7600, Chicago, Il. 60680.) Semi-annual (May and November). 4,900 pages. $85.00 single copy. With five-year contract, $75.00 per year for one copy; $130.00 per year for both copies. Complete listing of all U.S. banks and all foreign banks engaged in exchange. Arranged by country, city and alphabetically for speedy reference. Complete with addresses, principal officer, correspondents, financial figures.

International Boycotts. (Business Laws, Inc., P.O. Box 24162, Cleveland, Oh. 44124.) 1979. $45.00 per year.

The International Business Environment, A Management Guide. (Harold J. Peck, American Management Association, Inc., 135 W. 50th St., New York, N.Y. 10020.) 1969.

International Centre for Technical Expertise. (United States Council, International Chamber of Commerce, 1212 Avenue of the Americas, New York, N.Y. 10036.) 1977. $2.50. Experts at the International Centre for Technical Expertise assist in resolving legal disputes stemming from export contracts. This book describes the manner of intervention and how the experts are selected.

International Economics. Sixth Edition. (Charles P. Kindleberger, Richard D. Irwin, Inc., 1818 Ridge Road, Homewood, Il. 60430.) 1978. $18.25.

International Finance Corporation, General Policies. (International Finance Corp., 1818 H St., N.W., Wash., D.C. 20433.) 1977. Free. Published in Spanish, French and English.

International Jobs: Where They Are, How to Get Them. (Eric Kocher, Addison-Wesley Publishing Company, Reading, Mass. 01867.) 1979. $5.95 (paperback). Handbook for over 500 career opportunities around the world.

International Licensing: Opportunities and Challenges in Worldwide Technology Management. (Business International, One Dag Hammarskjold Plaza, New York, N.Y. 10017.) 1978. $150.00. Provides a broad and comprehensive analysis of the growing importance of licensing as an international business strategy, the benefits and limitations to the corporation when it acts as licensor and as licensee, and the licensing department in the context of organization, business management and personnel issues.

International Mail. (Superintendent of Documents, GPO, Wash., D.C. 20402.) $9.00. This book contains regulations and details about postage rates, prohibitions, import restrictions and other matters concerning postal service to foreign countries.

International Marketing. Second Edition. (Vern Terpstra, The Dryden Press, 901 N. Elm St., Hinsdale, Il. 60521.) 1978. $19.95 per copy.

International Marketing. Fourth Edition. (Philip R. Cateora and John M. Hess, Richard D. Irwin, Inc., 1818 Ridge Rd., Homewood, Il. 60430.) 1979. $16.00.

International Marketing. Fourth Edition. (Roland L. Kramer and Ruel C. Kahler, Southwestern Publishing Company, 5101 Madison Rd., Cincinnati, Oh. 45227.) 1977. 425 pages. $17.15. Focus is upon finding international opportunities via data analysis. Stresses managerial aspects of planning and decision-making for international marketing. Demonstrates the integration of international-related institutions, tools and techniques into the international marketing program.

International Monetary Fund Annual Report. (International Monetary Fund, 700 19th St., N.W., Wash., D.C. 20431.) Free. Describes the Fund's activities during the past fiscal year and surveys world economic developments.

International Policy Development and Business Diplomacy—Programs Staffed by the International Division (6273). (Chamber of Commerce of the U.S., 1615 H Street, N.W., Wash., D.C. 20062.) Free. Description of individual councils, committees and subcommittees—including purposes, objectives and activities—staffed by the International Division of the U.S. Chamber. 1980.

An International Rule of Law. (Eberhard P. Deutsch, University Press of Virginia, Box 3608 University Station, Charlottesville, Va. 22903.) 1977. 418 pages. $20.00. Examines the weaknesses of the International Court of Justice and argues for compulsory jurisdiction of the court over international disputes.

International Telex Directory. (International Publishing Service, 114 E. 32nd St., New York, N.Y. 10016.) 28th Edition, 6 volumes. 1979. $100.00. 1980 edition—$140.00.

International Trade. (UNIPUB, 345 Park Ave., S., New York, N.Y. 10010.) 1978. $18.00. This book contains the latest annual report and detailed analysis of world trade in commodities. Subjects covered are main trends in international trade, long-term outlook, commodity prices for foodstuffs, ores, petroleum and textiles. When ordering, cite symbol UNIPUB: G121.

International Trade Reporter's Export Shipping Manual. (Bureau of National Affairs, 1231 25th St., N.W., Wash., D.C. 20037.) Updated weekly. $186.00 per year, $174.00 for renewal. Market data and shipping information about foreign countries are covered in this manual. Topics such as major banks, principal cities and their populations, principal imports and exports, government information offices, tariff systems and summaries of required documents are included.

Investment Incentive Programs in Western Europe (5763). (Chamber of Commerce of the United States, 1615 H St., N.W., Wash., D.C. 20062.) 1978. $95.00 (looseleaf binder). Guide to forecasting profitability of investment in Europe; provides profiles of over 500 investment incentives in 18 European countries, including financial, fiscal, and factor programs; EC programs are covered as well. Updates planned.

Japan—A Growth Market for U.S. Consumer Products. (Superintendent of Documents, GPO, Wash., D.C. 20402.) 1978. $1.20. This book covers such topics as the need for a marketing plan, selecting an agent, domestic competition and retailing in Japan. A chart in it shows percentages of the types of U.S. products exported in Japan. When ordering, cite stock number 003-009-00253-2.

Johnson's World Wide Chamber of Commerce Directory. (Johnson Publishing Company, Inc., P.O. Box 455, Eighth and Van Buren, Loveland, Colorado 80537.) Annual. $12.00 plus $2.00 postage.

Legal Considerations Relating to U.S.-Brazilian Joint Ventures (6023). (Chamber of Commerce of the United States, 1615 H St., N.W., Wash., D.C. 20062.) 1979. $10.00. Prepared by a team of attorneys, this work analyzes the various legal considerations involved in establishing corporate joint ventures in Brazil, including tax implications.

Licensing Guide for Developing Countries. (UNIPUB, 345 Park Ave., S., New York, N.Y. 10010.) 1977. $22.50. This 184-page book by the World Intelligence Property Organization covers the legal aspects of industrial property licensing and technology transfer agreements. It includes discussion of the negotiation process, the scope of licensing agreements, technical services and assistance, production, trademarks, management, compensation, default and the expiration of agreements. When ordering, cite symbol WIPO: 53.

Literature Checklist. (Port Authority of New York and New Jersey, One World Trade Center, Ste. 62 West, New York, N.Y. 10048.) Free. The checklist lists free booklets and bulletins available from the port authority.

Local Chambers of Commerce Which Maintain Foreign Trade Services. (International Division, Chamber of Commerce of the United States, 1615 H St., N.W., Wash., D.C. 20062.) 1978. Free. This is a list of chambers of commerce that have programs to aid exporters.

Major Companies of the Arab World. (UNIPUB, 345 Park Ave., S., New York, N.Y. 10010.) 1978. $55.00. This Graham & Trotman book contains more than 4,000 entries about major companies in 27 countries and emirates, including company names and addresses; telephone, telex and cable numbers; principal activities; main branches and subsidiaries; names of chief executive officers and directors; principal shareholders; summary balance sheets and similar information. When ordering, cite symbol UNIPUB: MISC 52.

Manual for the Handling of Applications for Patents, Designs and Trademarks Throughout the World. (Octrooibureau Los En Stigter B.V., Amsterdam, the Netherlands.)

Maps of Port. (Port of Long Beach, P.O. Box 570, Long Beach, Ca. 90801.) Free. This is offered as a service by the Port of Long Beach.

Market Shares Reports. (National Technical Information Service, U.S. Dept. of Commerce, Box 1553, Springfield, Va. 22161.) Reports for over 88 countries, $4.75 each. 880 commodity reports at $3.25 each. Order number PB-271325. Provides basic data needed by exporters to evaluate overall trends in the size of markets for manufacturers; measure changes in the import demand for specific products; compare the competitive position of U.S. and foreign exporters; select distribution centers for U.S. products abroad; and identify existing and potential markets for U.S. components, parts and accessories.

Marking Country of Origin. (U.S. Customs Service, U.S. Dept. of Treasury, Superintendent of Documents, GPO, Wash., D.C. 20402.) 1976. 40 cents. Customs requirements for marking imported merchandise with name of country of origin.

Media Guide International. (Directories International, Inc., 1718 Sherman Ave., Evanston, Il. 60201.) $252.00 for complete guide. This guide, helpful in identifying media, is published in volumes that are two major publications groups: business, trade and professional magazines, and newspapers and news magazines. The first category is published in geographic editions.

Membership Directory. (American Importers Association, 420 Lexington Ave., New York, N.Y. 10017.) Updated every two years. 126 pages. $13.00. Alphabetical list of member firms, alphabetical and state product index and separate listing of member firms providing services to import trade. (Send written request with check.)

Membership Directory of the French Chamber of Commerce in the U.S. (French-American Chamber of Commerce, 1350 Avenue of the Americas, 17th Floor, New York, N.Y. 10019.) 1979. $30.00. Material on doing business in France is included in this membership directory.

Membership Roster. (National Customs Brokers and Forwarders Association of America, Inc., One World Trade Center, New York, N.Y. 10048.) 1978. 140 pages. Free. Lists approximately 400 firms—over 300 of them licensed U.S.-foreign freight forwarders and customs brokers—and the remainder are associate members located in foreign countries and engaged in a similar profession.

Moody's Industrial Manual. (Moody's Investors Service, 99 Church St., New York, N.Y. 10007.) Two volumes. Annual (July) with twice-weekly looseleaf bulletins. $450.00 per year. One of six manuals published yearly by this service. Contains detailed descriptions of 3,700 industrial companies in the United States and major foreign countries. Listings include summary of firm's interest and operation principal plants and subsidiaries, officers and directors, comparative income accounts, long-term record of earnings, and other financial and operating data. Other Moody manuals cover banks and finance, public utilities, government and municipals, over-the-counter industrials and transportation.

Multilateral Trade Negotiations: International Codes Agreed to in Geneva, Switzerland, April 12, 1979. (Superintendent of Documents, GPO, Wash., D.C. 20402.) $6.00. Stock number 052-070-04935-9.

The Multinational Corporation Regulatory Guidebook: A Review and Status Report on International Organization Activities Impacting MNCs. (International Business-Government Councellors, Inc., 1625 Eye St., N.W., Ste. 717, Wash., D.C. 20006.) 1979 edition. $75.00 per copy. An annual publication summarizing work under way in international organizations on technology transfer, codes of conduct, information disclosure/reporting and other key issues.

The Multinational Corporation: Studies in U.S. Foreign Investment. Volumes 1 & 2, March, 1972. (out of print). Available in libraries. Limited number available (free) from Investment Policy Division, U.S. Dept. of Commerce, Wash., D.C. 20230.

Multinational Executive Travel Companion—Your International Travel Encyclopedia, 1979. (World-Wide Business Centres, 575 Madison Ave., New York, N.Y.) 1979 edition, $20.00. 1980 edition, $30.00.

The Multinational Marketing and Employment Directory. (World Trade Academy Press, Inc., 50 E. 42nd St., New York, N.Y. 10017.) 1979. 1,300 pages. Two volumes, 8th edition. (In preparation.) Cloth, $125.00. The 8th edition will be published in two volumes, listing more than 7,500 American corporations operating in the United States and overseas. This Directory is recognized as an outstanding marketing source for products, skills and services in the United States and abroad. It is of particular value to manufacturers, distributors, international traders, investors, bankers, advertising agencies and libraries. Also, placement bureaus, executive recruiters, direct mail marketers and technical and management consultants. The specialized arrangement of the information expedites sales in domestic and foreign markets.

New York Port Handbook. (Maritime Association of New York, 80 Broad St., New York, N.Y. 10004.) $10.80.

1980 World Food and Agricultural Outlook and Situation Board Press Releases and Report Dates. (Division of Information; Economics, Statistics and Cooperative Service; Publications Unit, Room 0054 South; Department of Agriculture, Wash. D.C. 20250.) Free. This publication gives a schedule for release of reports and press releases on agricultural foreign trade.

Ocean Freight Rate Guidelines for Shippers. (Superintendent of Documents, GPO, Wash., D.C. 20402.) 1974. 75 cents. Factors to be considered in shipping goods by ocean freight are discussed in this book. When ordering, cite stock number 003-000-00423-6.

Ocean Liner Cargo Service—U.S. Ports to Europe, Africa, Middle East, Far East, Caribbean, South America. (International Transportation Services Branch, Dept. of Agriculture, Auditor's Bldg., Rm. 1405, Wash., D.C. 20250.) 1977. Supplement: January, 1978. Free. Available cargo ocean liner services are listed in this book. U.S. ports included are those from which most agricultural products are moved by ocean liner. The book lists foreign and domestic steamship companies, the types and frequency of cargo services, transit times and corporate addresses of U.S. flag carriers.

OECD Foreign Trade Bulletins. (Organization for Economic Cooperation and Development, 1750 Pennsylvania Ave., N.W., Wash., D.C. 20006.) Series A (1979) $45.00 with 12 issues per year; Series B (1978) $30.00 with 5 issues per year; and Series C (1977) $30.00 with 2 issues per year. Annual in two volumes. The bulletins provide country-by-country import and export data, itemized by product.

OGSM/POD Program Explanation, Public Law 480 Sales Program—A Brief Explanation of Title I. (Program Operations Division, Office of the General Sales Manager, Dept. of Agriculture, 14th & Independence Ave., S.W., Rm. 4548, Wash., D.C. 20250.) Free. This describes programs under the Trade Development and Assistance Act of 1954, which provides for U.S. government financing of agricultural commodity sales to foreign countries.

Operating in Latin America's Integrating Markets. (Business International, One Dag Hammarskjold Plaza, New York, N.Y. 10017.) 1978. $150.00. Indepth examination of the region's four principal integration movements—ANCOM, LAFTA, CACM and CARICOM. Provides facts on how to operate successfully in these markets.

Overseas Business Reports. (Superintendent of Documents, GPO, Wash., D.C. 20402.) Annual subscription rate: $40.00. Single copies at $1.25 each. Issued as a joint effort by the Dept. of Commerce and the U.S. Foreign Service, these booklets deal with trading or marketing in individual foreign countries or regions. The reports relating to trade prospects in regions state the reasons for improvement or worsening of trade; the status of agricultural and industrial sectors by country; inflation; trade deficits or surpluses; unemployment and consumer spending. Those focusing on single countries explain foreign trade outlook; industry trends; transportation; credit; distribution and sales channels; media and advertising; trade regulations and information for business travelers.

Overseas Export Promotion Calendar. (Export Awareness Division, Dept. of Commerce, 14th & Constitution Ave., N.W., Wash., D.C. 20230.) Quarterly publication. Free. Lists all export-related events sponsored by the Dept. of Commerce.

Patents and Trademarks. (National Association of Credit Management, George Kohlik, Editor, Oceana Publications, Inc., Dobbs Ferry, N.Y. 10522.) Material included dates from 1966 to the present. $110.00

Patents Throughout the World. (Trade Activities, Inc., 435 Hudson St., New York, N.Y. 10017.) Revised edition (1978) $60.00. Three supplements per year at $33.00 per year. Digests and data tables of patent law practice and details for filing patent applications in all countries.

Penetrating the International Market. (Robert Douglass Stuart, American Management Association, Inc., 135 W. 50th St., New York, N.Y. 10020.) 1965.

Pets, Wildlife, U.S. Customs. (U.S. Customs Service, U.S. Dept. of Treasury, Wash., D.C. 20229.) February, 1980. Free. Summary of Customs requirements for importing cats, dogs, birds and wildlife.

Pleasure Boats. (Superintendent of Documents, GPO, Wash., D.C. 20402.) 45 cents. Information for owners of yachts and pleasure boats on Customs procedures for importing a boat, entry and reporting requirements.

Polish-U.S. Economic Council, Fifth Plenary Session (6139). (Chamber of Commerce of the United States, 1615 H Street, N.W., Wash., D.C. 20062.) Contains highlights, joint communique and texts of reports presented at the most recent session of the council. 1979. Free.

Political Export Credit Risks. (Alexander and Alexander, Inc., 1185 Avenue of the Americas, New York, N.Y. 10036.) Free.

Port of New Orleans Annual Directory. (Port of New Orleans, P.O. Box 60046, New Orleans, La. 70160.) Annual. Free. The directory lists suppliers of services to the port during the past year.

Ports of the World. (Marine and Aviation Division, Insurance Company of North America, 1600 Arch St., 9th Floor, Philadelphia, Pa. 19101.) 1979. Free. This describes port conditions, packing and loss control recommendations.

Problems in Canadian Marketing. (American Marketing Association, 222 South Riverside Plaza, Chicago, Il. 60606.) 1977. $12.00 for members. $16.00 for nonmembers. This discusses distribution, communications, advertising, marketing research and environmental and public policy factors in the Canadian market.

Rand McNally Commercial Atlas and Marketing Guide. (Rand McNally & Company, P.O. Box 7600, Chicago, Il.) 1978. 669 pages. Leased at $110.00 a year. Comprehensive set of up-to-date reference maps and economic statistics for the United States, its states, countries and cities and for all of the countries of the world. Shows zip numbers for all post offices and nonpost office communities. Supplementary Rand McNally Road Atlas included.

Reference Book for World Traders. (Croner Publications, Inc., 211-05 Jamaica Ave., Queens Village, N.Y. 11428.) $65.00 per year, plus $4.95 postage and handling in the U.S. and Canada; add $8.95 for postage in other countries. A loose-leaf reference book for traders, this gives information about export documentation, steamship and airline companies, free trade zones, credit and similar matters. Supplements are issued monthly.

Report of the Ninth U.S.-E.C. Conference on Agriculture (6337). (Chamber of Commerce of the U.S., 1615 H St., N.W., Wash., D.C. 20062.) 1979. Single copy free. Contains discussion highlights from ninth conference on agriculture between agribusiness and farm organization leaders, plus representatives of particular commodity interests from the United States.

Report of the Sixteenth Japan-U.S. Businessmen's Conference (6176). (Chamber of Commerce of the U.S., 1615 H Street, N.W., Wash., D.C. 20062.) Free. Summary of most recent conference and of Joint Executive Committee meeting, including following issues: trade and investment, environmental pollution, natural resources, relations with the European Community and communications programs. 1979.

Report of the Sixth Annual Meeting, European Community-United States Businessmen's Council (6164). (Chamber of Commerce of the U.S., 1615 H Street, N.W., Wash., D.C. 20062.) Free. Contains summary of October 1979 conference discussions as well as joint council resolutions on energy, industrial policy and international trade issues.

Results of the Tokyo Round: Proceedings of a Conference on the Multilateral Trade Negotiations (6026). (Chamber of Commerce of the United States, 1615 H Street, N.W., Wash., D.C. 20062.) $10.00. Contains proceedings of an MTN conference held in January of 1979, and features talks by U.S. government officials, members of Congress and highlights from five workshops.

Sales Aids for Food Exporters. (Export Trade Services Division, Foreign Agricultural Service, Dept. of Agriculture, 14th & Independence Ave., S.W., Rm. 4945-S, Wash., D.C. 20250.) Free. This booklet lists all Foreign Agricultural Service programs to assist U.S. agricultural exporters.

SBA Business Loans. (Small Business Administration, Office of Public Information, 1441 L St., N.W., Rm. 100, Wash., D.C. 20416.) Free.

Service World Market Administrative Procedures. (International Trade Club of Chicago, 310 South Michigan Ave., Chicago, Il. 60604.) 1978. $25.00 nonmembers. This paperback manual discusses export sales, marketing and distribution, export trade support services, documentation, foreign trade definitions and similar matters.

Small Business Administration Publication Lists. (Small Business Administration, P.O. Box 15434, Fort Worth, Texas 76119.) Free. Two publications lists are issued, identifying Small Business Administration publications sold through the Government Printing Office.

Smaller Business, A Directory of Services for U.S. Investors in Developing Nations. (OPIC, 1129 20th St., N.W., Wash., D.C. 20527.) Free. Newly published brochure lists publications offered by the Overseas Private Investment Corporation (OPIC). Among them: *OPIC Guide for Executives of Smaller Companies, Finance Handbook, Investment Insurance Handbook,* the *OPIC Country List* and an annual report and a newsletter for overseas investors.

Sources of Aid and Information for U.S. Exporters. (Washington Researchers, 918 16th St., N.W., Wash., D.C. 20006.) 1979. $22.50.

Special and Administrative Provisions of the Tariff Act of 1930. (United States International Trade Commission, Wash., D.C. 20436.) 1971. Out of print; however, xerox copies are available at $21.00 per copy.

Standard & Poor's Corporation Records Service. (Standard & Poor's Corporation, 345 Hudson St., New York, N.Y. 10014.) Annual. $995.00. Six looseleaf volumes arranged alphabetically according to company.

State Government Conducted International Trade and Business Development Programs. (National Technical Information Service, 5285 Port Royal Rd., Springfield, Va. 22161.) $9.00. Prepared by the Council of State Governments, this technical report analyzes and evaluates international business programs conducted by states in the U.S. When ordering, cite number pb-271-006/9 ST.

Statistical Classification of Domestic and Foreign Commodities Exported From the United States (Schedule B). (Superintendent of Documents, GPO, Wash., D.C. 20402.) 1979. $13.00. Export classification numbers for products. Every product exported from the United States must carry such a number.

Summary and Collected Papers, Czechoslovak-U.S. Economic Council, Third Plenum (5990). (Chamber of Commerce of the United States, 1615 H St., N.W., Wash., D.C. 20062.) 1979. Single copy free. Contains highlights, joint communique and texts of reports of meeting between U.S. and Czechoslovak corporate executives.

Tax Free Trade Zones of the World. (Walter H. Diamond, Author. Matthew Bende & Co., 235 East 45th St., New York, N.Y. 12201.) 1977 edition with 1980 supplements. $120.00. Two volumes with supplements. This supplies current information about tax-free trade zones. Revisions are furnished free for six months after you buy the book.

Tentative Overseas Export Promotion Program. (Export Trade Services Division, Foreign Agricultural Service, Dept. of Agriculture, 14th & Independence Ave., S.W., Rm. 4945-S, Wash., D.C. 20250.) Free. This publication presents a schedule of foreign agriculture exhibits between October 1, 1979, and October 31, 1980.

39th Annual Report of the Foreign Trade Zones Board. (Superintendent of Documents, GPO., Wash., D.C. 20402.) $2.20.

Thomas' Register of American Manufacturers. (Thomas Publishing Co., 1 Penn Plaza, New York, N.Y. 10001.) Annual. $120.00. Comprehensive directory in 16 volumes, with separately bound finding guide to contents. Lists manufacturers, arranged geographically under product classifications, with street addresses and capital ratings; listed alphabetically with home office address, phone number, rating, indicating nature of products and interest in export business, directing officials, branches and subsidiaries; alphabetical trade name section.

Trade Directories of the World, 1977-1978. (Croner Publications, Inc., 211-05 Jamaica Ave., Queens Village, N.Y. 11428.) Annual $35.00; $3.95 postage and handling in the United States and Canada. Especially designed for advertising agents, industrial concerns, market researchers, public relations managers and all those who wish to compile their own mailing lists. Contains approximately 3,500 directories from 175 nations covering 687 categories. Kept up to date with monthly supplements.

Trade List: Sources of Credit Information in Foreign Countries. (International Trade Administration, Trade Facilitation, Information & Services Division, Dept. of Commerce, ECLS, Rm. 1033, 14th & Constitution Ave., N.W., Wash., D.C. 20230.) October, 1979. $3.00 (send check or money order payable to the Dept. of Commerce). This is a trade list in booklet form which gives the names and addresses of foreign sources of credit information. It lists about 300 foreign organizations that respond to requests from U.S. companies seeking credit information.

Trademarks Throughout the World. (Trade Activities, Inc., 435 Hudson St., New York, N.Y. 10014.) 1979 edition $85.00. 1980 supplements $33.00 (three supplements per year).

Travelers' Tips on Bringing Food, Plant and Animal Products Into the United States. (Superintendent of Documents, GPO, Wash., D.C. 20402.) September, 1979. 60 cents. U.S. Dept. of Agriculture Program Aide No. 1083.

Treaties in Force. (Superintendent of Documents, GPO, Wash., D.C. 20402.) 1979. $4.75. Annual. By the State Department's Office of the Legal Adviser, this lists by name and date all treaties and other international agreements of the United States. It tells where complete texts of treaties can be found. When ordering, cite stock number 044-000-01725-3.

Tourist Trademark Information. (Superintendent of Documents, GPO, Wash., D.C. 20402.) $1.10. List of the most popular tourist items prohibited importation because the trademark owners have recorded their marks with the Treasury Department.

Uniform Customs and Practice for Commercial Documentary Credit. (U.S. Council, International Chamber of Commerce, 1212 Avenue of the Americas, New York, N.Y. 10036.) Publication 290. Booklet $2.00. Leaflet $1.25. A detailed description of credits and the different kinds of letters of credit used to finance international sales.

Uniform Rules for Collection. (U.S. Council, International Chamber of Commerce, 1212 Avenue of the Americas, New York, N.Y. 10036.) 1979. $3.00 per copy. Leaflet, 75 cents per copy. This includes provisions and definitions applicable to all collections of remittances. When ordering, cite publication number 322.

United Nations Statistical Yearbook. (United Nations Sales Section, Rm. A-3315, New York, N.Y. 10017 or UNIPUB, 104 East 26th St., New York, N.Y. 10010.) 1978. Hardbound: $50.00. Paperback: $41.00. The yearbook presents 1977 country and worldwide data about social and economic subjects, including population, work forces, agriculture, forestry, fishing, mining and quarrying, manufacturing, construction, energy, trade, transportation, communications, consumption, wages and prices and balance of payments, as well as other matters. When ordering, cite symbol UNIPUB: UN78/17/1.

The United States and World Development: Agenda 1979. (Overseas Development Council, 1717 Massachusetts Ave., N.W., Wash., D.C. 20036.) 1979. $5.95. Annual.

United States Copyright Office "Circular R 38A." (Information & Publications, Copyright Office, Library of Congress, Wash., D.C. 20559.) Free. Information about international copyright relations and treaties of the United States.

United States Exports: World Area By Commodity Groupings. (Superintendent of Documents, GPO, Wash., D.C. 20402.) 1977. $8.75. Prepared by the Foreign Trade Division of the Bureau of the Census, this publication consists mainly of tables and statistics. When ordering, cite stock number 003-024-01587-1.

United States Government Manual. (Superintendent of Documents, GPO, Wash., D.C. 20402.) 1979-80. $7.50. Annual.

United States Oceanborne Foreign Trade Routes. (Superintendent of Documents, GPO, Wash., D.C. 20402.) 1979. $7.50. Compiled by the Maritime Administration of the Dept. of Commerce, this describes cargoes moving on U.S. foreign waterborne trade routes. It analyzes transportation patterns, trends and commodity flows. Tables show the commodity flow information for 1975 and 1976. The information is arranged by trade route and type of service. Maps show the geographic area covered by each trade route. When ordering, cite stock number 003-007-00098-7.

U.S. Chamber of Commerce Staff Specialists. (Chamber of Commerce of the United States, 1615 H St., N.W., Wash., D.C. 20062.) Free. This brochure lists the specialties of Chamber staff members and their telephone numbers.

U.S. Export Opportunities to Japan. (Superintendent of Documents, GPO, Wash., D.C. 20402.) 1978. $6.25. This book provides a marketing guide to 14 major industrial markets. It explains the large Japanese financial-industrial conglomerates, the process of decision-making in Japan and the debt-equity practices of Japanese firms. When ordering, cite stock number 003-009-00259-1.

U.S. Import Requirements. (U.S. Customs Service, 1301 Constitution Ave., N.W., Rm. 6303, Wash., D.C. 20229.) Free. General information of U.S. Customs requirements for imported merchandise.

U.S. Merchandise Trade. (Superintendent of Documents, GPO, Wash., D.C. 20402.) 1978. $4.75. This book presents U.S. exports and imports geographically and by end-use commodity. It is published by the Bureau of Economic Analysis of the Dept. of Commerce. When ordering, cite stock number 003-010-00058-9.

U.S. Service Industries in World Markets: Current Problems and Future Policy Development. (National Technical Information Service, 5285 Port Royal Rd., Springfield, Va. 22161.) 1977. $21.00 paperback; $3.50 microfiche. By the Dept. of Commerce, this study examines the U.S. service industry's participation and problems in international markets. There are detailed discussions about the following industries: accounting, advertising, automobile and truck rental, banking, building, construction and engineering, communications, computer services, education, employment services, equipment leasing, franchising, health services, hotel and motel services, insurance services, legal services, motion pictures, air transportation and maritime transportation. When ordering, cite stock number PB 262528-AS.

Visa Requirements of Foreign Governments. (Superintendent of Documents, GPO, Wash., D.C. 20402.) 75 cents.

Washington Information Directory (Congressional Quarterly, 1414 22nd Street, N.W., Wash., D.C. 20037.) $22.50. Covers the whole federal government, plus key state and local officials.

Webb-Pomerene Associations: A 50-Year Review. (Office of Public Reference, Federal Trade Commission, Rm. 130, Sixth St. and Pennsylvania Ave., N.W., Wash., D.C. 20580.) 1967. 113 pages. Free. Factual presentation of the nature and scope of Webb-Pomerene Association activity in international trade, including information on the number and activities of associations, the type of association activity, the extent of exports receiving Webb-Pomerene assistance, and the types of firms and products receiving such assistance.

World Aviation Directory. (Ziff-Davis Publishing Co., c/o Donald W. Dean, 1156 15th St., N.W., Wash., D.C. 20005.) $50.00 per copy.

The World Bank. (World Bank, 1818 H St., N.W., Wash., D.C. 20433.) 1977. 11 pages. Free. Leaflet summarizing the operations of the World Bank and IDA, provision of technical assistance, aid coordination, ownership and control.

World Bank Annual Report. (World Bank, 1818 H St., N.W., Wash., D.C. 20433.) Annual. Free. Review of operations during the fiscal year.

World Trade Annual. (Walker & Co., 720 5th Ave., New York, N.Y. 10019.) 1977. Annual: $209. Supplement: $477.00. Five volumes. This series by the Statistical Office of the United Nations gives world trade statistics by country and by Standard International Trade Classification code. Volumes focus on Eastern Europe and the Soviet Union, South and Central America, Africa, the Near East and the Far East.

World Trade Clubs in the United States. (International Division, Chamber of Commerce of the U.S., 1615 H St., N.W., Wash., D.C. 20062.) Free. This gives the names and addresses of the world trade clubs in the U.S.

World Trade Services Directory. (Port Promotion Division, Port Authority of New York and New Jersey, One World Trade Center, Ste. 62 West, New York, N.Y. 10048.) Free. This explains the roles of shippers, motor carriers, forwarders, drivers, terminal operators and steamship companies in the export process.

Yearbook of International Organizations. (Union of International Associations, 1 rue aux Laines, 1000 Brussels, Belgium.) 1978. 17th edition. $80.00.

Yearbook of International Trade Statistics. (United Nations Sales Section, Rm. A-3315, New York, N.Y. 10017.) 1978. $65.00. Two volumes. Volume I describes general industrial statistics, and Volume II deals with commodity production data.

You and Your Passport. (Superintendent of Documents, GPO, Wash., D.C. 20402.) $1.10.

Your Trip Abroad. (Superintendent of Documents, GPO, Wash., D.C. 20402.) 45 cents. Provides U.S. citizens traveling abroad with basic information on official documents, vaccinations, unusual travel requirements, dual nationality, drugs, modes of travel, customs, legal requirements abroad and other topics. Cat. No. S1.69:8872.

Periodicals

A number of excellent *periodicals,* devoted specifically to the field of export and import trade, are available to foreign traders, reporting current developments and providing directory and other working material essential to foreign business operation.

Such magazines carry instructive articles from authoritative sources in the many fields of foreign trading, news of developments at home and abroad, current regulations in export and import, conditions in foreign countries, market data, trade opportunities and directory material of shipping and other foreign trade services. Among publications in this class, the following are outstanding: *American Import and Export Bulletin; Brandon's Shipper and Forwarder; Business Abroad—The International Trade Review; Checklist of International Business Publications;* and *Shipping Digest.*

Of particular value for conditions in foreign countries are bulletins or magazines of American chambers of commerce abroad, foreign chambers of commerce in the United States, bulletins of foreign departments of banks, and bulletins of foreign government information services in the United States.

Government periodicals, including *Business America, Department of State Bulletin* and others, are especially helpful to foreign traders and those seeking information on many aspects of international relations.

Many monthly, weekly and daily periodicals are noted under subject headings in this chapter of the *Handbook* to which they particularly apply.

See also subject heading: Export Business Magazines.

ABD Monthly Operational Information. (Export Information Reference, Rm. 1325, Dept. of Commerce, 14th & Constitution Ave., N.W., Wash., DC 20320.) Free. Monthly. Lists proposed projects by the Asian Development Bank.

Advertising Age. (Publications Dept., Crain Communications, Inc., 740 Rush St., Chicago, Ill. 60611.) $30.00 per year, single issue, $1.00. Weekly. The magazine covers advertising news and one issue each month features a pull-out section on international advertising.

Advertising Age/Europe. (Publications Dept., Crain Communications, Inc., 740 Rush St., Chicago, Ill. 60611.) $20.00 per year in the United States; single issue, $2.00. Monthly. The magazine examines consumer product marketing and advertising news in Europe, and world development affecting European markets.

AEI Economist. (American Enterprise Institute, 1150 17th St., N.W., Wash. D.C. 20036.) $10.00 per year; single copy, $1.00. Monthly newsletter.

AEI Foreign Policy & Defense Review. (American Enterprise Institute, 1150 17th St., N.W., Wash., D.C. 20036.) $18.00 per year; 10 issues per year.

Aerospace Daily. (Aviation Division, Ziff-Davis Publishing Co., 1156 15th St., N.W., Wash., D.C. 20005.) $550.00 per year.

Air Cargo Guide. (Reuben H. Donnelley Corp., 2000 Clearwater Dr., Oak Brook, Ill. 50521.) $28.00 per year; single issue $3.00. Monthly. Index of all cargo airlines, their routes, flights, freight charges, etc.

Air Forwarders. (Reuben H. Donnelley Corp., 888 7th Ave., New York, N.Y. 10019.) $1.00 per copy. Quarterly.

Air Freight Weekly. (Aviation Division, Ziff-Davis Publishing Co., 1156 15th St., N.W., Wash., D.C. 20005.) $550.00 per year.

Airline Newsletter. (Roadcap Aviation Publications, 1030 South Green Bay Rd., Lake Forest, Ill. 60645.) $60.00 per year. Semi-monthly. News and analyses of trends in commercial air transportation.

Air Transport World. (Reinhold Publishing Co., Inc., 600 Summer St., Stamford, Ct. 06904.) $8.00 per year. Monthly.

American Aviation. (American Aviation Publications, Inc., 1156 15th St., N.W., Wash., D.C. 20005.) $10.00 foreign; $50.00 per year. Bi-weekly. In-depth reports covering world commercial air transportation, military aviation and business aviation.

American Banker. (525 West 42nd St., New York, N.Y. 10036.) $250.00 domestic; $275.00 foreign. Annual. A daily tabloid on banking and economics.

American Bulletin of International Technology Transfer. (International Advancement, P.O. Box 75537, Los Angeles, Ca. 90057.) $48.00 per year. Bi-monthly. A comprehensive listing of product and service opportunities offered and wanted for licensing and joint ventures agreements in the United States and overseas.

American Import/Export Bulletin. (North American Publishing Co., 401 N. Broad St., Philadelphia, Pa. 19108.) $5.00 per copy. Monthly.

American Shippers. (Howard Publications, Inc., P.O. Box 4728, Jacksonville, Fl. 32201.) $12.00 Inst., $1.00 per copy. Monthly. Direct line of communication from the maritime industry to those shippers who provide the major part of cargo revenues.

The Arbitration Journal. (American Arbitration Assoc., 140 W. 51st St., New York, N.Y. 10020.) $15.00 per year domestic subscription; $19.00 per year foreign subscription, $3.95 single copy. Quarterly. Contains articles by scholars and practitioners on labor, commercial, construction, accident claims and international trade arbitration. Other features include book reviews, significant arbitration court decisions, recent library acquisitions, letters to the editor and an opinion page.

Aviation Daily. (Ziff-Davis Publishing Co., 1156 15th St., N.W., Wash., D.C. 20005.) $325.00 yearly. $1.25 single copy. Management and marketing news of the entire worldwide air transportation industry.

Aviation Week & Space Technology. (McGraw-Hill, Inc., 1221 Ave. of the Americas, New York, N.Y. 10036.) $78.00/3 years; $55.00/2 years; $35.00/1 year. Weekly. Aerospace industry reporting.

Balance of Payments Reports. (Commerce Clearing House, Inc., 4025 W. Peterson Ave., Chicago, Il. 60640.) $210.00 per year. Weekly.

Balance of Payments Yearbook. (International Monetary Fund, 700 19th St., N.W., Wash., D.C. 20431.) $20.00 per year. Monthly. Contains quarterly, half-yearly or annual data on an up-to-date basis; annual issues contains updated revisions of data plus tables containing additional details and descriptive notes.

Barrons. (Dow Jones & Co., Inc., 200 Burnett Rd., Chicopee, Ma. 01021.) $43.00 per year. Weekly.

Barron's National Business and Financial Weekly. (Dow Jones & Co., Inc., 22 Cortlandt St., New York, N.Y. 10007.) $32.00 per year; $1.00 single copy. Weekly.

Belgian-American Trade Review. (Belgian-American Chamber of Commerce in the U.S., Inc., 50 Rockefeller Plaza, Ste. 1003-1005, New York, N.Y. 10020.) $15.00 per year airmail; $10.00 per year third class. Monthly. Contains new stories and other articles concerning Belgian industry, trade policy, legislation, economic and investment trends and reviews of current trade-related books and reports.

Brandon's Shipper and Forwarder. (Herbert Brandon, One World Trade Center, Ste. 1927, New York, N.Y. 10048.) $20.00 per year. Weekly. Ocean shipping and forwarding news. Separate supplements: *Intermodal World*, monthly; *Airfreight World*, weekly; and *Export Documents Required*, bi-annually.

Breve. (National Foreign Trade Council, Inc., 10 Rockefeller Plaza, New York, N.Y. 10020.) Free to members. Weekly. European news digest.

Brookings' Bulletin. (The Brookings Institution, 1775 Mass. Ave., N.W., Wash., D.C. 20036.) Free. Quarterly.

The Brussels Report Service. (International Business-Government Councellors, Inc. (IBGC), 1625 Eye Street, N.W., Ste. 717, Wash., D.C. 20006.) $240.00 per year. Biweekly. Covers developments in the European Economic Community institutions impacting corporate international trade and investment operations. Each issue also includes an in-depth supplement on a specific policy problem, or a "Who's Who" in the EEC.

Bureau of the Census Catalog. (Superintendent of Documents, GPO, Wash., D.C. 20402.) $19.00 per year. Four consecutive issues which are cumulative and monthly supplements. An annotated bibliography of publications issued by the Bureau of Census.

Business America. (Superintendent of Documents, GPO, Wash., D.C. 20402.) $34.00 a year; $8.50 additional for foreign mailing. Single copy $1.40. Biweekly. Principal Commerce Department publication for presenting domestic and international business news and news of the application of technology to business and industrial problems.

Business Asia. (Business International Corp., One Dag Hammarskjold Plaza, New York, N.Y. 10017.) $252.00 per year. Provides industry profiles, pointers for immediate action, profiles of foreign trade corporations, analyses of economic and political changes in terms of what they will mean to business, corporate case studies and specific opportunities for increased sales to or purchases from Asia's communist countries.

Business China. (Business International Corporation, One Dag Hammarskjold Plaza, New York, N.Y. 10017.) $252.00 per year. Provides industry profiles pointers for immediate action, profiles of foreign trade corporations, analyses of economic and political changes in terms of what they will mean to business, corporate case studies and specific opportunities for increased sales to or purchases from Asia's communist countries.

Business Eastern Europe. (Business International Corp., One Dag Hammarskjold Plaza, New York, N.Y. 10017.) $560.00 per year. Weekly. Country-by-country and industry-by-industry profiles. Includes a continuous analysis of current problem-solving experiences of Western firms on how to approach the local foreign trade organizations, negotiate contracts, clinch deals and secure payments.

Business Europe. (Business International Corp., One Dag Hammarskjold Plaza, New York, N.Y. 10017.) $560.00 per year. Weekly. Provides management information to executives responsible for

European, African and Middle Eastern operations. Contains indepth reporting and analysis of EEC and EFTA developments, country-by-country information on finance, marketing, taxation, personnel, organization, politics and actual corporate experience.

The Business Indicators. (The Australia and New Zealand Bank, Ltd., 63 Wall St., New York, N.Y. 10005.) Free. Monthly. This pamphlet examines business indicators in Australia and New Zealand.

Business International. (Business International Corp., One Dag Hammarskjold Plaza, New York, N.Y. 10017.) $385.00 per year. Weekly. Provides current information and sales-producing ideas in the form of news, analysis and actual corporate experience. Interprets developments in international management, marketing, finance, licensing, exporting, taxation, law, etc.

Business International Money Report. (Business International Corp., One Dag Hammarskjold Plaza, New York, N.Y. 10017.) $568.00 per year. Weekly. Analyzes latest developments in the world's financial and currency markets, their impact on borrowing decisions, cash management and foreign trade transactions, and how companies are responding to them. Includes interest and exchange rate updaters, with forecasts and hedged borrowing costs.

Business Latin America. (Business International Corp., One Dag Hammarskjold Plaza, New York, N.Y. 10017.) $395.00 per year. Weekly. Interprets new opportunities and obstacles being created by regional integration. Reports on political, economic and corporate trends and events in every Latin American country.

Business Service Checklist. (Superintendent of Documents, GPO, Wash., D.C. 20402.) $13.00 per year, $3.25 additional for foreign mailing. Single copy 60 cents. Biweekly. Lists news releases, books, pamphlets, reports and other materials of interest to industry and business that are published by the Department of Commerce.

Canada Commerce. (Canadian Business Center, Dept. of Industry, Trade and Commerce, Level 01 (Centre Area), 235 Queen St., Ottawa, Ontario K1A OH5). Free. Quarterly. This magazine contains news articles, book reviews, trade fair listings and other stories concerning international trade.

The China Business Review. (Publications Dept., The National Council for U.S.-China Trade, 1050 17th St., N.W., Ste. 350, Wash., D.C. 20036.) $60.00 for U.S. and Canada; $75.00 for other countries (price includes airmail postage).

Commerce Business Daily. (Superintendent of Documents, GPO, Wash., D.C. 20402.) $105.00 per year first class; $80.00 per year second class; six month trial subscriptions are $60.00 first class; $45.00 second class. A daily synopsis of U.S. government procurement invitations, subcontracting heads, contract awards, sales of surplus property and foreign business opportunities.

Congressional Record. (Superintendent of Documents, GPO, Wash., D.C. 20402.) $75.00 per year, 25 cents single copy. Daily while Congress is in session. A record of the proceedings of Congress.

Consumer Information Catalog. (General Services Administration, Consumer Information Center, Pueblo, Co. 81009.) Free. Quarterly.

Contacts for U.S. Food Products. (Export Trade Services Division, Dept. of Agriculture, 14th & Independence Ave., S.W., Rm. 4950-S, Wash., D.C. 20250.) Free. Monthly. Trade letter gives the names and addresses of U.S. agricultural suppliers and briefly describes their products. It announces trade shows and other events, and is distributed to potential foreign buyers. Distributed overseas.

Copyright. (World Intellectual Property Organization, 32 Chemin des Colombettes, 1211 Geneva 20, Switzerland.) Monthly. 10 Swiss francs each. 110 Swiss francs per year.

Copyright Bulletin. (United Nations Educational, Scientific and Cultural Organization, (UNESCO) from UNIPUB, Inc., Box 433, New York, N.Y. 10016.) $8.00 per year. Quarterly. Reports on developments in international copyright, including information on documentation, meetings and bibliographies.

Customs Bulletin. (Superintendent of Documents, GPO, Wash., D.C. 20402.) $65.00 per year, 65 cents single copy, $8.30 addition foreign mailing. Weekly. Contains regulations, rulings, decisions and notices concerning customs and related matter and the decisions of the U.S. Custom Court and the U.S. Court of Customs and Patent Appeals.

Customs Bulletin and Decisions. Vol. 13, No. 27, July 4, 1979. (Superintendent of Documents, GPO, Wash., D.C. 20402.) $1.30 per single copy. $65.00 per year. Includes regulations, decisions and notices concerning customs and related matters of the United States Court of Customs and Patent Appeals and the United States Customs Court.

Customs Regulations of the United States. (Superintendent of Documents, GPO, Wash., D.C. 20402.) $37.00 per year, $7.25 additional for foreign mailing. 1971 reprint includes amended text in revised pages nos. 1 through 130 (includes subscription to revised pages). Contains regulations for carrying out customs, navigation and other laws administered by the Bureau of Customs.

Department of State Bulletin. (Superintendent of Documents, GPO, Wash., D.C. 20402.) $12.00 per year, $1.40 single issue. Weekly. A bulletin, this includes statements about current U.S. foreign policy.

Department of State Newsletter. (Superintendent of Documents, GPO, Wash., D.C. 20402.) $12.00 per year, $1.35 per single issue. Acquaints the Department's officers and employees, at home and abroad, with developments of interest which may affect operations or personnel.

Development Forum Business Edition. (Subscription Dept., United Nations, CH-1211, Geneva 10, Switzerland.) $200.00, including airmail delivery costs. Twenty-four times yearly. This newspaper gives details about World Bank and United Nations Development Programmes projects.

Diplomatic List. (Superintendent of Documents, GPO, Wash., D.C. 20402.) $8.00 per year, $1.50 single copy. Quarterly. List of foreign diplomats in and around Washington, D.C.

Direction of Trade. (International Monetary Fund, 700 19th St., N.W., Wash., D.C. 20431.) $16.00 per year. Monthly and annual. Provides monthly information on each country's direction of trade with comparative data for corresponding period of preceding year. Provides annual, full-year data for several years and summary tables for various areas of the world and world aggregates.

Eastern Europe Report. (Business International Corp., One Dag Hammarskjold Plaza, New York, N.Y. 10017.) $560.00 per year. Twice monthly. Provides analysis of new opportunities for selling goods to the USSR, its six COMECN partners and Yugoslavia and explores the problem-solving experience of Western firms.

Economic Bulletin for Africa. (UNIPUB, 345 Park Ave., S., New York, N.Y. 10010.) $6.00. 1976 edition. This magazine is published irregularly. It provides economic news about Africa. When ordering, cite symbol UN 76/2K6.

Economic Outlook. (Organization for Economic Cooperation and Development, 1750 Pennsylvania Ave., N.W., Wash., D.C. 20006.) $8.50 per year, $2.50 single copy. Twice yearly. Periodic assessment of economic trends and prospects in the major trading nations. *Occasional Studies,* which treat selected topical problems in some depth, are included, or may be obtained separately ($2.50 each).

The Economist. (The Economist Newspaper, Ltd., London, England.) $75.00 per year. Weekly. Review of politics, international affairs, business and economics including special sections of overseas reports.

The Economist Financial Report. (The Economist Newspaper, Ltd., 75 Rockefeller Plaza, New York, N.Y. 10019.) $500.00 per year. Twenty-six issues a year. Provides a highly sophisticated analysis of news, trends and possible future developments in the world's banking and financial markets focusing on crucial information that is not available from normal sources.

European Trends. (The Economist Intelligence Unit Ltd., London, England from the Economist Newspaper Ltd., 75 Rockefeller Plaza, New York, N.Y. 10019.) $142.00 per year, $20.00 single copy. Quarterly. Provides information analysis and comment designed for use by international businessmen and administrators.

Europe, Magazine of the European Community. (European Community, 2100 M St., N.W., Ste. 707, Wash., D.C. 20037.) $6.00 per year. Issued every other month. Forum for discussion and analysis of European events and U.S.-E.C. relations.

Euro Statistics. (European Communities Information Service, 2100 M St., N.W., Ste. 707, Wash., D.C. 20037.) $27.35 by surface mail; airmail $25.75 more. Monthly. Published in English, Danish,

Italian, German, French and Dutch. Contains statistics on employment, industrial products, trade, prices, wages, salaries and similar matters for the European Economic Community and member countries, as well as the United States. Each edition also contains an indepth examination of a single industry.

EXIM Bank Record. (Export-Import Bank of the United States, 811 Vermont Ave., N.W., Wash., D.C. 20571.) Free. Ten issues per year. This newsletter describes Export-Import Bank activities.

Export Administration Regulations. (Superintendent of Documents, GPO, Wash., D.C. 20402.) $30.00 per year. Covers U.S. export control regulations and policies, with instructions, interpretations and explanatory material.

Export Briefs. (Export Trade Services Division, FAS, Dept. of Agriculture, 14th & Independence Ave., S.W., Rm. 4950-S, Wash., D.C. 20250.) Free. Weekly. Lists commodity items wanted by foreign purchasers. The data are supplied by U.S. agricultural attaches abroad.

Export Bulletin. (The Journal of Commerce, 110 Wall St., New York, N.Y. 10005.) $200.00 per year. Weekly. All U.S. exports listed by products and product groups by vessels and by destination. Shippers named.

Export Shipping Manual. (Bureau of National Affairs, Inc., 1231 25th St., N.W., Wash., D.C. 20037.) $186.00 per year. Indexed, loose-leafed reference binder; detailed current information on all areas of the world.

Export Licenses Approved and Reexportations Authorized. (Office of Export Administration, U.S. Dept. of Commerce, Wash., D.C. 20230.) $37.50 per year. Daily. Lists the commodity description, dollar value, and country of ultimate destination for each export license issued and for each ammendment to a license which increases the dollar value of an outstanding license and for each reexportation authorized.

Fairplay International Shipping Weekly. (Fairplay Publications Ltd., 52-42 Southwark St., London, SEI, England.) Weekly. $35.00 per year. Subscription includes: *World Ships on Order* (published quarterly).

FCIB Bulletin. (FCIB-NACM Corp., 475 Park Ave., S., New York, N.Y. 10016.) $100 per year; $10.00 per issue. Includes minutes of monthly Roundtable Conferences and Semi-Annual Survey of Terms and Conditions in Overseas Markets. Export credit information and review conditions and regulations in overseas markets.

FCIB International Bulletin. (FCIB-NACM Corp., 475 Park Ave., S., New York, N.Y. 10016.) $10.00 per issue. Twice monthly. Export credit information and review of conditions and regulations in overseas markets.

Federal Register. (Office of the Federal Register, Nat'l Archives and Records Service, GSA, GPO, Wash., D.C. 20402.) $75.00 per year. Daily. Contains executive orders, presidential proclamations and the general rules, regulations and notices issued by agencies of the Executive Branch. Microfilm edition available from the National Archives.

Federal Reserve Bulletin. (Board of Governors of the Federal Reserve System, Wash., D.C. 20552.) $20.00 per year. Monthly. Contains international financial statistics, domestic financial and commercial conditions and articles on domestic and foreign affairs.

Finance and Development. (International Monetary Fund and World Bank, 700 19th St., N.W., Wash., D.C. 20431.) Free. Quarterly. Articles by staff members to explain the policies and activities of the Fund and the Bank to the general public. Makes clear the character of current operations of the two institutions and the reasons for their choices of particular policies and programs. French, Spanish, German and English.

The Financial Times. (75 Rockefeller Plaza, New York, N.Y. 10019.) $365.00.

Foreign Affairs. (Subscriptions, Council on Foreign Relations, P.O. Box 2615, Boulder, Co. 80322.) $15.00 per year for five issues, domestic subscription. Indispensable for deeper understanding of major international issues and an active participant in formation of foreign policy.

Foreign Affairs Edition. (Capitol Services, Inc., 415 2nd St., N.W., Wash., D.C. 20002.) $430.00 per year. Daily while Congress is in session. Meant to be used with the *Congressional Record*.

Contains abstracts of foreign and international items in the *Congressional Record*. Loose-leaf form, averaging two to three pages daily.

FATUS-Foreign Agricultural Trade of the United States. (Division of Information, Dept. of Agriculture, Wash., D.C. 20250.) Free. Monthly with two annual supplements. Describes foreign agricultural trade of the United States, including statistics.

Foreign Agriculture. (Superintendent of Documents, GPO, Wash., D.C. 20402.) $34.35 per year. 70 cents single copy. Weekly. Includes *Foreign Crops and Markets*. Reviews foreign agricultural developments affecting U.S. trade.

Foreign Economic Trends and Their Implications for the United States. (U.S. Dept. of Commerce. From Superintendent of Documents, GPO, Wash., D.C. 20402.) 100 to 150 reports per year from Foreign Service posts abroad presenting current business and economic developments in every country that offers a present or potential market for U.S. goods. $50.00 per year.

Foreign Report. (The Economist Newspaper, Ltd., 75 Rockefeller Plaza, New York, N.Y. 10019.) $145.00 per year. Forty-eight issues with two indices. A confidential newsletter based on a continuous flow of information from high-level sources in business and politics containing items which are not reported in the major newspapers and magazines but which provide a vital background for political forecasting and business decision-making.

Foreign Service Journal. (The American Foreign Service Association, 2101 E St., N.W., Wash., D.C. 20037.) $7.50 per year. Monthly. Of special interest to foreign affairs personnel.

Foreign Trade Statistics. (Organization for Economic Cooperation and Development, 1750 Pennsylvania Ave., N.W., Wash., D.C. 20006). $64.20 per year, airmail (series A); $40.90 per year, airmail (series B). Series A, monthly. Series B, annual in six volumes. Contains country-by-country trade statistics. Series A provides currency figures and Series B gives information by broad product groupings.

Forex Service on Legislative Changes in International Finance. (International Reports. 200 Park Ave., S., New York, N.Y. 10003.) $220.00 per year. Monthly. (Available to *International Reports on Finance and Currencies* subscribers at $125.00 per year.) Covers economic-financial legislation and important developments affecting the policies of regional and international organizations.

Fortune. (Time, Inc., 541 N. Fairbanks Ct., Chicago, Il. 60611.) $28.00 per year. Monthly.

General Statistics. (Organization for Economic Cooperation and Development, 1750 Pennsylvania Ave., N.W., Wash., D.C. 20006.) $10.00 per year. Six times yearly with monthly supplement. Includes data on industrial production, population, wholesale and retail indices, salaries and wages, finance and economics.

German-American Trade News. (German-American Chamber of Commerce, 666 5th Ave., New York, N.Y. 10019.) $5.00 per year, $14.00 for three years. Bimonthly. Describes German trade relations, corporations, industrial and economic trends and similar matters. It is aimed at U.S. readers and includes features about traveling in Germany, investments, licensing, German trade fairs and a classified advertising section.

Headline Series. (Foreign Policy Association, 345 E. 46th St., New York, N.Y. 10017.) $7.00 per year. Five times a year. Current international problems analyzed by leading scholars in a popular, readable style. Includes maps, charts, discussion guides and reading references.

Highlights of U.S. Export and Import Trade. (Superintendent of Documents, GPO,Wash., D.C. 20402.) $34.00 per year and $3.00 single issue, domestic; $42.50 per year and $3.75 per single issue for foreign mailing. Monthly. Statistical book of U.S. exports and imports, compiled by the Bureau of the Census.

IEA International Communicator. (International Executives Association, Inc., Ste. 1014, 122 E. 42nd St., New York, N.Y. 10017.) Free to members. Monthly.

IEA Trade Highlights. (International Executives Association, Inc., Ste. 1014, 122 E. 42nd St., New York, N.Y. 10017.) Free to members. Monthly.

IMF Survey. (International Monetary Fund, 700 19th St., N.W., Wash., D.C. 20431.) $10.00 per year. Twenty-three issues. A topical report of Fund activities presented in broader context of developments in national economies and international finance. French, Spanish and English.

Import Alert. (American Importers Association, 11 W. 42nd St., New York, N.Y. 10036.) $300.00 per year. Six issues a year. Members only. Newsletter containing valuable information on rulings, regulations, activity affecting world trade.

Import Bulletin. (The Journal of Commerce, 110 Wall St., New York, N.Y. 10005.) $200.00 per year. Weekly. Imports listed by products and product groups, by vessels and by point of origin and port of arrival. Consignees named.

Index to Foreign Market Reports. (National Technical Information Service, 5285 Port Royal Rd., Springfield, Va. 22161.) $10.00 per year. Monthly. Lists of reports, useful because they let the exporter know what foreign market reports are available through the National Technical Service. The reports are listed by country and either Standard Industrial Classification code or general subject matter.

Industrial Property. (World Intellectual Property Organization, 32 Chemin des Colombettes, 1211 Geneva 20, Switzerland.) Monthly. 10 Swiss francs each. 110 Swiss francs per year.

International Business. (World Trade Associates, Inc., 14842 First Ave., S., Seattle, Wa. 98168.) $20.00, United States; $15.00 + $10.00 foreign airmail. Bimonthly. Magazine of the World Trade Clubs of America. Separate editions for the United States, the Middle East, Asia, Europe, South America and Africa. Topics include banking, transportation and sources of private and government assistance for foreign marketing.

International Business Intelligence. (International Reports, Inc., 200 Park Ave., S., New York, N.Y. 10003.) *Int'l Reports* subscribers—$220.00 annual; other, $250.00 and $75.00 three month trial. Report on important new international business trends, including advice on foreign investment possibilities and project financing. Subscribers also receive *Bulletin of the Institute of Seitch and Barter Trade, Foreign Letter and International Commercial Financing Guide.*

International Economic Indicators. (Superintendent of Documents, GPO, Wash., D.C. 20402.) $12.65 per year, plus $3.20 for foreign mailing; $3.20 single issue. Quarterly. Compares economic statistics for the United States and seven other major exporting nations. Data are arranged in four sections: economic prospects and recent trends; changes in key competitive indicators; basic data for indicators and notes and sources.

International Financial Statistics. (International Monetary Fund, 700 19th St., N.W., Wash., D.C. 20431.) $35.00 per year. Monthly. Reports for most countries of the world includes data on exchange rates, international liquidity, money and banking, international trade, prices, production, interest rates, government finance, etc.

International Report. (Chamber of Commerce of the United States, 1615 H St., N.W. Wash., D.C. 20062.) $30.00 per year. Monthly. Reports pending international trade and investment legislation, activities of international organizations and actions by the U.S. government that affect international business.

International Reports. (International Reports, Inc., 200 Park Ave., S., New York, N.Y. 10003.) $655.00; $175.00, three month trial period. Weekly. International report on finance and currencies, with German supplement.

International Trade Highlights. (International Executives Association, One World Trade Center, Ste. 1003, New York, N.Y. 10048.) Free to members; not available to nonmembers. Monthly. This newsletter covers trade news and international business opportunities.

International Trade Reporter—U.S. Export Weekly. (The Bureau of National Affairs, Inc., 1231 25th St., N.W., Wash., D.C. 20037.) $261.00 per year. Weekly newsletter containing important official action having impact on expanding U.S. export market.

Italian Trade Topics. (Commercial Office, Italian Embassy, 1601 Fuller St., N.W., Wash., D.C. 20009.) Free. Monthly. Pamphlet containing articles and news briefs describing Italian industry and economic conditions, plus a list of upcoming trade fairs in Italy.

The Japan Report. (United States-Japan Trade Council, 1000 Connecticut Ave., N.W., Wash., D.C. 20036.) $125.00 per year. Every third week. Contains commercial intelligence from various sources and specific business plans and decisions in numerous Japanese industries.

Journal of Commerce. (Twin Coast Newspapers, Inc., 110 Wall St., New York. N.Y. 10005.) $120 per year, $68.00 for 6 months and $36.00 for 3 months in the U.S. or U.S. possessions; $160.00 per year in foreign countries. Fees are payable in advance.

Journal of Commerce Export Bulletin. (Journal of Commerce, 110 Wall St., New York, N.Y. 10005.) $200.00 per year. Weekly. Newspapers that reports port and shipping developments. Lists products shipped from New York and ships and cargoes departing from 25 other U.S. ports. A "Trade Prospects" column lists merchandise offered and merchandise wanted.

Journal of Marketing. (American Marketing Association, 222 S. Riverside Plaza, Chicago, Ill. 60606.) $24.00 for nonmembers; $9.00 for members, $7.00 individual copy; $11.00 corporation single copy. Quarterly.

Key Officers of Foreign Service Posts. (Superintendent of Documents, GPO, Wash., D.C. 20402.) $4.50 per year, $1.50 per issue. Quarterly. Lists the names of ambassadors, economic and commercial officers and other chiefs at U.S. embassies and consulates.

Kiplinger Washington Letter. (Kiplinger Washington Editors, 1729 H St., N.W., Wash., D.C. 20006.) $42.00 per year. Weekly.

Lloyd's Maritime and Commercial Law. (Lloyds of London Press Ltd., Sheeper Place, Colchester, Essex C03, 3LP, England.) Quarterly. £19.

Main Economic Indicators. (Organization for Economic Cooperation and Development, 1750 Pennsylvania Ave., N.W., Wash., D.C. 20006.) $50.00 per year, $5.00 per month. Monthly. Statistical data concerning major economic indicators are presented country-by-country in this book. Countries include the U.S., Canada, Japan, Australia and New Zealand, and the European Community.

Marine Digest. (Marine Digest, 218 National Bldg., Seattle, Wa. 98104.) $10.00 per year. Weekly. Subscription includes *Marine Digest Directory* published annually.

Marine Engineering/Log. (Simmons-Boardman Publishing Corp., 350 Broadway, New York, N.Y. 10013.) $15.00 per year. Monthly.

Marine Engineering/Log (International Edition). (Simmons-Boardman Publishing Corp., 350 Broadway, New York, N.Y. 10013.) $22.00 per year. Monthly.

Marine Week. (IPC Industrial Press Ltd., Dorset House, Stamford St., London SEI 9LV, England.) $55.00 per year. Weekly. News journal of shipbuilding, shipping and marine equipment industries.

Maritime Research Weekly Charter Newsletter. (Maritime Research, Inc., 11 Broadway, New York, N.Y. 10004.) $150.00. $3.50 per copy. Weekly. Listing of all ship charter fixtures reported in N.Y. and London market.

Marketing in Europe. (Economist Intelligence Unit Ltd., 27 St. James Place, London SW1A INT, England.) $155.00 per year plus $13.00 airmail for one group; $310 per year plus $26.00 airmail for two groups; $310.00 per year plus $36.00 airmail for three groups. Monthly. This journal provides detailed analyses of the European market for consumer goods. The issues are published in three subject groups: food, drink and tobacco; clothing, furniture and leisure goods; and chemists' goods, such as pharmaceuticals and toiletries.

Marking Digest. (U.S. Customs Service Customs Information Exchange, Six World Trade Center, New York, N.Y. 10048.) Free. Last edition published January 1976. A digest of decisions relating primarily to the requirements of Section 304 of the Tariff Act of 1930, as amended (19 U.S.C. 1304), as to the marking of imported articles to indicate their origin.

Metric Reporter. (American National Metric Council, 1625 Massachusetts Ave., N.W., Wash., D.C. 20036.) Bi-weekly. $35.00 per year.

Middle East Report. (National Foreign Trade Council, Inc., 10 Rockefeller Plaza, New York, N.Y. 10020.) Free to members. Monthly. Middle East news digest.

Mideast Markets. (Financial Times, Braken House, Cannon St., London, EC4P 4BY, England.) $295.00 per year. Fortnightly. Guide to business opportunities and the factors affecting them in 20 countries in the Middle East and North Africa.

Minutes of Monthly Roundtable Conference. (FCIB-NACM Corp., 475 Park Ave. S., New York, N.Y. 10016.) $125.00 per year includes *FCIB Bulletin* and *Semi-Annual Survey of Terms and Conditions in Overseas Markets.* Verbatim report of discussions on problems exporters are currently having in world markets.

Monthly Bulletin of Statistics. (United Nations Publications, Rm. A-3315, New York, N.Y. 10017.) $84.00 per year, $8.50 per copy. Monthly. Statistics on 170 countries on over 60 subjects.

Monthly Catalog of United States Government Publications. (Superintendent of Documents, GPO, Wash., D.C. 20402.) $65.00 per year, $6.00 single copy. Monthly. Comprehensive listing of all publications issued by departments and agencies of the U.S. government.

Monthly Operational Summary of Proposed Projects. World Bank. (The Johns Hopkins University Press, Journals Division, Baltimore, Md. 21218.) $60.00 per year. Monthly.

Multinational Business. (The Economist Intelligence Unit Ltd., Spencer House, 27 St. James' Pl., London SWIA INT, England.) $130.00 per year, $49.00 single copy. Quarterly. Contains special reports ranging from analysis of economic and political conditions to aspects of government policies specifically relevant to the multinational corporation.

Nation's Business. (Chamber of Commerce of the United States, 1615 H St., N.W., Wash., D.C. 20062.) $13.50. Monthly. Magazine forecasting, analyzing and interpreting trends and developments in business and the government.

News Releases. (News Room, Dept. of Commerce, 14th & Constitution Ave., N.W., Rm. 5062, Wash., D.C. 20230.) Free. Monthly. News releases are issued showing exports and imports of selected product categories.

Noticias. (National Foreign Trade Council, Inc., 10 Rockefeller Plaza, New York, N.Y. 10020.) Free to members. Weekly. Latin American news digest.

OECD Financial Statistics. (OECD Publication Center, 1750 Pennsylvania Ave., N.W., Wash., D.C. 20006.) $107.30 annual, with five periodic supplements and monthly reports updating interest rates. A unique collection of data on financial markets in 16 European countries, the United States, Canada and Japan.

OECD Foreign Trade Bulletins. (OECD Publications Center, 1750 Pennsylvania Ave., N.W., Wash., D.C. 20006.) Series (A) $30.00 per year, $40.00 per year airmail; Series (B) $30.00 per year, $35.45 per year airmail; Series (C) $30.00 per year, $35.45 per year airmail, semiannual $14.50 per year. Series (C), a semiannual publication in two volumes (imports and exports) with details on quantity and value by countries of origin and destination given for 272 commodity categories.

Official Journal of the European Communities. (European Community Information Service, 2100 M St., N.W., Ste. 707, Wash., D.C. 20037.) Surface mail: $137.00. Airmail: $365.00 additional. Daily. Publishes all Community legislation and many communications. *The Official Journal.* Surface mail: $33.00. Airmail: $16.00 additional. Microfiche Edition. Surface mail: $137.00. Airmail: $12.50 additional. Monthly.

Operational Summary of Proposed Projects. (Journals Division, The Johns Hopkins University Press, Baltimore, Md. 21218.) $60.00 per year, 12 issues, including postage. Quarterly. By the World Bank, this magazine describes bank-financed projects.

Overseas Business Reports (OBR). (Superintendent of Documents, GPO, Wash., D.C. 20402.) $40.00 per year, 50 cents single copy. 75-80 reports each year providing background data on specific countries including basic economic data, foreign trade regulations, market factors, information on selling and establishing a business in that country, etc.

Overseas Export Promotion Calendar. (Program Development Office, Office of Int'l Marketing, Dept. of Commerce, 14th & Constitution Ave., N.W., Rm. 4009, Wash., D.C. 20230.) Free. Quarterly. Includes advertisements of exhibits at trade centers.

Pacific-Asia Report. (National Foreign Trade Council, Inc., 10 Rockefeller Plaza, New York, N.Y. 10020.) Free to members. Monthly. Pacific-Asia news digest.

Pacific Shipper. (Pacific Shipper, Inc., 1050 Mission St., San Francisco, Ca. 94111.) $14.00 per year. Compendium of Pacific Ocean shipping and foreign trade information. Contains news, schedules and directory material.

Patent and Trademark Review. (Trade Activities, Inc., 435 Hudson St., New York, N.Y. 10017.) $20.00 per year for 11 issues, always starts with January. Features articles on patents, trademarks and licensing, proposed legislation and enacted international statutes.

Port Record. (Port of New Orleans, P.O. Box 60046, New Orleans, La. 70160.) Free. Monthly. This magazine covers the past month's news at the port.

Postal Bulletin. (Superintendent of Documents, GPO, Wash., D.C. 20402.) $35.00 per year. Weekly.

Public Affairs Information Service Bulletin. (Public Affairs Information Service, Inc., 11 W. 40th St., New York, N.Y. 10018.) $180.00 full membership (annual bound volume, semimonthly and three cumulative bulletins), $120.00 associate membership (annual bound volume, three cumulative bulletins), $85.00 limited membership (annual bound volume only). Weekly and cumulative, per year. An index to pamphlets, periodical articles, government documents, etc.

Public Opinion. (American Enterprise Institute, 1150 17th St., N.W., Wash., D.C. 20036.) $12.00 per year, $2.50 single copy. Bimonthly.

Quota Information. (U.S. Customs Service, Wash., D.C. 20229.) Free. Monthly. Quota information on textiles, various commodities and dairy products.

Regulation (Journal on Government & Society). (American Enterprise Institute, 1150 17th St., N.W., Wash., D.C. 20036.) $12.00 per year, $2.50 single copy. Bimonthly.

Sea Trade. (Seatrade Publications Ltd., Fairfax House, Colchester, Essex, England.) £12 per year. Monthly.

Selected United States Government Publications. (Superintendent of Documents, GPO, Wash., D.C. 20402.) Free. Monthly.

Shipping Digest. (Geyer-McAllister Publications, Inc., 51 Madison Ave., New York, N.Y. 10010.) $18.00 per year. Weekly. Contains cargo sailing schedules from every U.S. port to every foreign port, as well as international air and sea commerce news.

Space Research and Technology. (American Elsevier Publishing Co., Inc., 32 Vanderbilt Ave., New York, N.Y. 10017.) Price varies.

Special Reports. (Foreign Agricultural Service Information Services Staff, Dept. of Agriculture, 14th & Independence Ave., S.W., Rm. 5918-S, Wash., D.C. 20250.) Free. About foreign agricultural markets.

Survey of Current Business. (Superintendent of Documents, GPO, Wash., D.C. 20402.) $22.00 monthly, $3.00 single copy. Provides the latest data on international transactions of the U.S., focusing on the balance of payments.

Tariffs and Trade. (Box 307, Ansonia Station, New York, N.Y. 10023.) $110.00. Semi-monthly. Newsletter detailing late developments in international trade news, legislation, policy, international credit, government services and similar matters.

Tariff Schedules of the United States. (Superintendent of Documents, GPO, Wash., D.C. 20402.) $19.00 base cost, supplements free of charge.

Tariff Schedules of the United States, Annotated. (Superintendent of Documents, GPO, Wash., D.C. 20402.) Subscription: $28.00 first-class mail; $23.00 fourth-class mail.

Tradelook. (Tradelook Publishing Company, 61 Woodhaven Blvd., Rego Pk., New York, N.Y. 11347.) $15.00 per year in the United States; $20.00 per year in foreign countries. Bimonthly. Concerned with investments, commodities and international trade.

The Trademark Reporter. (U.S. Trademark Association, 6 East 45th St., New York, N.Y. 10017.) Monthly. Available to members only, no charge. (Under special circumstances, they will make the publication available to government agencies, public libraries, law firms, schools, etc. $40.00 per year.)

Trade Policy Review. (Chamber of Commerce of the United States, 1615 H St., N.W., Wash., D.C. 20062.) $30.00 per year. Provides an in-depth analysis of key trade policy issues. Subscribers also have telephone access to chamber trade specialists.

Traffic World. (Traffic Service Corporation, 815 Washington Bldg., Wash., D.C. 20005.) $85.00 per year. Weekly.

Transportation Telephone Tickler. (Journal of Commerce, 445 Marshall St., Phillipsburg, N.J. 08865.) $25.00 for set of three books. Vol. I—metropolitan area (N.Y. and N.J.), Vols. II and III—U.S. and Canadian ports. Annual. Lists steamships lines, custom house brokers, freight forwarders, airlines.

TOP Bulletin—An Advisory Service. (Trade Opportunities Program, Office of Export Development, Dept. of Commerce, 14th & Constitution Ave., N.W., Rm. 2014, Wash., D.C. 20230.) $100.00 per year. Weekly. Describes overseas sales opportunities. Indexed by Standard Industrial Classification Code, Country of the opportunity and type of opportunity.

United Nations International Business Report. (International Business-Government Councellor, Inc., 1625 Eye Street, N.W., Ste. 717, Wash., D.C. 20006.) $120.00 per year. The subscription includes the special report entitled "The United Nations and International Business: A Road Map for Corporate Executives." A monthly newsletter focused on significant UN developments affecting international business in such areas as multinational corporations, technology, environment and natural resources, consumer relations.

U.S. Airborne Exports and General Imports. (Superintendent of Documents, GPO, Wash., D.C. 20402.) $14.90 per year. A series of foreign trade statistical reports by the Bureau of the Census. Titles and individual prices are: Summary of U.S. Export and Import Merchandise Trade, 30 cents, cite stock number FT 900; U.S. Waterborne Exports and General Imports, 50 cents, cite stock number FT 985; Vessel Entrances and Clearances, 25 cents, cite stock number FT 975; U.S. Airborne Exports and General Imports, 35 cents, cite stock number FT 986. $14.90 for an annual subscription to all four.

U.S.A.-R.O.C. Taiwan Economic News. (United States-Republic of China Economic Council, 200 Main St., Crystal Lake, Ill. 60014.) Free. Monthly. Covers the economic situation in the Republic of China.

U.S. Exports, Schedule E Commodity Groupings. (Superintendent of Documents, GPO, Wash., D.C. 20402.) $80.00 per year or $6.75 per single issue, domestic; $100.00 per year or $8.45 per single issue for foreign mailing. Monthly. Reports on U.S. exports by commodity, country, quantity and value. Includes an annual cumulative report.

U.S. Foreign Trade Reports. (Superintendent of Documents, GPO, Wash., D.C. 20402.) Monthly. U.S. General Imports, Schedule A Commodity, FT 135, $63.00 per year; U.S. Exports, Schedule E, FT 410, $80.00 per year; U.S. Trade with Puerto Rico and Their Possessions, FT 800, $16.30 per year; Highlights of U.S. Exports and Imports, FT 9090, $34.00 per year.

Washington International Business Report Service. (International Business-Government Councellors, Inc., 1625 Eye St., Ste. 717, Wash., D.C. 20006.) $264.00 per year. A biweekly newsletter service spotlighting major U.S. government policy, program and regulatory developments affecting foreign trade and investment.

World Traders Data Reports. (World Traders Data Report Section, U.S. Dept of Commerce, 14th & Constitution Ave., N.W., Wash., D.C. 20230.) $15.00 per report prepaid. Reports give basic commercial and descriptive background information on foreign firms. If information on a particular firm is not on file in Wash., it will be requested from the Foreign Service.

Export Business Magazines

Numerous *export business magazines* or catalogs are published in the United States, primarily for circulation in particular foreign countries as advertising media. Often they are printed in English and one or more foreign languages and carry advertising and descriptive material concerning American products or industries.

Some are general in their coverage, although frequently having a separate commodity department. Others specialize in certain commercial or industrial fields such as automobiles and industrial machinery.

A number of nontechnical magazines, especially international editions of popular American publications, also have wide circulation in many foreign countries. Some carry advertising particularly of branded consumer goods and are regarded by many as excellent advertising media for goods used in the home.

See subject headings: Advertising Abroad; and Foreign Marketing.

Aviation Week & Space Technology. (McGraw Hill, Inc., 1221 Ave. of the Americas, New York, N.Y. 10020.) $30.00 a year. Weekly. Aerospace industry reporting.

Boletin Internacional. (Banco de Vizcaya, Gran Via 1, Bilbao 1, Spain.) Free. Bimonthly. Published in Spanish and English editions, this magazine covers Spanish and international economic news.

Dirigente Constructor. (Represented outside Brazil by Vision, Inc., 641 Lexington Ave., New York, N.Y. 10022.) Monthly. Portuguese. Construction field.

Dirigente Industrial. (Represented outside Brazil by Vision, Inc., 641 Lexington Ave., New York, N.Y. 10022.) Monthly. Portuguese. Industrial management.

Dirigente Municipal. (Represented outside Brazil by Vision, Inc., 641 Lexington Ave., New York, N.Y. 10022.) Bimonthly. Portuguese. Municipal administration.

Dirigente Rural. (Represented outside Brazil by Vision, Inc., 641 Lexington Ave., New York, N.Y. 10022.) Bimonthly. Portuguese. Farming.

Embotellador, El. (Keller Publishing Corp., 10 Cutter Mill Rd., Great Neck, N.Y. 11021.) Bimonthly. Spanish. Soft drink, brewing industry, winery and distillery industries.

Energy International. (Miller Freeman Publications, Inc., 500 Howard St., San Francisco, Ca. 94105.) Free (outside the United States and Canada) to qualifying personnel of energy production, transmission and distribution organizations; officials of government departments and members of consulting firms. All others: $20.00 per year. Monthly. Provides summaries of events pertinent to the energy supply industry throughout the world, and deals with energy economics, technology utilization and reserves.

Instrumentacion Internacional. (Keller Publishing Corp., 10 Cutter Mill Rd., Great Neck, N.Y. 11021.) Spanish. New products and methods for the instrumentation and control fields.

International Hospital Equipment. (Miller Freeman Publications, Inc., 500 Howard St., San Francisco, Ca. 94105.) Free to qualifying personnel of administrative, professional and service departments in hospitals, and personnel or government health departments and medical research organizations. All others: $20.00 per year. Bimonthly tabloid plus *Buyers Guide* published in April. Presents news of products and services available to purchasers and specifiers of medical, surgical and hospital equipment throughout the world.

International Instrumentation. (Keller Publishing Corp., 10 Cutter Mill Rd., Great Neck, N.Y. 11021.) Bimonthly. English. New products and methods for the instrumentation and control fields.

International Management. (McGraw-Hill Publishing Co., Ltd., Maidenhead, England.) Free of charge to qualified senior management in large firms and government departments outside the United States and Canada. Monthly. English, Spanish, Arabic and Farsi. Management techniques and developments, company management stories, executive self-improvement.

Petroleo Internacional. (Petroleum Publishing Co., 1421 S. Sheridan Rd., P.O. Box 1260, Tulsa, Ok. 74101.) $5.00 per year. Monthly. Spanish.

Progreso. (Vision, Inc., 641 Lexington Ave., New York, N.Y. 10022.) $30.00. Nine times a year. Spanish. Business and development in Latin America.

Pulp and Paper International. (Miller Freeman Publications, Inc., 370 Lexington Ave., New York, N.Y. 10017.) Free to qualifying personnel in pulp, paper and paperboard manufacturing firms in all countries except U.S. and Canada. All others: $25.00 a year. Monthly plus *Annual Review*

Number published in July. Reports on news, interprets trends and provides semi-technical and technical information on the industry for operating personnel.

Reportero Industrial. (Keller Publishing Corp., 10 Cutter Mill Rd., Great Neck, N.Y. 11021.) Monthly. Spanish. New products and methods for industrial plants in Latin America.

Revista Aerea Latinoamerica. (Strato Publishing Co., Revista Aerea, 209 East 56th St., New York, N.Y. 10022.) Monthly. Spanish. Aviation industry.

Sugar Y Azucar. (Palmer Publications, 25 W. 45th St., New York, N.Y. 10036.) $5.00 a year; $1.00 per single copy. English, Spanish. Sugar industry.

Temas Magazine. (1650 Broadway, New York, N.Y. 10019.) $4.00 a year; 40 cents per copy. Monthly. Spanish.

Visao. (Vision, Inc., 641 Lexington Ave., New York, N.Y. 10022.) Bimonthly. Portuguese. News magazine.

Vision. (Vision, Inc., 641 Lexington Ave., New York, N.Y. 10022.) Twenty-four times a year. Spanish. News magazine.

Vision—The European Business Magazine. (Vision, Inc., 641 Lexington Ave., New York, N.Y. 10022.) $34 a year; $3.50 per copy. Eleven times a year. English, French, German, Italian.

World Coal. (Miller Freeman Publications, Inc., 500 Howard St., San Francisco, Ca. 94105.) Free to key management personnel in executive, production and engineering positions in U.S. coal companies and mines with annual production over 100,000 tons; also to consulting firms and key personnel in government departments concerned with coal mining. All others: $20.00 per year. Monthly, plus *Annual Review Number* published in November. Provides concise editorial coverage of worldwide coal industry developments.

World Industrial Reporter. (Keller Publishing Corp., 10 Cutter Mill Rd., Great Neck, N.Y. 11021.) Monthly. English. New products and methods for industrial plants.

World Mining. (Miller Freeman Publications, Inc., 500 Howard St., San Francisco. Ca. 94105.) $14.00, $1.00 per copy in the United States. Monthly, plus *Annual Catalog, Survey and Directory* published except in June. Reports techniques and developments in all branches of the metal and non-metallic mining and quarrying industry throughout the world.

World Wood. (Miller Freeman Publications, Inc., 500 Howard St., San Francisco, Ca. 94105.) Free to management production and technical personnel in logging, forestry, sawmilling, plywood and board manufacturing firms in all countries except U.S. and Canada. All others: $30.00 a year. United States and Canada: $35.00 a year. Monthly, plus *Annual Review Number* published in May. Emphasizes forestry and mill methods with detailed coverage of machinery and techniques.

Part IV. Appendix

Acronyms

A

AAA American Arbitration Association
AACCLA Association of American Chambers of Commerce in Latin America
ACDA United States Arms Control and Disarmament Agency
ACEP Advisory Committee on Export Policy
ADB Asian Development Bank
ADBF African Development Bank and Fund
ADTS Automated Data and Telecommunications System (GSA)
AEC Atomic Energy Commission
AEI American Enterprise Institute for Public Policy Research
AFL-CIO American Federation of Labor-Congress of Industrial Organizations
AIA American Importers Association
AID Agency for International Development
AIMU American Institute of Marine Underwriters
AmCham American Chamber of Commerce Abroad
ANCOM Andean Common Market
ANSI American National Standards Institute
APCAC Asia-Pacific Council of American Chambers of Commerce
APHIS Animal and Plant Health Inspection Service (USDA)
ARS Advanced Record System (GSA)
ASD/ISA Assistant Secretary of Defense for International Security Affairs
ASEAN Association of Southeast Asian Nations
ASEANCCI ASEAN Chambers of Commerce and Industry
ATA Admission Temporaire/Temporary Admission (carnet)

B

BEA Bureau of Economic Analysis (Dept. of Commerce)
BED Bureau of Export Development (Dept. of Commerce)
BIAC Business and Industry Advisory Committee (to the OECD)
BIE Bureau of Industrial Economics (Dept. of Commerce)
BSC Business Service Centers (GSA)

C

CAB Civil Aeronautics Board
CACM Central American Common Market
CAGNE Commerce Action Group for the Near East (Dept. of Commerce)

CARICOM   Caribbean Common Market
CCC   Commodity Credit Corporation
CCMS   Committee on Challenges to Modern Society
CDB   Caribbean Development Bank
CEA   Council of Economic Advisers
CED   Committee for Economic Development
CFF   Cooperative Financing Facility (Eximbank)
CFTC   Commodity Futures Trading Commission
CIC   Consumer Information Center (GSA)
CITA   Committee for the Implementation of Textile Agreements (Dept. of Commerce)
CMEA   Council for Mutual Economic Assistance
CoA   Council of the Americas
COGECA   General Committee for Agricultural Cooperation of the European Community
COGP   Commission on Government Procurement
COPA   Committee of Professional Agricultural Organizations of the European Community
CRS   Congressional Research Service

D

DEC   District Export Council (Dept. of Commerce)
DIBA   Domestic and International Business Administration (now International Trade Administration) (Dept. of Commerce)
DISC   Domestic International Sales Corporation
DOD   Department of Defense
DOE   Department of Energy
DOLITAC   Department of Labor International Technical Assistance Corps
DOT   Department of Transportation

E

EC   European Community
ECA   Economic Commission for Africa (ECOSOC)
ECAT   Emergency Committee for American Trade
ECE   Economic Commission for Europe (ECOSOC)
ECE/HBP   UN Economic Commission for Europe, Committee on Housing, Building and Planning
ECLA   Economic Commission for Latin America (ECOSOC)
ECOSOC   Economic and Social Council (UN)
ECS   Echantillons Commerciaux/Commercial Samples (carnet)
ECSC   European Coal and Steel Community
ECWA   Economic Commission for Western Asia (ECOSOC)
EEC   European Economic Community
EIA   Equipment Interchange Association
EIRR   Export Information Reference Room (Dept. of Commerce)
EFTA   European Free Trade Association
EMC   Export Management Company

EMS European Monetary System
EOP Executive Office of the President
EPA Environmental Protection Agency
ESCAP Economic and Social Commission for Asia and the Pacific (ECOSOC)
ESF Exchange Stabilization Fund (Dept. of the Treasury)
EuroMed Council of American Chambers of Commerce—Europe and Mediterranean
Eurotom European Atomic Energy Community
EXIM Export-Import Bank of the United States
Eximbank Export-Import Bank of the United States

F

FAA Federal Aviation Administration (Dept. of Transportation)
FAO Food and Agriculture Organization (UN)
FAS Foreign Agricultural Service (Dept. of Agriculture)
FCC Federal Communications Commission
FCIA Foreign Credit Insurance Association
FCIB formerly Foreign Credit Interchange Bureau
FCN Treaties of Friendship, Commerce and Navigation
FCS Foreign Commercial Service
FIATA International Federation of Forwarding Agents Association
FIC Federal Information Centers (GSA)
FIRS Foreign Information Retrieval System (HUD)
FIS Finance, Investment and Services (Dept. of Commerce)
FPRS Federal Property Resources Service (GSA)
FTC Federal Trade Commission
FTS Federal Telecommunications System (GSA)

G

GAO General Accounting Office
GATT General Agreement on Tariffs and Trade
GDR German Democratic Republic
GPO Government Printing Office
GSM-101 Noncommercial Risk Assurance Program (Dept. of Agriculture)
GSM-5 Export Sales Program (Dept. of Agriculture)
GSA General Services Administration
GSP Generalized System of Preferences
GPO Government Printing Office, U.S.

H

HEW Department of Health, Education, and Welfare (now Department of Health and Human Services and Department of Education)
HUD Department of Housing and Urban Development

I

IAA International Advertising Association, Inc.
IACAC International American Commercial Arbitration Commission

IATA International Air Transport Association
IBRD International Bank for Reconstruction and Development (World Bank)
ICA International Communication Agency
ICAO International Civil Aviation Organization (UN)
ICC International Chamber of Commerce
ICIE International Centre for Industry and the Environment
ICSID International Centre for Settlement of Investment Disputes (World Bank Group)
IDA International Development Association (World Bank Group)
IDB Inter-American Development Bank
IDCA United States International Development Cooperation Agency
IEA International Executives Association, Inc.
IEPA International Economic Policy Association
IFAD International Fund for Agricultural Development (UN)
IFC International Finance Corporation (World Bank Group)
ILAB Bureau of International Labor Affairs (Dept. of Labor)
ILO International Labor Organization (UN)
IMCO Inter-Governmental Maritime Consultative Organization (UN)
IMF International Monetary Fund
IMIC International Marketing Information Center (Dept. of Commerce)
INCOTERMS Foreign Trade Definitions
IOGA Industry-organized, government-approved (trade missions) (Dept. of Commerce)
IRS Internal Revenue Service
ISAC Industry Sector Advisory Committee (Dept. of Commerce)
ISTC Institute for Scientific and Technological Cooperation
ITA Industry and Trade Administration (now International Trade Administration) (Dept. of Commerce)
ITC United States International Trade Commission
ITC International Trade Centre (GATT/UNCTAD)
ITU International Telecommunications Union (UN)

L

LAFTA Latin American Free Trade Area

M

MarAd Maritime Administration (Dept. of Commerce)
MBEAP Minority Business Export Assistance Program (Dept. of Commerce)
MFN Most-Favored-Nation Tariff Status

MNC   Multinational Corporation
MTN   Multilateral Trade Negotiations

N

NAC   National Advisory Committee
NAFTA   New Zealand-Australia Free Trade Agreement
NAM   National Association of Manufacturers of the United States
NARS   National Archives and Records Service (GSA)
NASDA   National Association of State Development Agencies
NATO   North Atlantic Treaty Organization
NCBFAA   National Customs Brokers and Forwarders Association of America, Inc.
NCITD   National Committee on International Trade Documentation
NEP   National Export Policy
NEXCO   National Association of Export Management Companies, Inc.
NFTC   National Foreign Trade Council, Inc.
NIEO   New International Economic Order
NPA   National Planning Association
NPIS   New Product Information Service (Dept. of Commerce)
NSC   National Security Council
NTB   Nontariff Barrier
NTIS   National Technical Information Service (Dept. of Commerce)

O

OAS   Organization of American States
OBR   Overseas Business Reports
OCM   Office of Country Marketing (Dept. of Commerce)
ODC   Overseas Development Council
OEA   Office of Export Administration (Dept. of Commerce)
OECD   Organization for Economic Cooperation and Development
OEEC   Organization for European Economic Cooperation (now OECD)
OFPP   Office of Federal Procurement Policy
OGSM   Office of the General Sales Manager (Dept. of Agriculture)
OIA   Office of International Affairs (HUD)
OMB   Office of Management and Budget
OPEC   Organization of Petroleum Exporting Countries
OPIC   Overseas Private Investment Corporation
OSTP   Office of Science and Technology Policy

P

PBS   Public Buildings Service (GSA)
PEC   President's Export Council

PEFCO Private Export Funding Corporation
PPQ Plant Protection and Quarantine Programs (USDA)

S

SALT Strategic Arms Limitation Talks
SBA Small Business Administration
SDR Special Drawing Right
SEC Securities and Exchange Commission
SELA Latin American Economic System
SIC U.S. Standard Industrial Classification
SIS Special Industrial Services Program (UNIDO)
STR Special Trade Representative (now USTR, United States Trade Representative)

T

TEMPS Tailored Export Marketing Plan Service (Dept. of Commerce)
THE Technical Help to Exporters Program, NTIS (Dept. of Commerce)
TIR Transport International Routier (International Road Transport) (carnet)
TNC Transnational Corporation
TPC Trade Policy Committee (interagency)
TPUS Transportation and Public Utilities Service (GSA)
TRC Trade Relations Council of the United States, Inc.
TSUS Tariff Schedules of the United States

U

UN United Nations
UNCITRAL United Nations Commission on International Trade Law
UNCLOS United Nations Conference on the Law of the Sea
UNCTAD United Nations Conference on Trade and Development
UNCTC United Nations Centre on Transnational Corporations
UNCTSD United Nations Conference on Science and Technology for Development
UNDP United Nations Development Programme
UNEP United Nations Environment Programme
UNESCO United Nations Educational, Scientific and Cultural Organization
UNICE Union of Industrial Federations of the European Community
UNIDO United Nations Industrial Development Organization
UPU Universal Postal Union (UN)
USA-BIAC United States of America Business and Industry Advisory Committee (to the OECD)
USDA Department of Agriculture
USPS United States Postal Service
USTR United States Trade Representative

V

VAT   Value-Added Tax
VCE   Video-Catalog Exhibits

W

WARC   General World Administrative Radio Conferences (ITU)
WFC   World Food Council (UN)
WHO   World Health Organization (UN)
WIPO   World Intellectual Property Organization (UN)
WITS   Worldwide Information and Trade Service (Dept. of Commerce)
WMO   World Meteorological Organization (UN)
World Bank   International Bank for Reconstruction and Development

American Chambers of Commerce Abroad

ARGENTINA
Andrew Monteath, Executive
  Director
The American Chamber of
  Commerce in Argentina
Av. R. Saenz Pena 567
1352 Buenos Aires, Argentina
PHONE: 33-5591/5592
CABLE: USCHAMBCOM
TELEX: 22347 minag ar

AUSTRALIA
E. Kevin Bannon, Executive
  Director
The American Chamber of
  Commerce in Australia
8th Floor, 50 Pitt Street
Sydney, N.S.W. 2000,
  Australia
PHONE: 241-1907
CABLE: AMCHAM
  SYDNEY
TELEX: 22792 lincoln aa

Branch Offices
Suzie Bendall, Adelaide
  Manager
The American Chamber of
  Commerce in Australia
8th Floor, 50 Grenfell Street
Adelaide, S.A. 5000.
  Australia
PHONE: 212-5781

Mrs. Asta Johnston, Brisbane
  Manager
The American Chamber of
  Commerce in Australia
17th Floor
167 Eagle Street (G.P.O. Box
  439, 4001)
Brisbane, Queensland 4000,
  Australia
PHONE: 221-8542

C. C. Miller, Melbourne
  Manager
The American Chamber of
  Commerce in Australia
3rd Floor, 186 Exhibition
  Street
Melbourne, Victoria 3000,
  Australia
PHONE: 662-3535

Pat Maxwell, Perth Manager
The American Chamber of
  Commerce in Australia

6th Floor, 16 St. George's
  Terrace
Perth, W.A. 6000, Australia
PHONE: 25-9540

AUSTRIA
Dr. Patricia A. Helletzgruber,
  Manager
The American Chamber of
  Commerce in Austria
Turkenstrasse 9
A-1090 Vienna, Austria
PHONE: 31 57 51, 31 57 52
CABLE: USACHAMBER
TELEX: 33280 kodak a

BELGIUM
Anne Harrington, Executive
  Director
The American Chamber of
  Commerce in Belgium
Avenue des Arts 50, bte 5
B-1040, Brussels, Belgium
PHONE: (02) 512 12 62
TELEX: 61387 brunco b

BOLIVIA
Alfonso Revollo
Executive Secretary
American Chamber of
  Commerce of Bolivia
Casilla de Correo 8268
Avda. Arce #2071, of. 2
La Paz, Bolivia
PHONE: 34-2523

**BRAZIL—RIO DE
  JANEIRO**
Augusto de Moura Diniz, Jr.
Executive Vice President
American Chamber of
  Commerce for Brazil—Rio
  de Janeiro
Avenida Rio Branco 123, 21st
  Floor
P.O. Box 916-ZC-00
Rio de Janeiro, Brazil
PHONE: 222-1983
CABLE: AMERCHACOM

Branch Office
Paulo Emanuel Silva Lima
Executive Secretary
American Chamber of
  Commerce for Brazil—
  Filial—Salvador

Rua Conselheiro Dantas, 8,
Sala 706
Edificio Paraguassu
40000 Salvador, Bahia, Brazil
PHONE: 242-7293, 242-3048

BRAZIL—SAO PAULO
David M. Ventura
Executive Vice President
American Chamber of
   Commerce for Brazil—Sao
   Paulo
Rua Formosa 367, 29th Floor
P.O. Box 8109
01000 Sao Paulo, Brazil
PHONE: 222-6377
CABLE: AMERCHACOM

CHILE
Maria Isabel Jaramillo
Executive Secretary
Chamber of Commerce of the
   U.S.A. in the Republic of
   Chile
Hotel Sheraton San Cristobal,
   Loc. 11
Casilla de Correo 4131
Santiago, Chile
PHONE: 74-7167
CABLE: AMCHAMBER
TELEX: 3520004 (ITT)
   sheraton

COLOMBIA
Oscar A. Bradford
President
Colombian-American
   Chamber of Commerce
Bogota Hilton Hotel, Suite
   701
Carrera 7a, No. 32-16
Apartado Aereo 8008
Bogota, Colombia
PHONE: 329701/791
CABLE: CAMCOLAM
   BOGOTA
TELEX: 43326 and 45411
   camc co

Branch Office
Maria Elvira de Garces
Executive Director
Colombian-American
   Chamber of Commerce
Ave. 1-N No. 2N-97
Apartado 5943
Cali, Valle, Colombia
PHONE: 631812

COSTA RICA
Felicia M. Morales, Manager
American Chamber of
   Commerce of Costa Rica
Calle 3, Avenidas 1 y 3, 2o
   piso
Apartado Postal 4946
San Jose, Costa Rica
PHONE: 33-21-33
CABLE: AMCHAM

DOMINICAN REPUBLIC
Wilson A. Rood, Executive
   Director
American Chamber of
   Commerce of the
   Dominican Republic
P.O. Box 95-2
Hotel Santo Domingo
Santo Domingo, Dominican
   Republic
PHONE: 533-7292
CABLE: AMCHAM
TELEX: 3460033 hocosta

ECUADOR
Karl Newlands, Exec. Vice
   President
Ecuadorian-American
   Chamber of Commerce
Apartado 2432
Quito, Ecuador
PHONE: 543-512
CABLE: ECUAME
TELEX: 2298 ecuame ed

EL SALVADOR
Salvador I. Parada, Manager
American Chamber of
   Commerce of El Salvador
Apartado Postal (05) 9
Apt. "A," 9th Floor,
   Condominio Los Heroes
Blvd. Los Heroes
San Salvador, El Salvador
PHONE: 26-14-41; 26-35-44

FRANCE
W. Barrett Dower, Executive
   Director
The American Chamber of
   Commerce in France
21 Avenue George V
75008 Paris, France
PHONE: 723-80-26
CABLE: AMCHAM
TELEX: 650286 royale b

GERMANY
Paul G. Baudler, General
   Manager
American Chamber of
   Commerce in Germany
Rossmarkt 12
D-6000 Frankfurt 1, Germany
PHONE: (0611) 28-34-01
CABLE: AMECOC

Branch Offices
Robert H. Lochner,
   Representative
American Chamber of
   Commerce in Germany
Kurfurstenstrasse 114
1000 Berlin 30, Germany
PHONE: (030) 242646
CABLE: AMASCOT
   BERLIN

Dr. Leo M. Goodman,
   Representative
The American Chamber of
   Commerce in Germany
Zweibruckenstrasse 6
8000 Munich 2, Germany
PHONE: (089) 295953

Hans Jurgen Rosteck
ACC Representative
Geibelstr, 45
D-4000 Dusseldorf, Germany
PHONE: 0211/682343

Ed Becker
ACC Washington
   Representative
517 Meridian Street
Falls Church, Virginia 22046
   U.S.A.
PHONE: (703) 534-7237

GUATEMALA
Oliver Sause, Executive
   Manager
The American Chamber of
   Commerce in Guatemala
Etisa Building, 5th Floor
Calle Montaful y Av.
   Septima, Zona 9
Plazuela Espana
Apartado Postal 832
Guatemala City, Guatemala
PHONE: 312235; 61882
CABLE: AMCHAM
   GUATEMALACITY

HAITI
Executive Director
The Haitian-American
  Chamber of Commerce &
  Industry
Delmas P.O. Box 13486
Port-au-Prince, Haiti
PHONE: 204-42

HONG KONG
Raymond Purl, Executive
  Director
The American Chamber of
  Commerce in Hong Kong
1030 Swire House
Hong Kong
PHONE: 5-260165
CABLE: AMCHAM
TELEX: 83664 amcc hx

INDONESIA
Executive Director
American Chamber of
  Commerce in Indonesia
Tromol Pos 3060
3rd Floor, Oil Centre
  Building
Jl. M.H. Thamrin 55
Jakarta, Indonesia
PHONE: 357703
TELEX: 48116 cibsem

IRAN
Franklin T. Burroughs,
  Executive Director
The Iran American Chamber
  of Commerce
140 North Forsat Avenue
Bezrouke Building, 8th Floor
Tehran 15, Iran
PHONE: 895149
CABLE: IRANAMCHAM
  TEHRAN
TELEX: 212047 sard ir

IRELAND
Robert P. Chalker, Exec.
  Director
The U.S. Chamber of
  Commerce in Ireland
20 College Green
Dublin 2, Ireland
PHONE: 712733
CABLE: AMCHAM
  DUBLIN
TELEX: 24442 tai ei

ITALY
Herman H. Burdick, General
  Secretary
The American Chamber of
  Commerce in Italy
Via Agnello 12
20121 Milan, Italy
PHONE: 807955/6
CABLE: AMERCAM

JAPAN
William T. Panttaja,
  Executive Director
The American Chamber of
  Commerce of Japan
701 Tosho Building
2-2-3 Marunouchi
Chiyoda-ku, Tokyo 100,
  Japan
PHONE: (03) 211-5861/3
CABLE: AMCHAM TOKYO
TELEX: 28332 ernsttyo j

JAPAN, OKINAWA
Executive Director
The American Chamber of
  Commerce in Okinawa
Nansei Sekiyu Administration
  Bldg.
P.O. Box 191, Naha
Okinawa, Japan 900-91
PHONE: 09845-4558
CABLE: AMCHAM
  OKINAWA
TELEX: j79873 nansei ok

KOREA
BG. Frederick C. Krause
  (Ret.), Executive Director
The American Chamber of
  Commerce in Korea
3rd Floor, Chosun Hotel
Seoul, Korea
PHONE: 23-6471
CABLE: AMCHAMBER
TELEX: 28432 chosun

MALAYSIA
American Business Council of
  Malaysia
2-3 Bangunan Angkasa Raya
Jalan Ampang
Kuala Lumpur, Malaysia
PHONE: 428-347
TELEX: 31006 caltex (Attn:
  J.T. Franz ABC)

MEXICO
John M. Bruton, Executive
  Vice President
American Chamber of
  Commerce of Mexico
Lucerna 78-4
Mexico 6, D.F., Mexico
PHONE: 566-0866
CABLE: AMCHAMMEX
TELEX: 1777609 + 1771300
  achame
Al R. Wichtrich
President
American Chamber of
  Commerce of Mexico

Branch Offices
Eugene Delgado-Arias,
  General Manager
American Chamber of
  Commerce of Mexico
Avenida 16 de Septiembre
  730-1209
Guadalajara, Jalisco, Mexico
PHONE: 12-26-49; 12-51-81
CABLE: AMCHAMMEX

Kathleen Marks
Manager
American Chamber of
  Commerce of Mexico
Edif. de las Instituciones,
  Desp. 1005
Ocampo No. 250, Esq.
  Cuauhtemoc
Monterrey, Nuevo Leon,
  Mexico
PHONE: 44-00-90

MOROCCO
Susan Ouaknine
Executive Secretary
The American Chamber of
  Commerce in Morocco
53 rue Allal Ben Abdullah
Casablanca, Morocco
PHONE: 22-14-48
CABLE: AMCHAM
TELEX: 21947 pricewat m

NETHERLANDS
Adriana J. van der Graaf
General Manager
The American Chamber of
  Commerce in the
  Netherlands

Carneigieplein 5
2517 KJ The Hague, the
Netherlands
PHONE: 070-659808
CABLE: AMCHAM
TELEX: 31542 chevnl

NEW ZEALAND
Harry A. Purcell, Executive
Manager
The American Chamber of
Commerce in New Zealand
P.O. Box 3408
Wellington, New Zealand
PHONE: 727549
TELEX: 3514 inbusmac nz

NICARAGUA
Patricia Elizondo, Executive
Director
The American Chamber of
Commerce of Nicaragua
Apartado 2720
Managua, Nicaragua
PHONE: 8765; 8796
CABLE: AMCHAM
TELEX: 1234 hercasa

PANAMA
Lynda Richa, Executive
Secretary
American Chamber of
Commerce and Industry of
Panama
Apdo. 168
Estafeta Balboa
Panama City, Panama
PHONE: 69-3881
TELEX: 2283 bostonbk pa

PERU
Edwin McCain
Manager
American Chamber of
Commerce of Peru
Juan de Arona 830, 2nd Floor
Lima 27, Peru
PHONE: 40-3425
CABLE: AMCHAM PERU
TELEX: 21165 (Bank of
America)

PHILIPPINES
J. Marsh Thomson
Executive Vice-President
The American Chamber of
Commerce of the
Philippines

P.O. Box 1578, MCC
Manila, the Philippines
PHONE: 865-115
CABLE: AMCHAMCOM
TELEX: 45181 amcham ph

PORTUGAL
H. M. Brito do Rio, General
Secretary
Portuguese-American
Chamber of Commerce
Rua de D. Estefania, 155, 5Q
- E
Lisbon 1, Portugal
PHONE: 57 25 61

SINGAPORE
Wendy Edwards, Executive
Director
American Business Council of
Singapore
9th Floor, Shaw House
Orchard Road
Singapore 9
PHONE: 2350077
TELEX: 21460 conpac rs

SOUTH AFRICA
Clark Else, Executive Director
The American Chamber of
Commerce in South Africa
27th Floor, Life Centre
45 Commissioner Street
Johannesburg 2001, South
Africa
PHONE: 836-5622
TELEX: 8-7774

SPAIN
Jose Manrique, Executive
Director
The American Chamber of
Commerce in Spain
Avenida Generalisimo Franco
477, 8°
Barcelona 11, Spain
PHONE: 321 81 95/96
CABLE: AMCHAM SPAIN

Branch Office
Gabriela M. Tortosa, Staff
Officer
The American Chamber of
Commerce in Spain
Hotel EuroBuilding
Padre Damian 23
Madrid 14, Spain
PHONE: 4586520

SWITZERLAND
Walter H. Diggelman,
Executive Director
Swiss-American Chamber of
Commerce
Talacker 41
8001 Zurich, Switzerland
PHONE: (01) 211 24 54
CABLE: AMCHAMBER
TELEX: 812747 ipco ch

TAIWAN
Herbert Gale Peabody
Executive Director
The American Chamber of
Commerce in Taiwan
P.O. Box 17-277
Taipei, Taiwan
PHONE: 5512515
CABLE: AMCHAM TAIPEI
TELEX: 27841 amcham

THAILAND
Jack Scott, Executive Director
The American Chamber of
Commerce in Thailand
P.O. Box 11-1095
Bangkok, Thailand
PHONE: 2519266
CABLE: AMERCHAM
TELEX: 2778 kiangwan th

UNITED KINGDOM
Jack A. Herfurt, Director
General
The American Chamber of
Commerce (United
Kingdom)
75 Brook Street
London WIY 2EB, England
PHONE: 01-493-0381
CABLE: AMCHAM
LONDON WI
TELEX: 262969 intlawg

URUGUAY
John L. Micheloni, Manager
Chamber of Commerce of the
U.S.A. in Uruguay
Calle Bartolome Mitre 1337
Casilla de Correo 389
Montevideo, Uruguay
PHONE: 98-69-34; 90-60-52
CABLE: AMCHAM
TELEX: 820 bankame uy

Walter A. Vela
Executive Consultant
Chamber of Commerce of the
U.S.A. in Uruguay

VENEZUELA
Dr. Frank J. Amador
Executive Director
Venezuelan-American
  Chamber of Commerce &
  Industry
Centro Plaza, Torre A, Nivel
  15
Avenida Francisco de Miranda
Los Palos Grandes
Apartado 5181
Caracas, D.F. Venezuela
PHONE: 283-8355
CABLE: AMBERCO

**AMCHAM REGIONAL
  ORGANIZATIONS**

AACCLA
Keith L. Miceli, Executive
  Secretary

Association of American
  Chambers of Commerce in
  Latin America
1615 H Street, N.W.
Washington, D.C. 20062
PHONE: (202) 659-3055
CABLE: COCUSA
TELEX: 248302 ccus ur

APCAC
M. Barney Williamson
Chairman, Asia-Pacific
  Council of American
  Chambers of Commerce
President
Hercules Far East, Limited
5th Floor, Pola Aoyama Bldg.
5-17, Minami Aoyama
2-Chome, Minato—ku
Tokyo 107, Japan

EUROMED
Anne Harrington, Executive
  Director
The American Chamber of
  Commerce in Belgium
Avenue des Arts 50, bte 5
B-1040, Brussels, Belgium
PHONE: (02) 512 12 62
TELEX: 61387 brunco b

Department of Commerce District Office Directory International Trade Administration

- ● Denotes Trade Specialist.
- ● ● Denotes Change.
- ● ● ● Contact Trade Specialist in Frankfort, Kentucky.

ALABAMA
Birmingham—Gayle C. Shelton, Jr., Director, Suite 200-201, 908 South 20th Street 35205, Area Code 205 Tel 254-1331, FTS 229-1331

ALASKA
● ●**Anchorage**—Jack C. Wilburn, Director, 701 C Street, P.O. Box 32 99513, Area Code 907 Tel 271-5041, FTS Dial 8 399-0150, Ask for 271-5041

ARIZONA
Phoenix—Donald W. Fry, Director, Suite 2950 Valley Bank Center, 201 North Central Avenue 85073, Area Code 602 Tel 261-3285, FTS 261-3285

ARKANSAS
● ●**Little Rock**—Robert E. Kistler, Director, Savers Federal Bldg., 6th Flr. 72201, Area Code 501 Tel 378-5157

CALIFORNIA
● ●**Los Angeles**—Paul W. Leinenbach, Director, Room 800, 11777 San Vicente Boulevard 90049, Area Code 213 Tel 824-7591, FTS 799-7591
●**San Diego**—110 West C Street 92101, Area Code 714 Tel 293-5395
● ●**San Francisco**—Betty D. Neuhart, Director, Federal Building, Box 36013, 450 Golden Gate Avenue 94102, Area Code 415 Tel 556-5860, FTS 556-5868

COLORADO
Denver—Director, (Vacant) Room 165, New Customhouse, 19th & Stout Street 80202, Area Code 303 Tel 837-3246, FTS 327-3246

CONNECTICUT
Hartford—Richard C. Kilbourn, Director, Room 610-B, Federal Office Building, 450 Main Street 06103, Area Code 203 Tel 244-3530, FTS 244-3530

FLORIDA
Miami—Roger J. LaRoche, Director, Room 821, City National Bank Building, 25 West Flagler Street 33130, Area Code 305 Tel 350-5267, FTS 350-5267
●**Clearwater**—123 North Osceola Avenue 33515, Area Code 813 Tel 461-0011
●**Jacksonville**—815 S. Main Street, Suite 100 32207, Area Code 904 Tel 791-2796, FTS 946-2796
●**Tallahassee**—Collins Bldg., Rm. G-20 32304, Area Code 904 Tel 488-6469, FTS 946-4320

GEORGIA
Atlanta—Director, (Vacant) Suite 600, 1365 Peachtree Street, N.E. 30309, Area Code 404 Tel 881-7000, FTS 257-7000
Savannah—James W. McIntire, Director, 222 U.S. Courthouse & P.O. Box 9746, 125-29 Bull Street 31412, Area Code 912 Tel 232-4321, Ext. 204, FTS 248-4204

HAWAII
● ●**Honolulu**—H. Tucker Gratz, Director, 4106 Federal Building, P.O. Box 50026, 300 Ala Moana Boulevard 96850, Area Code 808 Tel 546-8694, FTS Dial 8, 556-0220, Ask for 546-8694

ILLINOIS
Chicago—Gerald M. Marks, Director, 1406 Mid Continental Plaza Building, 55 East Monroe Street 60603, Area Code 312 Tel 353-4450, FTS 353-4450
●**Commerce Business Daily** Room 1304, 433 West Van Buren Street 60607, Area Code 312 Tel 353-2950

INDIANA
Indianapolis—Mel R. Sherar, Director, 357 U.S. Courthouse

& Federal Office Building, 46 East Ohio Street 46204, Area Code 317 Tel 269-6214, FTS 331-6214

IOWA
Des Moines—Jesse N. Durden, Director, 817 Federal Building, 210 Walnut Street 50309, Area Code 515 Tel 284-4222, FTS 862-4222

KENTUCKY
● ● ●**Louisville**—Director, (Vacant), Room 636, U.S. Post Office and Court House Bldg. 40202
●**Frankfort**—Capitol Plaza Office Tower, Rm. 2425 40601, Area Code 502 Tel 875-4421

LOUISIANA
New Orleans—Edwin A. Leland, Jr., Director, 432 International Trade Mart, No. 2 Canal Street 70130, Area Code 504 Tel 589-6546, FTS 682-6546

MAINE
●**Augusta (Boston, Massachusetts District)**—1 Memorial Circle, Casco Bank Bldg., Area Code 207 Tel 623-2239, FTS 833-6249

MARYLAND
Baltimore—Carroll F. Hopkins, Director, 415 U.S. Customhouse, Gay and Lombard Streets 21202, Area Code 301 Tel 962-3560, FTS 922-3560

MASSACHUSETTS
Boston—Francis J. O'Connor, Director, 10th Floor, 441 Stuart Street 02116, Area Code 617 Tel 223-2312, FTS 223-2312

MICHIGAN
Detroit—Director (Vacant), 445 Federal Building, 231 West Lafayette 48226, Area Code 313 Tel 226-3650, FTS 226-3650

●**Grand Rapids**—350 Ottawa Street N.W. 49503, Area Code 616 Tel 456-2411/33 FTS 372-2411

MINNESOTA
Minneapolis—Glenn A. Matson, Director, 218 Federal Building, 110 South Fourth Street 55401, Area Code 612 Tel 725-2133, FTS 725-2133

MISSISSIPPI
● ●**Jackson**—Director (Vacant), P.O. Box 849, 1202 Walter Sillers Building 39205, Area Code 601 Tel 969-4388, FTS 490-4388

MISSOURI
St. Louis—Donald R. Loso, Director, 120 South Central Avenue 63105, Area Code 314 Tel 425-3302-4, FTS 279-3302
● ●**Kansas City**—Director (Vacant), Room 1840, 601 East 12th Street 64106, Area Code 816 Tel 374-3142, FTS 758-3142

MONTANA
●**Butte (Cheyenne, Wyoming District)**—225 S. Idaho Street, Room 101, P.O. Box 3809, 59701, Area Code 406 Tel 723-6561, Ext. 2317, FTS 585-2317

NEBRASKA
Omaha—George H. Payne, Director, Capitol Plaza, Suite 703A, 1815 Capitol Avenue 68102, Area Code 402 Tel 221-3665, FTS 864-3665

NEVADA
Reno—Joseph J. Jeremy, Director, 777 W. 2nd Street, Room 120 89503, Area Code 702 Tel 784-5203, FTS 470-5203

NEW JERSEY
Newark—Thomas J. Murray, Director, 4th Floor, Gateway Building, Market Street & Penn Plaza 07102, Area Code 201 Tel 645-6214, FTS 341-6214

NEW MEXICO
Albuquerque—William E. Dwyer, Director, 505 Marquette Ave., NW, Suite 1015 87102, Area Code 505 Tel 766-2386, FTS 474-2386

NEW YORK
Buffalo—Robert F. Magee, Director, 1312 Federal Building, 111 West Huron Street 14202, Area Code 716 Tel 846-4191, FTS 437-4191
New York—Arthur C. Rutzen, Director, Room 3718, Federal Office Building, 26 Federal Plaza, Foley Square 10007, Area Code 212 Tel 264-0634, FTS 264-0600

NORTH CAROLINA
Greensboro—Joel B. New, Director, 203 Federal Building, West Market Street, P.O. Box 1950 27402, Area Code 919 Tel 378-5345, FTS 699-5345

OHIO
Cincinnati—Gordon B. Thomas, Director, 10504 Federal Office Building, 550 Main Street 45202, Area Code 513 Tel 684-2944, FTS 684-2944
Cleveland—Charles B. Stebbins, Director, Room 600, 666 Euclid Avenue 44114, Area Code 216 Tel 522-4750, FTS 293-4750

OKLAHOMA
●**Oklahoma City (Dallas, Texas, District)**—4020 Lincoln Boulevard 73105, Area Code 405 Tel 231-5302, FTS 736-5302

OREGON
Portland—Lloyd R. Porter, Director, Room 618, 1220 S.W. 3rd Avenue 97204, Area Code 503 Tel 221-3001, FTS 423-3001

PENNSYLVANIA
Philadelphia—Patrick P. McCabe, Director, 9448 Federal Building, 600 Arch Street 19106, Area Code 215 Tel 597-2850, FTS 597-2866

222

Pittsburgh—William M. Bradley, Director, 2002 Federal Building, 1000 Liberty Avenue 15222, Area Code 412 Tel 644-2850, FTS 722-2850

PUERTO RICO
San Juan (Hato Rey)—Enrique Vilella, Director, Room 659-Federal Building 00918, Area Code 809 Tel 753-4555, Ext. 555, FTS Dial 9 472-6620, Ask for 753-4555

RHODE ISLAND
●**Providence (Boston, Massachusetts, District)**—1 Weybossett Hill 02903, Area Code 401 Tel 277-2605, Ext. 22, FTS 838-4482

SOUTH CAROLINA
Columbia—Margaret A. Patrick, Director, Strom Thurmond Fed. Bldg., Suite 571, 1835 Assembly Street 29201 Area Code 803 Tel 765-5345, FTS 677-5345
●**Charleston**—505 Federal Building, 334 Meeting Street 29403, Area Code 803 Tel 677-4361, FTS 677-4361

TENNESSEE
Memphis—Bradford H. Rice, Director, Room 710, 147 Jefferson Avenue 38103, Area Code 901 Tel 521-3213, FTS 222-3213
●**Nashville**—Room 1004, Andrew Jackson Office Building 37219, Area Code 615 Tel 251-5161 FTS 852-5161

TEXAS
Dallas—C. Carmon Stiles, Director, Room 7A5, 1100 Commerce Street 75242 Area Code 214 Tel 767-0542 FTS 729-0542
Houston—Felicito C. Guerrero, Director, 2625 Federal Bldg., Courthouse, 515 Rusk Street 77002, Area Code 713 Tel 226-4231, FTS 527-4231

UTAH
Salt Lake City—George M. Blessing, Jr., Director, 1201 Federal Building, 125 South State Street 84138, Area Code 801 Tel 524-5116, FTS 588-5116

VIRGINIA
Richmond—Philip A. Ouzts, Director, 8010 Federal Bldg., 400 North 8th Street 23240, Area Code 804 Tel 771-2246, FTS 925-2246

●**Fairfax**—8550 Arlington Blvd. 22031, Area Code 703 Tel 560-6460, FTS 235-1519

WASHINGTON
Seattle—Judson S. Wonderly, Director, Room 706, Lake Union Building, 1700 Westlake Avenue North 98109, Area Code 206 Tel 442-5615, FTS 399-5615

WEST VIRGINIA
Charleston—Roger L. Fortner, Director, 3000 New Federal Building, 500 Quarrier Street 25301, Area Code 304 Tel 343-6181, Ext. 375, FTS 924-1375

WISCONSIN
Milwaukee—Russell H. Leitch, Director, Federal Bldg/U.S. Courthouse, 517 East Wisconsin Avenue 53202, Area Code 414 Tel. 291-3473, FTS 362-3473

WYOMING
Cheyenne—Lowell O. Burns, Director, 6022 O'Mahoney Federal Center, 2120 Capitol Avenue 82001, Area Code 307 Tel 778-2220, Ext. 2151, FTS 328-2151

Federal Maritime Commission District Offices

ATLANTIC DISTRICT
6 World Trade Center, Suite 614
New York, New York 10048
Geoffrey Rogers, Director

GULF DISTRICT
P.O. Box 30550
New Orleans, Louisiana 70190
Harry T. Statham, Director

Savannah Office
P.O. Box 9927
Savannah, Georgia 31402

Miami Office
P.O. Box 59-2832
Miami, Florida 33159

PACIFIC DISTRICT
525 Market Street, 25th Floor
San Francisco, California 94105
Leonard J. Nordgren, Director

Los Angeles Office
U.S. Customs House
Building
P.O. Box 3184
Terminal Island Station
San Pedro, California
90731

PUERTO RICO DISTRICT
U.S. District Courthouse
Federal Office Building,
Room 762
Carlos Cardon Street
Hato Rey, Puerto Rico 00917
Rambel A. Cuprill, Director

GREAT LAKES DISTRICT
610 Canal Street
Chicago, Illinois 60607
Vera Paktor, Director

Foreign Chambers of Commerce and Associations in the United States

AFRICA
African-American Chamber of
  Commerce, Inc.
65 Liberty Street
New York, New York 10005
(212) 766-1343

ARGENTINA
Argentine-American Chamber
  of Commerce
Room 564
11 Broadway
New York, New York 10004
(212) 943-8753

ASIA
Association of Asian-
  American Chambers of
  Commerce
P.O. Box 1933
Washington, DC 20013
(202) 638-5595

AUSTRIA
U.S.-Austrian Chamber of
  Commerce, Inc.
120 Broadway

New York, New York 10005
(212) 571-0340

BELGIUM
Belgian-American Chamber of
  Commerce in the U.S.,
  Inc.
Suite 1003/1005
50 Rockefeller Plaza
New York, New York 10020
(212) 247-7613

BRAZIL
Brazilian-American Chamber
  of Commerce, Inc.
Room 610
22 West 48th Street
New York, New York 10036
(212) 575-9030

Brazil-California Trade
  Association
Suite 226
350 South Figueroa Street
Los Angeles, California
  90071
(213) 627-0634

CHILE
North American-Chilean
  Chamber of Commerce,
  Inc.
220 East 81st Street
New York, New York 10028
(212) 288-5691

CHINA
Chinese Chamber of
  Commerce of New York
Room C03
Confucius Plaza
33 Bowery
New York, New York 10002
(212) 226-2795

Chinese Chamber of
  Commerce of San Francisco
730 Sacramento Street
San Francisco, California
  94108
(415) 982-3000

COLOMBIA
Colombian-American
  Association, Inc.
Room 1110
115 Broadway
New York, New York 10006
(212) 233-7776

COSTA RICA
Costa Rica Export &
  Investment Promotion
  Center
Suite 400
200 S.E. First Street
Miami, Florida 33131
(305) 358-1891

DOMINICAN REPUBLIC
Dominican Republic Export
  Promotion Center
Room 86065
One World Trade Center
New York, New York 10048
(212) 432-9498

ECUADOR
Ecuadorean-American
  Association, Inc.
Room 1110
115 Broadway
New York, New York 10006
(212) 233-7776

FAR EAST
Far East-America Council of
  Commerce and Industry,
  Inc.
Room 1810
1270 Avenue of the Americas
New York, New York 10020
(212) 265-6375

FINLAND
The Finnish-American
  Chamber of Commerce
Fifteenth Floor
540 Madison Avenue
New York, New York 10022
(212) 832-2588

The Finnish-American
  Chamber of Commerce of
  the Midwest
Suite 1900
35 East Wacker Drive
Chicago, Illinois 60601
(312) 346-1150

FRANCE
French-American Chamber of
  Commerce in the U.S.
1350 Avenue of the Americas
New York, New York 10019
(212) 581-4554

GERMANY
German-American
  Chamber of Commerce,
  Inc.
666 Fifth Avenue
New York, New York 10019
(212) 582-7788

German-American Chamber
  of Commerce of Chicago
77 East Monroe Street
Chicago, Illinois 60603
(312) 782-8557

German-American Chamber
  of Commerce of Los
  Angeles, Inc.
Suite 2212
One Park Plaza Building
3250 Wilshire Boulevard
Los Angeles, California
  90010
(213) 381-2236

German-American Chamber
  of Commerce of the Pacific
  Coast, Inc.

Suite 910
465 California Street
San Francisco, California
  94104
(415) 392-2262

German-American Chamber
  of Commerce
Suite 606
One Farragut Square South
Washington, DC 20006
(202) 347-0247

GREECE
Hellenic-American Chamber
  of Commerce
Room 1145
25 Broadway
New York, New York 10004
(212) 943-8594

INDIA
India-America Chamber of
  Commerce
Suite 703
1101 Seventeenth Street,
  N.W.
Washington, DC 20036
(202) 659-1700

India-American Chamber of
  Commerce
Suite 1708
691 S. Irolo Street
Los Angeles, California
  90005
(213) 738-8800

Indo-American Chamber of
  Commerce
c/o The Bank of India
10 South LaSalle Street
Chicago, Illinois 60603
(312) 621-1200
(Attn: D. Roy, Assistant
  Manager)

INDONESIA
American-Indonesian
  Chamber of Commerce,
  Inc.
Room 3008
120 Wall Street
New York, New York 10005
(212) 344-1808

IRAN
Iran-American Chamber of
  Commerce, Inc.

225

Suite 834
50 Rockefeller Plaza
New York, New York 10020
(212) 757-9704

Iran-American Chamber of
Commerce and Industry
700 N. Sepulveda Boulevard
El Segundo, California 90245
(213) 967-2005

IRELAND
Ireland-United States Council
for Commerce and
Industry, Inc.
460 Park Avenue
New York, New York 10022
(212) 751-2660

ISRAEL
American-Israel Chamber of
Commerce and Industry,
Inc.
Room 5416
500 Fifth Avenue
New York, New York 10036
(212) 354-6510

American-Israel Chamber of
Commerce and Industry,
Inc.
Cleveland Center
10800 Brookpark Road
Cleveland, Ohio 44130
(216) 267-1200

American-Israel Chamber of
Commerce and Industry,
Inc.
Midwest Chapter
180 N. Michigan Avenue
Chicago, Illinois 60601
(312) 641-2937

Western States Chamber of
Commerce with Israel
Suite 806
6399 Wilshire Boulevard
Los Angeles, California
90048
(213) 658-7910

ITALY
Italian Chamber of Commerce
of Chicago
327 South LaSalle Street
Chicago, Illinois 60604
(312) 427-3014

Italy-America Chamber of
Commerce, Inc.
Suite 3015
350 Fifth Avenue
New York, New York 10001
(212) 279-5520

JAPAN
Honolulu Japanese Chamber
of Commerce
2454 South Beretania Street
Honolulu, Hawaii 96826
(808) 949-5531

Japan Business Association of
Southern California
350 S. Figueroa Street
Los Angeles, California
90071
(213) 628-1263

Japanese Chamber of
Commerce and Industry of
Chicago
Room 2108
230 N. Michigan Avenue
Chicago, Illinois 60601
(312) 332-6199

Japanese Chamber of
Commerce of New York,
Inc.
Room 1901
39 Broadway
New York, New York 10006
(212) 425-2513

Japanese Chamber of
Commerce of Northern
California
Room 408
World Affairs Center
312 Sutter Street
San Francisco, California
94108
(415) 986-6140

Japanese Chamber of
Commerce of Southern
California
Room 204
355 E. First Street
Los Angeles, California
90012
(213) 626-5116

KOREA
Korean-American Midwest
Association of Commerce
and Industry
c/o Estech General Chemicals
Corp.
30 N. LaSalle Street
Chicago, Illinois 60602
(312) 431-8315
(Attn: Edward R. Vrablik,
Pres.)

U.S.-Korea Economic Council
Suite 2-L
88 Morningside Drive
New York, New York 10027
(212) 749-4200

LATIN AMERICA
Central American Chamber of
Commerce in the U.S.,
Inc.
65 Liberty Street
New York, New York 10005
(212) 766-1348

Chamber of Commerce of
Latin America in the U.S.,
Inc.
Suite 3549
One World Trade Center
New York, New York 10048
(212) 432-9313

Latin Chamber of Commerce
601 Northwest 22nd Avenue
Miami, Florida 33125
(305) 642-3870

Latin American Chamber of
Commerce of Oregon
Room 429
Oregon Pioneer Building
320 S.W. Stark
Portland, Oregon 97204
(503) 221-1283

Latin American
Manufacturing Association
Suite 203
1325 Eighteenth Street, N.W.
Washington, DC 20036
(202) 467-5803

Pan American Chamber of
Commerce and Trade
Council

Business Information Center
315 Twelfth Avenue
San Francisco, California
94118
(415) 752-4093

Pan American Society of the
U.S., Inc.
680 Park Avenue
New York, New York 10021
(212) 628-9400

LEBANON
United States-Lebanese
Chamber of Commerce
Suite 6249
Five World Trade Center
New York, New York 10048
(212) 432-1133

MEXICO
Mexican-American Chamber
of Commerce of Chicago
3650 W. 26th Street
Chicago, Illinois 60623
(312) 762-5662
(Attn: Eusebio Arce)

Mexican Chamber of
Commerce of Arizona
1305 W. McDowell Road
Phoenix, Arizona 85001
(602) 252-6448

Mexican Chamber of
Commerce of the County of
Los Angeles
Room 404
125 Paseo de La Plaza
Los Angeles, California
90012
(213) 688-7330

The Mexican Chamber of
Commerce of the U.S.,
Inc.
Suite 6343
Five World Trade Center
New York, New York 10048
(212) 432-9332

Mexican Institute for Foreign
Trade
Fourth Floor
115 E. 57th Street
New York, New York 10022
(212) 371-3823

United States-Mexico
Chamber of Commerce
Suite 410
1800 K Street, N.W.
Washington, DC 20006
(202) 296-5198

U.S.-Mexico Quadripartite
Commission
c/o Adela
880 Third Avenue
New York, New York 10022
(212) 888-1215

MIDDLE EAST
American-Arab Association of
Commerce & Industry
Suite 1060
342 Madison Avenue
New York, New York 10017
(212) 986-7229

American-Arab Chamber of
Commerce
319 World Trade Building
Houston, Texas 77002
(713) 222-6152

MidAmerica-Arab Chamber of
Commerce, Inc.
Suite 2050
135 South LaSalle Street
Chicago, Illinois 60603
(312) 782-4654

U.S.-Arab Chamber of
Commerce (Pacific), Inc.
Suite 920
433 California Street
San Francisco, California
94104
(415) 397-5663

U.S.-Arab Chamber of
Commerce
Suite 4657
One World Trade Center
New York, New York 10048
(212) 432-0655

U.S.-Arab Chamber of
Commerce (Washington
Chapter)
Suite 627
1625 Eye Street, N.W.
Washington, DC 20006
(202) 293-6975

THE NETHERLANDS
The Netherlands Chamber of
Commerce in the U.S.,
Inc.
Eleventh Floor
One Rockefeller Plaza
New York, New York 10020
(212) 265-6460

NIGERIA
Nigerian-American Chamber
of Commerce, Inc.
65 Liberty Street
New York, New York 10005
(212) 766-1343

NORWAY
Norwegian-American
Chamber of Commerce,
Inc.
Suite 1908
Midwest Chicago Chapter
360 N. Michigan Avenue
Chicago, Illinois 60601
(312) 782-7750

The Norwegian-American
Chamber of Commerce,
Inc.
Suite 360
World Trade Center
350 S. Figueroa Street
Los Angeles, California
90071
(213) 626-0338

Norwegian-American
Chamber of Commerce,
Inc.
Upper Midwest Chapter
800 Foshay Tower
Minneapolis, Minnesota
55402
(612) 336-3338

The Norwegian-American
Chamber of Commerce,
Inc.
800 Third Avenue
New York, New York 10002
(212) 421-9210

Norwegian-American
Chamber of Commerce,
Inc.
1120 Fourth Avenue
Seattle, Washington 98101
(206) 682-5250

Norwegian-American
Chamber of Commerce
Suite 2609
One Embarcadero Center
San Francisco, California 94111
(415) 986-0766

PAKISTAN
Pakistani-American Chamber
of Commerce, Inc.
21 Vernon Street
P.O. Box 480
Floral Park, New York 11002
(516) 488-4100

PERU
Peruvian-American Association
Suite 564
11 Broadway
New York, New York 10004
(212) 943-8753

THE PHILIPPINES
The Philippine-American
Chamber of Commerce, Inc.
Room 809
565 Fifth Avenue
New York, New York 10017
(212) 972-9326

Philippine-American Chamber
of Commerce
c/o Philippine Consulate
447 Sutter Street
San Francisco, California 94108
(415) 391-3655

SPAIN
Spain-U.S. Chamber of
Commerce
Room 4220
500 Fifth Avenue
New York, New York 10036
(212) 354-7848

Spain-U.S. Chamber of
Commerce of the Pacific
Coast
Suite 944
World Trade Center
350 S. Figueroa Street
Los Angeles, California
90071
(213) 489-4459

SWEDEN
Swedish-American Chamber
of Commerce, Inc.
One Dag Hammarskjold Plaza
New York, New York 10017
(212) 838-5530

Swedish-American Chamber
of Commerce of the
Western U.S., Inc.
Suite 268
Ferry Building
World Trade Center
San Francisco, California
94101
(415) 781-4188

TRINIDAD
Trinidad and Tobago Chamber
of Commerce of the
U.S.A., Inc.
c/o Trinidad and Tobago Oil
Company
Room 400
1270 Avenue of the Americas
New York, New York 10020
(212) 541-4615

UNITED KINGDOM
British-American Chamber of
Commerce
Room 2805
10 E. 40th Street
New York, New York 10016
(212) 889-0680

British-American Chamber of
Commerce and Trade
Center of the Pacific
Southwest
Suite 562
350 S. Figueroa Street
Los Angeles, California 90071
(213) 622-7124

VENEZUELA
The Venezuelan-American
Association of the U.S.,
Inc.
Room 1110
115 Broadway
New York, New York 10006
(212) 233-7776

Foreign Embassies and Legations in the United States

AFGHANISTAN
Embassy
2341 Wyoming Avenue,
N.W.
Washington, D.C. 20008
(202) 234-3770

ALGERIA
Embassy
2118 Kalorama Road, N.W.
Washington, D.C. 20008
(202) 234-7246

ARGENTINA
Embassy
1600 New Hampshire
Avenue, N.W.
Washington, D.C. 20009
(202) 387-0705

AUSTRALIA
Embassy
1601 Massachusetts Avenue,
N.W.
Washington, D.C. 20036
(202) 797-3000

AUSTRIA
Embassy
2343 Massachusetts Avenue,
N.W.
Washington, D.C. 20008
(202) 483-4474

BAHAMAS
Embassy
Suite 865
600 New Hampshire Avenue,
N.W.
Washington, D.C. 20037
(202) 338-3940

BAHRAIN
Embassy
Suite 715
2600 Virginia Avenue, N.W.
Washington, D.C. 20037
(202) 965-4930

BANGLADESH
Embassy
3421 Massachusetts Avenue,
N.W.
Washington, D.C. 20007
(202) 337-6644

BARBADOS
Embassy
2144 Wyoming Avenue,
N.W.
Washington, D.C. 20008
(202) 387-7374

BELGIUM
Embassy
3330 Garfield Street, N.W.
Washington, D.C. 20008
(202) 333-6900

BENIN
Embassy
2737 Cathedral
Avenue, N.W.
Washington, D.C. 20008
(202) 232-6656

BOLIVIA
Embassy
3014 Massachusetts Avenue,
N.W.
Washington, D.C. 20008
(202) 483-4410

BOTSWANA
Embassy
Suite 404
4301 Connecticut Avenue,
N.W.
Washington, D.C. 20008
(202) 244-4990

BRAZIL
Embassy
3006 Massachusetts Avenue,
N.W.
Washington, D.C. 20008
(202) 797-0100

BULGARIA
Embassy
2100 16th Street, N.W.
Washington, D.C. 20009
(202) 387-7969

BURMA
Embassy
2300 S Street, N.W.
Washington, D.C. 20008
(202) 332-9044

BURUNDI
Embassy
2717 Connecticut Avenue,
N.W.
Washington, D.C. 20008
(202) 387-4477

CAMEROON
Embassy
2349 Massachusetts Avenue,
N.W.
Washington, D.C. 20008
(202) 265-8790

CANADA
Embassy
1746 Massachusetts Avenue,
N.W.
Washington, D.C. 20036
(202) 785-1400

CAPE VERDE
Embassy
Suite 300
1120 Connecticut Avenue,
N.W.
Washington, D.C. 20036
(202) 659-3148

**CENTRAL AFRICAN
EMPIRE**
Embassy
1618 22nd Street, N.W.
Washington, D.C. 20008
(202) 265-5637

CEYLON—(See Sri Lanka)

CHAD
Embassy
Suite 410
2600 Virginia Avenue, N.W.
Washington, D.C. 20037
(202) 331-7696

CHILE
Embassy
1732 Massachusetts Avenue,
N.W.
Washington, D.C. 20036
(202) 785-1746

CHINA
Embassy
2300 Connecticut Avenue,
N.W.
Washington, D.C. 20008
(202) 797-9000

COLOMBIA
Embassy
2118 Leroy Place, N.W.
Washington, D.C. 20008
(202) 387-5828

**CONGO, PEOPLE'S
REPUBLIC OF**
Embassy
14 E. 65th Street
New York, New York 10021
(212) 744-7840

COSTA RICA
Embassy
2112 S Street, N.W.
Washington, D.C. 20008
(202) 234-2945

CYPRUS
Embassy
2211 R Street, N.W.
Washington, D.C. 20008
(202) 462-5772

CZECHOSLOVAKIA
Embassy
3900 Linnean Avenue, N.W.
Washington, D.C. 20008
(202) 363-6315

DAHOMEY—(See Benin)

DENMARK
Embassy
3200 Whitehaven Street,
N.W.
Washington, D.C. 20008
(202) 234-4300

DOMINICAN REPUBLIC
Embassy
1715 22nd Street, N.W.
Washington, D.C. 20008
(202) 332-6280

ECUADOR
Embassy
2535 15th Street, N.W.
Washington, D.C. 20009
(202) 234-7200

EGYPT
Embassy
2310 Decatur Place, N.W.
Washington, D.C. 20008
(202) 232-5400

EL SALVADOR
Embassy
2308 California Street, N.W.
Washington, D.C. 20008
(202) 265-3480

ESTONIA
Legation
9 Rockefeller Plaza
New York, New York 10020
(212) 247-1450

ETHIOPIA
Embassy
2134 Kalorama Road, N.W.
Washington, D.C. 20008
(202) 234-2281

FIJI
Embassy
Suite 520
1629 K Street, N.W.
Washington, D.C. 20006
(202) 296-3928

FINLAND
Embassy
3216 New Mexico Avenue,
N.W.
Washington, D.C. 20016
(202) 363-2430

FRANCE
Embassy
2535 Belmont Road, N.W.
Washington, D.C. 20008
(202) 234-0990

GABON
Embassy
2034 20th Street, N.W.
Washington, D.C. 20009
(202) 797-1000

GAMBIA, THE
Embassy
Suite 300
2550 M Street, N.W.
Washington, D.C. 20037
(202) 785-1631

**GERMAN DEMOCRATIC
REPUBLIC**
Embassy
1717 Massachusetts Avenue,
N.W.
Washington, D.C. 20036
(202) 232-3134

**GERMANY, FEDERAL
REPUBLIC OF**
Embassy
4645 Reservoir Road, N.W.
Washington, D.C. 20007
(202) 331-3000

GHANA
Embassy
2460 16th Street
Washington, D.C. 20009
(202) 462-0761

GREAT BRITAIN
Embassy
3100 Massachusetts Avenue,
N.W.
Washington, D.C. 20008
(202) 462-1340

GREECE
Embassy
2221 Massachusetts Avenue,
N.W.
Washington, D.C. 20008
(202) 667-3168

GRENADA
Embassy
Suite 802
1101 Vermont Avenue, N.W.
Washington, D.C. 20005
(202) 347-3198

GUATEMALA
Embassy
2220 R Street, N.W.
Washington, D.C. 20008
(202) 332-2865

GUINEA
Embassy
2112 Leroy Place, N.W.
Washington, D.C. 20008
(202) 483-9420

GUINEA-BISSAU
Embassy
211 E. 43rd Street
Suite 604
New York, New York 10017
(212) 661-3977

GUYANA
Embassy
2490 Tracy Place, N.W.
Washington, D.C. 20008
(202) 265-6900

HAITI
Embassy
4400 17th Street, N.W.
Washington, D.C. 20011
(202) 723-7000

HUNGARY
Embassy
3910 Shoemaker Street, N.W.
Washington, D.C. 20008
(202) 362-6730

ICELAND
Embassy
2022 Connecticut Avenue,
N.W.
Washington, D.C. 20008
(202) 265-6653

INDIA
Embassy
2107 Massachusetts Avenue,
N.W.
Washington, D.C. 20008
(202) 265-5050

INDONESIA
Embassy
2020 Massachusetts Avenue,
N.W.
Washington, D.C. 20036
(202) 293-1745

IRAN
Embassy
3005 Massachusetts Avenue,
N.W.
Washington, D.C. 20008
(202) 797-6500

IRELAND
Embassy
2234 Massachusetts Avenue,
N.W.
Washington, D.C. 20008
(202) 483-7639

ISRAEL
Embassy
1621 22nd Street, N.W.
Washington, D.C. 20008
(202) 483-4100

ITALY
Embassy
1601 Fuller Street, N.W.
Washington, D.C. 20009
(202) 234-1935

IVORY COAST
Embassy
2424 Massachusetts Avenue,
N.W.
Washington, D.C. 20008
(202) 483-2400

JAMAICA
Embassy
1666 Connecticut Avenue,
N.W.
Washington, D.C. 20009
(202) 387-1010

JAPAN
Embassy
2520 Massachusetts Avenue,
N.W.
Washington, D.C. 20008
(202) 234-2266

JORDAN
Embassy
2319 Wyoming Avenue,
N.W.
Washington, D.C. 20008
(202) 265-1606

KENYA
Embassy
2249 R Street, N.W.
Washington, D.C. 20008
(202) 387-6101

KOREA
Embassy
2320 Massachusetts Avenue,
N.W.
Washington, D.C. 20008
(202) 483-7383

KUWAIT
Embassy
2940 Tilden Street, N.W.
Washington, D.C. 20008
(202) 966-0702

LAOS
Embassy
2222 S Street, N.W.
Washington, D.C. 20008
(202) 332-6416

LATVIA
Legation
4325 17th Street, N.W.
Washington, D.C. 20011
(202) 726-8213

LEBANON
Embassy
2560 28th Street, N.W.
Washington, D.C. 20008
(202) 462-8600

LESOTHO
Embassy
Caravel Building, Suite 300
1601 Connecticut Avenue,
N.W.
Washington, D.C. 20009
(202) 462-4190

LIBERIA
Embassy
5201 16th Street, N.W.
Washington, D.C. 20011
(202) 723-0437

LIBYA
Embassy
1118 22nd Street, N.W.
Washington, D.C. 20037
(202) 452-1290

LITHUANIA
Legation
2622 16th Street, N.W.
Washington, D.C. 20009
(202) 234-5860

LUXEMBOURG
Embassy
2200 Massachusetts Avenue,
N.W.
Washington, D.C. 20008
(202) 265-4171

MADAGASCAR
Embassy
2374 Massachusetts Avenue,
N.W.
Washington, D.C. 20008
(202) 265-5525

MALAWI
Embassy
Bristol House
1400 20th Street, N.W.
Washington, D.C. 20036
(202) 296-5530

MALAYSIA
Embassy
2401 Massachusetts Avenue,
N.W.
Washington, D.C. 20008
(202) 234-7600

MALI
Embassy
2130 R Street, N.W.
Washington, D.C. 20008
(202) 332-2249

MALTA
Embassy
2017 Connecticut Avenue,
N.W.
Washington, D.C. 20008
(202) 462-3611

MAURITANIA
Embassy
2129 Leroy Place, N.W.
Washington, D.C. 20008
(202) 232-5700

MAURITIUS
Embassy
Suite 134
4301 Connecticut Avenue,
N.W.
Washington, D.C. 20008
(202) 244-1491

MEXICO
Embassy
2829 16th Street, N.W.
Washington, D.C. 20009
(202) 234-6000

MOROCCO
Embassy
1601 21st Street, N.W.
Washington, D.C. 20009
(202) 462-7979

NEPAL
Embassy
2131 Leroy Place, N.W.
Washington, D.C. 20008
(202) 667-4550

NETHERLANDS
Embassy
4200 Linnean Avenue, N.W.
Washington, D.C. 20008
(202) 244-5300

NEW ZEALAND
Embassy
37 Observatory Circle, N.W.
Washington, D.C. 20008
(202) 328-4800

NICARAGUA
Embassy
1627 New Hampshire
Avenue, N.W.
Washington, D.C. 20009
(202) 387-4371

NIGER
Embassy
2204 R Street, N.W.
Washington, D.C. 20008
(202) 483-4224

NIGERIA
Embassy
2201 M Street, N.W.
Washington, D.C. 20037
(202) 223-9300

NORWAY
Embassy
2720 34th Street, N.W.
Washington, D.C. 20008
(202) 333-6000

OMAN
Embassy
2342 Massachusetts Avenue,
N.W.
Washington, D.C. 20008
(202) 387-1980

PAKISTAN
Embassy
2315 Massachusetts Avenue,
N.W.
Washington, D.C. 20008
(202) 332-8330

PANAMA
Embassy
2862 McGill Terrace, N.W.
Washington, D.C. 20008
(202) 483-1407

PAPUA NEW GUINEA
Embassy
Suite 631
1800 K Street, N.W.
Washington, D.C. 20006
(202) 659-0856

PARAGUAY
Embassy
2400 Massachusetts Avenue,
N.W.
Washington, D.C. 20008
(202) 483-6960

PERU
Embassy
1700 Massachusetts Avenue,
N.W.
Washington, D.C. 20036
(202) 833-9860

PHILIPPINES
Embassy
1617 Massachusetts Avenue,
N.W.
Washington, D.C. 20036
(202) 483-1414

POLAND
Embassy
2640 16th Street, N.W.
Washington, D.C. 20009
(202) 234-3800

PORTUGAL
Embassy
2125 Kalorama Road, N.W.
Washington, D.C. 20008
(202) 265-1643

QATAR
Embassy
Suite 1180
600 New Hampshire Avenue,
N.W.
Washington, D.C. 20037
(202) 338-0111

ROMANIA
Embassy
1607 23rd Street, N.W.
Washington, D.C. 20008
(202) 232-4747

RWANDA
Embassy
1714 New Hampshire
Avenue, N.W.
Washington, D.C. 20009
(202) 232-2882

SAUDI ARABIA
Embassy
1520 18th Street, N.W.
Washington, D.C. 20036
(202) 483-2100

SENEGAL
Embassy
2112 Wyoming Avenue,
N.W.
Washington, D.C. 20008
(202) 234-0540

SEYCHELLES
Embassy
8th Floor
201 E. 42nd Street
New York, New York 10017
(212) 867-5157

SIERRA LEONE
Embassy
1701 19th Street, N.W.
Washington, D.C. 20009
(202) 265-7700

SINGAPORE
Embassy
1824 R Street, N.W.
Washington, D.C. 20009
(202) 667-7555

SOMALIA
Embassy
Suite 710
600 New Hampshire Avenue,
N.W.
Washington, D.C. 20037
(202) 234-3261

SOUTH AFRICA
Embassy
3051 Massachusetts Avenue,
N.W.
Washington, D.C. 20008
(202) 232-4400

SPAIN
Embassy
2700 15th Street, N.W.
Washington, D.C. 20009
(202) 265-0190

SRI LANKA
Embassy
2148 Wyoming Avenue,
N.W.
Washington, D.C. 20008
(202) 483-4025

SUDAN
Embassy
Suite 400
600 New Hamsphire Avenue,
N.W.
Washington, D.C. 20037
(202) 338-8565

SURINAM
Embassy
Suite 711
2600 Virginia Avenue, N.W.
Washington, D.C. 20037
(202) 338-6980

SWAZILAND
Embassy
4301 Connecticut Avenue,
N.W.
Washington, D.C. 20008
(202) 362-6683

SWEDEN
Embassy
Suite 1200
600 New Hampshire Avenue,
N.W.
Washington, D.C. 20037
(202) 298-3500

SWITZERLAND
Embassy
2900 Cathedral Avenue,
N.W.
Washington, D.C. 20008
(202) 462-1811

SYRIA
Embassy
2215 Wyoming Avenue,
N.W.
Washington, D.C. 20008
(202) 232-6313

TANZANIA
Embassy
2139 R Street, N.W.
Washington, D.C. 20008
(202) 232-0501

THAILAND
Embassy
2300 Kalorama Road, N.W.
Washington, D.C. 20008
(202) 667-1446

TOGO
Embassy
2208 Massachusetts Avenue,
N.W.
Washington, D.C. 20008
(202) 234-4212

TRINIDAD AND TOBAGO
Embassy
1708 Massachusetts Avenue,
N.W.
Washington, D.C. 20036
(202) 467-6490

TUNISIA
Embassy
2408 Massachusetts Avenue,
N.W.
Washington, D.C. 20008
(202) 234-6644

TURKEY
Embassy
1606 23rd Street, N.W.
Washington, D.C. 20008
(202) 667-6400

UGANDA
Embassy
5909 16th Street, N.W.
Washington, D.C. 20011
(202) 726-7100

**UNION OF SOVIET
 SOCIALIST REPUBLICS**
Embassy
1125 16th Street, N.W.
Washington, D.C. 20036
 (202) 628-7551

**UNITED ARAB
 EMIRATES**
Embassy
Suite 740
600 New Hampshire Avenue,
 N.W.
Washington, D.C. 20037
(202) 338-6500

UPPER VOLTA
Embassy
5500 16th Street, N.W.
Washington, D.C. 20011
(202) 726-0992

URUGUAY
Embassy
1918 F Street, N.W.
Washington, D.C. 20006
(202) 331-1313

VENEZUELA
Embassy
2445 Massachusetts Avenue,
 N.W.
Washington, D.C. 20008
(202) 797-3800

WESTERN SAMOA
Embassy
Room 303
820 Second Avenue
New York, N.Y. 10017
(212) 682-1482

YEMEN
Embassy
Suite 860
600 New Hampshire Avenue,
 N.W.
Washington, D.C. 20037
(202) 965-4760

YUGOSLAVIA
Embassy
2410 California Street, N.W.
Washington, D.C. 20008
(202) 462-6566

ZAIRE
Embassy
1800 New Hampshire
 Avenue, N.W.
Washington, D.C. 20009
(202) 234-7690

ZAMBIA
Embassy
2419 Massachusetts Avenue,
 N.W.
Washington, D.C. 20008
(202) 265-9717

**DELEGATION OF THE
 COMMISSION OF THE
 EUROPEAN
 COMMUNITIES**
Embassy
Suite 707
2100 M Street, N.W.
Washington, D.C. 20037
(202) 862-9500

Local Chambers of Commerce with Foreign Trade Services

ALABAMA

Birmingham Area Chamber of Commerce
P.O. Box 10127
Birmingham, Alabama 35202
International Trade Department
(205) 323-5461

Mobile Area Chamber of Commerce
P.O. Box 2187
Mobile, Alabama 36601
Trade Development
M.B. Rambeau, Manager
(205) 433-6951

Alabama State Chamber of Commerce
P.O. Box 76
Montgomery, Alabama 36101
James J. Britton, Executive Vice President
(205) 834-6000

Selma and Dallas County Chamber of Commerce
P.O. Drawer D
Selma, Alabama 36701
James D. Bradley, Executive Vice President
(205) 875-7241

ALASKA

Greater Juneau Chamber of Commerce
200 N. Franklin Street
Juneau, Alaska 99801
R.A. Derr, Executive Vice President
(907) 586-2201

ARIZONA

Nogales-Santa Cruz County Chamber of Commerce
P.O. Box 578
Nogales, Arizona 85621
Charles V. Fowler, Executive Director
(602) 287-3685

Phoenix Metropolitan Chamber of Commerce
34 West Monroe Street, Ninth Floor
Phoenix, Arizona 85003
Arizona World Trade Association

Gayle Allen, Operations Manager
(602) 254-5521

ARKANSAS

Fort Smith Chamber of Commerce
613 Garrison Avenue
Fort Smith, Arkansas 72901
Paul Latture, Manager
(501) 783-6118

Metropolitan Chamber of Commerce
No. 1 Spring Street
Little Rock, Arkansas 72201
Economic Development
Nolan Fleming, Vice President
(501) 374-4871

CALIFORNIA

Fresno County and City Chamber of Commerce
P.O. Box 1469
Fresno, California 93716
Les Dabritz, Executive Vice President
(209) 233-4651

Gardena Valley Chamber of Commerce
1551 W. Redondo Beach Boulevard
Gardena, California 90247
Anita E. Bell, General Manager
(213) 532-9905

Huntington Beach Chamber of Commerce
18582 Beach Boulevard
Huntington Beach, California 92648
Ralph C. Kiser, Executive Manager
(714) 962-6661

CONNECTICUT

Greater Hartford Chamber of Commerce
250 Constitution Plaza
Hartford, Connecticut 06103
Arthur J. Lumsden, President
(203) 525-4451

Greater Meriden Chamber of Commerce, Inc.
17 Church Street
Meriden, Connecticut 06450
Sanford S. Shorr, Executive Vice President
(203) 235-7901

New Britain Chamber of Commerce
Central Park Plaza
127 Main Street
New Britain, Connecticut 06051
Robert T. MacBain, Executive Vice President
(203) 229-1665

The Greater New Haven Chamber of Commerce
P.O. Box 1445
New Haven, Connecticut 06506
Research and Economic Development, Domestic and Foreign
Fred Meisenkothen, Manager
(203) 787-6735

Southwestern Area Commerce & Industry Association of Connecticut, Inc.
Suite 100, One Landmark Square
Stamford, Connecticut 06901
John Mitovich, President
(203) 359-3220

Greater Waterbury Chamber of Commerce
P.O. Box 1469
32 N. Main Street
Waterbury, Connecticut 06721
Frank D. Fulco, President
(203) 757-0701

DELAWARE
Delaware State Chamber of Commerce, Inc.
1102 West Street
Wilmington, Delaware 19801
(302) 655-7221

DISTRICT OF COLUMBIA
The Metropolitan Washington Board of Trade
Board of Trade Building
1129 20th Street, N.W.
Washington, D.C. 20036
John R. Tydings, Executive Vice President
(202) 857-5900

FLORIDA
Fort Lauderdale Area Chamber of Commerce
Box 14516
Fort Lauderdale, Florida 33302
World Trade Council, Community Development
Michael V. Frey, Group Manager
(305) 462-6000

Jacksonville Area Chamber of Commerce
P.O. Drawer 329
Jacksonville, Florida 32201
Business and Industry Services
Arnie Frankel, Manager
(904) 396-0100

Greater Miami Chamber of Commerce
1200 Biscayne Boulevard
Miami, Florida 33132
G. Lester Freeman, Executive Vice President
(305) 374-1800

Orlando Area Chamber of Commerce
P.O. Box 1234
Orlando, Florida 32804
Economic Research Department
Margie E. Varney, Manager
(305) 425-1234

Pensacola Area Chamber of Commerce
P.O. Box 550
Pensacola, Florida 32593
Transportation
Fred Donovan, Vice President
(904) 438-9691

Florida Chamber of Commerce
P.O. Box 5497
Tallahassee, Florida 32301
Louis Polatty, Executive Vice President
(904) 222-2831

Greater Tampa Chamber of Commerce
P.O. Box 420
Tampa, Florida 33601
Tampa World Trade Council
Eugene E. Paredes, Executive Director
(813) 228-7777

GEORGIA
Atlanta Chamber of Commerce
1300 North Omni International
Atlanta, Georgia 30303
International Department
Carol Martel, Director
(404) 521-0845

Georgia Chamber of Commerce
1200 Commerce Bulding
Atlanta, Georgia 30303
International Council
(404) 524-8481

Columbus Chamber of Commerce
P.O. Box 1200
Columbus, Georgia 31902
Joe F. Ragland, Executive Vice President
(404) 327-1566

Emanuel County Chamber of Commerce
124 N. Main Street
Swainsboro, Georgia 30401
Randolph B. Cardoza, Executive Director
(912) 237-6426

GUAM
Guam Chamber of Commerce
P.O. Box 283
107 ADA Plaza Center
Agana, Guam 96910
James B. McDonald, President
(671) 472-6202

HAWAII
The Chamber of Commerce of Hawaii
735 Bishop Street
Honolulu, Hawaii 96813
Robert B. Robinson, President
(808) 531-4111

IDAHO
Greater Boise Chamber of Commerce
P.O. Box 2368
Boise, Idaho 83701
Paul Ralston, Executive Vice President
(208) 344-5515

ILLINOIS
Chicago Association of Commerce and Industry
130 South Michigan Avenue
Chicago, Illinois 60603
World Trade Division
Robert L. Bean, Director
(312) 786-0111

Chicago South Chamber of Commerce
11145 South Michigan Avenue
Chicago, Illinois 60628
Robert Swaney, President
(312) 928-3200

Chamber of Commerce of Upper Rock Island County
622-19th Street
Moline, Illinois 61265
Executive Manager
(309) 762-3661

Peoria Chamber of Commerce
230 SW Adams Street
Peoria, Illinois 61602
Philip L. Carlson, President
(309) 676-0477

Rockford Area Chamber of Commerce
815 East State Street
Rockford, Illinois 61101
World Trade Club of Illinois
Roland W. Stebbins, Manager
(815) 987-8100

INDIANA
Anderson Chamber of Commerce
P.O. Box 469
Anderson, Indiana 46015
(317) 642-0264

The Greater Elkhart Chamber of Commerce, Inc.
P.O. Box 428
514 S. Main Street
Elkhart, Indiana 46514
Keith E. Meade, Executive Vice President
(219) 293-1531

Metropolitan Evansville Chamber of Commerce
329 Main Street
Evansville, Indiana 47708
Economic Development
Michael R. Hinton, Director
(812) 425-8147

Greater Fort Wayne Chamber of Commerce
826 Ewing Street
Fort Wayne, Indiana 46802
D.J. Petruccelli, Executive Vice President
(219) 424-1435

Indianapolis Chamber of Commerce
320 N. Meridian Street
Indianapolis, Indiana 46204
World Trade and Economic Research
Robert W. Palmer, Director
(317) 635-4747

Kokomo-Howard County Chamber of Commerce
P.O. Box 731
Kokomo, Indiana 46901
Herman L. Stine, Executive Vice President
(317) 457-5301

Marion Area Chamber of Commerce
215 S. Adams Street
Marion, Indiana 46952
J.R. Choate, Executive Director
(317) 664-5107

South Bend-Mishawaka Area Chamber of Commerce
230 West Jefferson
South Bend, Indiana 46601
David Major, Executive Vice President
(219) 234-0051

IOWA
Cedar Falls Chamber of Commerce
P.O. Box 367
10 Main Street
Cedar Falls, Iowa 50613
Sam Scherf, Executive Vice President
(319) 266-3593

Cedar Rapids-Marion Area Chamber of Commerce
127 Third Street, N.E.
Cedar Rapids, Iowa 52401
International Trade Bureau
Richard J. Petska, Manager
(319) 364-5135

Greater Des Moines Chamber of Commerce
Eighth and High Streets
Des Moines, Iowa 50307
World Trade Department
Chester W. Good, Manager
(515) 283-2161

Fort Madison Chamber of Commerce
P.O. Box 277
Fort Madison, Iowa 52627
Michael L. Howard, General Manager
(319) 372-5471

Waterloo Chamber of Commerce
P.O. Box 749
Waterloo, Iowa 50704
Jim Lawrence, General Manager
(319) 233-8431

KANSAS
Kansas City, Kansas, Area Chamber of Commerce
P.O. Box 1310
Kansas City, Kansas 66117
Forrest Halter, General Manager
(913) 371-3070

Wichita Area Chamber of Commerce
350 W. Douglas Avenue
Wichita, Kansas 67202
Industrial Development
Jerry M. Mallot, Manager
(316) 265-7771

KENTUCKY
Ashland Area Chamber of Commerce
Winchester Avenue at
 Eighteenth Street
Ashland, Kentucky 41101
Ray B. Graeves, Executive
 Vice President
(606) 324-5111

Louisville Area Chamber of Commerce
300 W. Liberty Street
Louisville, Kentucky 40202
Economic Development
Department
Stanley R. Bowling, Manager
(502) 582-2421

LOUISIANA
Greater Lafayette Chamber of Commerce, Inc.
P.O. Drawer 51307
Lafayette, Louisiana 70505
Ralph U. Thomas, Executive
 Vice President
(318) 233-2705

Greater Lake Charles Chamber of Commerce
P.O. Box 3109
Lake Charles, Louisiana
 70602
Adolph J. Janca, Executive
 Vice President
(318) 433-3632

Chamber of Commerce of the New Orleans Area
P.O. Box 30240
New Orleans, Louisiana
 70190
International Business
 Development
Economic Development
 Council
James B. Whitnell, Manager
(504) 527-6900

Shreveport Chamber of Commerce
P.O. Box 20074
Shreveport, Louisiana 71120
William T. Hackett, Jr.,
 Executive Vice President
(318) 226-8521

MAINE
Biddeford-Saco Chamber of Commerce
P.O. Box 305
Biddeford, Maine 04005
Clayton W. Cartmill,
 Executive Vice President
(207) 282-1513

Maine State Chamber of Commerce
One Canal Plaza, P.O. Box
 65
Portland, Maine 04112
Paul C. Emerson, President
(207) 774-9871

MARYLAND
Maryland State Chamber of Commerce
60 West Street
Annapolis, Maryland 21401
Labor and Employment Laws
 and Regulations
Samuel W. Christine,
 Director
(301) 269-0642

Chamber of Commerce of Metropolitan Baltimore
22 Light Street
Baltimore, Maryland 21202
Economic Development
Allen Anders, Manager
(301) 539-7600

Greater Baltimore Committee, Inc.
Suite 900, 2 Hopkins Plaza
Baltimore, Maryland 21201
William Boucher, III,
 Executive Director
(301) 727-2820

Hagerstown-Washington County Chamber of Commerce, Inc.
14 Public Square
Hagerstown, Maryland 21740
John E. Ritchey, Executive
 Director
(301) 739-2015

Salisbury Area Chamber of Commerce
P.O. Box 510
Salisbury, Maryland 21801
G. Barton Middleton,
 Executive Director
(301) 749-0144

MASSACHUSETTS
Greater Gardner Chamber of Commerce
301 Central Street
Gardner, Massachusetts 01440
Nicholas D. Rudziak,
 Executive Vice President
(617) 632-1780

New Bedford Area Chamber of Commerce
P.O. Box G-827
New Bedford, Massachusetts
 02742
Frederick A. Rubin,
 Executive Vice President
(617) 999-5231

Greater Northampton Chamber of Commerce
62 State Street
Northampton, Massachusetts
 01060
Paul J. Walker, Executive
 Director
(413) 584-1934

South Shore Chamber of Commerce
36 Miller Stile Road
Quincy, Massachusetts 02169
Ronald E. Zooleck, Executive
 Vice President
(617) 479-1111

Greater Springfield Chamber of Commerce
Suite 600, 1500 Main Street
Springfield, Massachusetts
 01115
Robert J. Schwarz, Executive
 Vice President
(413) 734-5671

Waltham West Suburban Chamber of Commerce
663 Main Street
Waltham, Massachusetts
 02154
T.L. Manning, Executive
 Vice President
(617) 894-4700

238

Worcester Area Chamber of Commerce
Suite 350, 100 Front Street
Worcester, Massachusetts
01608
Economic Development
Department
James J. Donoghue, Manager
(617) 753-2924

MICHIGAN
Greater Detroit Chamber of Commerce
150 Michigan Avenue
Detroit, Michigan 48226
World Trade and Port
Development Departments
George C. Kiba, General
Manager
(313) 964-4000

Grand Rapids Area Chamber of Commerce
17 Fountain Street, N.W.
Grand Rapids, Michigan
49503
Stuart E. Cok, Executive Vice
President
(616) 459-7221

Michigan State Chamber of Commerce
Suite 500, 501 S. Capitol
Avenue
Lansing, Michigan 48933
Martin Rauscher, Vice
President
(517) 371-2100

Macomb County Chamber of Commerce
10 North Avenue, P.O. Box
855
Mount Clemens, Michigan
48043
David L. Walters, Executive
Vice President
(313) 463-1528

MINNESOTA
Greater Minneapolis Chamber of Commerce
15 S. Fifth Street
Minneapolis, Minnesota
55402
World Trade
John F. Moon, Research
Director
(612) 339-8521

St. Paul Area Chamber of Commerce
Suite 300, The Osborn
Building
St. Paul, Minnesota 55102
Economic Action Group
Peter Oberle, Assistant
Manager
(612) 222-5561

St. Peter Chamber of Commerce
214 Grace Street
St. Peter, Minnesota 56082
Robert W. Wettergren,
Manager
(507) 931-3400

MISSISSIPPI
Jackson Chamber of Commerce
P.O. Box 22548
Jackson, Mississippi 39205
Mendell Davis, Executive
Vice President
(601) 948-7575

Mississippi Marketing Council
P.O. Box 849
Jackson, Mississippi 39205
International Business
Development
Bill McGinnis, Director
(601) 354-6707

MISSOURI
Chamber of Commerce of Greater Kansas City
600 TenMain Center, 920
Main Street
Kansas City, Missouri 64105
International Department
Marilyn Weil, Manager
(816) 221-2424

St. Louis Regional Commerce and Growth Association
10 Broadway
St. Louis, Missouri 63102
World Trade Department
Joseph M. de Rotaeche
(314) 231-5555

MONTANA
Montana Chamber of Commerce
P.O. Box 1730
Helena, Montana 59601
Forrest Boles, President
(406) 442-2405

NEBRASKA
Beatrice Chamber of Commerce
P.O. Box 703
Beatrice, Nebraska 68310
James E. Bradley, Executive
Vice President
(402) 223-2338

Crete Chamber of Commerce
P.O. Box 264
Crete, Nebraska 68333
Marilyn McElravy, Manager
(402) 826-2136

Lincoln Chamber of Commerce
1221 N Street
Lincoln, Nebraska 68508
Transportation Department
John DuPont, Manager
(402) 432-7511

Greater Omaha Chamber of Commerce
1620 Dodge Street
Omaha, Nebraska 68102
Economic Development
Council
Rod Moseman, Executive
Director
(402) 341-1234

NEVADA
Henderson Chamber of Commerce
152 Water Street
Henderson, Nevada 89015
Gary Johnson, Executive
Director
(702) 565-8951

Greater Las Vegas, Nevada, Chamber of Commerce
2301 E. Sahara Avenue
Las Vegas, Nevada 89105
Ken O'Connell, Executive
Vice President
(702) 457-4664

Greater Reno Chamber of Commerce
P.O. Box 3499
Reno, Nevada 89505
Jud Allen, General Manager
(702) 786-3030

Nevada State Chamber of Commerce
P.O. Box 2806
Reno, Nevada 89505
Fred Davis, Executive
Director
(702) 323-1877

NEW HAMPSHIRE
Greater Nashua Chamber of Commerce
P.O. Box 1123
Nashua, New Hampshire
03061
James J. Archey, Executive
Vice President
(603) 882-8106

NEW JERSEY
Greater Atlantic City Chamber of Commerce
10 Central Pier
Atlantic City, New Jersey
08401
William H. Eames, Executive
Director
(609) 345-5600

Eastern Union County Chamber of Commerce
P.O. Box 300
Elizabeth, New Jersey 07207
International Trade Committee
Thomas K. Spear, Manager
(201) 352-0900

Hudson County Chamber of Commerce and Industry
911 Bergen Avenue
Jersey City, New Jersey
07306
Ellsworth C. Salisbury, Jr.,
Executive Vice President
(201) 653-7400

Morris County Chamber of Commerce
330 South Street, P.O. Box
122M
Morristown, New Jersey
07960
Joseph Cironi, President
(201) 539-3882

New Jersey State Chamber of Commerce
5 Commerce Street
Newark, New Jersey 07102
Gerald D. Hall, Vice
President
(201) 623-7070

South Jersey Chamber of Commerce
North Park Drive
Pennsauken, New Jersey
08109
Leighton Williams, President
(609) 964-3400

Plainfield Central Jersey Chamber of Commerce
120 West Seventh Street
Plainfield, New Jersey 07060
Leonard M. Menhart,
Executive Vice President
(201) 754-7250

Vineland Chamber of Commerce
P.O. Box 489
Vineland, New Jersey 08360
James S. Moffatt, Director
(609) 691-7400

Woodbridge Metropolitan Chamber of Commerce
655 Amboy Avenue
Woodbridge, New Jersey
07095
Roger W. Johnson, Executive
Vice President
(201) 636-4040

NEW MEXICO
Greater Albuquerque Chamber of Commerce
401 Second Street, N.W.
Albuquerque, New Mexico
87102
Trade Expansion Program
Carol Meyer, Project Director
(505) 842-0220

NEW YORK
Albany Area Chamber of Commerce
Suite 200, 90 State Street
Albany, New York 12207
Community Development
James E. Grant, Manager
(518) 434-1214

Broome County Chamber of Commerce, Inc.
P.O. Box 995
Binghamton, New York
13902
International Commerce
Committee
H.J. Kammerer, Executive
Vice President
(607) 772-8860

Brooklyn Chamber of Commerce
26 Court Street
Brooklyn, New York 11242
D.J. Speert, Foreign Trade
Secretary
(212) 875-1000

Long Island Association of Commerce and Industry
425 Broad Hollow Road
Melville, New York 11747
C. William Gaylor, Executive
Vice President
(516) 752-9600

Chamber of Commerce of the Borough of Queens
24-16 Bridge Plaza South
Long Island City, New York
11101
Business Development
Albert E. Bruchac, Director
(212) 784-7700

Orange County Chamber of Commerce
26 North Street
Middletown, New York
10940
(914) 342-2522

Mount Vernon Chamber of Commerce
Suite 308, 26 E. First Street
Mount Vernon, New York
10550
Salvatore Quaranta, Executive
Vice President
(914) 664-7500

New York Chamber of Commerce and Industry
65 Liberty Street
New York, New York 10005
International Affairs
Gil Weinstein, Vice President
(212) 766-1346

Niagara Falls Area Chamber of Commerce
468 Third Street
Niagara Falls, New York 14301
James D. Phillips, President
(716) 285-9141

Rochester Area Chamber of Commerce, Inc.
55 St. Paul Street
Rochester, New York 14604
World Trade Department
William F. Freiert, Manager
(716) 454-2220

Schenectady County Chamber of Commerce
Suite 6, 243 State Street
Schenectady, New York 12305
Economic Development
S. Earl Snyder
(518) 372-5656

Greater Syracuse Chamber of Commerce
1500 One Mony Plaza
Syracuse, New York 13202
Economic Development
Robert F. Valentine, Director
(315) 422-1343

NORTH CAROLINA
Greater Charlotte Chamber of Commerce
P.O. Box 32785
Charlotte, North Carolina 28232
William J. Veeder, President
(704) 377-6911

High Point Chamber of Commerce
P.O. Box 5025
High Point, North Carolina 27262
Calvin T. Rice, President
(919) 882-8151

Raleigh Chamber of Commerce
P.O. Box 2978
Raleigh, North Carolina 27602
Economic Development
Steve Kelly, Director
(919) 833-3005

Greater Winston-Salem Chamber of Commerce
P.O. Box 1408
Winston-Salem, North Carolina 27102
Economic Development Department
Paul W. Spain, Manager
(919) 725-2361

NORTH DAKOTA
Fargo Chamber of Commerce
321 N. Fourth Street, P.O. Box 2443
Fargo, North Dakota 58108
Industrial Development
Robert Everson, Manager
(701) 237-5678

OHIO
Akron Regional Development Board
Eighth Floor, One Cascade Plaza
Akron, Ohio 44308
Economic Development
Robert H. Schmidt, Director
(216) 376-5550

Greater Canton Chamber of Commerce
229 Wells Avenue, N.W.
Canton, Ohio 44703
Harlan D. Dobry, Executive Vice President
(216) 456-7253

Greater Cincinnati Chamber of Commerce
120 W. Fifth Street
Cincinnati, Ohio 45202
Economic Development
Charles E. Webb, Group Executive
(513) 721-3300

Greater Cleveland Growth Association
690 Union Commerce Building
Cleveland, Ohio 44115
International Division
Lothar A. Koeberer, Vice President
(216) 621-3300

The Columbus Area Chamber of Commerce
50 West Broad Street, P.O. Box 1527
Columbus, Ohio 43216
International Affairs
Kathleen Walsh
(614) 221-1321

Ohio Chamber of Commerce
Eighth Floor, 17 South High Street
Columbus, Ohio 43215
Economic Development
Edmond M. Loewe, Director
(614) 228-4201

Dayton Area Chamber of Commerce
1980 Winters Bank Tower
Dayton, Ohio 45423
World Trade Council
Jeanne Eickman, Manager
(513) 226-1444

Defiance Area Chamber of Commerce
P.O. Box 130
Defiance, Ohio 43512
E.M. Hanks, Executive Manager
(419) 782-7946

Lima Area Chamber of Commerce
53 Public Square
Lima, Ohio 45801
Larry A. DeFries, Executive Vice President
(419) 222-6045

Toledo Area International Trade Association
218 Huron Street
Toledo, Ohio 43604
(an affiliate of Toledo Area Chamber of Commerce)
(419) 243-8191

241

Youngstown Area Chamber of Commerce
200 Wick Building
Youngstown, Ohio 44503
Weston O. Johnstone,
President
(216) 744-2131

OKLAHOMA
Oklahoma City Chamber of Commerce
One Santa Fe Plaza
Oklahoma City, Oklahoma 73102
International Trade Development
Earl Nichols, Manager
(405) 232-6381

Metropolitan Tulsa Chamber of Commerce
616 South Boston Avenue
Tulsa, Oklahoma 74119
Economic Development Division
Ray Vella, Assistant Manager
(918) 585-1201

OREGON
Portland Chamber of Commerce
824 S.W. Fifth Avenue
Portland, Oregon 97204
World Trade and Commerce Department
Norma L. Eikenberry, Manager
(503) 228-9411

PENNSYLVANIA
Butler Area Chamber of Commerce
P.O. Box 1082
Butler, Pennsylvania 16001
Barry L. Racey, Executive Director
(412) 285-3208

Erie Area Chamber of Commerce
1006 State Street
Erie, Pennsylvania 16501
Bernard D. Gorniak,
Executive Vice President
(814) 454-7191

Lower Bucks County Chamber of Commerce
409 Hood Boulevard
Fairless Hills, Pennsylvania 19030

Warren R. Likens, Executive
Vice President
(215) 943-7400

Greater Philadelphia Chamber of Commerce
Suite 1960, 1617 J.F.K. Boulevard
Philadelphia, Pennsylvania 19103
Henry H. Reichner, Jr.,
Executive Vice President
(215) 568-4040

Greater Pittsburgh Chamber of Commerce
411 Seventh Avenue
Pittsburgh, Pennsylvania 15219
Civic Affairs
John R. Rumisek, Manager
(412) 391-3400

Chamber of Commerce of Reading and Berks County
541 Court Street, P.O. Box 1698
Reading, Pennsylvania 19603
W.R. McIlvain, Executive Director
(215) 376-6766

Greater Scranton Chamber of Commerce
426 Mulberry Street
Scranton, Pennsylvania 18503
World Trade Division
Kenneth S. Dolph, Staff Services
(717) 342-7711

State College Area Chamber of Commerce
131 Sowers Street
State College, Pennsylvania 16801
Patricia L. Calahan, Executive Director
(814) 237-7644

Warren County Chamber of Commerce
Pennsylvania Bank & Trust Co. Building
Warren, Pennsylvania 16365
Thomas P. McKeever,
Executive Vice President
(814) 723-3050

Greater Washington Area Chamber of Commerce
Millcraft Center, 90 W. Chestnut Street
Washington, Pennsylvania 15301
Robert W. Sperring,
Executive Director
(412) 225-3010

RHODE ISLAND
Greater Providence Chamber of Commerce
10 Durrance Street
Providence, Rhode Island 02903
Economic Development
William E. Harper, Vice President
(401) 521-5000

SOUTH CAROLINA
Spartanburg Chamber of Commerce
P.O. Box 1636
Spartanburg, South Carolina 29301
Membership Services
Ruth Wilson Calvert,
Manager
(803) 585-8722

TENNESSEE
Greater Chattanooga Area Chamber of Commerce
1001 Market Street
Chattanooga, Tennessee 37402
James W. Hunt, Executive Vice President
(615) 756-2121

Greater Knoxville Chamber of Commerce
P.O. Box 2229
Knoxville, Tennessee 37901
Urban Affairs
David M. Jensen, Group Manager
(615) 637-4550

Memphis Area Chamber of Commerce
P.O. Box 224
Memphis, Tennessee 38101
Business and Industrial Services Department
M.S. Worsham, Manager
(901) 523-2322

242

Nashville Area Chamber of Commerce
161 Fourth Avenue, N.
Nashville, Tennessee 37219
International Affairs
Larry Stephenson, Director
(615) 259-3900

TEXAS
Amarillo Chamber of Commerce
301 Polk Street
Amarillo, Texas 79101
Don Hileman, Executive Vice
President
(806) 374-5238

Beaumont Chamber of Commerce
P.O. Box 3150
Beaumont, Texas 77704
Transportation Department
Doyle G. Owens, Manager
(713) 838-6581

Dallas Chamber of Commerce
1507 Pacific
Dallas, Texas 75201
International Programs
Robert W. Dean, Director
(214) 651-1020

Fort Worth Chamber of Commerce
700 Throckmorton Street
Fort Worth, Texas 76102
Business Development
Norman Robbins, Jr.,
Manager
(817) 336-2491

Galveston Chamber of Commerce
315 Tremont Street
Galveston, Texas 77550
Charles K. Lawrence,
Executive Vice President
(713) 763-5326

Harlingen Area Chamber of Commerce, Inc.
311 E. Tyler, P.O. Box 189
Harlingen, Texas 78550
David E. Allex, President
(512) 423-5440

Houston Chamber of Commerce
25th Floor, 1100 Milam
Building
Houston, Texas 77002
International Business
C. Baldwin, Manager
(713) 651-1313

Lubbock Chamber of Commerce
P.O. Box 561
Lubbock, Texas 79408
John A. Logan, Executive
Vice President
(806) 763-4666

Odessa Chamber of Commerce
P.O. Box 3626
Odessa, Texas 79760
Arthur A. Roberts, Executive
Vice President
(915) 332-9111

Greater San Antonio Chamber of Commerce
P.O. Box 1628
San Antonio, Texas 78206
International Affairs
George Laird, Manager
(512) 227-8181, Ext. 37

UTAH
Salt Lake Area Chamber of Commerce
#19 East Second South
Salt Lake City, Utah 84111
Economic Development
Department
Kay Dimas, Director
(801) 364-3631

VERMONT
Rutland Region Chamber of Commerce
One Mead Building
Rutland, Vermont 05701
C.R. Barnes, Executive Vice
President
(802) 773-2747

VIRGINIA
Charlottesville-Albemarle Chamber of Commerce
P.O. Box 1564
Charlottesville, Virginia
22902

Fred E. Ferguson, Executive
Vice President
(804) 295-3141

Fairfax County Chamber of Commerce
USAA Building
8550 Arlington Boulevard
Fairfax, Virginia 22031
(703) 560-4000

Norfolk Chamber of Commerce
420 Bank Street
Norfolk, Virginia 23501
James D. Fairchild, Executive
Vice President
(804) 622-2312

Metropolitan Richmond Chamber of Commerce
201 E. Franklin Street
Richmond, Virginia 23219
Carlton P. Moffett, President
(804) 649-0373

Virginia State Chamber of Commerce
611 E. Franklin Street
Richmond, Virginia 23219
Edwin C. Luther, III,
Executive Manager
(703) 643-7491

Winchester-Frederick County Chamber of Commerce
P.O. Box 667
Winchester, Virginia 22601
Wade D. Ferguson, Executive
Director
(703) 662-4118

WASHINGTON
Greater Renton Chamber of Commerce
300 Rainier Avenue North
Renton, Washington 98055
Kay F. Johnson, Manager
(206) 226-4560

Seattle Chamber of Commerce
215 Columbia Street
Seattle, Washington 98104
Trade & Transportation
Carl Jesberg, Manager
(206) 447-7263

Tacoma Area Chamber of Commerce
P.O. Box 1933
Tacoma, Washington 98401
Business/Industry Relations Department
Gary D. Brackett, Manager
(206) 627-2175

WEST VIRGINIA
West Virginia Chamber of Commerce
P.O. Box 2789
Charleston, West Virginia 25330
John D. Hurd, Executive Vice President
(304) 342-1115

WISCONSIN
Greater La Crosse Chamber of Commerce
P.O. Box 219
La Crosse, Wisconsin 54601

Quinn Johnson, Executive Vice President
(608) 784-4880

Metropolitan Milwaukee Association of Commerce
756 N. Milwaukee Street
Milwaukee, Wisconsin 53202
John R. Duncan, President
(414) 273-3000

World Trade Association of Milwaukee
756 Milwaukee Street
Milwaukee, Wisconsin 53202
Peter W. Beitzel, Executive Secretary
(414) 273-3000

Marinette Area Chamber of Commerce
P.O. Box 512
Marinette, Wisconsin 54143
George S. Robbins, Manager
(715) 735-6681

Racine Chamber of Commerce
731 Main Street
Racine, Wisconsin 53403
Darrell Wright, President
(414) 633-2451

WYOMING
Casper Area Chamber of Commerce
P.O. Box 399
Casper, Wyoming 82602
Dorothy Perkins, Executive Manager
(307) 234-5311

Port Authorities and Services

The Port Authority of New York and New Jersey operates a Port Commerce program that provides information to exporters and importers.

The program complements the services of freight forwarders, customhouse brokers, export packers, banks, warehouse services and others.

It also offers more than 25 publications. Its *World Trade Services Directory,* a free publication, contains an "Export Guide" page that shows the respective roles of the shipper, motor carrier, forwarder, driver, terminal operator and steamship company in the exporting process. Another page of the directory lists common export documents.

The Port Authority *Literature Checklist* lists other free booklets and bulletins available.

Contact the main office at the address above or the regional office of the Port of New York and New Jersey Trade Development at the following offices:

**CARIBBEAN—LATIN
 AMERICA**
Port Authority of New York
 and New Jersey
One World Trade Center,
 Room 86021
New York, New York 10048
(212) 466-8333

CHICAGO
Port Authority of New York
 and New Jersey
Prudential Plaza
Chicago, Illinois 60601
(312) 236-0075

CLEVELAND REGION
Port Authority of New York
 and New Jersey
Terminal Tower Building
Cleveland, Ohio 44113
(216) 621-3188

LONDON
Port Authority of New York
 and New Jersey
St. Olaf House, Tooley
 Street, 3rd Floor
London SEI 2PH England
011-44-1 403-1844

CONTINENTAL EUROPE
Port Authority of New York
 and New Jersey
Talstrasse 66
8001 Zurich
Switzerland
211.06.15

**FAR EAST—PACIFIC
 AREA**
Port Authority of New York
 and New Jersey
Kokusai Building,
 Marunouchi
Chiyoda-ku, Tokyo 100
Japan

The Port of Los Angeles also has representatives across the country. Contact:
Port of Los Angeles
Director, Trade Development
P.O. Box 151
San Pedro, California 90733
(213) 548-7962

Free publications from the port include *Freight Shipping Directory*, a port-to-port guide showing which shipping lines travel from the Port of Los Angeles to all other ports in the world, and *Facilities Folder*, a pamphlet giving general information about facilities available at the port.

The Port of Long Beach has overseas representatives for Australia, New Zealand, Japan, Singapore, Hong Kong, Korea,

Taiwan and Europe. To find out more about them and other Long Beach port services, contact:

Director, Trade Development
Port of Long Beach
P.O. Box 570
Long Beach, California 90801
(213) 437-0041

From this office you also can obtain free publications, including *Harbor Handbook,* which describes port facilities; *Trade and Service Guide,* a port-to-port directory; and *Maps of Port and Tide Tables.*

The Port of New Orleans has a massive, 20-year expansion program underway. It offers free publications such as the *Annual Directory* which lists suppliers of services to the port.

The main office address is:
Port of New Orleans
P.O. Box 60046
New Orleans, Louisiana 70160
(504) 522-2551

Information can also be obtained from the regional sales managers at:

SOUTHERN REGION
Port of New Orleans
P.O. Box 60046
New Orleans, Louisiana
  70160
(504) 522-2551
Telex: 547496

MIDWEST
Port of New Orleans
Suite 1225-26
327 LaSalle Street
Chicago, Illinois 60604
(312) 939-0722

EASTERN REGION
Port of New Orleans
25 Broadway, Suite 557
New York, New York 10004
(212) 422-0786

WESTERN REGION
Port of New Orleans
Railway Exchange Building,
  Suite F18
St. Louis, Missouri 63101
(314) 241-6320

The Port of New Orleans operates the following overseas sales offices:

EUROPE
Port of New Orleans
416 Avenue Louise
Box 7
1050 Brussels, Belgium
0-1-322-648-1995
Telex: 61250

LATIN AMERICA
Port of New Orleans
Apartado 8520
Panama 5, Republic of
  Panama
258780
Telex: 368745

FAR EAST
Port of New Orleans
World Trade Center Building
P.O. Box 96
Tokyo 105, Japan
435-5381
Telex: 26613

AUSTRALIA
Port of New Orleans
94 Baden Powell Drive
Mount Eliza
3930
Victoria, Australia
787-3714

Small Business Administration Field Offices Addresses and Telephone Numbers

REGION		CITY	STATE	ZIP CODE	ADDRESS	(TELEPHONE NUMBERS FOR PUBLIC USE ONLY)
I	RO	Boston	Mass.	02110	60 Battery March, 10th Fl.	(617) 223-3891
	DO	Boston	Mass.	02114	150 Causeway St., 10th Floor	(617) 223-2234
	POD	Holyoke	Mass.	01050	302 High Street, 4th Floor	(413) 536-8770
	DO	Augusta	Maine	04330	Federal Building, 40 Western Ave., Room 512	(207) 622-6171
	DO	Concord	N.H.	03301	55 Pleasant St., Room 213	(603) 224-4041
	DO	Hartford	Conn.	06103	One Financial Plaza	(203) 244-3600
	DO	Montpelier	Vt.	05602	Federal Building, 87 State St., Rm. 204, P.O. Box 605	(802) 229-0538
	DO	Providence	R.I.	02903	40 Fountain St.	(401) 528-4580
II	RO	New York	N.Y.	10007	26 Federal Plaza, Room 29-118	(212) 264-1468
	DO	New York	N.Y.	10007	26 Federal Plaza, Room 3100	(212) 264-4355
	POD	Melville	N.Y.	11746	425 Broad Hollow Rd., Rm. 205	(516) 752-1626
	DO	Hato Rey	Puerto Rico	00919	Chardon and Bolivia Streets, P.O. Box 1915	(809) 763-6363
	DO	Newark	N.J.	07102	970 Broad St., Room 1635	(201) 645-2434
	POD	Camden	N.J.	08104	1800 East Davis Street	(609) 757-5183
	DO	Syracuse	N.Y.	13260	Federal Building Room 1071, 100 South Clinton Street	(315) 423-5383
	BO	Buffalo	N.Y.	14202	111 West Huron St., Room 1311, Federal Building	(716) 846-4301
	BO	Elmira	N.Y.	14901	180 State Street, Rm. 412	(607) 733-4686
	POD	Albany	N.Y.	12210	99 Washington Ave., Twin Towers Bldg., Rm. 301-mezz.	(518) 472-6300
	POD	Rochester	N.Y.	14614	Federal Building, 100 State Street, Room 601	(716) 263-6700
III	RO	Philadelphia	Bala Cynwyd, Pa.	19004	231 St. Asaphs Rd., 1 Bala Cynwyd Plaza, Suite 646 West Lobby	(215) 596-5901
	DO	Philadelphia	Bala Cynwyd, Pa.	19004	231 St. Asaphs Rd., 1 Bala Cynwyd Plaza, Suite 400 East Lobby	(215) 596-5889
	BO	Harrisburg	Pa.	17101	100 Chestnut Street, 3rd Floor	(717) 782-3840
	BO	Wilkes-Barre	Pa.	18702	Penn Place, 20 N. Pennsylvania Ave.	(717) 826-6497
	BO	Wilmington	Del.	19801	844 King Street, Federal Building, Rm. 5207	(302) 573-6294
	DO	Baltimore	Towson, Md.	21204	Oxford Bldg., 8600 LaSalle Road, Rm. 630	(301) 962-4392
	DO	Clarksburg	W. Va.	26301	109 North 3rd St., Room 301, Lowndes Bank Building	(304) 623-5631
	BO	Charleston	W. Va.	25301	Charleston National Plaza, Suite 628	(304) 343-6181
	DO	Pittsburgh	Pa.	15222	Federal Building, 1000 Liberty Ave., Room 1401	(412) 644-2780
	DO	Richmond	Va.	23240	Federal Building, 400 North 8th St., Room 3015, Box 10126	(804) 782-2617
	DO	Washington	D.C.	20417	1030 15th St. N.W., Suite 250	(202) 655-4000
IV	RO	Atlanta	Ga.	30309	1375 Peachtree St., N.E.	(404) 881-4943
	DO	Atlanta	Ga.	30309	1720 Peachtree Street, N.W., 6th Floor	(404) 881-4325
	DO	Birmingham	Ala.	35205	908 South 20th St., Room 202	(205) 294-1344
	DO	Charlotte	N.C.	28202	230 S. Tryon Street, Suite 700	(704) 372-0711
	POD	Greenville	N.C.	27834	215 South Evans Street, Rm. 206	(919) 752-3798
	DO	Columbia	S.C.	29201	1801 Assembly St., Room 131	(803) 765-5376
	DO	Jackson	Miss.	39201	Providence Capitol Bldg., Suite 690, 200 E. Pascagoula St.	(601) 969-4371
	BO	Biloxi	Miss.	39530	111 Fred Haise Blvd., Gulf Nat. Life Insurance Bldg. 2nd Floor	(601) 435-3676
	DO	Jacksonville	Fla.	32202	Federal Building, 400 West Bay St., Room 261, P.O. Box 35067	(904) 791-3782
	DO	Louisville	Ky.	40202	Federal Building, 600 Federal Pl., Room 188	(502) 582-5971
	DO	Miami	Coral Gables, Fla.	33134	2222 Ponce De Leon Blvd., 5th Floor	(305) 350-5521
	POD	Tampa	Fla.	33602	700 Twiggs Street, Suite 607	(813) 228-2594
	DO	Nashville	Tenn.	37219	404 James Robertson Parkway, Suite 1012	(615) 251-5881
	BO	Knoxville	Tenn.	37902	502 South Gay St., Room 307, Fidelity Bankers Building	(615) 637-9300
	POD	Memphis	Tenn.	38103	Federal Building, 167 North Main St., Room 211	(901) 521-3588
	POD	West Palm Beach	Fla.	33402	Federal Building, 701 Clematis St., Room 229	(305) 659-7533
V	RO	Chicago	Ill.	60604	Federal Building, 219 South Dearborn St., Room 838	(312) 353-0355
	DO	Chicago	Ill.	60604	Federal Building, 219 South Dearborn St., Room 437	(312) 353-4528
	BO	Springfield	Ill.	62701	One North, Old State Capital Plaza	(217) 525-4416
	DO	Cleveland	Ohio	44199	1240 East 9th St., Room 317	(216) 522-4180
	DO	Columbus	Ohio	43215	Federal Bldg., U.S. Courthouse, 85 Marconi Blvd.	(614) 469-6860
	BO	Cincinnati	Ohio	45202	Federal Building, 550 Main St., Room 5028	(513) 684-2814
	DO	Detroit	Mich.	48226	477 Michigan Ave., McNamara Building	(313) 226-6075
	BO	Marquette	Mich.	49855	540 W. Kaye Ave., Don H. Bottum University Center	(906) 225-1108
	DO	Indianapolis	Ind.	46204	575 North Pennsylvania St., Rm. 552 New Fed. Bldg.	(317) 269-7272
	DO	Madison	Wis.	53703	212 East Washington Ave., 2nd Floor	(608) 252-5261
	BO	Milwaukee	Wis.	53202	Federal Bldg. Rm. 246, 517 East Wisconsin Ave.	(414) 291-3941
	POD	Eau Claire	Wis.	54701	500 South Barstow St., Room 89AA, Fed. Off. Bldg. & U.S. Courthouse	(715) 834-9012
	DO	Minneapolis	Minn.	55402	12 South 6th St., Plymouth Building	(612) 725-2362

RO—Regional Office   POD—Post of Duty Station
DO—District Office   BO—Branch Office

State and Territory International Business Offices

The following list gives the addresses and telephone numbers of international business offices in the states, territories and the District of Columbia.

ALABAMA
Industrial Development Division
Alabama Development Office
3734 Atlanta Highway
c/o State Capitol
Montgomery, Alabama 36130
(205) 832-6980

ALASKA
Alaska Department of Commerce & Economic Development
Pouch EE
Juneau, Alaska 99801
(907) 465-2020

ARIZONA
International Trade
Office of Economic Planning & Development
Executive Towers, Room 505
1700 W. Washington
Phoenix, Arizona 85007
(602) 255-3737

ARKANSAS
International Marketing Division
Arkansas Industrial Development Commission
205 State Capitol
Little Rock, Arkansas 72201
(501) 371-1121

CALIFORNIA
Department of Economic & Business Development
1120 N Street
Sacramento, California 95814
(916) 322-5665

Los Angeles Office:
Office of International Trade
World Trade Center, Suite 550
350 South Figueroa Street
Los Angeles, California 90071
(213) 620-3474

COLORADO
Domestic & International Office
Colorado Division of Commerce & Development

1313 Sherman Street, Room 500
Denver, Colorado 80203
(303) 839-2205

CONNECTICUT
International Division
Connecticut Department of Commerce
210 Washington Street
Hartford, Connecticut 06106
(203) 566-3842

DELAWARE
Division of Economic Development
Delaware Dept. of Community Affairs & Economic Development
630 State College Road
Dover, Delaware 19901
(302) 678-4254

DISTRICT OF COLUMBIA
Office of Business & Economic Development
District Building, Room 201
14th & E Streets, N.W.
Washington, D.C. 20004
(202) 727-6600

FLORIDA
Bureau of Trade Development
Florida Department of Commerce
107 West Gaines Street
Collins Building, Room G26
Tallahassee, Florida 32304
(904) 488-9050

GEORGIA
International Division
Georgia Department of Industry & Trade
1400 North Omni International
P.O. Box 1776
Atlanta, Georgia 30304
(404) 656-3577

HAWAII
International Service Agency
Suite 910 - Hawaii Department of Planning & Economic Development
Financial Plaza of the Pacific
Honolulu, Hawaii 96804
(808) 548-4621

IDAHO
Idaho Division of Industrial
Development & Tourism
Capitol Building, Room 108
Boise, Idaho 83720
(209) 384-2470

ILLINOIS
Direct Foreign Investments
Suite 1122 - Department of
Business & Economic
Development
205 West Wacker Drive
Chicago, Illinois 60606
(312) 793-3130

INDIANA
International Trade Division
Department of Commerce
336 State House
Indianapolis, Indiana 46204
(317) 633-4538

IOWA
International Division
Iowa Development
Commission
250 Jewett Building
Des Moines, Iowa 50309
(515) 281-3251

KANSAS
International Trade Division
Kansas Department of
Economic Development
503 Kansas Avenue, 6th Floor
Topeka, Kansas 66603
(913) 296-3481

KENTUCKY
International Division
Kentucky Department of
Commerce
Capitol Plaza Tower
24th Floor
Frankfort, Kentucky 40601
(502) 564-2170

LOUISIANA
International Division
Department of Commerce &
Industry
343 International Trade Mart
New Orleans, Louisiana
70130
(504) 568-5255

MAINE
Maine State Development
Office

State House
193 State Street
Augusta, Maine 04333
(207) 289-2656

MARYLAND
Division of Business &
Industrial Development
Department of Economic
Development
1748 Forest Drive
Annapolis, Maryland 21401
(301) 269-3514

MASSACHUSETTS
Office of International
Business
Massachusetts Department of
Commerce & Development
Saltonstall Building, 13th
Floor
100 Cambridge Street
Boston, Massachusetts 02202
(617) 727-3205

MICHIGAN
International Division
Office of Economic
Development
Michigan Department of
Commerce
P.O. Box 30225
Lansing, Michigan 48909
(517) 373-6390

MINNESOTA
International Division
Minnesota Department of
Economic Development
Hanover Building
480 Cedar Street
St. Paul, Minnesota 55101
(612) 296-4039

MISSISSIPPI
International Business
Development
Mississippi Marketing Council
1202 Walter Sillers State
Office Building
P.O. Box 849
Jackson, Mississippi 39205
(601) 354-6707

MISSOURI
International Business
Development

Missouri Division of
Commerce & Industrial
Development
P.O. Box 118
Jefferson City, Missouri
65102
(314) 751-4241

MONTANA
Montana International Trade
Commission
Suite 415 - Power Block
Helena, Montana 59601
(406) 443-7910

NEBRASKA
Nebraska Department of
Economic Development
P.O. Box 94666
301 Centennial Mall South
Lincoln, Nebraska 68509
(402) 471-3111

NEVADA
Nevada Department of
Economic Development
Capitol Complex
Carson City, Nevada 89710
(702) 885-4322

NEW HAMPSHIRE
New Hampshire Office of
Industrial Development
Department of Resources &
Economic Development
6 Park Street
Concord, New Hampshire
03301
(603) 271-2591

NEW JERSEY
New Jersey Office of
International Trade
Room 508
1101 Raymond Blvd.
Newark, New Jersey 07102
(201) 648-3518

NEW MEXICO
International Trade
Development
Department of Commerce &
Industry
Bataan Memorial Building
Santa Fe, New Mexico 87503
(505) 827-5571

249

NEW YORK
New York State Department
of Commerce
Division of International
Commerce
230 Park Avenue
New York, New York 10017
(212) 949-9290

NORTH CAROLINA
International Division
North Carolina Department of
Commerce
Dobbs Building
430 N. Salisbury Street
Raleigh, North Carolina
27611
(919) 733-7193

NORTH DAKOTA
Business & Industrial
Development Department
523 E. Bismark Avenue
Bismark, North Dakota 58501
(701) 224-2810

OHIO
International Trade Division
Ohio Department of Economic
& Community Development
P.O. Box 1001
Columbus, Ohio 43216
(614) 466-5017

OKLAHOMA
Department of Industrial
Development
500 Will Rogers Building
Oklahoma City, Oklahoma
73105
(405) 521-3501

OREGON
International Trade Division
Oregon Department of
Economic Development
317 South Alder Street
Portland, Oregon 97204
(503) 229-5535

PENNSYLVANIA
Bureau of International
Commerce
Pennsylvania Department of
Commerce
408 South Office Building
Harrisburg, Pennsylvania
17120
(717) 787-7190

RHODE ISLAND
International Trade Director
Department of Economic
Development
One Weybosset Hill
Providence, Rhode Island
02903
(401) 277-2605

SOUTH CAROLINA
International Division
South Carolina State
Development Board
P.O. Box 927
Columbia, South Carolina
29202
(803) 758-2235

SOUTH DAKOTA
South Dakota Industrial
Development
P.O. Box 5004
Sioux Falls, South Dakota
57101
(605) 339-6779

TENNESSEE
International Marketing
Department of Economic &
Community Development
1004 Andrew Jackson
Building
Nashville, Tennessee 37219
(615) 741-2549

TEXAS
International Development
Division
Texas Industrial Commission
410 E. Fifth Street
Austin, Texas 78701
(512) 472-5059

UTAH
Division of Industrial
Development
2 Aero Press Square, Suite
200
165 So. West Temple
Salt Lake City, Utah 84101
(801) 533-5325

VERMONT
Department of Economic
Development
Agency of Development &
Community Affairs

Pavilion Office Building
109 State Street
Montpelier, Vermont 05602
(802) 828-3221

VIRGINIA
International Trade &
Development
Virginia Division of Industrial
Development
1010 State Office Building
Richmond, Virginia 23219
(804) 786-3791

VIRGIN ISLANDS
Industrial Development
Commission
Virgin Islands Department of
Commerce
P.O. Box 1692
Charlotte Amalie
St. Thomas, Virgin Islands
00801
(809) 774-1331

WASHINGTON
Department of Commerce &
Economic Development
Room 101
General Administration
Building
Olympia, Washington 98504
(306) 753-5641

WEST VIRGINIA
Governor's Office of
Economic & Community
Development
Rotunda Room 150
Charleston, West Virginia
25305
(304) 348-0190

WISCONSIN
Industrial Location Services
Wisconsin Department of
Business Development
123 West Washington Avenue
Madison, Wisconsin 53702
(608) 266-1767

WYOMING
Department of Economic
'Planning and Development
Barrett Building
Cheyenne, Wyoming 82002
(307) 777-7284

250

COMMONWEALTH OF PUERTO RICO
Secretary of Commerce
Department of Commerce
P.O. Box 4275
San Juan, Puerto Rico 00905

COMMONWEALTH OF PUERTO RICO, NEW YORK OFFICE
Economic Development
  Administration
1290 Avenue of the Americas
35th Floor
New York, New York 10019
(212) 245-1200

State Economic Development Officials Responsible for International Trade

AMERICAN SAMOA
Coleman, Peter Tali
Governor
Pago Pago, AS 96799
633-4116

ALABAMA
Hope, Robert M.
Director
State Docks Dept.
Mobile, AL 36602
(202) 690-6112

ALASKA
Eakins, Richard H.
Alaska Dept. of Commerce
and Economic Development
Pouch EE
Juneau, AK 99801

ARIZONA
W.F. Kane
Director of International
Trade
Office of Economic Planning
& Development
1700 W. Washington Street
Room 505
Phoenix, AZ 85007
(602) 271-3737

ARKANSAS
Dyke, James T.
Director
Dept. of Economic
Development
Rm. 4C-300, #1 Capitol Mall
Little Rock, AR 72201
(501) 371-2052

CALIFORNIA
Richard C. Kirp
Director
Office of International Trade
350 S. Figueroa
Suite 550
Los Angeles, CA 90071
(213) 620-3474

COLORADO
Charles Brand
Colo. Dept of Commerce and
Development
Room 500
1313 Sherman Street
Denver, CO 80203

CONNECTICUT
Miller, Gary H.
Director
International Div.
Dept. of Economic
Development
210 Washington Street
Hartford, CT 06106
(203) 566-3842

DELAWARE
Gilliam, James H., Jr.
Secretary
Dept. of Community Affairs
& Economic Development
N. du Pont Hwy.
ETV Bldg.
Dover, DE 19901
(302) 678-4456

FLORIDA
Brock, Dick
Chief
Bureau of Trade Development
Dept. of Commerce
Collins Bldg.
Tallahassee, FL 32301
(904) 488-6124

GEORGIA
Welsh, John D.
Director
International Trade Div.
Dept. of Industry & Trade
1400 N. Omni International
Atlanta, GA 30303
(404) 656-3577

GUAM
Diego, Jose D.
Director
Dept. of Commerce
P.O. Box 682
Agana, GU 96910
6461250

HAWAII
Sakata, Thomas S.
Administrator
Hawaii International Services
Agency
Dept. of Planning &
Economic Development
Financial Plaza of the Pacific,
#910
130 Merchant Street
Honolulu, HI 96813
(808) 548-4621 or 548-3048

ILLINOIS
Ferguson, Tom
Manager
Business Services Div.
Dept. of Commerce &
    Community Affairs
222 S. College
Springfield, IL 62706
(217) 782-6861

INDIANA
Grebe, Phillip M.
State Forester
International Trade Div.
Dept. of Commerce
336 State House
Indianapolis, IN 46204
(317) 232-8845

IDAHO
Jan Hammer
Director
State of Idaho
Office of International Trade
P.O. Box 790
Boise, ID 83701
(208) 384-2240

IOWA
Schissel, John
Director of Foreign Trade
Development Commission
250 Jewett Bldg.
914 Grand Street
Des Moines, IA 50309
(515) 281-3251

KANSAS
Loveless, Roland
Director
Div. of Development
Dept. of Economic
    Development
6th Floor
503 Kansas Avenue
Topeka, KS 66603
(913) 296-3336

KENTUCKY
Savage, William E.
Director
International Trade
Dept. of Commerce
Capital Plaza Tower
Frankfort, KY 40601
(502) 564-2170

LOUISIANA
Breaux, Clarence
Director
International Development
Office of Commerce &
    Industry
Dept. of Commerce
343 International Trade Mart
New Orleans, LA 70130
(504) 568-5255

MAINE
Campbell, George
Director
Development Office
Executive Dept.
State House
Augusta, ME 04333
(207) 289-2656

MARYLAND
McDonald, Gerald L.
Director
Office of Business &
    Industrial Development
Dept. of Economic &
    Community Development
1748 Forest Dr.
Annapolis, MD 21401
(301) 269-3514

MICHIGAN
Workman, Wayne L.
Director
Office of Economic
    Development
Dept. of Commerce
5th Fl., Law Bldg.
Lansing, MI 48909
(517) 373-3530

MINNESOTA
Printy, David
Commissioner
Dept. of Economic
    Development
480 Cedar Street
St. Paul, MN 55101
(612) 296-2755

MISSISSIPPI
Caraway, William
Exec. Director
Agricultural & Industrial
    Board
12th Fl., Sillers Bldg.
Jackson, MS 39202
(601) 354-6710

MISSOURI
Hurst, Steven
Director
Div. of Commerce &
    Industrial Development
Dept. of Consumer Affairs,
    Regulation & Licensing
Jefferson State Office Bldg.
P.O. Box 118
Jefferson City, MO 65102
(314) 751-3600

NEBRASKA
Costello, Dominick
Chief
Marketing Div.
Dept. of Agriculture
P.O. Box 94947
Lincoln, NE 68509
(402) 471-2358

MONTANA
John Lopoch,
Director
Gov's Office of Commerce &
    Small Business Development
State Capitol
Helena, MT 59601
(406) 499-3823

NEVADA
John Buchanan,
Director
Dept. of International
    Development
Capitol Complex
Carson City, NV 89710
(702) 885-4322

NEW HAMPSHIRE
Parks, James N.
Supervisor
Foreign Trade & Commercial
    Development
Dept. of Resources &
    Economic Development
6 Park Street
Concord, NH 03301
(603) 271-2591

NEW JERSEY
Brady, Joseph F.
Chief
Office of International Trade
Div. of Economic Development
Dept. of Labor & Industry
John Fitch Plaza
Trenton, NJ 08625
(609) 292-2323

NEW MEXICO
R.E. McDowell
International Trade Specialist
Department of Commerce and
Industry
113 Washington Avenue
Santa Fe, NM 87503
(505) 827-5571

NEW YORK
Hassett, William D., Jr.
Commissioner
Dept. of Commerce
Twin Towers
99 Washington Avenue
Albany, NY 12245
(518) 474-4100

NORTH CAROLINA
Hinkle, James R.
Director
International Div.
Dept. of Commerce
430 N. Salisbury Street
Raleigh, NC 27611
(919) 733-7196

NORTH DAKOTA
Harward, Stewart
Director
European Office
Old West Regional
Commission
c/o Business & Industrial
Development Dept.
523 E. Bismarck Avenue
Bismarck, ND 58505
(701) 224-2810

OHIO
Sexton, Fred
Deputy Director
Div. of International Trade
Dept. of Commerce
30 E. Broad Street
Columbus, OH 43215
(614) 466-5017

OKLAHOMA
Matthews, Steve
Director
International Trade
Dept. of Industrial
Development
4020 N. Lincoln Blvd.
Oklahoma City, OK 73105
(405) 521-2401

OREGON
Frengle, Douglas
Manager
International Trade
Dept. of Economic
Development
5th Fl.
921 SE Washington
Portland, OR 97205
(503) 229-5535

PENNSYLVANIA
Newlin, John
Director
Bureau of International
Development
Dept. of Commerce
408 South Office Bldg
Harrisburg, PA 17120
(717) 787-7190

PUERTO RICO
Arroyo, Noel A.
Auxiliary Secretary
Box 4275
San Juan, PR 00905
(809) 725-7254

SOUTH CAROLINA
Heller, Max
Chairman
State Development Board
1301 Gervais Street
Box 927
Columbia, SC
29202
(803) 758-3145

SOUTH DAKOTA
Garness, Richard
Director
Div. of Industrial
Development
Dept. of Economic &
Tourism Development
P.O. Box 5004
620 S. Cliff
Sioux Falls, SD 57101
(605) 339-6779

TEXAS
Alagna, Antonito F.
Director
International Development
Div.

Industrial Commission
P.O. Box 12728
Capitol Station
Austin, TX 78711
(512) 472-5059

TENNESSEE
Gardner, Dick
Director, Export Trade
Dept. of Economic &
Community Development
1004 Andrew Jackson Bldg.
Nashville, TN 37219
(615) 741-2549

UTAH
Cooke, Peter S.
Director
Industrial Development Div.
Office of Community &
Economic Development
165 S. West Temple, #200
Salt Lake City, UT 84101
(801) 533-5325

VERMONT
Dworshak, Louis R.
Director
International Business
Economic Development Dept.
Agency of Development &
Community Affairs
Pavilion Office Bldg.
Montpelier, VT 05602
(802) 828-3221

VIRGINIA
Kessener, Fred G.
Director
International Trade &
Development
Div. of Industrial
Development
1010 State Office Bldg.
Richmond, VA 23219
(804) 786-4486

WASHINGTON
Nordell, Alan
Manager
Trade Development
Dept. of Commerce &
Economic Development
312 First Avenue, N.
Seattle, WA 98109
(206) 464-6282

WISCONSIN
Brunner, Robert
Secretary
Dept. of Business
    Development
123 W. Washington Avenue,
    #650
Madison, WI 53702
(608) 266-3222

WYOMING
Tony Roso
Department of Economic
    Planning & Development
Barrett Building
Cheyenne, WY 82002
(307) 777-7284

U.S.-Foreign Trade Zones

Zone No. 1, New York City. Brooklyn Navy Yard, Brooklyn, New York 11205, Tel. (212) 834-1300.

Zone No. 2, New Orleans. P.O. Box Z0046, New Orleans, Louisiana 70160, Tel. (504) 897-0189.

Zone No. 3 and Subzone 3-A, San Francisco. Ferry Building, San Francisco, California 94111, Tel. (415) 391-8000.

Zone No. 5, Seattle. P.O. Box 1209, Seattle, Washington 98111, Tel. (206) 587-4964.

Zone No. 7, Mayaquez, Puerto Rico. G.P.O. 2350, San Juan, Puerto Rico 00936, Tel. (809) 767-4747.

Zone No. 8, Toledo. 3332 St. Lawrence Drive, Toledo, Ohio 43605, Tel. (419) 729-3704.

Zone No. 9 and Subzone 9-A, Honolulu. Pier 39, Honolulu, Hawaii 96817, Tel. (808) 548-5435.

Zone No. 10, Bay County, Michigan. Port of Bay County, P.O Box 391, Bay City, Michigan 48707, Tel. (517) 892-4578.

Zone No. 12, McAllen, Texas. P.O. Box 1988, McAllen, Texas 78501, Tel. (512) 682-2875.

Zone No. 14, Little Rock, Arkansas. Little Rock Port Authority, 7500 Lindsey Road, Little Rock, Arkansas 72206, Tel. (501) 372-4114.

Zone No. 15, Kansas City, Missouri. 425 Volcker Blvd., Kansas City, Missouri 64110, Tel. (816) 421-7666.

Zone No. 16, Sault Ste. Marie, Michigan. Sault Industrial Park, Sault Ste. Marie, Michigan 49783, Tel. (906) 635-9131.

Zone No. 17, Kansas City, Kansas. 425 Volcker Blvd., Kansas City, Missouri 64110, Tel. (816) 421-7666.

Zone No. 18, San Jose, California. 2001 Fortune Drive, San Jose, California 95131, Tel. (408) 263-5000.

Zone No. 19, Omaha, Nebraska. Omaha Douglas Civic Center #401, 1819 Farnam Street, Omaha, Nebraska 68102, Tel. (402) 344-4636.

Zone No. 20, Portsmouth, Virginia. 1600 Maritime Tower, Norfolk, Virginia 23510, Tel. (804) 622-1671.

Zone No. 21, Dorchester County, South Carolina. P.O. Box 1498, Summerville, South Carolina 29483, Tel. (803) 871-4870.

Zone No. 22, Chicago, Illinois. 12700 Butler Drive, Lake Calumet Harbor, Chicago, Illinois 60633, Tel. (312) 646-4400.

Zone No. 23, Buffalo, New York. 901 Fuhrmann Blvd., Buffalo, New York 14203, Tel. (716) 856-4436.

Zone No. 24 and Subzone 24-A, Pittston, Pennsylvania. Wilkes-Barre/Scranton Airport Terminal, Avoca, Pennsylvania 18641, Tel. (717) 655-5563.

Zone No. 25, Port Everglades, Broward County, Florida. P.O. Box 13136, Port Everglades, Florida 33316, Tel. (305) 523-3404.

Zone No. 26, Shenandoah, Coweta County, Georgia. Atlanta Foreign Trade Zone, P.O. Box 1157, Shenandoah, Georgia 30625, Tel. (404) 577-4820.

Zone No. 27, Boston, Massachusetts. 99 High Street, Boston, Massachusetts 02110, Tel. (617) 482-2930.

Zone No. 28, New Bedford, Massachusetts. Industrial Development Commission, 1213 Purchase Street, New Bedford, Massachusetts 02740, Tel. (617) 997-6501.

Zone No. 29, Louisville, Kentucky. Suite 103, Vermont American Building, 100 E. Liberty Street, Louisville, Kentucky 40202, Tel. (502) 583-9731.

Zone No. 30, Salt Lake City, Utah. 209-A City and County Building, Salt Lake City, Utah 84111, Tel. (801) 535-7902.

Zone No. 31, Granite City, Illinois. 2801 Rock Road, Granite City, Illinois 62040, Tel. (618) 877-8444.

Zone No. 32, Miami, Florida. 1200 Biscayne Blvd., Miami, Florida 33132, Tel. (305) 374-1800.

Zone No. 33 and Subzone 33-A, Pittsburgh, Pennsylvania. 534 Union Trust Building, Pittsburgh, Pennsylvania 15219, Tel. (412) 471-3939.

Zone No. 34, Niagara County, New York. County Office Building, 59 Park Avenue, Lockport, New York 14094, Tel. (716) 434-2871.

Zone No. 35, Philadelphia, Pennsylvania. 940 Public Ledger Building, 6th and Chestnut Street, Philadelphia, Pennsylvania 19106, Tel. (215) 925-9301.

Zone No. 36, Galveston, Texas. Galveston Wharves, P.O. Box 328, Galveston, Texas 77550, Tel. (713) 765-5996.

Zone No. 37, Orange County, New York. Foreign Trade Development Company of Orange County, Inc., P.O. Box 6147, Stewart Airport, Newburgh, New York 12550, Tel. (914) 564-7700.

Zone No. 38, Spartanburg County, South Carolina. P.O. Box 817, Charleston, South Carolina 29402, Tel. (803) 723-8651.

Zone No. 39, Dallas/Fort Worth, Texas. Dallas/Fort Worth Airport, P.O. Drawer DFW, Dallas/Fort Worth Airport, Texas 75261, Tel. (214) 574-6720.

Zone No. 40, Cleveland, Ohio. 101 Erieside Avenue, Cleveland, Ohio 44114, Tel. (216) 241-8004.

Zone No. 41, Milwaukee, Wisconsin. Suite 513, 110 East Wisconsin Avenue, Milwaukee, Wisconsin 53202, Tel. (414) 276-6969.

Zone No. 42, Orlando, Florida. Orlando International Airport, P.O. Box 19127, Orlando, Florida 32814, Tel. (305) 855-4000.

Zone No. 43, Battle Creek, Michigan. BC/CA1/KAL Inland Port Authority of South Central Michigan Development Corporation, P.O. Box 1438, Battle Creek, Michigan 49016, Tel. (616) 968-8197.

Zone No. 44, Morris County, New Jersey. Office of International Trade, 1100 Raymond Boulevard, Room 508, Newark, New Jersey 07102, Tel. (201) 648-3518.

Zone No. 45, Portland, Oregon. P.O. Box 3529, Portland, Oregon 97208, Tel. (503) 231-5000.

Zone No. 46 and Subzones 46a & 46b, Cincinnati, Ohio. 120 West Fifth Street, Cincinnati, Ohio 45202, Tel. (513) 721-3300.

Zone No. 47, Campbell County, Kentucky. N. Kentucky Port Authority, 400 Licking Pike, Wilder, Kentucky 41071, Tel. (606) 581-1444.

Zone No. 48, Tucson, Arizona. Broadway Realty and Trust, P.O. Box 12863, Tucson, Arizona 85732, Tel. (602) 747-5700.

Zone No. 49, Newark/Elizabeth, New Jersey. One World Trade Center, New York, New York 10048, Tel. (212) 466-7985.

APPLICATIONS PENDING

Boonville, Missouri. Greater Kansas City Foreign Trade Zone, Inc., Crown Center, 2440 Pershing Road, Kansas City, Missouri 64108, Tel. (816) 421-7666.

Long Beach, California. Board of Harbor Commissioners of the Port of Long Beach, P.O. Box 570, Long Beach, California 90801, Tel. (213) 437-0041.

World Trade Clubs in the United States

ALABAMA
International Trade Club
P.O. Box 283
Mobile, Alabama 36601

ARIZONA
Arizona World Trade Association
3811 East McKellips Road
Mesa, Arizona 85205

ARKANSAS
Arkansas Exporters Roundtable
c/o Brooks-Pollard Company
1650 Union National Plaza
Little Rock, Arkansas 72201

CALIFORNIA
Long Beach Area Chamber of Commerce
International Business
Association
50 Oceangate Plaza
Long Beach, California 90802

Foreign Trade Association of Southern California
Los Angeles World Trade
Center
350 South Figueroa Street,
Room 226
Los Angeles, California
90071

International Club of Los Angeles
Los Angeles World Trade
Center
350 South Figueroa Street
Los Angeles, California
90071

Los Angeles World Affairs Council
900 Wilshire Boulevard, Suite
230
Los Angeles, California
90017

Oakland World Trade Association
1939 Harrison Street, Suite
400
Oakland, California 94612

California Council for International Trade
1333 Gough Street
San Francisco, California
94109

Junior World Trade Association
465 California Street
San Francisco, California
94104

San Francisco Area World Trade Association
465 California Street
San Francisco, California
94104

World Trade Club
World Trade Center
Ferry Building
San Francisco, California
94111

Santa Clara Valley World Trade Club
P.O. Box 6178
San Jose, California 95150

COLORADO
International Trade Association of Colorado
P.O. Box 18398
Denver, Colorado 80218

CONNECTICUT
Connecticut Business and Industry Association
60 Washington Street, Suite
1202
Hartford, Connecticut 06106

WESTCONN International Trade
P.O. Box 406
Stamford, Connecticut 06904

Connecticut Foreign Trade Association
c/o Manufacturers Association
of Southern Connecticut
608 Ferry Road
Stratford, Connecticut 06497

Connecticut International
Trade Association
c/o C.H. Dexter Division
Dexter Corporation
1 Elm Street
Windsor-Locks, Connecticut
06096

FLORIDA
**Tampa World Trade
Council**
The Greater Tampa Chamber
of Commerce
International Department of
the Greater Tampa
Chamber of Commerce
P.O. Box 420
Tampa, Florida 33601

GEORGIA
**Atlanta Chamber of
Commerce**
International Department
P.O. Box 1740
Atlanta, Georgia 30301

**Southern Center for
International Studies**
Lenox Towers, Suite 1239
3400 Peachtree Road, N.E.
Atlanta, Georgia 30326

HAWAII
**Hawaii World Trade
Association**
Chamber of Commerce of
Hawaii
Dillingham Transportation
Building
735 Bishop Street
Honolulu, Hawaii 96813

ILLINOIS
**International Trade Club of
Chicago**
310 S. Michigan Avenue
Chicago, Illinois 60604

**Foreign Trade Credit Group
of the Chicago Midwest
Credit Management
Association**
315 South Northwest
Highway
Park Ridge, Illinois 60068

**World Trade Club of
Northern Illinois**
c/o Rockford Area Chamber
of Commerce
815 East State Street
Rockford, Illinois 61101

INDIANA
**World Trade Club of
Indiana, Inc.**
928 Chamber of Commerce
Building
Indianapolis, Indiana 46204

**International Trade
Committee of the
Indianapolis Chamber of
Commerce**
320 North Meridian Street
Indianapolis, Indiana 46204

Michiana World Trade Club
230 West Jefferson Boulevard
South Bend, Indiana 46601

IOWA
**Iowa-Illinois International
Trade Association**
c/o Davenport Chamber of
Commerce
404 Main Street
Davenport, Iowa 52801

**World Trade Council of
Iowa**
Eighth and High Streets
Des Moines, Iowa 50307

KANSAS
Wichita World Trade Club
350 West Douglas Avenue
Wichita, Kansas 67202

KENTUCKY
**Kentuckiana World
Commerce Council, Inc.**
300 West Liberty Street
Louisville, Kentucky 40202

LOUISIANA
**Southern United States
Trade Association**
International Trade Mart
2 Canal Street, Suite 338
New Orleans, Louisiana
70130

**World Trade Club of
Greater New Orleans**
242 International Trade Mart
2 Canal Street
New Orleans, Louisiana
70130

MASSACHUSETTS
**The International Business
Center of New England,
Inc.**
470 Atlantic Avenue
Boston, Massachusetts 02210

**The Foreign Commerce
Club of Boston, Inc.**
99 Buckskin Path
Centerville, Massachusetts
02632

**Western Massachusetts
International Trade
Association**
c/o B & G Associates
P.O. Box 71
Holyoke, Massachusetts
01041

MICHIGAN
**West Michigan World Trade
Club**
P.O. Box 1238
Grand Rapids, Michigan
49501

MINNESOTA
**Minnesota World Trade
Association, Inc.**
5235 Xerxes Avenue South
Minneapolis, Minnesota
55410

MISSISSIPPI
**International Trade Club of
Mississippi**
P.O. Box 849
Jackson, Mississippi 39205

MISSOURI
**International Trade Club of
Greater Kansas City**
2440 Pershing Road, Suite
266
Kansas City, Missouri 64108

**World Trade Club of St.
Louis, Inc.**
7912 Bonhomme, Room 209
St. Louis, Missouri 63105

St. Louis Regional
Commerce and Growth
Association
World Trade Department
10 Broadway
St. Louis, Missouri 63102

Greater Ozarks
International Trade Club
c/o Springfield Area Chamber
of Commerce
P.O. Box 1036
Springfield, Missouri 65805

NEBRASKA
Midwest International Trade
Association
c/o International Banking
P.O. Box 82408
Lincoln, Nebraska 68501

NEW JERSEY
International Commerce
Club of Morris County
Warner Lambert International
Division
201 Tabor Road
Morris Plains, New Jersey
07950

NEW YORK
International Industrial
Marketing Club
150 Great Neck Road
Great Neck, New York 11021

The Long Island Association
of Commerce and
Industry
425 Broad Hollow Road,
Suite 205
Melville, New York 11746

Foreign Commerce Club of
New York, Inc.
One World Trade Center,
Suite 3811
New York, New York 10048

International Association,
Inc.
122 East 42nd Street, Suite
1014
New York, New York 10017

Overseas Automotive Club,
Inc.
44 East 23rd Street
New York, New York 10010

World Trade Club of New
York, Inc.
c/o The New York Chamber
of Commerce and Industry
65 Liberty Street
New York, New York 10005

World Trade Council
c/o Rochester Area Chamber
of Commerce, Inc.
55 St. Paul Street
Rochester, New York 14604

World Commerce
Association of Central
New York
1500 One Mony Plaza
Syracuse, New York 13202

Buffalo World Trade
Association
146 Canterbury Square
Williamsville, New York
14221

NORTH CAROLINA
Triad World Trade Club
c/o Jim Garst
Mid Atlantic Shipping
Company
P.O. Box 19012
Greensboro, North Carolina
27410

North Carolina World
Trade Assocation
P.O. Box 10387
Raleigh, North Carolina
27605

OHIO
International Trade Council
Akron Regional Development
Board
One Cascade Plaza, Eighth
Floor
Akron, Ohio 44308

World Trade Club
c/o Greater Cincinnati
Chamber of Commerce
120 West Fifth Street
Cincinnati, Ohio 45202

The Columbus Area
Chamber of Commerce
International Trade Committee
Department of Economic
Development
50 W. Broad Street
Columbus, Ohio 43215

World Trade Council
c/o The Dayton Area
Chamber of Commerce
1980 Winters Bank Tower
Dayton, Ohio 45423

OKLAHOMA
Oklahoma City Chamber of
Commerce
World Trade Council
One Santa Fe Plaza
Oklahoma City, Oklahoma
73102

Tulsa World Trade
Association
616 South Boston Avenue
Tulsa, Oklahoma 74119

PENNSYLVANIA
International Trade
Development Association
P.O. Box 113
Furlong, Pennsylvania 18925

World Trade Association of
Philadelphia, Inc.
Land Title Building
Philadelphia, Pennsylvania
19110

Chamber of Commerce of
Greater Pittsburgh
Civic Affairs Department
411 Seventh Avenue
Pittsburgh, Pennsylvania
15219

Reading Foreign Trader
Association
P.O. Box 142
Reading, Pennsylvania 19603

World Trade Council
c/o York Area Chamber of
Commerce
P.O. Box 1229
13 East Market Street
York, Pennsylvania 17405

PUERTO RICO
The International Trade
Association of Puerto Rico
c/o Manuel T. Hidalgo
1319 Ashford Avenue
Santurce, Puerto Rico 00907

RHODE ISLAND
The World Trade Club of Rhode Island
Howard Building-Box 1
10 Dorrance Street
Providence, Rhode Island 02903

SOUTH CAROLINA
Western South Carolina International
Trade Club
P.O. Box 5823
Greenville, South Carolina 29606

TENNESSEE
International Group of Memphis
P.O. Box 81290
Memphis, Tennessee 38152

Mid-South Exporters' Roundtable
P.O. Box 3521
Memphis, Tennessee 38103

World Trade Club of Memphis
P.O. Box 3577
Memphis, Tennessee 38103

TEXAS
International Trade Association of Dallas, Inc.
P.O. Box 672
Dallas, Texas 75221

Fort Worth Export-Import Club
P.O. Box 17372
Fort Worth, Texas 76101

Traffic Club of Galveston-Texas City
P.O. Box 343
Galveston, Texas 77550

Houston World Trade Association
World Trade Center, Suite 1013
1520 Texas Avenue
Houston, Texas 77002

San Antonio Export-Import Club
P.O. Box 17032
San Antonio, Texas 78217

UTAH
Utah World Trade Association
c/o U.S. Department of Commerce
1203 Federal Building
Salt Lake City, Utah 84138

VIRGINIA
Hampton Roads Foreign Commerce Club
7432 North Shore Road
Norfolk, Virginia 23505

Richmond Export-Import Club
8010 Federal Building
400 North Eighth Street
Richmond, Virginia 23240

WASHINGTON
World Trade Club
Mayflower Park Hotel
405 Olive Way
Seattle, Washington 98101

WISCONSIN
World Trade Association of Milwaukee, Inc.
756 N. Milwaukee Street
Milwaukee, Wisconsin 53202

Southeastern Wisconsin World Trade Association
P.O. Box 291
Racine, Wisconsin 53401

Part V. Index

A

B

C

264

D

E

F

G

H

I

O

P

Q

R

S

T

U

V

W

International Division Activities

International Economic Policy Section

The International Division staffs a system of committees, sub-committees and task forces whose business members develop positions on international trade, investment and economic development issues for the U.S. Chamber. These positions are the basis for congressional testimony and policy and program recommendations to the administration. Issues of current concern include: export controls; multilateral trade negotiations; the Arab boycott; export financing; trade with socialist economies; trade in services; export promotion; codes of conduct; overseas business payments; transfer of technology; foreign investment in the United States; U.S. investment abroad; expropriation; tax treaties; foreign investment taxation; energy and resource needs; commodity agreements; Law of the Sea; foreign source income taxation; overseas voting rights; the human rights issue in international economic policy; and social security agreements.

The International Economic Policy Section monitors and analyzes legislation affecting American business abroad, prepares testimony on the most significant bills before congress and advises U.S. Chamber members on crucial legislative developments. Close contacts are maintained with key congressional staff and executive branch officials on matters affecting international business.

In addition, the Section offers practical guidance and assistance to member firms, local chambers of commerce and other organizations in their efforts to expand international trade and investment and seeks to improve and expand national export promotion programs. It also works for more effective import adjustment mechanisms and promotes two-way investment.

International Economic Affairs Section

The International Division develops and conducts the foreign relations of the U.S. Chamber. Through a process of business diplomacy involving business leaders in the United States and overseas, the Division develops recommendations on international economic problems to assure that government policy makers in the United States and foreign countries are well advised of business attitudes. Also, it is responsible for the U.S. Chamber's important working relationships with AmChams and for maintaining close contacts with foreign counterpart business organizations and foreign agencies involved in international economic matters.

The International Economic Affairs Section's activities are divided into six regional areas:

African Affairs:

Efforts are being made to facilitate American business relations with all countries of Africa. This program includes efforts to establish American chambers of commerce in key countries. AmCham Morocco has been operating since 1966, and AmCham South Africa was inaugurated in November 1977. In addition, practical workshops and other initiatives for business development throughout the continent are emphasized.

Asian-Pacific Affairs:

In addition to providing liaison for the 12 AmChams comprising the Asian-Pacific Council of American Chambers of Commerce (APCAC), the U.S. Chamber provides the secretariat for the Advisory Council on Japan-U.S. Economic Relations. The Council is composed of chief executive officers of fifty major U.S. corporations who meet annually with their Japanese counterparts. The two groups also cosponsor a series of "quadrilateral" businessmen's conferences with representatives from Europe and the Middle East to address the wide range of trade, investment, monetary and natural resource issues facing both developed and developing countries. The U.S. Chamber also staffs the India-U.S. Business Council, involving U.S. business leaders and their Indian counterparts in discussions on economic and commercial policies designed to strengthen the bilateral relationship, promote expanded trade and encourage U.S. investment in the Indian economy. A council linking the business communities of the United States and the five member nations of the Association of Southeast Asian Nations (ASEAN)—the Philippines, Indonesia, Singapore, Malaysia and Thailand—began operating in 1979.

East-West Trade:

The U.S. Chamber provides staff support for U.S.-Eastern European economic councils with Romania, Hungary, Poland, Czechoslovakia and Bulgaria. These councils serve as recognized channels for communication between key U.S. business leaders and their East European counterparts. In an effort to expand trade and industrial cooperation, the councils closely examine legal and economic bottlenecks that hinder commercial interchange between the United States and selected Eastern European non-market economies. The U.S. Chamber also holds a permanent seat on the board of directors of the U.S.-U.S.S.R. Trade and Economic Council—a business organization formed to facilitate U.S.-Soviet trade.

European Affairs:

The U.S. Chamber maintains close liaison with 13 AmChams in the Western European and Mediterranean area and with their regional council, the Council of American Chambers of Commerce—Europe and Mediterranean (EuroMed)— communicating relevant trade and investment news to this region and tracking those aspects of Europe's political and economic evolution, inside the European Community (EC) and out, which may be significant for American business. The U.S. Chamber staffs the E.C.-U.S. Businessmen's Council—a body of top American and Western European business leaders who deal on a continuing basis with economic issues affecting the Atlantic Community and who advise their respective governments on how to deal with them. In addition, annual, formal conferences between private sector agricultural leaders from the EC and the United States are organized by the U.S. Chamber.

Hemispheric Affairs:

The U.S. Chamber staffs three important institutions which reflect the special geographical and historical ties between the United States and other Western Hemisphere nations. They are: the Association of American Chambers of Commerce in Latin America (AACCLA) representing over 17,000 corporate and individual AmCham members in 15 Latin American countries, which was founded in 1967; the Committee on Canada-United States Relations, jointly sponsored with the Canadian Chamber of Commerce, which has met biannually since 1933; and the Brazil-U.S. Business Council, established in 1976 as a channel of communication between business leaders of the two countries. AACCLA, the Committee on Canada-United States Relations and the Brazil-U.S. Business Council formulate recommendations on economic relations between these countries and the United States.

Middle East Affairs:

Reflecting the rapidly growing importance of the countries of the Middle East to U.S. economic interests, and as part of the U.S. Chamber's effort to address the energy and natural resource problems facing the business community and the trade, investment and monetary implications of these problems, the U.S. Chamber staffs various activities involving the Middle East. In addition to monitoring developments in the area relevant to American business and advising members of emerging trade and investment opportunities in the region, the U.S. Chamber administers four bilateral business councils with Egypt, Israel, Iran and the Sudan. These councils involve prominent American business leaders with their counterparts in discussions of trade and economic policy issues to improve bilateral commercial relations and to expand mutually beneficial flows of trade and investment.

International Research and Special Projects

The International Research and Special Projects Section is responsible for the study, analysis and preparation of research reports and issue papers that are used for policy development and implementation by the Division's International Economic Policy and International Economic Affairs Sections. In addition, this Section monitors legislative developments and activities of intergovernmental organizations that have an international economic impact on the U.S. business community.

A variety of reports, surveys and other publications are produced by this Section to educate and mobilize the public on important international commercial and economic questions, including the monthly *International Report* and the *Trade Policy Review,* which is published on an *ad hoc* basis in the form of updated bulletins and special reports on the implementation of the multilateral trade negotiations and on U.S. trade policy and bilateral trade negotiations.

This Section organizes conferences, seminars and symposia to publicize topical trade and investment issues and to help frame solutions to related international economic questions. Also, it provides sources of information for certain business and cultural inquiries on the international level, including importing and exporting, employment overseas and technical associations.